P9-CFC-918

LEGAL WRITING

How to use your Connected Casebook

Step 1: Go to www.CasebookConnect.com and redeem your access code to get started.

Access Code:  STXT92116145416

Step 2: Go to your **BOOKSHELF** and select your Connected Casebook to start reading, highlighting, and taking notes in the margins of your e-book.

Step 3: Select the **STUDY** tab in your toolbar to access a variety of practice materials designed to help you master the course material. These materials may include explanations, videos, multiple-choice questions, flashcards, short answer, essays, and issue spotting.

Step 4: Select the **OUTLINE** tab in your toolbar to access chapter outlines that automatically incorporate your highlights and annotations from the e-book. Use the My Notes area for copying, pasting, and editing your book notes or creating new notes.

Step 5: If your professor has enrolled your class, you can select the **CLASS INSIGHTS** tab and compare your own study center results against the average of your classmates.

Is this a used casebook? Access code already scratched off?

You can purchase the Digital Version and still access all of the powerful tools listed above. Please visit CasebookConnect.com and select Catalog to learn more.

PLEASE NOTE: Each access code can only be used once. This access code will expire one year after the discontinuation of the corresponding print title and must be redeemed before then. CCH reserves the right to discontinue this program at any time for any business reason. For further details, please see the Casebook Connect End User Agreement.

PIN: 9111149710

32447

Editorial Advisors

Rachel E. Barkow
Segal Family Professor of Regulatory Law and Policy
Faculty Director, Center on the Administration of Criminal Law
New York University School of Law

Erwin Chemerinsky
Dean and Professor of Law
University of California, Berkeley School of Law

Richard A. Epstein
Laurence A. Tisch Professor of Law
New York University School of Law
Peter and Kirsten Bedford Senior Fellow
The Hoover Institution
Senior Lecturer in Law
The University of Chicago

Ronald J. Gilson
Charles J. Meyers Professor of Law and Business
Stanford University
Marc and Eva Stern Professor of Law and Business
Columbia Law School

James E. Krier
Earl Warren DeLano Professor of Law
The University of Michigan Law School

Tracey L. Meares
Walton Hale Hamilton Professor of Law
Director, The Justice Collaboratory
Yale Law School

Richard K. Neumann, Jr.
Professor of Law
Maurice A. Deane School of Law at Hofstra University

Robert H. Sitkoff
John L. Gray Professor of Law
Harvard Law School

David Alan Sklansky
Stanley Morrison Professor of Law
Faculty Co-Director, Stanford Criminal Justice Center
Stanford Law School

ASPEN COURSEBOOK SERIES

LEGAL WRITING
Process, Analysis, and Organization

SEVENTH EDITION

LINDA H. EDWARDS
E. L. Cord Foundation Professor of Law
William S. Boyd School of Law
University of Nevada, Las Vegas

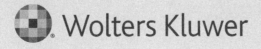

Copyright © 2018 CCH Incorporated. All Rights Reserved.

Published by Wolters Kluwer in New York.

Wolters Kluwer Legal & Regulatory U.S. serves customers worldwide with CCH, Aspen Publishers, and Kluwer Law International products. (www.WKLegaledu.com)

No part of this publication may be reproduced or transmitted in any form or by any means, electronic or mechanical, including photocopy, recording, or utilized by any information storage or retrieval system, without written permission from the publisher. For information about permissions or to request permissions online, visit us at www.WKLegaledu.com, or a written request may be faxed to our permissions department at 212-771-0803.

To contact Customer Service, e-mail customer.service@wolterskluwer.com, call 1-800-234-1660, fax 1-800-901-9075, or mail correspondence to:

> Wolters Kluwer
> Attn: Order Department
> PO Box 990
> Frederick, MD 21705

Printed in the United States of America.

1 2 3 4 5 6 7 8 9 0

ISBN 978-1-4548-9591-6

Library of Congress Cataloging-in-Publication Data

Names: Edwards, Linda Holdeman, 1948- author.
Title: Legal writing : process, analysis, and organization / Linda H.
  Edwards, E. L. Cord Foundation Professor of Law, William S. Boyd School of
  Law, University of Nevada, Las Vegas.
Description: Seventh edition. | New York : Wolters Kluwer, [2018] | Series:
  Aspen coursebook series | Includes bibliographical references and index.
Identifiers: LCCN 2017060731 | ISBN 9781454895916
Subjects: LCSH: Legal composition.
Classification: LCC KF250 .E38 2018 | DDC 808.06/634--dc23
LC record available at https://lccn.loc.gov/2017060731

SUSTAINABLE FORESTRY INITIATIVE   Certified Sourcing
www.sfiprogram.org
SFI-00756

About Wolters Kluwer Legal & Regulatory U.S.

Wolters Kluwer Legal & Regulatory U.S. delivers expert content and solutions in the areas of law, corporate compliance, health compliance, reimbursement, and legal education. Its practical solutions help customers successfully navigate the demands of a changing environment to drive their daily activities, enhance decision quality and inspire confident outcomes.

Serving customers worldwide, its legal and regulatory portfolio includes products under the Aspen Publishers, CCH Incorporated, Kluwer Law International, ftwilliam.com and MediRegs names. They are regarded as exceptional and trusted resources for general legal and practice-specific knowledge, compliance and risk management, dynamic workflow solutions, and expert commentary.

To Dan

Words fail.

SUMMARY OF CONTENTS

PART I

THE PROCESS OF WRITING PREDICTIVELY: THE OFFICE MEMO · 15

STAGE ONE
ORGANIZING FOR ANALYSIS: OUTLINING YOUR WORKING DRAFT · 17

STAGE TWO
DRAFTING FOR ANALYSIS: WRITING THE WORKING DRAFT · 73

STAGE THREE
CONVERTING YOUR WORKING DRAFT TO AN OFFICE MEMO · 121

CONTENTS

CHAPTER 3
USING RULES TO ORGANIZE YOUR ANALYSIS   27

CHAPTER 4
FINDING A RULE IN A STATUTE   37

CHAPTER 5
FINDING A RULE IN A CASE   45

CHAPTER 6
FINDING A RULE FROM MULTIPLE AUTHORITIES   57

STAGE TWO
DRAFTING FOR ANALYSIS: WRITING THE WORKING DRAFT

CHAPTER 7
ANALYZING A SINGLE ISSUE: RULE EXPLANATION

CHAPTER 8
ANALYZING A SINGLE ISSUE: RULE APPLICATION

CHAPTER 9
ANALYZING A SINGLE ISSUE: USING MULTIPLE AUTHORITIES

CHAPTER 15
REVISING FOR USAGE AND STYLE

PART II
PROFESSIONAL LETTER WRITING

CHAPTER 16
WRITING PROFESSIONAL LETTERS

PREFACE TO THE SEVENTH EDITION

Like prior editions, the seventh edition of *Legal Writing* adopts a process-based approach, not a document-based approach. Learning to write using a document-based approach is like learning to cook by reading a description of the finished dish: how it looks, how it tastes, how it smells. The description of the finished dish is important because the cook needs to understand her goal. But the description of the dish doesn't tell her what she needs to *do* to get there.

Learning to write using a process-based approach is like learning to cook that same dish by reading the recipe. The recipe takes the cook through the stages of preparation ("chop the carrots into quarter-inch slices; sauté the onions in one tablespoon of olive oil"). In those early stages, the elements of the dish don't look, taste, or smell the way they will when the cooking process is completed ("cook over low heat, stirring constantly until thickened; then pour into the chicken stock mixture and simmer for one hour"). But those intermediate stages are critical to achieving the end result.

Like a recipe, this book consciously tracks the stages in the writing process. Concepts are introduced at the points where they become relevant to a writer's process of creating and communicating content. In this new edition, the rule structure is still the starting point. Earlier expansions in the treatment of analogical reasoning and narrative are maintained, but the material is significantly streamlined to meet the needs of modern students. A streamlined approach also preserves the primary pedagogical role of the professor and the student's actual writing assignment. After all, a student can't learn too much by reading about how to write. The real action happens in the writing itself. This book aims to convey the crucial information without adding unnecessary distraction or reading time.

Other changes improve the book's substance. As adult learners, law students need to understand why they are being asked to learn in certain ways. Chapter 1, then, begins with a section on adult learning, the writing process, incremental learning, and "flipped" classrooms. Some content has been combined with other sections, making room for a new Chapter 4 on working with statutes. These days, most legal questions begin with statutes, so this new chapter gives statutes a more prominent place. The citation chapter has been updated as well. Chapter 16's treatment of letter writing has been streamlined to better match the needs of a first-year course.

The section on brief writing has been restructured and supplemented to provide more guidance in fewer pages. Chapter 18 uses the rule to help students identify issues, begin to organize a draft, and sketch out working headings. Chapter 19 teaches the skill of reworking a rule statement into a more favorable expression—not just accepting the most obvious rule statement from the authorities. Chapter 20 covers the first steps in writing the working draft, and Chapter 21 helps the student refine arguments, especially with the Question Presented and the standard of review. Chapters 22 (facts statements) and 23 (remaining components) complete the initial writing process. Revision and oral argument are covered in Chapters 24 and 25.

Appendices: The sample documents are designed, of course, for critique, not for mimicry. The samples in this edition are:

- *Appendix A:* An office memo applying a three-element conjunctive rule and using rule-based reasoning, analogies, policy, and factual inferences.
- *Appendix B:* An office memo applying a rule with factors and making significant use of factual analogies.
- *Appendix C:* Sample letters.
- *Appendix D:* A trial-level brief applying a procedural rule (setting aside a default judgment) that incorporates the substantive rule. A subpart of the analysis uses a set of factors.
- *Appendix E:* An appellate brief addressing a pure question of law setting out two alternative arguments.
- *Appendix F:* An appellate brief making extensive use of statutory construction tools, including the definition of terms used in the rule and arguments based on applicable policy rationales.

Linda H. Edwards
November 2017

ACKNOWLEDGMENTS

No book is the product of the author alone—certainly not this one. My former Mercer colleagues encouraged and supported the book from its inception. Mercer legal writing faculty Susan Bay, Jim Hunt, Lenora Ledwon, Gus Lehouck, Adam Milani, Kathy Sampson, Kevin Shelley, Michael Smith, Greg Spicer, David Walter, and Stasia Williams have taught me much and have made the learning fun. Three deans, Phil Shelton, Dick Creswell, and Larry Dessem, paved the way. Suzanne Cassidy, Sarah McPherson, Cary Gonzalez, Michelle Davis, Jane Burns, and Barbara Blackburn, worked faithfully and without glory. Special thanks to Jack Sammons for bold ideas, to Hal Lewis and Reynold Kosek for wise counsel, and to Sidney Watson and Joe Claxton for their faith in the project.

Like all teachers of legal writing, I am blessed by being part of the national legal writing community. No list could identify all the colleagues who have shared generously of their vision, enthusiasm, wisdom, and experience. I am especially indebted to Deirdre Alfred, Jan Armon, Mary Beth Beazley, Joel Cornwell, David Drueding, Alice Dueker, K.K. Duvivier, Neal Feigenson, Dennis Hynes, Steve Jamar, Katie McManus, Phil Meyer, Teresa Phelps, Terry Pollman, Leslie Reed, and the anonymous reviewers who made such perceptive comments on early drafts. Particular thanks to Mary Lawrence, Richard Neumann, and Marilyn Walter for their steadfast support of their legal writing colleagues, including me.

I gratefully acknowledge my debt to Emilie and Katie Edwards for their forbearance; to Cathi Reinfelder for redeeming the text from many errors; and to Carol McGeehan for nurturing and enlarging my vision of the book.

I would also like to thank the following copyright holder for permission to reprint the map of the federal judicial circuits: *2009 Summer Judicial Staff Directory* 963 (CQ Press 2000). Copyright © 2009 by Congressional Quarterly, Inc. Phone: (202) 729-1863; URL: *http://directories.cqpress.com*.

Before you begin your first legal writing assignment, take a moment to consider yourself, the nature of the authorities you'll be using, and your professional responsibilities.

I. WHO ME? A WRITER?

Most new law students wouldn't call themselves writers. They wouldn't say that in three years they plan to take a job as a professional writer, earning most of their income by writing for publication. But that's exactly what lawyers do. Most lawyers write and publish more pages than a novelist, and with much more hanging in the balance.

You are studying to be a professional writer, even if you don't think your skills are good enough yet to justify the title. If you think of yourself as a writer working on ways to improve your own craft, you'll find it much easier to learn the skills you need. You'll start to notice good and bad writing everywhere you look and imagine ways to improve it. You'll take the time to look up a pesky grammar rule. You'll be more willing to revise and edit. In other words, good writing will be important to you, and you'll soon find that it is within your grasp. In the long run, your determination to write well will make much more difference than your entry-level writing skills. What's the message? You can do this. All it takes is hard work.

> You'll earn most of your income by writing for publication.

II. PLIABLE AUTHORITY

Many of us arrive at law school thinking that learning the law will be like learning the rules of Monopoly™. But the law is not like Monopoly™. Many legal rules are created in a series of judicial opinions, so you'll find different versions of the rule written by different judicial writers, not just one official statement in the Rules booklet. And when they wrote those opinions, the judges were focused on deciding the case before them, not explaining future situations. What's more, some of those judges are not great writers, or perhaps they were too busy with a heavy caseload to think and write as clearly as they would have liked. Statutes can be unclear as well, and even the clearest statutes are later subjected to comment and explanation by multiple judges.

Even more fundamentally, a legal rule must use general verbal descriptions to identify the people and situations to which it applies. It isn't just a matter of who draws the card. Nor can the descriptions always be as concrete as "a player who lands on Park Place." The law often relies on such vague standards as "reasonable care" or "the best interests of the child."

Understanding the law is actually more like a detective's job than a Monopoly™ game. You're going to have to interpret what you find. You'll take clues from the language of courts, legislatures, agencies, and commentators. You'll have to evaluate the meaning and significance of it all to try to reach an answer that makes sense of those clues. In other words, understanding the law is a constructive act, and you will be the one doing the constructing.

This book will help you recognize and work with these legal clues so your legal analysis will be more accurate and thorough. Even so, adjusting to the uncertainty of the law and the pliability of authorities can be unsettling. Just remember that this frustration and confusion is part and parcel of beginning law study. Soon you'll be used to the uncertainty, and you'll even come to like the opportunities it can give you to influence the law's development.

III. ETHICS

Like everything else you do in law practice, your legal writing will be governed by the ethical standards your state has adopted. Most states use a version of either the ABA's Model Rules of Professional Conduct or the earlier Model Code of Professional Responsibility. Sanctions for violating these rules range from private censure to public disbarment. No matter the version your state uses, however, your objective legal writing[1] must meet at least these standards:

- *Competence* (including legal knowledge, skill, thoroughness, and preparation)[2];
- *Diligence*[3];
- *Promptness*[4];
- *Candid, unbiased advice.*[5]

It should go without saying that you must never advise or assist a client to commit a crime or a fraud.[6] Short of illegality or fraud, however, you might still disapprove of some of your client's options or views. For those uncomfortable situations, you'll have two points of comfort. First, while your advice must include an accurate assessment of the law, it can also include relevant moral, economic, social, and political considerations.[7] In fact, an important part of

---

1. The ethical rules governing *persuasive* legal writing are covered in Chapter 17.
2. ABA Model R. Prof. Conduct 1.1.
3. *Id.* at 1.3.
4. *Id.* at 1.3.
5. *Id.* at 1.7.
6. *Id.* at 1.2(d).
7. *Id.* at 2.1.

your counseling role is to help your client consider all factors—not just the law—before deciding a difficult question. Second, remember that advising a client doesn't mean that you personally endorse the client's activities or views.[8] It means only that you are providing the client with all the relevant information so that the client can make her own decision.

These ethical standards should apply to your legal writing starting now, not just after you are a lawyer. They apply to the work you'll do as a law clerk, and they'll be among the standards your legal writing professor will use to evaluate your law school writing. Be sure that every document you write meets these standards of professional responsibility.

IV. PLAGIARISM

A writer commits plagiarism if she presents as her own the words or ideas she has found in another source. Most of us first learned of plagiarism in school. There, plagiarism happens primarily when a writer (1) doesn't attribute an *idea* to its source, or (2) doesn't use quotation marks to show that the *words themselves* came from another source. In an academic setting, an author implicitly represents that she is the source of all ideas and words not otherwise attributed. Failure to attribute borrowed words or ideas constitutes plagiarism. It is both a lie and a theft.

In law practice, though, the concept of plagiarism can be confusing. Lawyers and judges often use, without attribution or quotation marks, language and ideas drawn from other lawyers' work. Firms keep form files and brief banks so documents prepared by one lawyer can be "recycled" by another. Law clerks write opinions to be signed by their judges. Judges incorporate into their opinions whole sections of briefs filed by lawyers. Associates write briefs to be signed by partners. Law publishers publish books of pleadings and other legal forms.

Some people question whether the concept of plagiarism applies in a practice setting. They argue that writing in law practice does not carry a representation that the author is the source of all unattributed ideas and words, especially not when the document is asserting a legal point. In legal practice, the writer's goal is not to take personal credit for originating ideas. Instead, in law practice, the goal is to serve the client efficiently and well. The identity of the writer is irrelevant. Proponents of this position argue that service to a client requires presenting the most effective material in the most effective manner for the least cost.

No matter what standards may apply in law practice, though, your law school writing is being done in an academic environment where the writing assignment has pedagogical goals. Each assignment focuses on helping

---

8. *Id*. at 1.2(b).

students learn and teachers evaluate that learning. To learn how to write good legal documents, you need to write them yourself, and your teacher needs to be able to identify your ideas and text to be able to evaluate them.

Your school's honor code probably prohibits plagiarism, which may include even "mere" carelessness. An honor code charge is serious business for any student, but especially for law students. In a couple of years, you'll be applying for admission to the bar, and most Character and Fitness Committees ask questions about honor code violations. You'll have to report any honor code proceeding. You may have to appear personally to explain yourself, and your bar admission may be delayed or denied.

So carefully follow your teacher's instructions about using material from another source or working with another student. Be precise in your note taking so you can tell where each idea came from and distinguish between paraphrases and quotes. *Unless you have explicit instructions to the contrary, do not use the words or ideas of another without proper attribution and, where appropriate, quotation marks.*[9]

Now that you understand your own status as a professional writer, the nature of the authorities you'll be working with, and the ethical standards you must meet, it's time to begin working out your analysis of the legal issue you've been assigned.

---

9. For a discussion of when quotation marks are appropriate, see Chapter 14, section III.

CHAPTER 1

FIRST THINGS FIRST

I. ADULT LEARNING: THE WRITING PROCESS, INCREMENTAL LEARNING, AND "FLIPPED" CLASSROOMS

Students from first grade through high school and even some in college might be able to learn well by simply doing whatever the teacher asks them to do, but adult learners are different. Adult learners both need and deserve to understand the point of what they are being asked to do. So how does adult learning work in law school? How should it?

Incremental Learning

Much of law school learning traditionally has been done by immersion. New law students are invited to jump into the pool, flail around, and try to keep their heads above water until they figure out how to swim. We show up on the first day, start reading cases, try to respond to questions in class, and feel generally lost for months on end. We're supposed to learn by finding our own way, by responding to questions in class, and especially by listening to the dialog our professor has with our classmates. Dean Michael Hunter Schwartz has called this the Vicarious Learning/Self-Teaching Model. We're supposed to learn primarily by listening to others talk in class and by teaching ourselves the law outside of class.

Thankfully, most extreme forms of this learning model have all but disappeared. Today, many professors supplement a gentler version of the traditional method with explanation, handouts, and even some exercises. Still, in most nonskills classrooms, a version of the traditional model predominates. But in a legal writing class, the primary course goal is different. The primary goal of a legal writing class is to teach new skills, and learning theory experts know that we best learn a new skill by taking small steps and gradually moving toward expertise. Luckily, legal writing fits this incremental learning model well.

Writing as a Process

Writing is a process with naturally occurring stages and distinct goals at each stage. As you move step by step toward a finished document, you learn new material at the time it becomes relevant to your work. That's why this book is *organized by those writing stages, not by the components of a finished document*. The book will take you through four main stages of a writing assignment and help you use each stage as your own writing coach. Look at the Table of Contents to notice the chapters in each of the following stages:

Stage 1. Before you think about your reader and about the finished document, you'll need to work out your own analysis. You'll need to figure out your answer to the question you've been asked. Stage 1 helps you take the first steps toward that analysis by identifying the issues and organizing them in a manageable way. In Stage 1, you'll learn how to read statutes and cases, synthesize them, and use the structure of a legal rule to organize your own thinking. You'll learn about the legal system in Stage 1, so you can evaluate the precedential values of the authorities you've found.

Stage 2. Once you've identified the issues and roughed out an organization, you'll need to work out your answers. Stage 2 shows you how to do that. Here is where you'll learn about explaining and applying a rule (a version of the famous "IRAC" organization) and how to organize your thoughts into the kind of structured, linear thought that lawyers use. Many of us come to law school without much prior experience in this sort of organization. The discipline of Stages 1 and 2 will help you develop this vital lawyering skill and use the writing process to guide, deepen, and test your ideas.

Stage 3. After your analysis is solid—and only then—Stage 3 helps you convert your analysis into a document designed for your reader. Here you'll tweak your organization to meet your reader's needs and add the other components of the document, like a heading, a question presented, a brief answer, a fact statement, and a conclusion.

Stage 4. Finally, in Stage 4, it's time to pay attention to the fine points of writing, like grammar, punctuation, clarity, and citation form. These matters may seem like technicalities compared to accurate analysis, but they are the first things your reader will notice. A sloppy document invites a reader to doubt its accuracy, so Stage 4 helps you make the document as technically perfect as it can be.

This book is organized by these writing stages *because the writing process is a thinking process*. In each stage, that process helps you think more clearly. Here are some hints for using this writing process to its greatest advantage:

- *Be willing to revisit earlier stages.* A completed document should take the reader on a linear journey, but you'll find the process of creating the document to be far from linear. It circles you back to earlier stages again and again as you understand more about the issue, the facts, and the law. The dynamic nature of this process makes it alive, challenging, even fun. If you're willing to construct, dismantle, and reconstruct your writing, you'll produce a good document.
- *Experiment with different writing strategies* and observe your own writing process. What works well for you at each stage and what doesn't? Do you work better if you dictate a draft first? Does free-writing help you? How about charts or colored pens? Each writer's process is unique. Try to learn as much as possible about your own.
- *Be patient.* On your first few writing assignments, don't try to combine or compress the writing stages. Your goal is to let each stage teach you some critical skills. Soon you'll be able to speed up each stage. For instance, you might find that you can accomplish the goals of the working draft stage with some other, quicker form of prewriting, like a detailed and annotated outline. When you're ready, you can customize each stage to fit your own skill level, the assignment's complexity, and your unique process.
- *Learn the general principles before you decide to try something new.* Learning legal writing is a little like learning music theory. In college, music students take courses in music theory. They first learn the principles most composers use in most situations. After they understand those principles, they can learn when and how to depart from them. This is an introductory course on legal writing, so it teaches the basic principles that apply in most situations. First learn those basic principles. Soon you'll develop the judgment to know when and how to choose a different strategy.

Legal Writing in a "Flipped" Classroom

Adult learning theory shows that adults learn better by active (experiential) learning activities—by applying new ideas to relevant situations. A "flipped" classroom is just such an opportunity. It means that your professor will expect you to have understood the reading material before you come to class. Don't expect her to just lecture about the same material you've just read. Instead, in class you'll often work on the exercises in each chapter or apply the concepts to your own writing assignment. Flipped classrooms provide the very best opportunities for learning, so welcome those class times when you and your classmates are actively working together.

Now, before you begin your first legal writing assignment, take a moment to consider your role, what to look for in a case opinion, and how lawyers reason about a legal question.

> Don't expect your professor to just lecture about the same material you've just read.

II. UNDERSTANDING YOUR ROLE

As a lawyer, you'll likely write many kinds of documents—court papers, letters, legal instruments, and internal working documents for the law firm. As different as these documents are from each other, they all fall roughly into one of three categories defined by your role when writing them. Your writing will differ significantly depending on which of these three roles you're performing.

- Planning and Preventive Writing
- Predictive Writing
- Persuasive Writing

Planning and Preventive Writing.   You'll do planning and preventive writing when you draft transactional documents like wills, trusts, leases, mortgages, partnership agreements, and contracts. Planning documents like these define the rights of the parties and the limits of their conduct, much as case law and statutes do for society at large. Planning and preventive writing can be very satisfying. You can create and structure some of the most important transactions and relationships in someone's life or in the commercial world. Also, with careful planning, you can prevent future disputes. Most lawyers would rather help clients prevent injury than recover from injury.

Predictive Writing.   Predictive writing is part of another satisfying task—client counseling. Clients and other lawyers will often seek your advice when they face an important decision. You'll need to research the law, predict the most likely result of each possible choice, and help your client or colleague choose wisely.

You'll write predictively in both transactional and litigation settings. In transactional settings, you'll predict legal outcomes to analyze and prevent possible problems. Litigation requires deciding many questions as well, ranging from relatively routine matters of litigation management to such fundamental matters as whether to settle the case.

In predictive writing, you'll often write an *office memo* (addressed to another lawyer who has requested your help) or an *opinion letter* (addressed to your client). Your job is to analyze the relevant law objectively, as a judge would do. In predictive writing, you weigh the strengths and weaknesses of each possible argument. You don't take a side. The answer might not be the answer your client or colleague wants to hear, but it's the answer they need in order to make a good decision.

Persuasive Writing.   Legal problems can't always be prevented, of course, and some end up in litigation. When that happens, you become an advocate, taking on a persuasive role. No matter what result you might have predicted, your job now is to persuade the judge to reach the result most helpful to your client. You'll marshal the strongest arguments and refute opposing arguments. The most common persuasive document is the *brief* (also called a *memorandum of law*).

Although the goals of prediction and persuasion differ, on a fundamental level they can't be separated. To predict a result, you'll have to understand the arguments each advocate would present. To persuade, you'll have to understand how the argument will strike a neutral reader. So improving your predictive analysis improves your persuasive analysis too, and vice versa.

Before you go on, turn to Appendices A and B, which contain sample office memos, and to Appendices D-F, which contain sample briefs. We'll study the parts of each document in more detail later. For now, just notice the function of each kind of document and how it will eventually appear.

EXERCISE 1-1

Recognizing Your Role
Identify the primary lawyering role called for in each of the following situations:

1. A client (a widower) has been diagnosed with a fatal form of cancer.
   a. The client asks you to draft a will and trust to protect his assets for his children.
   b. The client asks you whether there is a procedure by which he can designate someone to care for his children after his death and whether it would be wise for him to do so.
   c. The client asks you to file a lawsuit seeking recovery against his employer for exposure to carcinogens in the workplace.
2. A client has located a piece of real property she wishes to buy and then lease to a commercial tenant. The title registry lists an easement allowing the owner of the property next door to use the driveway along the back of the property. But the client would like to expand the existing structure on the property and eliminate the driveway.
   a. The client asks you whether the easement can be challenged legally.
   b. The client asks you to approach the owner of the property next door and seek the release of the easement.
   c. The client asks you to draft both the release of the easement and a lease for the new commercial tenant to sign.

III. READING CASES: INTRODUCTION

Even if your legal issue is controlled by a statute, you'll probably find yourself reading cases about that statute. In law school's first few weeks, reading cases may be the most important skill to practice. It's helpful to get an early overview of the parts of a case opinion so you know what information to notice and where to find it. Judicial opinions don't follow an established formula, but most of them roughly follow this format:

- Case name, court, citation, date (at the top of the opinion)
- Facts (what happened to raise the legal issue)
- Procedural history (what happened in prior courts or agencies)
- Legal issue(s) to be decided
- Rule(s) of law (the court's statement of the applicable legal standard)
- Reasoning (the court's reasons for deciding the case as it did)
- Holding (the court's decision on the relevant facts)
- Order (what will happen next (e.g., remanded for trial)

Notice the difference between the governing rule of law, the holding, and the court's reasoning. The *rule* sets out the legal test the court used to decide the case (e.g., to revoke a will, a testator must take some action that demonstrates her intent). The *holding* states the court's conclusion about whether the facts of this case meet that legal test (e.g., merely marking a large "X" across only the first page of a five-page will, as the decedent did here, is enough if the other evidence of intent is sufficiently strong). The *reasoning* is the full discussion of why the court decided the legal issue as it did. The court's reasons may include multiple forms of reasoning, including the language of the governing rule of law, comparisons to prior cases, policy rationales, and the court's interpretation of the facts. The final section in this chapter gives you an overview of legal reasoning. First, though, practice case reading with this exercise.

EXERCISE 1-2

Finding the Parts of a Case
Exercises in later chapters will use the case of *Coffee System of Atlanta v. Fox*, found in App. G. Read the case now and identify the parts of the opinion. Be ready to discuss your answers in class.

IV. HOW LAWYERS THINK

Lawyers and judges argue and decide cases by using several kinds of reasoning. Here are the most important:

- rule-based reasoning
- analogical (or counteranalogical) reasoning
- policy-based reasoning
- narrative

We'll study each more closely in later chapters, but we'll start with an overview. As you read cases in all your classes, notice how judges are using these kinds of reasoning.

(1) *Rule-based reasoning* applies a rule of law directly to the facts of the case. It says, "*X* is the answer because *the applicable rule of law* requires it." What is it about the following sentence that makes it an example of rule-based reasoning?

> **RULE-BASED REASONING**
> Harold Collier should not be bound by the contract he signed because he is a minor, and the case of *A v. B* held that minors can't execute binding contracts.

(2) *Analogical reasoning* shows factual similarities between earlier cases and the client's situation. It says, "*X* is the answer because *the facts of this case are just like the facts of* A v. B, *and* X *was the result there.*" What is it about the following sentence that makes it an example of analogical reasoning? How is it different from the example of rule-based reasoning using the same case in the prior example?

> **ANALOGICAL REASONING**
> Harold Collier should not be bound by the contract he signed because, like the successful defendant in *A v. B*, he is only sixteen.

Counteranalogical reasoning is the opposite of analogical reasoning. You show *differences* between case authority and the client's facts—differences that justify a different result in the client's case. What is it about the following sentence that makes it an example of counteranalogical reasoning?

> **COUNTERANALOGICAL REASONING**
> Harold Collier's situation is unlike the situation in *C v. D*, where the minor lost. The minor in *C. v. D.* had deliberately misrepresented his age, but Harold Collier never made any statement about his age.

(3) *Policy-based reasoning* asks which answer would be best for society at large. It says, "*X* should be the answer, because *that rule will encourage good results for our society and discourage bad results.*" What is it about the following sentence that makes it an example of policy-based reasoning?

> **POLICY-BASED REASONING**
> Harold Collier should not be bound by the contract he signed because he is only sixteen, and people that young should be protected from the harmful consequences of making important decisions before they are old enough to understand what they are doing.

(4) *Narrative* implies an answer *by telling a story whose theme calls for a certain result*. It uses storytelling techniques like characterization, context, description, dialogue, and perspective to appeal to commonly shared notions of justice, mercy, fairness, reasonableness, and empathy.

Sometimes the relevant legal rule incorporates a narrative theme. For example, in Harold's case, maybe the rule allows enforcement against minors only if the other party didn't use undue influence. Narrative would use storytelling techniques to show that the other party's conduct did or did not amount to undue influence. What is it about the following sentences that make them an example of narrative?

> **NARRATIVE**
> (where the narrative theme is part of the governing rule)
> Harold Collier should not be bound by the contract he signed because Jenkins, a car dealer for twenty-two years, pressured Harold, discouraging him from calling his parents to ask advice and telling him that another purchaser was looking at the car at that very moment. Jenkins lowered his voice, said, "I'll tell you what I'll do. I'll knock off $1,000 just for you—just because this is your first car. But you can't tell anyone how low I went. This will be our secret."

Even if the rule doesn't use a narrative theme, you can still use narrative to show the fairness of a certain result. A judge might exercise any available discretion in favor of the client or might create an exception to, reinterpret, or even overturn the rule. Narrative appeals to commonly shared notions of justice, mercy, fairness, reasonableness, and empathy. Because these values underlie many policy rationales, narrative can partner with policy-based reasoning, showing a real-life example of the policy that justifies the rule.

For example, remember that the rule about contracts made by minors is supported by the policy that minors should be protected from the harmful consequences of making important decisions before they are old enough to know better. Narrative can bolster that policy point. What is it about the following paragraph that makes it an example of narrative? And what is it about that narrative that relates to the policy-based argument?

> **NARRATIVE**
> (where the narrative theme provides an example of a policy point)
> Harold Collier should not be bound by the contract he signed. He is only sixteen; he has never shopped for a car; he was pressured by a sophisticated sales agent; he did not have the benefit of advice from any advisor; and the car purchase will exhaust the funds he has saved for college.

Each method of reasoning has persuasive power, and they work best together. Rule-based reasoning establishes the structure of the analysis (Chapters 2–6, 18, and 19). Within that structure, you'll want to use reasoning based on rules, analogies, policy, and narrative (Chapters 7–10, 19, 20). Start now to notice the kinds of reasoning you find in the cases you read, the arguments you hear your classmates make, and your own analysis of hypotheticals.

EXERCISE 1-3

Forms of Reasoning
Read section I-A of the sample office memo in App. A. Identify each form of reasoning you find.

Now you have a glimpse of the process that lies ahead, the concepts of incremental learning and flipped classrooms, your lawyering roles, the parts of a case opinion, and the forms of reasoning you'll use. It's time to begin working out your analysis of the legal issue you've been assigned. As we'll see in the next chapter, the first thing to do is to identify and outline the legal rule that will answer the question you've been asked.

THE PROCESS
OF WRITING
PREDICTIVELY:
THE OFFICE MEMO

ORGANIZING FOR ANALYSIS: OUTLINING YOUR WORKING DRAFT

CHAPTER 2

OUTLINING RULES

The first step in the writing process is identifying and outlining the legal rule that will answer your question. The good news is that this outline of the rule will give you the outline of your analysis. Later in the writing process, your analysis will become a document designed for your reader, but first it will go through several stages. Don't worry yet about your reader. First work out your own analysis.

I. OUTLINING A RULE: OVERVIEW

The foundation of your legal analysis is the relevant rule of law. By *rule of law* we mean a statement that explains the test for deciding a legal issue.[1] Begin by finding the rule that will govern your issue and outlining it.

This chapter introduces rule outlining first by outlining a rule in the abstract—that is, without reference to a set of facts or a legal question. *This is how you'll outline rules to make a "course outline" and to study for a final exam.* For a course outline, you'll outline rules in the abstract because you don't yet know the exam questions.

For the purposes of this chapter, skip Roman numerals; we'll add those in Chapter 3. Otherwise, though, just use traditional outline form: large-case letters, Arabic numerals, and small-case letters, as necessary. For example, imagine you are working on a course outline for your criminal law class. You are about to outline the rule that defines burglary:

---

1. Sometimes you can express a rule in more than one way. In Chapters 5 and 19, we'll explore the flexibility of legal rules.

Burglary is the breaking and entering of the dwelling of another in the night-time with the intent to commit a felony therein.

How might you outline this rule—that is, write it out in a way that makes its structure visible? As you can see, this rule contains a batch of elements, and *each* must be proven before a set of facts can constitute burglary. Here is an outline of this rule:

> To establish a burglary, the state must prove *all* the following elements:
>
> A. breaking
> B. entering
> C. dwelling
> D. of another
> E. in the nighttime
> F. intent to commit felony therein

Notice how this outline of the burglary rule will let you focus on each element in an orderly way, not forgetting any element and not mixing your analysis of any one element with any other.

II. COMMON RULE STRUCTURES

As you learn to outline rules you'll begin to see certain common structures. Noticing these structures helps you recognize them quickly and outline rules easily. As you see rules of law later in this book or in your other law school courses, develop the habit of noticing the rule structure. These structures will be fundamental to your legal analysis in all settings—legal writing assignments, course outlines, and exams.

1. A mandatory elements structure (a conjunctive test).   This kind of rule lists a set of elements, all required. Do you see that the burglary rule above is an example of a mandatory elements structure?

2. An either/or structure (a disjunctive test).   This kind of rule sets out two or more subparts, either of which is enough to answer the question. Here is an either/or rule:

An easement can be created by a deed, by an exception to the statute of frauds, by implication, or by prescription.

In outline form, the rule looks like this:

An easement can be created in any of the following ways:

A. by deed
B. by an exception to the statute of frauds
C. by implication, or
D. by prescription

Notice that the first two rule structures are different only because the introductory language tells us whether all subparts are required or whether any single subpart is enough to answer the question by itself.

3. A factors (aggregative) test. This kind of rule gives us a flexible standard guided by multiple criteria (factors). Some rules use an objective standard. The burglary statute, for example, defines burglary using a set of relatively objective criteria. Was it a dwelling? Did it belong to another? Did the defendant enter it? But some rules use a much more flexible standard, giving more leeway (discretion) to the judge. To help judges exercise their discretion wisely and uniformly, rules using flexible standards often identify factors (criteria) to guide the decision. Here's an example:

Child custody shall be decided in accordance with the best interests of the child. Factors to consider in deciding the best interests of the child are: the fitness of each possible custodian; the appropriateness for parenting of the lifestyle of each possible custodian; the relationship between the child and each possible custodian; the placement of the child's siblings, if any; living accommodations; the district lines of the child's school; the proximity of extended family and friends; religious issues; any other factors relevant to the child's best interests.

In outline form, the rule looks like this:

Child custody shall be decided in accordance with the best interests of the child, to be determined by considering relevant factors such as the following:

A. the fitness of each possible custodian
B. the appropriateness for parenting of the lifestyle of each possible custodian
C. the relationship between the child and each possible custodian
D. the placement of the child's siblings, if any
E. living accommodations
F. the district lines of the child's school
G. the proximity of extended family and friends
H. religious issues
I. any other factors relevant to the child's best interests

Notice the difference between this rule structure and a rule with mandatory elements (a conjunctive test). In a conjunctive test, all the subparts must be met. But here the subparts are just factors to consider together, not separate individual requirements. One or more can be absent without necessarily changing the result. The judge gauges the importance of each factor.

4. A balancing test. This kind of rule balances opposing considerations against each other. A balancing test is also inherently flexible, so it often includes factors or guidelines to help the judge weigh each side of the balance.

For example, consider this procedural question: Before trial, parties in civil litigation exchange information with each other by using interrogatories (written questions calling for answers under oath). A party receiving a set of interrogatories might object, arguing that answering would be unduly burdensome. To decide whether the party must answer the interrogatories, the judge applies the following rule:

> A party must respond to interrogatories unless the burden of responding substantially outweighs the questioning party's legitimate need for the information.

To measure "burden," the judge might consider a variety of factors, including the time and effort required, the cost, any privacy concerns, and any other circumstances. To measure "legitimate need," the judge might consider a variety of other factors, such as how important the information would be to the trial, whether the information is available from another source, and any other circumstances relating to the party's need. In outline form, the rule looks like this:

A party must respond to interrogatories unless the burden of responding substantially outweighs the questioning party's legitimate need for the information.

A. The burden of answering:
1. the time and effort necessary to answer
2. the cost of compiling the information
3. any privacy concerns of the objecting party
4. any other circumstances raised by that party's situation
B. The questioning party's need for the information:
1. how important the information would be to the issues of the trial
2. whether it would be available from another source or in another form
3. any other circumstances relating to the party's need for the information

Compare this rule structure with a factors test. In a factors test, the judge uses factors to decide a single standard (e.g., best interests of the child). In a balancing test, the judge balances two competing interests, using factors to gauge the strength of each interest as compared to the other.

5. **A rule with exception(s) (a defeasible rule).**   Any of these rule structures also might include exceptions. Here is an example of a rule with two exceptions:

> A lawyer shall not prepare any document giving the lawyer a gift from a client except where the gift is insubstantial or where the client is related to the lawyer.

In outline form, the rule looks like this:

> A lawyer shall not prepare any document giving the lawyer a gift from a client except:
>
> A. where the gift is insubstantial, or
> B. where the client is related to the lawyer.

Again, notice the difference between this structure and the others. The introductory language defines the subparts as exceptions to a general principle.[2]

6. **Rules combining several structures.**   Most of your early assignments will use relatively simple rules, but sometimes a rule might combine more than one rule structure. The larger structure will fit one of our examples, but within a subpart, the rule might use a different structure. We'll see more of how this works in Chapter 3, Part III. For now, just focus on the basic idea of rule outlining.

III. A FEW HINTS ABOUT OUTLINING RULES

Outlining a rule helps you understand the rule clearly. Outlining is a tool for careful, critical reading—perhaps the most important of all lawyering skills. Here are a few pointers for outlining rules:

1. **Follow traditional principles of outlining.**   Two outlining principles especially apply to outlining legal rules. (1) Each subdivision must have at least two parts; (2) Each subpart should include the whole analysis of that point and nothing more. For instance, in the burglary rule, notice that each subpart covers one and only one element.

2. **Notice relationships among subparts.**   Double check the relationships among subparts. If your rule has factors, how do they interrelate? Do they all count equally or might some be more important than others? You'll find clues

---

2. Sometimes (but rarely) the relevant rule might be a simple declarative statement with no subparts (e.g., to be valid, a will must be signed).

to these questions in the cases that apply the rule, and you can also use your common sense. The point here is to remember to ask yourself these questions as you formulate the rule.

3. Notice whether the list of elements or factors is meant to be exclusive. The rule might answer that question expressly, using language like "and any other relevant factors." Or the rule might merely imply whether the list is exclusive, such as by introducing the list with the word "including" to indicate that other factors may be relevant too. If the rule's language doesn't tell you whether the list is exclusive, check other authorities and use your common sense.

4. Consider restating the rule in your own words. Using your own words helps you understand the rule, and you can often state the rule more simply and clearly than its original writer did. But don't rephrase the *key terms* of the statute (e.g., "best interests of the child"), and be sure that your rephrasing is accurate.

5. Ask what you'd have to prove to show that the requirements of the rule are met (or not). For example, a rule might provide that a speaker's words will be considered an offer if the hearer had a reasonable belief that the speaker intended by the words to make an offer. The words "reasonable belief" would require the hearer to prove not one thing, but two: (1) that she believed that the speaker intended to make an offer, and (2) that her belief was reasonable.

6. You can sometimes change the tabulation (numbering and lettering scheme). You might be able to organize the rule more simply and clearly than its original writer did, but don't change the tabulation unless your version will be easier to understand and the original structure isn't so well known that the cases all use it in discussing the rule.

7. Convert layered negatives to affirmative statements if it won't change the meaning. Layered negatives often occur in rules with exceptions—rules where the main clause says that something is *not* permitted *unless* certain facts are true. For example, find the layered negatives here:

A lawyer shall *not* prepare any document giving the lawyer a gift from a client *except*:

A. where the gift is insubstantial, or
B. where the client is related to the lawyer.

Layered negatives are hard to understand. They make the rule structure needlessly complicated. Get rid of them when you can.

A lawyer *can* prepare a document giving the lawyer a gift from a client *only if*:

A. the gift is insubstantial, or
B. the client is related to the lawyer.

Exercises in Formulating a Rule from a Statutory Format

Use the rule structures above to outline the following rules about professional responsibility. These rules aren't easy, so you'll need to read each one carefully. Also, be prepared to see a variety of approaches among your classmates' answers. Think of these exercises as a game rather than a test,[3] and don't expect to find a "right" answer. Also, keep a copy of your answers. We'll be working with most of these same rules again at the end of Chapter 3.

EXERCISE 2-1 *7 factors*

A lawyer shall not . . . collect an unreasonable fee. . . . The factors to be considered in determining the reasonableness of a fee include the following: the time and labor required, the novelty and difficulty of the questions involved, and the skill requisite to perform the legal service properly; the likelihood, if apparent to the client, that the acceptance of the particular employment will preclude other employment by the lawyer; the fee customarily charged in the locality for similar legal services; the amount involved and the results obtained; the time limitations imposed by the client or by the circumstances; the nature and length of the professional relationship with the client; the experience, reputation, and ability of the lawyer or lawyers performing the services; and whether the fee is fixed or contingent.[4]

EXERCISE 2-2 *disjunc.*

(b) A lawyer may reveal information relating to the representation of a client to the extent the lawyer reasonably believes necessary. . . .

(5) to establish a claim or defense on behalf of the lawyer in a controversy between the lawyer and the client, to establish a defense to a criminal charge or civil claim against the lawyer based upon conduct in which the client was involved, or to respond to allegations in any proceeding concerning the lawyer's representation of the client.[5]

---

3. Learning theory teaches us that we learn better when we approach learning lightheartedly, as play.

4. Based on ABA Model R. Prof. Conduct 1.5(a).

5. ABA Model R. Prof. Conduct 1.6(b).

↗ conjunctive

EXERCISE 2-3

A contingent fee[6] agreement shall state the method by which the fee is to be determined, including the percentage or percentages that shall accrue to the lawyer in the event of settlement, trial or appeal, litigation and other expenses[7] to be deducted from the recovery, and whether such expenses are to be deducted before or after the contingent fee is calculated.[8]

exception ↗

EXERCISE 2-4

A lawyer who has formerly represented a client in a matter shall not thereafter represent another person in the same or a substantially related matter in which that person's interests are materially adverse to the interests of the former client unless the former client gives informed consent, confirmed in writing.[9]

Hint: Under what circumstances must the lawyer decline representation?

An Exercise in Formulating a Rule from a Statement in a Case

EXERCISE 2-5

A contract in partial restraint of trade and reasonably limited as to time and territory and otherwise reasonable is not void. *Coffee System of Atlanta v. Fox* (App. G) (paraphrased).

---

6. A contingent fee is a fee that is due only if the lawyer achieves a favorable result. For instance, the fee for representing a plaintiff in a personal injury suit might be 33 percent of any funds recovered. If nothing is recovered, the lawyer's fee is zero.

7. Such expenses can include court filing fees, costs of depositions, expert witness fees, transcript preparation charges, travel costs, and the cost of creating trial exhibits.

8. Based on ABA Model R. Prof. Conduct 1.5(c).

9. ABA Model R. Prof. Conduct 1.9(a).

CHAPTER 3

USING RULES
TO ORGANIZE YOUR
ANALYSIS

Chapter 2 introduced rule outlining. There you outlined rules in the abstract—without trying to answer a legal question. That's how you'll outline rules to create a course outline and study for a law school exam. Now we'll turn to rule outlining to answer a specific legal question. The rule outline will organize both your own analysis (your working draft) and, ultimately, the office memo (or brief) you'll write.

I. ORGANIZING A WORKING DRAFT

The first step toward creating your working draft is creating its organization, and the most important principle is this: *Use an outline of the rule as the outline of the analysis.*

For a simple example, we'll return to the burglary rule. Assume that you work in a prosecutor's office. Gerald Shaffer has been arrested for striking his estranged wife. The police have charged him with criminal assault. Because Mr. Shaffer forcibly entered his estranged wife's house, the police want to know whether they can also charge Mr. Shaffer with burglary. In other words, did Mr. Shaffer commit burglary? Assume that you have located and outlined this rule as we did in Chapter 2:

To establish a burglary, the state must prove *all* the following elements:

A. breaking
B. entering
C. dwelling

> D. of another
> E. in the nighttime
> F. intent to commit felony therein

It's easy to see how the rule's outline will organize your legal analysis. Using this outline as a guide, your analysis of the Shaffer question would discuss each element separately, completing the discussion of one element before proceeding to the next.

II. HINTS FOR ORGANIZING THE DRAFT

Outlining a rule to answer a legal question is almost the same as outlining a rule in the abstract. Here are the few differences and a couple of hints to make the process easier:

1. Begin with a Roman numeral devoted to the question you've been asked. Generally in predictive legal writing you'll be answering one or more questions. In the working draft, reserve the Roman numerals for these questions. For the Shaffer question, the Roman numeral would be:

> I. Did Mr. Shaffer's acts constitute burglary?

If you've been asked several questions, use a Roman numeral for each. If you've been asked only one question, use a Roman numeral "I" for that question, and don't worry that you have only one Roman numeral. Let the use of the Roman numeral assure you that this is the issue you were given and, therefore, that this is the point of connection between the question and your own analysis.

2. Immediately after the question, state the whole rule. For instance, in the burglary example the sentence would be:

> I. Did Mr. Shaffer's acts constitute burglary?
>
> To establish a burglary, the state must prove that the defendant's acts constituted a breaking and entering of the dwelling of another in the nighttime with the intent to commit a felony therein.

3. Now add the rule's subparts in outline form. These subparts will be the headings and subheadings of the corresponding parts of your analysis. Headings provide an important thinking and writing discipline. They help you stay on track as you write, not mixing the discussions of separate issues, ending up with fuzzy thinking (and writing). Here is the Shaffer outline with its subparts:

I. Did Mr. Shaffer's acts constitute burglary?

To establish a burglary, the state must prove that the defendant's acts constituted a breaking and entering of the dwelling of another in the nighttime with the intent to commit a felony therein.

A. breaking
B. entering
C. dwelling
D. of another
E. in the nighttime
F. intent to commit felony therein

4. Be sure that the outline answers the question you have been asked. The rule might not be phrased exactly as the answer to your question. For instance, assume that two lawyers from different firms, Janice Colby and James Kraft, are married to each other. Colby represents the owner of a parcel of real property listed for sale. Prospective buyers of the real property ask Kraft to represent them in negotiating a better price. Kraft wants to know if he must tell the prospective buyers that the lawyer for the owners is his wife. Here is the rule, phrased as you find it in the applicable code:

> A lawyer related to another lawyer as parent, child, sibling, or spouse shall not represent a client in a representation directly adverse to a person who the lawyer knows is represented by the other lawyer except upon the consent by the client after consultation regarding the relationship.

You could outline this rule, phrased just as you found it, like this:

A. A lawyer may not represent a client if *all* the following are true:
   1. the lawyer is related to another lawyer as parent, child, sibling, or spouse
   2. the lawyer's relative represents another party to the legal matter
   3. the interests of the two clients are directly adverse

B. Despite section A, the lawyer may represent the client if both the following requirements are met:

> 1. the lawyer discloses to the client the relationship with the opposing lawyer, and
> 2. the client consents

But this outline doesn't *directly* answer the question you were asked. You were asked whether Kraft must disclose his relationship, not whether he can represent the client. So rephrase the rule to directly answer the question you were asked, like this:

> I. Must Kraft disclose to the prospective buyers his relationship to Colby?
>
> A lawyer must disclose his relationship to another lawyer if the two lawyers are related as parent, child, sibling, or spouse; the other lawyer represents another party in the same legal matter; and the interests of the two clients are directly adverse.
>
> A. The lawyer is related to the other lawyer as parent, child, sibling, or spouse.
> B. The lawyer's relative represents another party to the same legal matter.
> C. The interests of the two clients are directly adverse.

Now the rule outline answers the question you were asked. The question asks whether the lawyer must tell his client about his relationship, and the rule begins "A lawyer must disclose to his client his relationship to another lawyer if . . ." The outline of the rule still accurately communicates the rule's meaning, but its subparts are rearranged to answer your question.

5. Personalize the outline. The rules you'll be working with are written to apply to everyone, so they don't refer to individual names or facts. To outline a rule as part of a course outline, this generalized version is fine. But to answer a legal question, personalize the outline by substituting the relevant names and key facts, as we've done with the Shaffer example below.

6. Phrase the subheadings as questions. In the working draft stage, the outline will be easier to use if you phrase the subheadings as questions, like this:

> I. Did Mr. Shaffer's acts constitute burglary?
>
> To establish a burglary, the state must prove that the defendant's acts constituted a breaking and entering of the dwelling of another in the nighttime with the intent to commit a felony therein.

> A. Did Shaffer's acts constitute a breaking?
> B. Did Shaffer's acts constitute an entry?
> C. Was the premises a dwelling?
> D. Did it belong to another?
> E. Did it happen in the nighttime?
> F. When he committed these acts, did Shaffer intend to commit felony inside?

Using questions reminds you to stay objective as you work out the analysis. They help you avoid slipping into advocating for your preliminary conclusions. Later, when you revise for your reader, you can change these questions into your conclusions on each subpart.

7. Don't be too quick to leave out part of the rule. If you're outlining the rule to apply it to a set of facts, you might be tempted to leave out part of the outline (an element or a factor perhaps) because that part doesn't seem to apply to your facts or maybe because, on that element or factor, the answer seems obvious. For example, return to the rule about preparing a will:

> A lawyer shall not prepare a will for a client if:
>
> A. the will gives the lawyer a bequest,
> B. the bequest is substantial, and
> C. the client is not related to the lawyer.

You might be tempted to assume that a parcel of real property is a bequest of substantial value and thus omit *B* from your outline because you take it as a given. Since *B* seems obviously true on these facts, maybe there is no point in discussing *B*. The only points at issue seem to be *A* and *C*.

But don't be so ready to assume. Let the outlining process teach you about how the rule works. You'll need to find out what the authorities say about the rule's meaning. Once you've researched both law and facts, you can decide how the rule will apply to your client. Only then will you know whether you can treat any parts of the rule as given.

III. RULES WITHIN AN UMBRELLA RULE

One more reminder: Every time you're working with a rule containing subparts, you'll be working with more than one rule. In the burglary case, for instance, the rule stating all of burglary's elements is a rule of law. But in each subsection, you'll have to work with the rule defining that element. The rule defining the "nighttime" element, for example, might be "a time between thirty minutes after sunset and thirty minutes before sunrise." Here's how our outline looks now:

I. Did Mr. Shaffer's acts constitute burglary?

To establish a burglary, the state must prove that the defendant's acts constituted a breaking and entering of the dwelling of another in the nighttime with the intent to commit a felony therein.

A. Did Shaffer's acts constitute a breaking?
   [state the rule on what constitutes a breaking]

B. Did Shaffer's acts constitute an entry?
   [state the rule on what constitutes an entry]

C. Was the premises a dwelling?
   [state the rule on what constitutes a dwelling]

D. Did it belong to another?
   [state the rule on what it means to belong to another]

E. Did it happen in the nighttime?
   [state the rule on what constitutes nighttime]

F. When he committed these acts, did Shaffer intend to commit felony inside?
   [state the rule on how to determine intent to commit a felony]

As you can see, you'll often be working with rules within a larger rule. We might call the larger rule—the one that establishes the relationships among the subrules—the "umbrella" rule. The subrules are like the spokes of an umbrella. As you've probably guessed, the umbrella rule will provide your overall structure. Look at the rule outlines in Chapters 2 through 4, and notice how the umbrella rules create the relationships among the subrules.

All the subrules might be set out in the same opinion or statute that states the umbrella rule (see the rules in Chapters 2 through 4). But sometimes you'll have to look in other cases or statutes for the subrules. The point is that when a rule has subparts, your analysis will need to account for the rule defining each subpart.

Exercises in Rule Outlining

These exercises revisit most of the exercises at the end of Chapter 2. Now, though, we add facts and a question to answer. For each exercise, outline a legal discussion of the question, using an outline of the rule as this chapter has explained. In other words:

- use a Roman numeral for the question
- draft a sentence stating the rule
- add the outline of the rule's subparts

- be sure the outline directly answers the question
- personalize the outline
- phrase the subheadings as questions and
- don't omit any relevant subparts.

Don't try to *answer* the legal issue. Just draft the *outline*.

EXERCISE 3-1

Rule Outlining

Wallace Luttrell, a lawyer, is considering raising his customary fees. He wants to know whether charging a fee of $4,000 for an uncontested divorce would be unethical. You researched the governing ethical rules and found the following rule:

ABA MODEL RULES OF PROFESSIONAL CONDUCT — RULE 1.5(a)

A lawyer's fee shall be reasonable. The factors to be considered in determining the reasonableness of a fee include the following: the time and labor required, the novelty and difficulty of the questions involved, and the skill requisite to perform the legal service properly; the likelihood, if apparent to the client, that the acceptance of the particular employment will preclude other employment by the lawyer; the fee customarily charged in the locality for similar legal services; the amount involved and the results obtained; the time limitations imposed by the client or by the circumstances; the nature and length of the professional relationship with the client; the experience, reputation, and ability of the lawyer or lawyers performing the services; and whether the fee is fixed or contingent.[1]

EXERCISE 3-2

Rule Outlining

Janice Tobin represents Victor Carletta in a divorce. While discussing the property issues of the divorce, Carletta told Tobin that he doesn't want to disclose certain financial accounts to his wife's attorney because he doesn't plan to report the income from those accounts on his income tax return. Intentionally not reporting income is a crime. Tobin is not comfortable with knowing and not disclosing Carletta's plans. She isn't sure what to do. May Tobin ethically reveal her client's plans? You researched the issue and found the following rule:

---

1. Based on ABA Model R. Prof. Conduct 1.5(a).

> **ABA MODEL RULES OF PROFESSIONAL CONDUCT—RULE 1.6(b)**
>
> (b) A lawyer may reveal information relating to the representation of a client to the extent the lawyer reasonably believes necessary. . .
>
> (5) to establish a claim or defense on behalf of the lawyer in a controversy between the lawyer and the client, to establish a defense to a criminal charge or civil claim against the lawyer based upon conduct in which the client was involved, or to respond to allegations in any proceeding concerning the lawyer's representation of the client.

Note: This rule covers only the question of whether Tobin can *reveal confidential information*. Other rules govern whether Tobin can *continue to represent* Carletta despite his plans. The general rule would require that she stop representing him if he persists.

EXERCISE 3-3

Rule Outlining

Matthew Willett has agreed to represent Juanita Bautista in a civil claim against another driver in a car accident. The fee will be a *contingent fee*, that is, a percentage of the recovery in the case. Willett has drafted a letter to Bautista describing the fee arrangement. He wants to know if his letter sufficiently describes the fee agreement. You have researched the applicable ethical rules and found the following:

ABA MODEL RULES OF PROFESSIONAL CONDUCT—RULE 1.5(c)

(c) . . . A contingent fee agreement shall state the method by which the fee is to be determined, including the percentage or percentages that shall accrue to the lawyer in the event of settlement, trial or appeal, litigation and other expenses to be deducted from the recovery, and whether such expenses are to be deducted before or after the contingent fee is calculated. . . .

EXERCISE 3-4

Rule Outlining

Several years ago, Clifford Foodman defended Carson on hit-and-run charges. Now a new client, Janoff, has asked Foodman to defend her on a contract dispute. Carson is the plaintiff in the case. Foodman wants to know whether he must get Carson's consent to represent Janoff in the case of *Carson v. Janoff* after formerly representing Carson on the hit-and-run charges.

ABA MODEL RULES OF PROFESSIONAL CONDUCT—RULE 1.9(a)

(a) A lawyer who has formerly represented a client in a matter shall not thereafter represent another person in the same or a substantially related matter in which that person's interests are materially adverse to the interests of the former client unless the former client gives informed consent, confirmed in writing.

IV. ORGANIZING BY RULE: SPECIAL CIRCUMSTANCES

Once you get the hang of it, organizing by rule will become straightforward and even easy, but the process might be a bit more complicated if

- your rule combines several structures;
- your issue uses rules from different sources;
- your issue requires analyzing separate rules with no umbrella rule;
- your issue requires two rules—one substantive and one procedural; or
- your state hasn't decided which rule to adopt.

Your professor will help you know whether your legal issue falls within any of them.

CHAPTER 4

FINDING A RULE IN A STATUTE

As we've been working on rule outlining, you might have noticed that most of our examples and exercises have been based on statute-like sources. These days, most legal issues are controlled, in one way or another, by statutes, so our next step is learning to find and state rules from statutes. In this chapter, we'll work on

- reading a statute
- identifying the issues the statute raises
- interpreting the statute's language.

I. READING STATUTES

First, let's be clear about the relationship between legislatures and courts. A statute binds the courts of that jurisdiction, but a court has the authority to interpret the statute's language.[1] If the legislature disagrees, it can amend the statute, and the court is then bound by the newly amended statute. But the court interprets the new statute in future cases, so to state an accurate rule, we'll need to read both the statute and the cases interpreting it.

Start with the statute. Reading statutes can be difficult because they can be complicated and even badly written. It's helpful to begin with a version of the famous five Ws that guide a journalist:

---

1. A court has the authority to rule a statute unconstitutional, and on that question, the court has the last word. Other nuances apply as well. We'll learn more about how all this works in Chapter 6, where we'll deal with multiple authorities.

The Five Ws of Reading a Statute

Who? Whose actions are covered?
What? What kinds of actions are required, prohibited, or permitted?
When? When did the statute become effective?
Where? Where must the actions have taken place to be covered?
What then? What consequences follow?

To find the answers to these questions, you might need to read more than the provision itself. If your statute is part of an act with multiple parts, you'll need to carefully read at least these parts:

- the individual provisions that seem to deal directly with the legal issue;
- any other provisions expressly cross-referenced by those provisions;
- the titles of all the provisions of the entire act;
- any definitions of terms used in the relevant provisions;
- any statement of purpose and preamble to the act;
- if length is not prohibitive, read the entire act;
- the dates of enactment and effective dates of the act and its relevant provisions;
- all this information for any amendments to relevant provisions;
- the same information, if available, for any prior versions of relevant provisions (to understand what changes the legislature intended to make when it enacted the current version).

Read word by word and phrase by phrase, paying attention to every detail. Even the internal tabulation (numbering or lettering) can be significant. Notice especially whether any list set out in the statute is meant to be exclusive. The statute might tell you expressly, by using language like "and any other factors relevant to the child's best interests." Or the statute might merely imply whether the list is exclusive, for instance, by introducing the list with a word like "including."

Some Important Words

and	unless
or	other
either	outweighs
all	limited to
include	may
except	shall

EXERCISE 4-1

Read this statute and answer the questions that follow it. If you would need more information to answer the question, identify the information you would need.

> A lawyer who has formerly represented a client in a matter shall not thereafter represent another person in the same or a substantially related matter in which that person's interests are materially adverse to the interests of the former client unless the former client gives informed consent, confirmed in writing.[2]

1. Assume that Lawyer Abbott previously represented Former Client Jones. Abbott is now representing New Client Harris in a matter involving Former Client Jones. Former Client Jones has filed a complaint with the state bar, alleging that Lawyer Abbott has violated the applicable professional rule (above). In your own words, make a list of what the state bar investigator would have to find out to decide whether Lawyer Abbott violated the professional rule.

2. Assume that last year Lawyer Cole represented client *A* in a car accident case. That case is now closed. Today *A*'s wife asked Lawyer Cole to represent her in a divorce proceeding against *A*. Must Lawyer Cole seek *A*'s consent to the representation? If *A* refuses to consent, can Lawyer Cole ethically accept the case anyway?

II. IDENTIFYING ISSUES

We've already been practicing outlining rules from statutes. Outlining a rule is how you identify the issues you'll need to analyze. To double check your rule outline, read the statute again, this time with a pencil in your hand. Look for key words or phrases. Look for language that helps you answer the Five Ws. You're looking for the answer to this question: What would someone have to prove to show that the statute has been violated (or not)? Circle each word that helps you answer that question. Include words that tell you something about the relationships among the statute's key terms (words like "and," or "or"). Here is an example:

---

2. Model R. Prof. Conduct 1.9(a) (2013).

THE STATUTE:
No cemetery shall be hereafter established within the corporate limits of any city or town; nor shall any cemetery be established within two hundred and fifty yards of any residence without the consent of the owner of the legal and equitable title of such residence.[3]

KEY TERMS:

cemetery	hereafter	established	within	corporate limits
city	town	250 yards	residence	
consent	owner	legal title	equitable title	

RELATIONAL TERMS:

or	nor	and

Can you see that each key term raises an issue? For example, only cemeteries are covered by this statute, so you'll have to find out what the term "cemetery" means. "Hereafter" raises an issue too. The statute doesn't prohibit all cemeteries—only those established "hereafter." After what? The date of the statute's passage? Or the date on which the statute became effective? What are those dates?

And what does the term "established" mean? Is a cemetery "established" when construction begins? Ends? When the cemetery first opens for business? When the first body is buried? Each key term raises an issue.

Are you surprised to find so many issues raised in one statutory sentence? Statutes are packed tightly with key terms, and each of them raises an issue. If you were analyzing whether and how this statute applies to your client's facts, you would have at least twelve issues to consider. Some of them would be easy to deal with and some might not be, but you'd have to think through them all.

One word of caution: Watch out for phrases that might sound like a single key term but might, in fact, be several. For example, a statute might provide that to make a valid gift, a donor must transfer possession of the gifted item with "manifested intent." You might first think of the words "manifested intent" as a single key term, but think again. To prove that something was a valid gift, you'd have to prove two things, not one: (1) that the donor intended to part with ownership, and (2) that this intent was sufficiently "manifested" to others. Your list of key terms should treat these words separately.

---

3. Va. Code, § 56 (Michie 1942), construed in *Temple v. Petersburg*, 29 S.E.2d 357 (Sup. Ct. Apps. Va. 1944).

EXERCISE 4-2

The Fair Housing Act, 42 U.S.C. §§ 3601–3619, prohibits housing discrimination. Underline the words or phrases that raise potential legal issues in the following portion of the Act:

> [I]t shall be unlawful . . . to refuse to sell or rent after the making of a bona fide offer, or to refuse to negotiate for the sale or rental of, or otherwise make unavailable or deny, a dwelling to any person because of race, color, religion, sex, familial status, or national origin.

III. INTERPRETING STATUTORY LANGUAGE

If binding case authority has already told you what the statute means, you can rely on that case law. But if not, you'll have to use other tools. Here are the most important:

The Text Itself. The most important tool is the "plain meaning" of the statute. If that meaning is not ambiguous, a court usually enforces it unless the result would be absurd. Also look for other parts of the statute or act that might tell you more about the language you're concerned with, such as the section explaining the act's purpose. Many acts contain separate definition sections. Even when your term isn't defined, other parts of the statute might give you clues about what the term means.

The Legislature's Intent. If the text of the statute is unclear, many courts will try to decide what the legislature intended,[4] perhaps by considering the legislative history of the statute. Legislative history consists primarily of the documents made by the legislative body during its deliberations. Legislative history comes in many forms, such as committee reports, speeches, witness testimony, or studies introduced into the record. Your research text will tell you more about legislative history and how to find it.

Policy. Courts can also consider the policy concerns implicated by various interpretations. Some of those policies may have been part of the legislature's intent, but the legislature might not have foreseen all policy concerns. If the legislature hasn't spoken on the issue, a court can consider its own view of which interpretation would produce the best overall results.

---

4. Figuring out what the legislature intended isn't easy. The statute was probably enacted by a large group of elected officials who were serving in that office years ago. The text was probably produced by political compromise, and various legislators might have had vastly different intentions for that language. Quite possibly, your question never occurred to them at all. How can we decide the intent of the legislature as if the legislature were an entity with one mind? But when a statute's language is unclear, a court must have some basis for a decision, and legislative intent can be a part of that rationale.

Also, some *kinds* of statutes carry a general policy leaning that applies to all statutes of that kind. These policies call for either a broad or a narrow interpretation of that kind of statute. Here are the most common of these policy leanings:

- Statutes that change long-standing case law (statutes "in derogation of the common law") should be strictly construed (read narrowly, so that doubt is resolved in favor of less change).
- Statutes intended to remedy a problem ("remedial statutes") should be liberally construed (read broadly to include more kinds of situations than a narrow reading would allow) so they can accomplish their remedial purpose.
- Statutes making certain conduct a crime ("penal statutes") should be narrowly construed, out of concern for the rights of the accused.

Finally, courts are guided by the general policy that, if possible, the meaning of any statute should be construed in a way that will render the statute constitutional.

Agency Interpretation.　If an agency is responsible for enforcing a statute, that agency won't be able to do its job without deciding what the statute means. Courts often look to such an agency as the entity with the most expertise in the relevant issues. If so, the court is likely to give deference to the agency's interpretation. The court also might consider the interpretation of an agency that has no authority to enforce the statute but nonetheless works with the statute routinely. Look for agency interpretations in the agency's regulations, in the agency's decisions, and in case law.

Commentators and Other Courts.　Finally, as with any other legal question, courts may see persuasive value in the opinions of other courts and of respected commentators.

IV. CANONS OF CONSTRUCTION

In case of ambiguity, a court may also consider commonly accepted maxims of interpretation known as "canons of construction." Here are some of the most generally applicable:

- Give effect to rules of grammar and punctuation.
- Use the technical meaning of technical terms and the ordinary (person on the street) meaning for nontechnical terms.
- If the same words appear in various parts of an act, we presume that the words have the same meaning throughout.
- If the statute sets out a list that ends with a phrase like "and any other," these "other" items should refer only to things that are relevantly similar to the items in the list.[5]

---

5. This principle is sometimes called the principle of "ejusdem generis," meaning literally "of the same genus."

- Modifying words generally modify the first possible referent immediately prior to the modifier.[6]
- Where a statute from state X is adopted in state Y, the interpretation by the courts of state X should be followed in state Y.
- If the statute doesn't contain an exception for a certain situation, the courts shouldn't create one.
- Absent clear indication, the court should presume that the legislature didn't intend to enact a statute that contravenes fundamental shared societal values.
- Specific description of one or more situations in the text of a statute implies the exclusion of other kinds of situations not mentioned.
- Different statutes on the same legal issue (statutes "in pari materia") should be read consistently, especially where the legislature intended to create a consistent statutory scheme.
- Sometimes the courts of state X will have interpreted a word in a certain way. If the legislature of that state later enacts a different statute that uses that same word and doesn't define it, we should presume that the legislature meant to use the court's preexisting interpretation of that word.
- Although not technically part of the statute's text, such items as titles, preambles, and section headings are evidence of legislative intent.
- If a court has interpreted a statute in a certain way and the legislature later amends the statute but doesn't change that language, we could conclude that the legislature was satisfied with the court's interpretation.

These canons of construction may be treated as legal principles in and of themselves, so if you use one or more of them, you should try to cite to a case that applied that canon. But even if you can't find case authority that adopts the maxim, a court still might be persuaded by the canon's logic.

None of these guidelines for interpreting statutes can provide a certain answer. As a matter of fact, when you apply several, they might support contradictory results.[7] But because most courts will consider these guidelines, they'll help you predict what a court might decide.

---

6. For example, consider a statute that uses the phrase "relating to aggravated sexual abuse, sexual abuse, or sexual conduct involving a minor or ward." Does an offense relating to aggravated sexual abuse have to involve a minor or ward? Probably not. The modifying phrase ("involving a minor or ward") should refer only to the possible referent immediately prior ("sexual conduct"). See *Lockhart v. United States*, 136 S. Ct. 958 (2016).

7. Karl N. Llewellyn, *Remarks on the Theory of Appellate Decision and Rules or Canons About How Statutes Are to Be Construed*, 3 VAND. L. REV. 395 (1950).

CHAPTER 5

FINDING A RULE IN A CASE

Now that you've had some practice with outlining rules from statutes, it's time to turn our attention to formulating and outlining rules from a case opinion.

I. WHY FORMULATE A RULE FROM A CASE?

So you've found a case right on point. Why not just apply that case to your client's facts and be done with it? To answer that question, let's look at an example.

Facts: Your firm represents Sharon Watson, a sales employee of Carrolton Company, headquartered in Atlanta, Georgia. Watson had previously owned Carrolton and sold it to its present owners. She stayed on as an employee and signed a covenant not to compete (an agreement promising not to compete with Carrolton in certain ways for a certain span of time after her job ended). Now Watson is considering leaving Carrolton to form a new business that would compete with Carrolton. She needs to know whether Carrolton would be able to enforce the covenant against her. You've been asked to write an office memo predicting how a court would answer that question.

You research the issue and find *Coffee System of Atlanta v. Fox*, a Georgia case dealing with enforcement of covenants not to compete. *Fox* appears in Appendix G. Take a moment to read it.

A beginning legal writer finding the *Fox* case might write out a legal analysis like this:

- Describe the facts and the court's conclusion in *Fox* (that the covenant was enforceable).

- Compare those facts to Watson's facts.
- Conclude that the Watson covenant is or is not enforceable (because the Watson facts are/are not similar to the *Fox* facts).

This analyses is based on whether the two sets of *facts* are similar. But without identifying the rule, we can't know which of these similarities or differences matter—that is, which would make any difference to the outcome. For example, in *Fox*, the plaintiff was in the business of selling coffee systems. Did that affect the court's decision? Would it matter if the next litigants were disputing a covenant that prevented the defendant from manufacturing shoes? Or selling real estate? Without identifying a rule of law, we can't tell.

In legal analysis, the rule of law tells us which factual similarities or differences matter. The rule is the bridge between the facts of the precedent case and the facts of the present situation. So to use a case opinion as authority, you've got to articulate a *rule of law* from that opinion and then apply that *rule* to the client's facts.

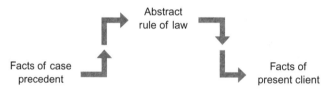

This is not to say that you'll ignore factual comparisons. As we saw in Chapter 1, using an analogy to a similar case is an important kind of legal reasoning. When the facts of the two cases are strikingly similar, the analogy is probably the most powerful analytical tool of all. But you'll still need to articulate a rule of law connecting the two cases. The analogy can then show that the rule of law from *Fox* would apply to Watson's case in the same way the court applied it to the facts in *Fox*.

So instead of organizing by factual comparisons, organize by the outline of the legal rule from *Fox*. Let's say that you've read *Fox* and formulated its rule like this:[1]

A covenant is enforceable if all the following elements are reasonable:

1. the kind of activity restrained,
2. the geographical area of the restraint, and
3. the time span of the restraint.

---

1. You could formulate other versions of the rule from *Fox*, as we'll soon see.

Do you recognize the structure of that rule? It's a conjunctive rule—a rule that sets out a test with required elements. Now, use it to draft the outline of your analysis of the Watson question just as Chapter 3 explained.

I. Is the Watson/Carrolton covenant not to compete enforceable?

The covenant is enforceable if the activity restrained, the geographic area of the restraint, and the time span of the restraint are all reasonable.

A. Is the kind of activity restrained reasonable?
B. Is the geographical area reasonable?
C. Is the time span reasonable?

II. A SLIPPERY TASK

Formulating a rule from a statute, as we have mostly done in prior chapters, is not always straightforward, but at least a statute's drafter was engaged in that same task—the task of drafting a rule of law to be applied to future situations. A statute drafter's goal is to write out the whole rule in one spot using something resembling a rule structure.

Not so with case opinions. Judges try to do a good job of writing opinions, but they have too few law clerks, too many cases, and too little time. These handicaps can't be overcome completely, even by perfect people, and judges aren't perfect. They are human, just like the rest of us. Some of them are not superlative legal writers, and even the best legal writers sometimes write unclearly.

Also, a judge's primary job is to resolve the dispute before her. It's customary to explain the decision by discussing legal principles, but a judge doesn't have to use a certain format or comply with standards of thoroughness or clarity. Also, the judge is writing in prose—a less precise genre than legislation. And even if the judge tries to write with legislative precision, she doesn't have the benefit of a legislative review process to edit her text.

Finally, a statute creates one authoritative statement, but for rules from cases, you might find many case opinions with each judge restating the rule in her own words. Sometimes the language variations are dramatic. So, formulating and outlining a rule from a case can be challenging, but you'll soon develop the skills and experience you'll need for the task. We'll start here with a way to understand the significance of a single case: the inherited rule and the processed rule.

III. INHERITED RULES AND PROCESSED RULES

Early in a judicial opinion, most judges will state a rule from earlier cases or from a statute. The opinion then applies that rule to the facts before the court and reaches a result. Reading that result and understanding how the court got there tells us new information about the rule and what it means.

Notice that we're using the word "rule" to refer both to the rule of law the opinion inherits from prior authorities and the complete rule as it appears when the opinion concludes. You might think of these as "the inherited rule" and "the processed rule." The opinion usually inherits a rule from earlier authorities and processes it by applying it to a new set of facts, explaining more about the rule in the process. The opinion might change the inherited rule in some way. Or it might simply add more information, so the rule coming out of the case is the same rule but now with new information about what it means. Either way, the rule you are primarily interested in is the processed rule.

To formulate a rule from a case, start by identifying:

- the inherited rule
- the relevant facts
- the new information the judge gives us about the rule
- the judge's decision about how the rule applies to the new facts
- the processed rule

The inherited rule. This is the starting point of the opinion's analysis—the legal principle the court takes from prior authorities. For a contracts case dealing with whether a certain communication was complete enough to be a valid offer, the inherited rule might be that an effective offer must include all essential terms. For a negligence case where the plaintiff knowingly entered a burning building, the inherited rule might be that a person assumes the risk of injury when he makes a voluntary choice to subject himself to known danger.

The facts relevant to the rule. These are the facts the court used to decide how to apply the inherited rule in that case. For the contracts case, a relevant fact might be that this communication didn't include a statement of price. For the torts case, the fact might be that the plaintiff entered the burning building to save his child.

The new information about the rule. This is anything new the opinion teaches us about the rule. In the contracts case, the court might tell us that price is an essential term. In the torts case, the court might tell us that a choice isn't voluntary where a father must choose between entering the burning building or not saving his child.

The court's decision about how the rule applies to these facts. This is the result the court reached after applying the inherited rule and the new information to the new situation. For the contracts case, the decision might be that the plaintiff had not made an effective offer. For the torts case, the decision might be that the plaintiff had not assumed the risk of injury.

The processed rule.   This is the inherited rule modified or supplemented by the new information about the rule. Your notes distilling these parts of the opinion might look like this:

CONTRACTS CASE

Inherited rule	An effective offer must include all the essential terms of the proposed contract.
Relevant facts	The plaintiff's communication did not include a price, and the parties had no prior course of dealing to determine price.
New information	Price is an essential term of a valid contract. The term must be stated expressly or it must be discernible from the past dealings of the parties or from some other accepted standard.
Decision	The plaintiff did not make an effective offer here because the price was unstated and the parties had no past dealings.
Processed Rule	An effective offer must include all essential terms. Price is an essential term of a valid contract. The price must be stated expressly, or it must be discernible from the past dealings of the parties or from some other accepted standard.

TORTS CASE

Inherited rule	Assumption of the risk requires a voluntary choice.
Relevant facts	The plaintiff entered the burning building to save his child.
New information	A choice is not voluntary when a father must choose between entering the building or not saving his child.
Decision	The plaintiff did not assume the risk of injury.
Processed Rule	?

Before you continue reading, try your hand at formulating the processed rule from the torts case.

IV. TOOLS FOR FINDING NEW INFORMATION

To find the new information a case gives you about a rule, ask yourself these questions:

- What did the court *say* about the rule?
- How did the court *apply* the rule?
- How did the court *not* apply the rule?
- What *facts* did the court emphasize?
- What *policy* considerations did the court discuss (if any)?

1. Notice what the court said about the rule. The judge usually gives us some explanation of the rule before applying it to the facts of that case. Here the judge's main goal is to tell us about the rule. Begin with this part of the opinion. The *court's* explicit explanation of the rule gives you the most important new information.

2. Notice how the court applied the rule. After noticing what the court *said* about the rule, look at how the court *applied* the rule to the facts before it. If the rule requires that an action must be "reasonable," the opinion will decide whether the facts before it meet that standard.

3. Notice how the court did *not* apply the rule. If you're wondering whether a certain fact from your client's situation would affect the outcome, ask whether that kind of fact seemed to affect the judge's ruling in the earlier case. A judge's silence usually can't be considered a binding rule of law. But if the most likely reason for the silence is that the ignored fact wasn't relevant to the outcome, the silence can be helpful information. After all, your goal here is to figure out what accounted for the judge's decision.

4. Notice any facts the court emphasized. When a judge describes the facts or applies the law, she might emphasize a certain fact. Usually, she explains why that fact is important, but sometimes not. Even if the judge didn't directly explain whether or why that fact was important, the opinion's emphasis on it implies that the judge found it significant somehow. Your job is to figure out why the court emphasized that fact. Think about what else the opinion tells you and use your common sense.

5. Look for any policy considerations that explain the rule. Sometimes the authorities will explain *why* this rule is better than other possible approaches. Maybe the reasons include a lofty constitutional concern for a citizen's civil rights. Maybe the reasons are utterly pragmatic, such as recognizing that a different rule isn't realistic. As we saw in Chapter 1, these reasons are called "policies." When the court discusses underlying policies, we learn more about what the court meant by the rule and how the rule would apply in new situations. Again, use your common sense. What mischief is the rule designed to prevent? What social good is the rule designed to encourage? Even if the opinion doesn't identify relevant policies, you can imagine what they might have been.

V. CHOOSING THE RULE'S BREADTH

Remember from this and earlier chapters that rules can be formulated in different ways. One way rule formulations can differ is in breadth. For instance, in the torts opinion above (let's call it *Cantwell v. Denton*), you might have formulated a rule that looks something like this:

> Assumption of the risk requires a voluntary choice. A father's choice to enter a burning building is not voluntary.

This rule formulation describes the situations to which the rule would apply, and the description is narrow. It says that this rule applies to fathers who are choosing between entering a burning building and the lives of their children. It tells us nothing about whether the rule would apply to persons other than fathers, to situations other than burning buildings, or to saving people other than children. It certainly tells us nothing about whether the rule would include saving property rather than lives. But you might need to predict how a court would rule in one of those situations.

Facts of Example

Mr. and Mrs. Gregory have asked your firm to represent them in litigation against Jerico Auto Works, an auto repair business. Jerico advertised oil changes completed in twenty minutes, "while you wait." On the fateful day, the Gregorys put a turkey in their oven, set the temperature at 325 degrees, and left for town to have Jerico change the oil in their car. Jerico completed the job, and the Gregorys began driving the rural road toward their home.

They were only halfway home when they noticed the internal engine heat beginning to climb. They realized that they were running low on oil and guessed—correctly, as it turned out—that Jerico hadn't tightened the oil plug. But they also realized that the turkey in their oven was nearly done. They had few neighbors on this rural road, so the odds were small that they would be able to flag another driver and get home before the burning turkey might cause a fire in their kitchen.

They decided to drive on, hoping to make it home before their kitchen (and perhaps their house) burned. The Gregorys got close enough to walk the rest of the way and so saved their kitchen, but at the cost of serious engine damage. Jerico refuses to pay for the damage because the Gregorys continued driving after noticing the engine temperature.

As part of deciding whether to accept the case, an attorney in your firm has asked you to predict whether the decision to continue driving would be considered an assumption of the risk. If so, recovery would be jeopardized.

Figuring Out a Rule

Assume that your only authority is *Cantwell v. Denton*. Suppose you stated the rule of *Cantwell* as we did above:

> Assumption of the risk requires a voluntary choice. A father's choice to enter a burning building is not voluntary where he must choose between entering the building and failing to save his child.

This rule won't tell you much about whether the Gregorys' decision would constitute assumption of the risk. But what if you could state the rule more broadly? Maybe a judge deciding the Gregory case might agree that the *Cantwell* rule is broader than just fathers, burning buildings, and children. Do you think the court in *Cantwell* meant to limit its holding to such a narrow situation?

Most opinions will contain at least several paragraphs explaining the court's decision. The language the court used is your main evidence, but also consider how the court actually applied its rule and what authorities the court cited for support. Consider these versions of the relevant part of the *Cantwell* opinion:

VERSION 1
A father's choice to enter a burning building is not voluntary where he must choose between entering the building and failing to save his child. The bond between a parent and a child is the strongest human bond. In situations that otherwise would constitute assumption of the risk, the law should not penalize a plaintiff for fulfilling the duties of a parent to a child.

VERSION 2
A father's choice to enter a burning building is not voluntary where he must choose between entering the building and failing to save his child. Our law places the highest value on human life, and the highest form of courage is to risk one's own life to save another. The doctrine of assumption of the risk was not designed to penalize one who demonstrates this kind of courage.

VERSION 3
A father's choice to enter a burning building is not voluntary where he must choose between entering the building and failing to save his child. We must remember, after all, that it was the defendant's negligence that placed the plaintiff in the position of having to choose between the threatened harm and an equal or greater harm. A defendant cannot subject the plaintiff to such a Hobson's choice and then defend against his own negligence by pointing to the plaintiff's response.

What broader rule might you formulate if *Cantwell*'s discussion reads like Version 1? What about Version 2? Version 3? Which version would allow you to formulate a rule to address the Gregorys' concern about their kitchen?

Version 1 grounds the rule in the special obligations of a parent to a child. In Version 1, you can formulate a rule that applies to parents, not just fathers. Maybe you could even formulate a rule that would cover property damage if protection of the property was a clear parental duty. But the Gregorys' dilemma didn't involve parental duty, so Version 1 won't tell the Gregorys much.

Version 2 grounds the rule in the special value we place on trying to save human life. In Version 2, your rule wouldn't be limited to a parental obligation, but it still might not cover property damage.

Version 3 grounds the rule in the results of the defendant's negligence. That negligence put the plaintiff in the difficult position of choosing between two threatened harms. Version 3 allows you to formulate a rule like this:

> Assumption of the risk requires a voluntary choice. When the defendant's negligence forces the plaintiff to choose between the threatened harm and another equal or greater harm, the plaintiff's choice is not voluntary.

Figure 5-1 demonstrates how this broader formulation of the rule would allow the Gregorys to argue that they did not assume the risk of damage to their car by continuing to drive.

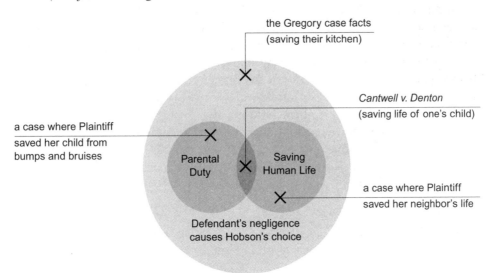

Figure 5-1 **Situations Covered by Each Rule Formulation**

VI. HOLDING VERSUS DICTA

You'll need to understand one more idea before you tackle rule formulation from a case opinion: the difference between *holding* and *dicta*.[2] Only a holding

---

2. The full term is *"obiter dictum,"* literally meaning "a remark made in passing."

is binding on future courts. If the language you want to rely on is dicta,[3] a judge in a future case might *choose* to follow it, but isn't *bound* by it.

How can we tell? A statement of law necessary to the court's result is part of the holding. The judge might make many statements about the law. Some will be necessary to the decision, and some may not. Statements of law not essential to the outcome are dicta.[4]

> **Example:** Remember the contracts opinion (described above) dealing with whether a communication without a price could be a valid offer. In that opinion, the court might have made some other statements about other rules of law. The judge might have mentioned that a valid contract requires an offer, acceptance, and consideration. But the judge didn't decide that case by considering whether there had been a valid acceptance or sufficient consideration, so any statements about acceptance or consideration would be dicta.

Is the language you're interested in holding or dicta? If it's part of the holding, you can use it to formulate a rule of law without wondering whether it is binding in future cases. If it's dicta but it's the only authority you can find, you can still use it to formulate a rule. Though dicta isn't binding, a lower court often gives it great deference. Since many trial and intermediate appellate court judges view their role as applying the law as the higher court would, dicta is persuasive evidence of what the higher court would hold. But be careful not to mislead the court or another lawyer by presenting your formulation of the rule as if it were part of the holding.

The distinction between holding and dicta is sometimes clear, as in the contracts example above. But sometimes the distinction is debatable. You won't always know for sure whether a certain statement of law was necessary to the court's decision.

> **Example:** Back to *Cantwell v. Denton*, our hypothetical case about assumption of the risk. What if the *Cantwell* opinion included all three versions? What if the opinion reads like this:
>
> A father's choice to enter a burning building is not voluntary where he must choose between entering the building and failing to save his child. The bond between a parent and a child is the strongest human bond. In situations that

---

3. Technically, "dictum" is singular and "dicta" is plural, but it's common to simply use the plural version. That's what we'll do here.

4. Don't confuse dicta with the "inherited rule." Inherited rules can be dicta or they can be part of the holding, depending entirely on whether the inherited rule is part of the law necessary to the court's result. If the court describes an inherited rule and relies on it to reach the result, the inherited rule is part of the holding. If the court describes an inherited rule but the inherited rule is not a necessary component of the court's reasoning in reaching the case's result, the inherited rule is a dicta.

> otherwise would constitute assumption of the risk, the law should not penalize a plaintiff for fulfilling the duties of a parent to a child.
>
> Further, our law places the highest value on human life, and the highest form of courage is to risk one's own life to save another. The doctrine of assumption of the risk was not designed to penalize one who demonstrates this kind of courage.
>
> We must remember, after all, that it was the defendant's negligence that placed the plaintiff in the position of having to choose between the threatened harm and an option of equal or greater evil. A defendant cannot subject the plaintiff to such a Hobson's choice and then defend against his own negligence by pointing to the plaintiff's decision.

If you are trying to persuade the judge that the Gregorys didn't assume the risk by continuing to drive, you'll argue that the rule drawn from the third paragraph is *Cantwell*'s holding. But if you represent Jerico, you'll argue that the statements in the third paragraph are dicta. You'll argue that the narrower statements of law in the first and second paragraphs were all that were necessary to decide *Cantwell*, so the broad statements in the third paragraph are "mere dicta."

If you are writing an office memo predicting the judge's decision on the Gregory facts, you'll want to account for both possibilities.

EXERCISE 5-1

Formulating and Outlining a Rule from an Opinion
Facts
Attorney Karen Berry provided her client with $50,000 in financing for a business venture. In exchange, Berry received a security interest in several of the assets of the business and assumed partnership status. The relationship between Berry and her client went bad, and the client has reported Berry to attorney disciplinary authorities, alleging that Berry unethically took advantage of the lawyer-client relationship in the transaction. The investigating lawyer has asked you to figure out whether Berry complied with the ethical duties applying to business transactions with a client. Assume that *Goldman v. Kane* is your only authority. The relevant parts of the opinion are found in Appendix G. Formulate the governing rule, and write it out in an outline form.

EXERCISE 5-2

Distinguishing Holding from Dictum
Based on what you learned about *Goldman v. Kane* in Exercise 5-1, which of the following is part of the holding and which is dictum?

1. The court's statements about the requirement that the attorney refrain from misrepresenting or concealing any material fact.
2. The court's statements about the requirement that any advice the attorney gives the client must be the same advice that the attorney would be expected to give if the transaction were between the client and a stranger.
3. The court's statements about the requirement that the client be fully informed of the nature and effect of the transaction.
4. The court's statements about the requirement that the transaction not be fundamentally unfair or egregiously overreaching.

CHAPTER 6

FINDING A RULE FROM MULTIPLE AUTHORITIES

I. THE CONTINUING SEARCH FOR A RULE

Sometimes a case or a statute sets out the rule in a clear, well-organized way. If so, be grateful, formulate the rule, use it to organize your analysis, and start to write. But sometimes the rule is not so clear. Maybe you'll find several cases that use different words for the rule or that even seem to articulate different rules for the same issue. You might have to return to the cases to get a clearer understanding of the rule. To demonstrate why, let's return to Ms. Watson's covenant not to compete.

Assume that while you were researching Georgia law on the Watson issue from Chapter 5, you found not only *Fox*, but also *Clein v. Kapiloff*. *Clein* appears in Appendix G. Stop now and read it.

You could formulate several slightly different rules from *Clein*. Let's assume that you formulated this one:

To be enforceable, a covenant not to compete:

1. must be supported by sufficient consideration, and
2. must be reasonable. The test for determining reasonableness is:
   a. whether the covenant is reasonably necessary to protect the interests of the party who benefits by it,
   b. whether it unduly prejudices the interests of the public, and
   c. whether it imposes greater restrictions than are necessary.

But remember that in Chapter 5 we formulated this rule from *Fox*:

A covenant is enforceable if all the following elements are reasonable:

1. the kind of activity that is restrained,
2. the geographical area where it is restrained, and
3. the time period of the restraint.

Fox and *Clein* are from the same jurisdiction, but they seem to lay out different rules. You need to organize according to the structure of the rule, but here you seem to have two different rules. What to do?

You might be tempted to organize the analysis by describing and applying, one at a time, the "rules" set out in *Fox* and *Clein*. The discussion would first give a sort of "case brief" of *Fox*, describing the facts and the rule the court described. After applying the rule from *Fox* to the Watson facts, you'd do the same thing with *Clein*, setting out the rule you got from that case and applying it to the Watson facts. The organization would look something like this:

I. Is the Watson covenant not to compete enforceable?
   A. The rule in the *Fox* case
      The covenant is enforceable if the activity restrained, the geographical area of the restraint, and the time period of the restraint are all reasonable.
      1. Is the kind of activity restrained reasonable?
      2. Is the geographical area of the restraint reasonable?
      3. Is the duration of the restraint reasonable?
   B. The rule in the *Clein* case
      The covenant is enforceable if it is supported by sufficient consideration and its terms are reasonable.
      1. Is the covenant supported by sufficient consideration?
      2. Are its terms reasonable? Reasonableness is judged by the following criteria:
         a. Is the covenant reasonably necessary to protect Carrolton's interests?
         b. Does the covenant unduly prejudice the interests of the public?
         c. Does the covenant impose greater restrictions than are necessary?

But your reader needs to know *Georgia's* rule on enforcing covenants not to compete. Organizing by the separate cases here would give your reader two possible rules and two possible outcomes. Is Georgia's rule one of these? Which? If the Georgia rule is a combination of these rules, how are they combined?

A writer who organizes around separate cases instead of a single rule hasn't completed the analysis. Here, you'll have to wrestle with these two opinions until you can predict the rule a Georgia court would apply.

If you find seemingly inconsistent authorities like these, you'll need to (1) compare the relative precedential value of each authority, and (2) study each case to see if you can reconcile or distinguish them.

II. COMPARING PRECEDENTIAL VALUES

Cases serve as precedent for the rules they articulate, but not all cases carry the same precedential value. The degree of deference a court will give to a prior case can depend on many factors.

A. Primary Authority: Is This Really "Law"?

Some authorities are "law," and some are simply commentary on the law or suggestions about what the law ought to be. Authorities that are actually law are called "primary authorities." Authorities that explain or comment on the law are called "secondary authorities."

Primary authority is created by an entity that has the legal power to create law. The most common kinds of law are

- constitutions (federal and state)
- statutes enacted by legislatures
- case law created by courts
- administrative law created by governmental agencies

These authorities are primary authorities, that is, they constitute "law." Situations governed by Michigan law are governed by these primary authorities:

- the U.S. and Michigan constitutions
- the statutes the Michigan legislature enacts
- the case law the Michigan courts create
- the administrative law the Michigan state agencies create
- applicable federal case law, statutes, and administrative law.

Secondary authority comes in many forms, such as:

- treatises
- legal encyclopedias
- law review articles
- uniform laws

These sources are created by private individuals, organizations, or businesses. They may help you locate primary law or understand it better once you've found it. For some, respect for the author or for the drafting process will cause judges to pay deference to the source's content. But those private individuals, organizations, or businesses don't have the authority to create law. So, generally, when a secondary source conflicts with a primary source from that jurisdiction, the primary source controls.

B. Mandatory Authority: Is It Binding?

Not all primary authorities will bind the Georgia court on Watson's question. For example, an Iowa statute or case opinion would not bind the Georgia court. The Georgia court might find the Iowa opinion persuasive, perhaps because of the strength of its reasoning or because it represents the rule in a majority of states or because the judge who wrote the opinion is particularly well respected. But the Georgia court would not be *required* to follow it. The Iowa court will be explaining Iowa law, and Georgia is not bound to follow Iowa law so the Iowa opinion would be *persuasive* authority, but not *mandatory* authority.

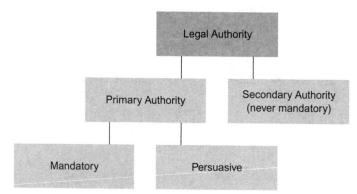

As you probably know from your legal research text, each state has two court systems—a state system and a federal system. Each of those systems has a trial-level court and at least one appellate-level court. The federal court system is the same for each state. It is structured like this:

Highest appellate court	United States Supreme Court
Intermediate appellate court	United States Court of Appeals (for that circuit)
Trial-level court	United States District Court (for that district)

A case is filed in the trial court (here the District Court). Eventually it might be appealed to the intermediate appellate court (here the Court of Appeals for that circuit). Finally, it might be appealed to the Supreme Court, the highest appellate court in the federal system.

Figure 6-1

The Federal Judicial Circuits, as Shown in 2009 Summer Judicial Staff Directory 963 *(C.Q. Press 2009).*

State court systems follow a similar pattern, though the courts have different names. Cases are filed first in the trial court and then may be appealed to an intermediate appellate court (if one exists) and eventually to that state's highest appellate court.

On issues of state law, the decisions of a state's highest court are mandatory authority for all other courts of that state and for all federal courts applying that state's law. The state's highest court is not bound by its own decisions. Its role in developing the law requires it to be free to overrule itself. But reluctance to change the law without compelling reason causes even the highest court to pay great deference to its own prior holdings.

Decisions of intermediate appellate courts are binding on trial courts within the geographic boundaries of the intermediate appellate court's jurisdiction. Decisions of courts from other states or decisions of federal courts, including even the United States Supreme Court, are persuasive but not mandatory.

On issues of federal law, decisions of the United States Supreme Court are binding on all federal and state courts in the country. Decisions of the intermediate-level federal appellate court (the United States Court of Appeals for that circuit) are binding on all federal district courts in that circuit. Figure 6-1 shows the geographic jurisdictions of the federal circuit courts of appeal.

On issues of federal law, decisions of federal intermediate appellate courts (circuit courts) and federal trial courts are not mandatory authority for state courts, but as a practical matter, state courts generally give the opinions of those courts significant weight. This is especially true of state courts within the geographical boundaries of the federal court.

C. Subsequent Treatment: Is It Still "Good Law"?

Before using any authority, you'll have to update it to be sure it's still valid, still "good law." A case opinion can be reversed by a higher court or overruled (expressly or implicitly) by a later opinion in a different case.[1] A statute can be repealed or amended by a later statute. The effect of a statute may be limited or expanded by a later court interpreting the statute. A court may have nullified the statute on constitutional grounds. Your research text will explain how to update your sources. Never rely on authority you haven't updated.

D. Any Other Factors?

Mandatory authority is, of course, binding, but strange as it sounds, occasionally you might find two conflicting sources of mandatory authority. For example, you might find a statute and a conflicting case opinion from that state's highest court. If the legislature has enacted a valid statute governing the issue, a court is bound by it.[2] But courts often interpret statutes—they tell us what the statute means. If an opinion has interpreted the statute in a certain way, the opinion's interpretation controls.[3] In that sense, the opinion controls the statute.

For non-binding case law, precedential value can be affected by other factors, including these:

- **The relative level of the issuing court.** The more prestigious the court, the more persuasive its opinions. For instance, a decision of the United States Supreme Court is powerful persuasive authority, even when it isn't mandatory.
- **The date of the opinion.** All other things being equal, more recent opinions are more persuasive.
- **The strength of the opinion's reasoning.** A well-reasoned opinion is more persuasive than a poorly reasoned opinion. An opinion that includes a thorough discussion of policy is more persuasive than an opin-

---

1. An opinion is reversed when that *same* case is appealed to a higher court and that court reverses the opinion of the court below. Once a case has completed the litigation process and is closed, it can't be reversed except by reopening proceedings in that same case. But the opinion in that case can be overruled. An opinion is overruled if, in a later opinion in a *different* case, the issuing court or a higher court recants the law set out in the earlier opinion.

2. A court can declare a statute invalid if the statute suffers from some constitutional infirmity, but if the statute is valid, it controls.

3. If the legislature disagrees with the court's interpretation, the legislature can and sometimes does amend the statute to correct the court's interpretation. Then the new statute controls, at least until the court speaks again.

ion that simply applies existing legal authorities without exploring the policy rational.

- **The subsequent treatment of the opinion by other authorities.** Later authorities, both primary and secondary, might comment on your authority. For example, later case opinions might discuss and rely on the case. Or a later opinion might question or reject the reasoning of the earlier case. Other writers might comment on the case in treatises or law review articles. An opinion that has received favorable notice is usually more persuasive than an opinion receiving critical or no notice.

- **Whether the court's statements about your issue are part of the holding or dicta.** Statements that are dicta are not as persuasive as statements that are part of the holding.[4]

- **How factually similar the opinion is to your facts.** The more similar the facts, the more sure the judge can be that the authority was meant to apply to situations like yours.

- **The number of subscribing judges.** Most federal intermediate-level appellate cases are decided by a panel of the court, usually three judges. Far less frequently a case will be decided by all judges of that court (the court sitting "en banc"). En banc opinions are binding on future panels of the same court. They are generally more persuasive to other courts than are panel decisions. Unanimous opinions are more persuasive than split decisions (opinions with dissents). A majority opinion generally is more persuasive than a concurring opinion, which is in turn more persuasive than a dissenting opinion.[5]

En banc opinion	An opinion issued in a case heard by all the judges of that particular court.
Majority opinion	An opinion subscribed to by a majority of the judges who heard the case.
Concurring opinion	An opinion that agrees with the result reached by the majority opinion but for different reasons than those of the majority opinion.
Dissenting opinion	An opinion that disagrees with the result reached by the majority opinion.

- **Whether the opinion is published.** If the opinion does not appear in an official collection of published opinions (an official case reporter

---

4. See Chapter 5, section VI.

5. Be careful with concurring or dissenting opinions. Is the statement that caught your eye part of the disagreement between the concurring or dissenting opinion and the majority opinion? If so, the statement in the concurring or dissenting opinion may actually prove that what it says is *not* the law. After all, the opinion is disagreeing with the majority opinion on that point, and it is the majority opinion that controls.

published in hard copy), it might not be "published." In some states, an unpublished opinion has no precedential value, and some courts have local rules that prohibit even citing it. Some other courts will consider an unpublished opinion, though its precedential value is weak. But even if the court declines to give the unpublished opinion any precedential weight, an unpublished opinion may still help you predict how that same court would approach a similar situation.

- **The judge's reputation.**   Some judges have earned respect separate from the position they hold. The opinions of those judges may have added persuasive value.
- **Trends in the law.**   If you can discern a trend among other courts in the nation or in your state, opinions consistent with that trend may have greater precedential value than inconsistent opinions. For example, if, over the past several years your state's highest court has been extending the liability of manufacturers in various situations, a case opinion consistent with that trend may have more precedential weight than an opinion from some other state questioning that trend.

EXERCISE 6-1

Comparing Precedential Values

Your firm represents Kay Lang, who sold a piece of Los Angeles commercial property to Adam Kornfeld. Kornfeld claims that Lang failed to disclose defects in the property, and he has filed suit against her for damages in the state trial court. You are researching whether California law requires a seller to disclose the condition of real property.

You've found the following authorities. Which are primary authorities? For each authority, describe the precedential value it likely will carry for the Kornfeld/Lang dispute.

a. An opinion of the California Supreme Court deciding the duty of a seller to disclose to the buyer the condition of the property;
b. An article in the University of California at Los Angeles (UCLA) Law Review discussing the applicable California rule on the seller's duty to disclose to the buyer the condition of the property;
c. An opinion of the United States Court of Appeals for the Ninth Circuit applying the applicable California rule on the duty of a seller to disclose to a buyer the condition of the property;
d. A California statute on the duty of a seller to disclose to a buyer the condition of the property;
e. An unpublished opinion of another California state trial court applying the California rule on the duty of a seller to disclose to a buyer the condition of the property;

f. A section from a California legal encyclopedia explaining the applicable California rule on the duty of a seller to disclose to a buyer the condition of the property; and

g. An opinion of the United States Supreme Court applying the California rule on the duty of a seller to disclose to a buyer the condition of the property.

EXERCISE 6-2

Comparing Precedential Values

Your firm represents Marietta Jones, a plaintiff in an employment discrimination action. You filed suit on her behalf against Treemart, your client's former employer, alleging that Treemart selected Jones for layoff because of her race. The suit is filed in the United States District Court for the Southern District of New York. The complaint alleges violations of the Civil Rights Act of 1964, 42 U.S.C. § 2000e-17, a federal statute that prohibits employment discrimination based on race.

But before Jones can file a lawsuit in court, the federal statute requires her to first file a charge with the applicable administrative agency. Her charge must be filed within 300 days of the discriminatory act.

On January 3, Treemart notified Jones that she had been selected for layoff. The layoff was to be effective on February 3. Treemart has filed a motion to dismiss the Jones complaint, arguing that Jones did not file the agency charge within 300 days after January 3, the date Treemart notified Jones of her selection for layoff. Jones argues that she filed suit within 300 days after February 3, the date her layoff became effective. The legal issue is whether the 300 days began to run when Jones was notified of her selection or when the layoff became effective.

You research the issue and find the following authorities. Which are primary authorities? For each authority, describe how much precedential value it is likely to carry in *Jones v. Treemart*.

a. An explanation of the rule on when the time period begins to run found in the leading treatise on the Civil Rights Act of 1964;

b. An opinion of the United States Court of Appeals for the Second Circuit discussing whether the time period begins to run from the notification date or the effective date of an employment decision;

c. An opinion of the United States Court of Appeals for the Fifth Circuit discussing whether the time period begins to run from the notification date or the effective date of an employment decision;

     d. An opinion of the New York Court of Appeals (the highest state court for New York) applying the Civil Rights Act of 1964 and deciding whether the time period begins to run from the notification date or the effective date of the employment decision; and

     e. An opinion of the New York Court of Appeals applying the comparable provision of the New York statute that also prohibits employment discrimination.

III. RECONCILING AUTHORITIES: PULLING THEM ALL TOGETHER

The second way to deal with inconsistent cases is to reconcile them. You might be able to combine the language in the cases into one rule of law. This process is called "synthesizing" or "harmonizing" opinions. A more careful reading of the court's language might resolve the apparent conflict. Perhaps you initially misread one opinion. Perhaps one opinion uses careless language. If so, the way the court *applied* the rule it articulated might help you see what the court really meant. Or the rule in one case might be a more complete explanation of one of the elements of the rule from the other case.

If you decide that the opinions really do set out different rules, maybe they were meant to apply to different situations. Look for factual or procedural differences. Showing that the rules in two opinions apply to different situations is called "distinguishing" cases. For example, one rule might apply when a business is a "lending institution" and the other might apply to other kinds of businesses. Maybe one rule is meant to be an exception to the other. If the rules are meant to apply to different situations, then the rule in one of the cases will apply to your client's case while the other won't.

When you reconcile cases, you're looking for clues to tell you whether one of these resolutions is possible. Reread all the language in both opinions. Look for later cases that might help solve the mystery. Even if the later cases don't mention the inconsistency, they'll probably state and apply a rule, giving you important clues about whether reconciliation is possible.[6]

---

6. In theory, though rarely, two rules may be irreconcilable. Lawmakers seldom *mean* to maintain two inconsistent rules in a single jurisdiction, but an inconsistency might have developed nonetheless. For example, two courts of equal rank might adopt differing rules until a higher court resolves the question. If you're predicting a result, you'll have to decide which rule the judge is more likely to apply. Consider such factors as the direction in which the court seems to be moving, which rule is better reasoned, and which rule produces a more reasonable result under the facts of your case.

Example: We'll return to *Fox* and *Clein* for an example of how to reconcile cases. First, gauge the precedential value of each case. You'll find that both opinions are mandatory authorities issued by the highest court in the same state. Both are factually similar to Watson's situation. *Fox* is more recent, though, and it doesn't mention *Clein*. This may be significant since *Fox* does cite several other earlier cases as support for its own articulation of the rule.

Further, *Fox* lays out a test in tabulated form, which seems to indicate that the court was intentionally announcing something important. Compare this tabulation with the more rambling discussion in *Clein*. The *Clein* court even drops factual conclusions about time and territory into the middle of this rambling discussion.

Finally, one of the differences between the rules the two opinions seem to lay out—*Clein*'s statement that the covenant must be supported by consideration—is dicta. Thus, it appears that the precedential value of *Fox* outweighs *Clein*, especially for the part of *Clein* that is dicta.

Next, try to distinguish the two opinions. You only find one potentially significant distinction—the covenant in *Fox* was part of an employment contract and the covenant in *Clein* (like the Watson facts) was part of the sale of a business. But *Clein* explains that this distinction simply means that more latitude is allowed when a covenant is part of the sale of a business. Neither opinion indicates that the test for determining reasonableness (the rule) would be different based on this distinction.

Trying to harmonize the opinions causes you to wonder whether perhaps *Clein* implies two of the three *Fox* elements (time and territory). After all, those two aspects of the covenant are mentioned in the court's discussion of the *Clein* facts. Although the *Clein* opinion doesn't include "time and territory" as part of the rule it seems to announce, *Clein*'s factual conclusions do seem to imply that those facts are legally significant.

Also, while *Fox* doesn't specifically mention consideration (a *Clein* element), *Fox* does state that "the contract [must] be valid in other essentials," citing to two earlier cases. So maybe *Fox* isn't inconsistent with the first element of the rule you formulated from *Clein*, since *Fox* seems to refer to all essential elements of a contract, which would surely include consideration.

So, you try to formulate the most likely rule. Since you've noticed that the first element from your *Clein* rule (consideration) is actually part of an additional element announced in *Fox*, one you had originally missed (valid in other essentials), you can include that additional element.

The second half of your *Clein* rule (interests of parties and public) seem to conflict with *Fox*, and no distinguishing feature of *Clein* implies that the *Clein* rule rather than the *Fox* rule would apply to the Watson facts. So, the apparent greater precedential value of *Fox* seems to trump the second half of the *Clein* rule. You decide that this is the Georgia rule on enforcing covenants not to compete[7]:

I.　Is the Watson covenant not to compete enforceable?

The covenant is enforceable if the contract is valid in all other essentials and if the activity restrained, the geographical area of the restraint, and the time period of the restraint are all reasonable.

A. Is the contract valid in all other essentials, including sufficiency of consideration?

[Discuss any relevant cases pertaining to contract essentials including *Fox* and *Clein*.]

B. Is the kind of activity restrained reasonable?

[Discuss any relevant cases pertaining to the nature of the restrained activity, including *Fox* and *Clein*.]

C. Is the geographical scope reasonable?

[Discuss any relevant cases pertaining to the geographical limits of a restrained activity, including *Fox* and *Clein*.]

D. Is the duration of the restraint reasonable?

[Discuss any relevant cases pertaining to the duration of a restraint, including *Fox* and *Clein*.]

Under each element, you'll discuss all cases that tell you something important about that element. Notice that cases could and should appear under more than one element when those cases contribute to the analysis of more than one element. For example, under element D, you'll discuss what *Fox* and *Clein* each tell you about whether the duration of the restraint is reasonable. You'll also discuss both cases under sections B and C (geography and kind of activity).

This organization serves the dual functions of a working draft. It helps you analyze, and it serves as the starting point for organizing the draft you ultimately provide to your reader.

No matter what you decide, remember that if you're struggling with the large-scale organization of your first draft, you're struggling with formulating the rule. If you are struggling with formulating the rule, you haven't yet mastered the authorities. When you are sitting in front of the computer keyboard, you'll be on your own, without a teacher there to offer advice. Your working draft structure can offer important counsel. Don't forget to listen to it.

---

7. Several other reconciliations of *Fox* and *Clein* are possible. As a matter of fact, in Chapter 19 we'll revisit these two cases, exploring a way to salvage some additional precedential value from *Clein*.

EXERCISE 6-3

Reconciling Opinions

Reconcile the following four summaries of case opinions setting out the requirements for recovery under the attractive nuisance doctrine. Use them to formulate one rule of law, if possible. For each part of the rule you formulate, identify the case(s) you would cite for support of that part of the rule.

Then use that rule to create an outline for a working draft about whether a client's facts would allow recovery for an attractive nuisance claim. You might find that your answers differ from those of your classmates. Part of the benefit (and fun) of these exercises is to compare these differing answers, identifying those that are most accurate and complete.

Bell v. Grackin (state's highest appellate court, 1959)

Facts: A piece of wire was lying in a neighbor's yard. A child walking by saw the wire and went into the yard to get it. As he was playing with the wire, the child bent it and then let it go. The wire recoiled, hitting the child in the eye. The child sought recovery from the neighbor based on the doctrine of attractive nuisance. The court denied recovery, stating:

> The doctrine underlying the attractive nuisance cases applies only where the instrument or artificial condition is within itself inherently dangerous even while being used properly, such as weapons, explosives, or power tools. It would be extending the doctrine entirely too far to apply it to such commonplace objects as a piece of wire, a pencil, a coat hanger, or a hammer, all objects so commonplace as to be found around any house or yard, but not dangerous in themselves, although they might be attractive to children and capable of inflicting injury if misused.

Andersonville v. Goodden (state's intermediate-level appellate court, 1961)

Facts: A neighbor's pickup truck was parked unattended in the neighbor's yard. A child came into the yard to sell the neighbor candy bars for a school fund-raising project. The child saw the truck, climbed on it, fell, and impaled himself on a hook attached to the rear of the truck. The child sought recovery from the neighbor based on the doctrine of attractive nuisance. The court denied recovery, stating:

> The attractive nuisance doctrine was developed for the benefit of children coming upon property even though trespassing. However, the courts of this state have been reluctant to extend the doctrine beyond its restricted application to situations in which the dangerous instrument is found to be one of actual and compelling attraction for children. The courts have not expanded

the doctrine to cases where the instrument or artificial condition did not actually draw the children onto the property.

Newcomb v. Roberts (state's highest appellate court, 1982)

Facts: A swimming pool was located in a backyard with no fence, unshielded from view. A child visiting next door and playing hide-and-seek came into the backyard seeking a hiding place. She hid behind a utility shack for a while. Then she began to wonder whether her friends were still looking for her. She decided to go investigate the status of the game. As she was leaving the backyard, walking alongside the pool, she accidentally fell into the pool and suffered serious injury. She brought suit against the property owner under the doctrine of attractive nuisance. The court allowed recovery, stating:

> A landowner is liable for physical harm to trespassing children by an artificial condition if the place where the condition exists is one upon which the possessor knows or has reason to know that children are likely to trespass; if the risk posed by the condition is one that children, because of their youth, will not realize; and if the landowner fails to exercise reasonable care to eliminate the danger or otherwise to protect the children. This landowner should have known that neighborhood children were likely to trespass and that such children would not appreciate the risks posed by a swimming pool. The landowner did not enclose the pool in a fence or take any steps to shield the pool from view. Thus, the landowner is liable for the injuries to the child.

McDaniels v. Lanier (state's highest appellate court, 1987)

Facts: A natural pond lay behind a house located on two acres of property. The pond was visible to passersby, and no fence prevented access. A child saw the pond and decided to swim in the pond. The child suffered abdominal cramps and drowned. The court denied recovery, stating:

> An owner who has reason to know that children are likely to trespass is liable, under the doctrine of attractive nuisance, for injuries sustained by a child if the risk is one that children will not appreciate and if the owner has failed to exercise reasonable care to protect the child [cite to Newcomb]. However, here the condition that caused the injury was a naturally occurring condition rather than an artificial condition. While landowners have a duty to protect trespassing children from artificially created conditions on their property, they do not have the duty to protect trespassing children from naturally occurring conditions. Such a duty would often require landowners to take unreasonable or impossible actions such as fencing off huge tracts of land. Thus, the owner is not liable for the injuries to the trespassing child.

You've now taken your first run at *organizing* your working draft. Next you'll *write* the working draft, filling in content beneath each heading and subheading. The next chapters tell you how to write each of those parts. But remember that if you find yourself struggling with which authorities go where, return to those authorities and revisit your organization. You might rethink the tasks of Chapters 2 through 10 several times before your analysis is accurate and complete.

DRAFTING FOR ANALYSIS: WRITING THE WORKING DRAFT

CHAPTER 7

ANALYZING A SINGLE ISSUE: RULE EXPLANATION

After you've used the rule to create a structure, the next step is to write out the analysis, putting flesh on the structure's bones. Fortunately, there is a paradigm (a commonly used organizational plan) to get you started. You may have heard it referred to as "IRAC" or "CREAC"[1] or a similar, mysterious-sounding acronym. We'll look at the details soon, but for now, the basic idea is that you'll first *explain* the law and then *apply* the law to your client's facts.

We'll begin simply, with a single-issue analysis using only one case. This chapter covers the first half of the paradigm—explaining the rule. The next chapter covers the second half of the paradigm—applying the rule.[2]

One suggestion before we continue: You might decide to write out a working draft of the facts before you begin writing about the law. Writing the facts may help you understand both the law and the facts better and earlier. Also, if you're having trouble getting started, writing a draft of the fact statement can help overcome "writer's block." If you think it might help, write out a draft of the legally significant facts now, before you begin writing the analysis of the law. This working draft of the facts doesn't need to follow any special format, but if you want to see what the fact statement will ultimately look like, review the fact statement in Appendix A.

I. WHAT IS A SINGLE-ISSUE DISCUSSION?

Let's first clarify what we mean by a "single-issue discussion." As you worked through the preceding chapters, you outlined the rule and used it

---

1. "Issue, Rule, Application, Conclusion" or "Conclusion, Rule, Explanation, Application, Conclusion."
2. After working with a single issue and only one case, see Chapters 9 and 10 to show you how to work with multiple authorities and multiple issues.

to create an organizational plan. For example, remember the burglary rule from Chapter 2:

> To establish a burglary, the state must prove *all* the following elements:
>
> A. breaking
> B. entering
> C. dwelling
> D. of another
> E. in the nighttime
> F. intent to commit felony therein

Should you explain all these requirements together before you start to apply any of them to your client's facts?   Or should you divide your discussion of the burglary rule into six subsections, explaining and applying each element (A through F) one at a time?

The rule itself will tell us the answer. Are all these elements necessary? In other words, must the prosecutor prove each one to prove a burglary? Yes. The defendant must have "broken" and "entered." The structure entered must have been a "dwelling" belonging to "another." The entry must have been "in the nighttime" and with the "intent to commit a felony therein." The question of whether the structure was a dwelling has nothing to do with whether the entry was in the nighttime. Each element is a separate requirement that must be met independently. If the defendant can prove the absence of any one of them, the prosecution fails.

For a rule like this one (a list of required elements), each element is a separate issue, and you'll discuss each separately, using a separate subheading for each one. For a full analysis of the burglary rule, then, you'd have six separate issues. You'd explain and apply one before you begin to explain the next. The organizational paradigm described in this chapter and the next would be written out separately for each of them.

The same would be true for the second kind of rule structure from Chapter 2 (a disjunctive test). There we used the example of the possible ways to create an easement:

> An easement can be created in any of the following ways:
>
> A. by deed
> B. by an exception to the statute of frauds
> C. by implication, or
> D. by prescription

Those creation methods are all separate from each other. The easement either was created in a deed or it wasn't. The answer to whether it was created by a deed has nothing to do with any of the other possible ways to create an easement. So, each of the subparts can be (and should be) decided separately. The working draft analysis would have four separate issues, and the organizational paradigm described in this chapter and the next would be written out separately for each of them.

But the third rule structure from Chapter 2 (the child custody rule) is different. It has nine subparts, but they are all factors to be considered only together, as *part* of deciding the best interests of the child. None has any legal effect other than as part of the mix of factors determining the child's best interests. A healthy dose of one might make up for a shortage of another. Maybe one parent has better living arrangements but the other parent lives near extended family. The rule requires the judge to consider all the factors together. So at least for the working draft, you'd treat all the factors together as one large issue. You'd write out only one paradigm, explaining all the factors first before applying any of them.[3]

II. THE PARADIGM FOR LEGAL ANALYSIS

Legal issues are decided by first figuring out what the rule of law means and then applying that rule to a set of facts.

Overview: Explaining comes before applying. In the rule explanation half of the paradigm, you'll state the issue,[4] state the rule you believe will govern it, explain that rule, and use case authority to illustrate it. Then, in the rule application half of the paradigm, you'll apply the rule to your client's facts, perhaps using analogies to the facts of the cases. This rule application leads directly to the conclusion—your answer to the question you were asked. Here is an overview of the basic paradigm:

PARADIGM FOR A WORKING DRAFT

RULE EXPLANATION

1. State the issue.
2. State the governing rule of law.
3. Explain what it means and use case(s) to illustrate it.

---

3. Remember that we're just writing out a working draft to analyze a legal question. You might later decide to separate the the factors, but for now, let the structure of the rule help you be sure that you understand both the rule and how it would apply.

4. When you revise your draft to prepare it for your reader, you'll change the question to your answer to that question. See Chapter 12.

RULE APPLICATION

4. Explain how the rule applies to your client's facts, using analogies if possible.
5. State your conclusion.

This reasoning process uses both inductive and deductive reasoning. In the first half of the process, a lawyer figures out what the rule is by using the results in earlier cases to formulate a general rule. This is *inductive reasoning*—reasoning from the specific to the general.

EXAMPLE OF INDUCTIVE REASONING
In the *Fox* opinion, the court decided the enforceability of the covenant not to compete by evaluating the reasonableness of the duration, the geographical scope, and the nature of the activity restrained. Therefore covenants not to compete are enforceable if these three terms are reasonable.

In the second half of the process, the lawyer applies that general rule to the client's facts using *deductive reasoning*—reasoning from the general to the specific.

EXAMPLE OF DEDUCTIVE REASONING
Covenants not to compete are enforceable if the duration, the geographical scope, and the nature of the activity restrained are reasonable. These three terms of the Watson/Carrolton covenant are reasonable. Therefore, the Watson/Carrolton covenant is enforceable.

The interplay of these two kinds of reasoning should remind you of the ladder of abstraction illustration in Chapter 5.

You can use this illustration as a mental map while you write. It can help you remember where you are in the paradigm. It can remind you not to let your client's facts (the second half of the paradigm) slip into the first half of the paradigm (the explanation of the rule itself).

Why keep the two halves separate?   Many new writers find it hard to write a comprehensive rule explanation. Part of the challenge is learning to recognize and evaluate rule explanation—learning what it is and the kind of information it covers.

Mixing explanation and application contributes to the confusion. You might state the rule and then proceed to write several pages about the rule and how it applies to the facts. It "feels" like a thorough analysis, but how can you tell? To evaluate your own draft, you'll need to check the depth and breadth of both halves of the reasoning process, but that's hard to do when they are mixed together. Learning what rule explanation is *not* (and moving that material out of the spot reserved for rule explanation) can help you learn what rule explanation *is* (and clear space to insert it).

Keeping the halves distinct doesn't mean that you must finish writing the first half before you can write the second half. For early versions of the working draft you can write more freely. Many writers find this unstructured prewriting helpful. Using the paradigm simply means that when you finish your writing process, the working draft should explain fully first, before applying the rule.

EXERCISE 7-1

Identifying and Labeling the Parts of the Paradigm
Read the "Facts" section of the office memo in Appendix A. Then read section A of the office memo (a single-issue discussion). Identify and label each part of the paradigm for a single-issue discussion.

III. EXPLAINING THE RULE

Now that you have an overview of the paradigm in mind, it is time to examine each part more closely. In the next few sections we'll work through the first half of the paradigm. We'll use examples based on the following situation:

Facts of Example: Linda Pyle owns a commercial horse stable, which is located on land Pyle recently bought. Howard Gavin was Pyle's lawyer in the land purchase. He is a well-respected partner in a medium-sized general practice firm, with seventeen years of practice experience, all in litigation. Pyle's land purchase was Gavin's first venture into real property transactions. Gavin tried to handle Pyle's purchase carefully because he was nervous about working outside his usual practice area.

Before completing the sale, Pyle had asked Gavin whether there would be any problem with using this land to stable horses. Gavin checked the zoning regulations and assured Pyle that there would be no problem. But Gavin hadn't thought to check the title for possible easements.

The sale was completed and Pyle built a house and stable. About three months after she and the horses moved in, huge gravel trucks from the quarry on the other side of the hill began to rumble through her property and out to the county road. They quickly wore a rutted path right through Pyle's front yard and close beside the stable. The horses become upset each time a truck goes by. Pyle contacted the quarry owners and discovered that they own an easement across her property and expect to continue using it for the foreseeable future.

Pyle has come to a partner in your firm to find out what she can do. The partner has concluded that the easement is valid. The only option left is a claim against Gavin. You've been asked whether Gavin's failure to check the title for possible easements constituted legal malpractice.

Assume that your research turned up only one case, *Jacobson v. Kamerinsky*, an opinion from the highest appellate court in your jurisdiction. The opinion appears in Appendix G. Stop now and read it.

As Chapters 3 through 6 described, state the issue you'll analyze.[5] Next, state the rule that governs the issue. Follow it with citations to the primary source(s) for the rule. You'll be refining your understanding of this rule as you write the rest of the discussion, so don't be surprised if you need to revise your rule statement as you write.

I. Did Howard Gavin commit malpractice when he failed to check the deed for easements?

A lawyer has a duty to provide a client with representation that meets or exceeds the standard of professional skill and diligence commonly possessed and exercised by a reasonably prudent lawyer in this jurisdiction. *Jacobson v. Kamerinsky* [citation].

---

5. Later, when you convert your working draft to a document designed for a reader, you might decide to begin with a statement of your conclusion (your answer to the issue). For now, though, begin by stating the issue and let the process of writing your working draft help you reach the best conclusion.

Usually the rule statement should go in the first paragraph after the heading.[6] The discipline of concisely stating the rule within the first paragraph is an important part of your analytical process. It helps you articulate the focal point of the first half of the analysis, and it focuses your attention on the rule you're about to explain.

After you've typed your rule statement, identify for yourself the rule's key term or standard. Just for the working draft, you may even want to use italics for those words so you remember to focus on them. Your rule explanation will define that term or standard. Can you identify the key term or standard in our example? The term or standard the analysis must define and apply? Check your answer against the answer in the footnote.[7]

Now explain where you got the rule and what it means. You can think of this as using the available authorities to "prove" to yourself (and later to your reader) that the rule is what you think it is and means what you think it means. When you're dealing with a rule based primarily on a case, the most important tools for "proving" the rule are:

- describing what the court said about the rule
- describing how the court applied the rule
- pointing out any relevant information about how the court did *not* apply the rule
- pointing out any relevant facts the court emphasized
- describing the policy considerations that support the rule

The idea isn't just to report this information but, instead, to use it to make a point about the rule.

IV. RULE EXPLANATION USING A SINGLE CASE

No generic format fits each situation, but this approach can get you started. As you read this section, refer to the sample rule explanation at the end of this chapter.

Start by making a list of the points you've learned about the rule. Organize the points into categories starting with general information and proceeding to more specific information. For example, here are three common categories:

- what you know about how the rule functions generally
- what you know about each identified subpart (factor or guideline), if any
- what you know about how the rule functions in specific kinds of situations.

---

6. Occasionally, the issue is complex enough to require a little context or clarification. If so, *briefly* set out the necessary context or clarification, but even in these unusual cases, be sure to get to the rule statement as quickly as you can.

7. The heart of this standard is "skill and diligence commonly possessed and exercised by a reasonably prudent lawyer in this jurisdiction."

Use the categories as your basic order for the explanation, beginning with how the rule functions *generally*. You've already stated the rule and cited the case, so now set out the facts and the part of the holding that establishes the rule. Use the tools for case law analysis to explain the rule's general functioning. If an illustration would be helpful, use a case to illustrate the rule. Include any relevant policy rationale you find in the authorities.

Next, if your rule has identified factors or guidelines, take each relevant factor or guideline, one at a time, and follow the same procedure.[8] Finally, state and explain any relevant points about how the rule functions in specific relevant situations. If it would be helpful, you can use a case to illustrate how the rule would apply in that situation. Follow the same procedure for each of these points. Include any policy rationale that applies especially to that situation.

As you write, you'll probably think of additional points. Simply add them in an appropriate place. Don't worry if you don't have information in one of the categories. For example, your rule might not have factors or guidelines, so you wouldn't have a second category. Sometimes the case doesn't tell you any relevant information about how the rule applies in certain situations, so you might not have a third category. But intentionally looking for information in each category will help you notice points you might have missed.

Here are some general principles to follow for the rule explanation section:

1. Use all relevant tools of case law analysis.   Reread the case, using each tool of analysis described in Chapter 5. Note all the relevant information the tools helped you locate and ask yourself what each piece of information teaches you about the rule.

2. Cite to the relevant authorities when you make a point about the law, the reasoning behind the law, or the facts of a case.   Notice the precedential value of each source and confirm that the source said what you think it said. Chapter 14 will explain the details of proper citation form. For now, just be sure to identify the authorities in whatever way will allow you to relocate that source.

3. Keep your focus on the key term or standard.   Most legal analysis is an exercise in defining terms, so focusing on those key terms will keep you focused on the heart of your issue.

4. Discuss only the topics that will be relevant to your client's situation.   Don't include everything one might ever want to know about the rule. Include only information that might pertain to your client's situation.

5. Use only very short quotes of key language.   It's common for new legal writers to overquote. If you quote freely, you may fill up several pages with nothing but quotations and your introductions to them. But merely retyping

---

8. State each point you've learned about how that factor or guideline functions; (2) state the facts and holding relevant to *that* point; and (3) use any other tools for case law analysis to explain your point about that factor or guideline.

material from the sources isn't analysis. The sources should be your starting point, but your analysis begins only when you draw conclusions from the sources and explain the basis for them.

6. Use proper paragraphing techniques.   A paragraph should have a topic or a thesis sentence, which usually appears as the first sentence of the paragraph. The paragraph should be limited to information about that topic or thesis and should fit smoothly and logically between its neighbors. These principles are more than just principles of style—they're important to the substance of your analysis. They'll help you flesh out and order your thoughts and think of new points you want to add.

7. Use thesis sentences instead of topic sentences.   A topic sentence identifies the topic the paragraph will discuss, but that's all it does. A thesis sentence asserts a position, and the content of the paragraph focuses on "proving" that point.[9] The thesis might be the rule itself, a part of the rule, or a point about how the rule functions.

Compare these paragraphs. Which has a thesis sentence? Identify it. Notice how it articulates the paragraph's point and leads to analysis rather than merely a report on the case.

Cantwell v. Denton [citation] dealt with the issue of when a choice is sufficiently voluntary to constitute assumption of the risk. In that case, the defendant negligently caused a fire in an apartment building, and a father entered the burning building to save his child. The court held that the father's action was not sufficiently voluntary to constitute assumption of the risk. [citation]	A choice is not sufficiently voluntary to constitute assumption of the risk if the defendant's negligence has forced the plaintiff to choose between the threatened harm and another equal or greater harm. *Cantwell v. Denton* [citation]. In *Cantwell*, the defendant had negligently caused a fire in an apartment building. A father had to choose between entering the burning building and standing by while his child's life was in danger. The court held that standing by while the child was in danger would have been an equal or greater harm. [citation] Under such circumstances, the court held, the choice to subject one's self to danger is not "voluntary" in the sense necessary to constitute assumption of the risk. [citation]

---

9. Occasionally a paragraph or even several paragraphs can refer to the thesis sentence of the prior paragraph by using a clear relational word or phrase (for example, "similarly") or when the context otherwise clearly communicates that the point of the subsequent paragraph is to provide additional evidence for the prior paragraph's thesis.

Identifying the thesis might show you that the *topic* contains several different *theses,* each deserving its own supporting material. Or it might help you find the gaps in your reasoning and in the "proof" you've found in the authorities. If you're careful to limit the paragraph to material that supports the thesis you've stated, you'll notice if you lack support for that thesis and need to go back to the authorities to find stronger support.

8. Use a transitional word, phrase, or sentence each time you move on to a new point.   Be explicit about the relationships between paragraphs and points. Here is a list of commonly used transitions:

TRANSITIONS[10]

ADDITIONS

additionally	in addition	not only
along with	in fact	in any event
also	moreover	
and	nor	
another reason	even more relevant	
further		

SEQUENCE

first	next	finally
second	not only, but also	

COMPARISON

both	likewise	in comparison
here		in the same way
		similarly
		so too here

CONTRAST

but	despite	Nevertheless
in contrast	instead	rather
while	still	however
instead	even though	notwithstanding
on the other hand	even so	
in contrast	though	

---

10. Adapted from David Angell & Brent Heslop, *The Elements of E-Mail Style,* 62–64 (Addison-Wesley Publ. 1994), and Ross Guberman, *Point Made,* 274–277 (Oxford Univ. Press 2014).

CAUSATION

as a result
because
for that reason
predictably
that is why
thus

CONCESSION

although	even though	though
that said	even assuming	on the other hand
even so	even if	

ILLUSTRATION

as in	in particular	specifically
for instance	for example	to illustrate
to illustrate	like	

RESULT

accordingly	consequently	as a result
therefore	for	since
because	thus	

SUMMARY

accordingly	the bottom line is that	therefore
at its core	thus	put another way
in summary	in other words	

EMPHASIS

above all	more important	chiefly
in fact	all the more reason	especially
in particular	simply put	

9. Keep paragraphs fairly short—less than half of a double-spaced page.   Short paragraphs keep you focused on the thesis of that paragraph. When a paragraph gets long, it may have begun to wander or it may be lumping together several subpoints. Not discussing subpoints separately usually leads to mixing information more or less randomly and a more cursory analysis.

V. COUNTERANALYSIS

Ask yourself whether there is another reasonable interpretation of the rule. If so, say so. Explaining the other interpretation helps you double-check your assessment of its strength. Also, your reader will need to understand what other possibilities exist. This explanation of other possible interpretations is called "counteranalysis."

If your large-scale organization hasn't already provided a place for discussing the counteranalysis,[11] you can place it here, following the interpretation you think more likely. ("Another possible interpretation exists, however. . . .")

Match the depth of the discussion to your assessment of its strength. If it's possible but unlikely that a court would adopt it, cover it briefly, summarizing the rationale behind it. But if it's a closer call, discuss the counteranalysis in more depth so you can be sure you haven't underestimated its support. Either way, conclude your counteranalysis with your reasons for believing that the interpretation you predicted is more likely.

Milk the authority for all you can learn about the rule and include the parts that might be relevant to your client's facts. Remember that the rule explanation section explains *only* the rule itself—not how the rule applies to the facts of your client's situation. The application section comes next. *Don't include rule application in the rule explanation section.* As a discipline, draw a line between rule explanation and rule application on your working draft, to remind yourself to keep your discussion of your client's facts below the line.

Here is an example of rule explanation for the Pyle/Gavin issue.

A WORKING DRAFT OF RULE EXPLANATION

I. Did Howard Gavin commit legal malpractice in his representation of Linda Pyle? ISSUE

A lawyer has a duty to provide a client with representation that meets or exceeds the standard of professional skill and diligence *commonly possessed and exercised by a reasonably prudent lawyer in this jurisdiction. Jacobson v. Kamerinsky* [citation]. RULE

---

11. See, for example, the large-scale organization of the warranty issue in Chapter 10 Section II.

In *Jacobson,* the lawyer failed to file a timely claim before the medical malpractice screening panel. By statute, a medical malpractice claim cannot be pursued unless it has been filed before the screening panel within the applicable time limit. [citation] Therefore the client's claim was barred. Because a reasonably prudent lawyer would research and comply with the statutory requirements for bringing a particular kind of claim, the court held that the lawyer was liable to his client for the losses that resulted from the failure to file the claim. [citation]

One gauge of the prudent lawyer standard is whether the task is something general practitioners are familiar with doing. In *Jacobson,* the court had pointed out that the enactment of the screening panel requirement had been widely publicized in newspapers, electronic media, and the state bar journal. However, the court explained that even without publicity, a prudent lawyer would comply with filing requirements because filing lawsuits is something general practitioners are familiar with doing. [citation] Therefore if the task is familiar to general practitioners, the court need not ask whether the lawyer should have been aware of the particular requirement.

Another gauge of the prudent lawyer standard is whether the error could have been prevented by research. In *Jacobson,* the court observed that an "error in judgment" does not constitute malpractice. [citation] While *Jacobson* did not expressly define the difference between an error in judgment and a breach of the prudent lawyer standard, the court distinguished the *Jacobson* facts from an "error in judgment" by pointing out that in *Jacobson* the correct answer would have been apparent had the lawyer done the necessary research. [citation] Therefore, although a prudent lawyer can make an error in judgment, a prudent lawyer does not make errors preventable by proper research.

The "prudent lawyer" standard is not reduced for lawyers operating outside their area of special knowledge. In *Jacobson,* the lawyer-defendant had been in practice only ten weeks when he accepted the medical malpractice case. The court held that the lawyer's lack of experience did not excuse his failure. [citation] Clients should be entitled to at least the minimum standard of skill and diligence, according to the court. [citation] Also, a contrary rule would offer no incentive to lawyers to gain necessary knowledge or experience. [citation]

RULE EXPLANATION
Key facts

Holding

Thesis sentence (a characteristic the court found significant)

Key facts

Court's statement about those facts

How court's statement supports thesis

Thesis sentence (another significant characteristic)

Disclosure that thesis is an inference

Reasoning from the court's observation about the facts

Thesis sentence (how rule applies to a particular situation)

Relevant facts

Holding on this point

Court's two policy reasons

The standard probably would not be affected by facts indicating that the lawyer intended to be particularly careful, or that he was otherwise skilled and diligent, or that he was a well-respected partner of a well-respected firm. Although no facts like these were present in *Jacobson*, the court's language and policy statement explained in the previous paragraph would seem to apply to this question as well.

> Thesis sentence anticipating another issue
>
> Disclosure of lack of facts in *Jacobson*
>
> Reasoning from policy

It is unclear whether the court would rely on expert testimony or would make its own judgment about what a prudent lawyer would do in a certain situation. This question was not at issue in *Jacobson*. However, the opinion does not mention the testimony of any expert witness, and the court's statements that a prudent lawyer would research the requirements for bringing a claim seemed to be statements of the court's own opinion rather than statements based on someone's testimony. The court's repeated references to the standard as "the minimum" that "any client should be entitled to expect" [citations] seem to indicate that the court considered itself competent to decide the standard.

> Thesis sentence; kind of evidence necessary
>
> Disclosure key to evaluating strength of thesis
>
> Inferring a point from the court's language

Thus, whether certain conduct falls short of the "prudent lawyer" standard appears to be determined on a case-by-case basis, by what the judge thinks a prudent lawyer would do. However, two ways to gauge whether the failure falls below the standard are: (1) whether the task is something general practitioners are familiar with doing; and (2) whether the problem could have been prevented by doing proper research.

> Summary of points made in rule explanation

CHECKLIST FOR RULE EXPLANATION

State the Issue
- ☐ Place it in the heading with a Roman numeral.

State the Applicable Rule of Law
- ☐ Place it within the first paragraph.
- ☐ Highlight the key terms.

Explain Where the Rule Comes From and What It Means
- ☐ Set out the facts of the case.
- ☐ Explain what the court held about the rule.

☐ Explain any important dicta.
☐ Explain how the court applied the rule.
☐ Where appropriate, explain how the court did *not* apply the rule.
☐ Point out any facts the court emphasized.
☐ Explain what legal commentators have said about the case or the rule.
☐ Explain the policies that underlie the rule.

General Principles

☐ Cite a source for each statement of a rule, a holding, the court's reasoning, or facts from a case.
☐ Do not discuss your client's facts in this section.
☐ Where possible, use thesis sentences.
☐ Limit paragraphs to one topic or thesis.
☐ Connect each topic or thesis to the prior material.
☐ Check paragraph length (yardstick: one-half of a double-spaced page, maximum).
☐ Include counteranalysis if necessary and not already covered.
☐ Conclude counteranalysis by explaining reasons the predicted interpretation is more likely.

Overall Evaluation

☐ Have you cited a source for each statement of a rule, a holding, a court's reasoning, or the facts of a case?
☐ Have you used thesis sentences where possible?
☐ Have you limited each paragraph to a single thesis?
☐ Have you signaled each transition to a new thesis?
☐ Have you kept paragraphs to less than half of a double-spaced page?
☐ In each section, have you checked for logical organization by reading all the thesis sentences in order?
☐ Have you remained as objective as possible?

EXERCISE 7-2

Writing the Rule Explanation
Write out the rule explanation section for the following memo assignment, using *Lucy v. Zehmer*[12] as your only authority. One of the most common errors in legal writing is rushing into rule application before writing a sufficiently thorough rule explanation. This exercise, which requires you to write the rule explanation section only, is good practice in learning how to write a thorough rule explanation section.

---

12. 84 S.E.2d 516 (Va. 1954). Opinion reprinted in Appendix G.

Facts

Virginia Ryan is the owner of an antique shop. She has come to your firm asking for advice.

Ryan is acquainted with Stewart Kaplan and his older sister, Julia Kaplan. Stewart and Julia are not on good terms. Their mother recently died, bequeathing to Stewart an old quilt and to Julia their deceased father's World War II medals. During the settling of the estate, relations between Stewart and Julia became even more strained when Julia gave the medals to a local historical organization without offering them to Stewart first. Stewart had a strong sentimental attachment to the medals, and he believes that Julia gave them away on purpose to spite him.

Ryan knew the facts of the dispute about the war medals, and she knew that the relationship between Stewart and Julia was strained. Ryan did not get along well with Julia either, and she and Stewart felt a common bond in this respect.

Several weeks after learning that Julia had donated the medals, both Stewart and Julia happened to attend a community carnival. Stewart saw Ryan there, and said to her, "Let's have a little fun." Ryan said, "OK. What do you have in mind?" Stewart said, "Follow me. We'll give my dear sister a scare." He took Ryan by the arm and led her to within earshot of Julia. Stewart winked at Ryan and, in a stage voice, offered to sell her the old quilt. Ryan said she was interested and asked what price Stewart had in mind. Stewart said, "How about $150?" Ryan said, "That's pretty steep for an old quilt. How about $25?"

Both Stewart and Ryan could tell that Julia had heard the conversation. However, Ryan believed that Stewart was serious about selling the quilt. Stewart and Ryan continued negotiating the price, through several offers and counteroffers, finally settling on a price of $75. "Done!" said Stewart, winking at Ryan. He said, "Let's do this right. Here, let me write out the terms." He wrote (reading aloud as he went along), "Stewart Kaplan hereby sells to Virginia Ryan the old quilt he inherited from his mother for the price of $75." They both signed it. Still enjoying the game, Stewart said, "Wait, we need today's date and the date I'll deliver the quilt to you." He inserted the date and added (reading aloud), "Delivery to occur next Wednesday." He also wrote (without reading aloud), "Thanks for playing along. This was fun." Both parties initialed the additional writing, and Ryan put it in her pocket. She told Stewart that it was great doing business with him and then left.

The following Wednesday Ryan called Stewart to tell him that she had the check ready and to ask when he planned to deliver her quilt. Stewart stuttered that he had never actually intended to sell the quilt. Ryan said, "I thought you wanted to get revenge on Julia." "Yes," said Stewart, "but just by letting her know how it feels to be ignored." "Well, that's not what I thought. I thought you wanted to get revenge by selling the quilt. I want that quilt, Stewart. It is an antique and $75 is a fair price. Besides I already promised it to one of my customers."

Ryan wants to know whether she can enforce what she thought was Stewart's agreement to sell the quilt. An attorney in the firm has asked you to analyze Ryan's question. The attorney has told you to assume that a judge would find that Ryan genuinely believed that Kaplan was serious.

Issue

Was there an enforceable contract for the sale of the quilt?

CHAPTER 8

ANALYZING A SINGLE ISSUE: RULE APPLICATION

Now that you've explained the rule, you're ready to apply it to your client's facts. Remember that this half of the paradigm relies on deductive, syllogistic reasoning—that is, applying a general, often abstract principle to a specific situation.

General principle	Covenants not to compete are enforceable if the duration, the geographical scope, and the nature of the activity restrained are reasonable.
Application to facts	These three terms of the Watson/Carrolton covenant are reasonable.
Result	Therefore, the Watson/Carrolton covenant is enforceable.

Although rule-based reasoning is still important in the second half of the paradigm, analogical, narrative, and policy-based reasoning are at least as important to the analysis. You might also need to draw inferences from the facts (inferential reasoning).

I. TWO APPROACHES TO WRITING THE APPLICATION SECTION

The point of the paradigm is to apply the rule you've just explained, so the application section should roughly track the explanation section. You could begin by applying each point you discussed in the explanation section, knowing that you'll supplement those points with analogies and other forms of reasoning. This way you are sure to apply the rule you just explained instead of allowing your application section to wander.

You might find, though, that a slightly different approach works better for you. While your analysis ultimately should be framed in tightly reasoned logic, it should also embrace a flowing narrative, and plugging into the narrative can give you insights that rule-based reasoning misses.

So, some writers find it more natural to begin writing rule application by focusing on the narrative (the facts), without looking back to the rule explanation section. As they write the first draft of the application section, they have the rule explanation in mind, but more impressionistically so. This strategy frees them to think like a storyteller thinks, and thus be more tuned in to the facts of their case.

If you choose this approach, you might need to revise your initial draft of each section so the rule explained in the first half matches the rule applied in the second half. But just as often, you'll return to the explanation section to add or edit the discussion of a point you hadn't noticed until you began to write about your client's facts. No matter which way you approach the writing process, the result should be the same—a logical analysis applied to your client's narrative.

II. CONTENT OF RULE APPLICATION

The organization of each rule application section will be unique, but here are some general principles for getting started:

Use thesis sentences.   For each point you made about the rule in the explanation section, *write a thesis sentence stating how you think that point will apply to your client's facts.*

Use facts to support conclusions.   In one or more paragraphs following the thesis sentence, *use your client's facts to support why the thesis sentence is an accurate prediction.* Explain the inferences and factual conclusions you think a judge or jury would draw from these facts, and use your common sense. Imagine the situation. What would it have looked like? Seemed like? What other things might have been true if these are the facts? How might the scenario look to a judge or a jury? Could someone else paint a different picture using the same facts?

Try to support your thesis with direct fact-to-fact comparisons.   Identify the similarities between your client's situation and the precedent case. Explain how these similarities show the likely result for your client. Also, identify any significant factual *differences*, and explain how these differences demonstrate your prediction.

Apply the rule's underlying policies to your client's situation.   Your client's facts might raise precisely the concerns that the rule was designed to address. If so, a court will be more likely to apply the rule strictly to your client's situation. But if not and if the court has any discretion, a court might be more likely to interpret and apply the rule as you would prefer.[1]

Include any necessary counter-application.   Just as you might need to discuss other reasonable interpretations of the rule (in the explanation section), you might need to discuss other possible interpretations of the facts (in the application section). Match the depth of your discussion to the strength of the other interpretation. If it's possible but unlikely that a judge or jury would see the facts that way, cover it briefly. But if it's a closer call, discuss the other interpretation of the facts more thoroughly. Either way, conclude your counter-application with your reasons for believing that the interpretation you predicted is more likely.

State your conclusion.   After you've explained how the rule applies to your client's facts, end by stating your conclusion. If the analysis has been long or complex, summarize the key reasons supporting that conclusion.

III. ANALOGIES

Analogies are often the heart of a rule application section. Chapter 1 introduced analogies. Now we'll explore them in greater depth. Analogies point out similarities between two things. They compare the facts of a prior case with the client's facts, to show similarities pointing toward a similar result (*"analogizing"* cases). Counter-analogies point out *differences* between two things. They compare the facts to find differences that might point toward a different result (*distinguishing"* cases).

A. Which Similarities and Differences Matter?

Not all similarities and differences are legally significant. A similarity or difference is legally significant if it relates to:

- a key term used in the rule
- a policy implicated by the rule

Comparisons relating to a key term are the most important. The rule is the key part of the analysis. No matter how compelling the situation, the rule is still the rule. If a factual similarity or difference would help a court decide how the rule might apply to that situation, the comparison will be important.

---

1. Reread the sample office memo in Appendix A, noticing how policy-based reasoning can help predict a result.

For example, in most jurisdictions, a seller of real property who knows or should know of material defects in the property must disclose those defects to a potential buyer. Notice that this rule has two elements:

A seller must disclose if:

1. the seller knows or should know of the defect, and
2. the defect is material.

Therefore, factual similarities or differences would be most important if they would help the judge decide either of these two elements—what kind of "knowledge" is enough to raise the duty and how to gauge whether a defect is "material."

B. Choosing a Format for Your Analogies

For each analogy (case comparison) you want to make, you'll need to decide how much to say about it. Professor Michael Smith has identified two formats for case comparisons: the short form and the long form.[2] Use the long form for important or complicated comparisons and the short form for all other circumstances. In either format, though, be sure to give direct, fact-to-fact comparisons. Notice how the examples below make direct factual comparisons.

Short-form case comparison.   Usually this format begins with a thesis sentence stating the point of the comparison. Then, in roughly this order, the text gives a factual overview of the cited case (if not already provided); the specific facts to be compared; and the result in the cited case. Then a thesis sentence states the relevant similarities or differences; identifies the specific comparable facts from the client's situation; and uses that comparison to show why the result in the client's situation would (or wouldn't) be the same.

Examples: Here are two examples of a short-form case comparison, one showing differences and another showing similarities. Identify the sentences that match the case comparison format:

[Differences]

Buckley's representation that she was old enough to buy a car is significantly different from the representations in *Carney*. There, a minor entered into a contract to purchase a car. The minor affirmatively stated to the sales agent that he was twenty-two, and the agent recorded that information on the loan application, which the minor then signed. The court affirmed the trial

---

2. Michael R. Smith, 1992–1994 Class Handouts "Techniques for Using Case Authority to Discuss 'Points' in a Memo," on file with the author.

court's holding that the minor had fraudulently misrepresented his age and was therefore estopped from disaffirming the contract. *Id.* at 807–808.

Buckley, however, never stated her age at all. Further, her answer, taken to mean what she intended it to mean, was not even false. The sales agent had asked her whether she was old enough to buy a car. Buckley misunderstood the question, thinking that the agent was asking whether she was old enough to drive. She truthfully answered the question she thought the agent was asking. She said "yes," meaning that she was old enough to have a driver's license.

[Similarities]

Buckley's statement is much closer to the situation in *Woodall*, in which the minor made the representation "unknowingly." In *Woodall*, the minor did not realize that he was making a representation of majority because he did not read the form contract he was signing. *Id.* at 97. Similarly, Buckley did not realize that she might be making a representation of majority because she misunderstood the agent's question. In both cases, the requisite intent to deceive is absent. Therefore, the result in Buckley's situation should be the same as the result in *Woodall*—an order permitting disaffirmance.

Long-form case comparison.   The long-form case comparison uses a similar format but gives the reader more information about the cited case and the factual comparisons.

Example: Here is an example of a long-form case comparison[3] that points out many factual similarities and also a factual difference. Identify the sentences that match the case comparison format:

> *Fahmie v. Wulster*, 408 A.2d 789 (1979), provides the closest analogy to Frimberger's situation. In *Fahmie*, a corporation that originally owned a parcel of property requested permission from the Bureau of Water to place a nine-foot diameter culvert on the property to enclose a stream. The Bureau required instead that a sixteen-foot diameter culvert should be installed. The corporation, however, went ahead with its original plan and installed the nine-foot culvert.
>
> The property was later conveyed to Wulster, the CEO of the corporation, who had no knowledge of the installation of the nine-foot culvert. Nine years later, Wulster conveyed the property, by warranty deed, to Fahmie.
>
> In anticipation of the subsequent resale of the property, Fahmie made application to the Economic Development Commission to make additional improvements to the stream and its banks. It was then that the inadequate nine-foot culvert was discovered and the plaintiff was required to replace it with a sixteen-foot diameter pipe.
>
> Fahmie sued Wulster for the cost to correct the violation, claiming a breach of the deed's warranty against encumbrances. The New Jersey Supreme Court

---

3. Adapted from Frimberger v. Anzellotti, 594 A.2d 1029 (1991).

concluded that a claim for breach of a covenant against encumbrances cannot be predicated on the necessity to repair or alter the property to conform with land use regulations.

[Similarities]

The *Fahmie* case is remarkably similar to Frimberger's situation. Like the plaintiff in *Fahmie*, Frimberger is also alleging a breach of the covenant against encumbrances based on the necessity of bringing the property into compliance with a state environmental land use regulation. Just as in *Fahmie*, neither the current owner nor his immediate predecessor knew of the violation of the regulation. In both cases, the violation was created by a remote owner. In both cases, this remote owner knew or should have known that he was creating a violation of the regulation. In neither case did the current owner's deed contain an exception for violations of land use statutes. In both cases, the current owner discovered the violation upon filing an application with the relevant regulatory agency to make further improvements to the property.

[Difference]

The only relevant difference between the two situations results in an even weaker case for Frimberger. In *Fahmie*, the state agency actually required the plaintiff to replace the inadequate culvert with the larger culvert, thus causing the plaintiff significant expense. In Frimberger's situation, however, the state agency has taken no action to require abatement of the violation. As a matter of fact, the agency has invited Frimberger to apply for an exception to the relevant requirement. Therefore, it is even less likely that Frimberger's facts establish a breach of the covenant than did the facts in *Fahmie*.

IV. COMMON TROUBLE SPOTS IN RULE APPLICATION

The three most common weaknesses in rule application sections are these:

- not applying the rule as the first half of the paradigm explained it;
- announcing an outcome without sufficiently explaining the supporting reasoning; and
- not accounting for different possible interpretations of the facts.

Understanding these three weaknesses will help you avoid falling victim to them.

Not applying the rule as the explanation section described it.   We've already discussed this potential weakness, but it merits a reminder. The explanation section has included only relevant information, so match the application section to that coverage and approach. Equally important, revise the explanation section to reflect any new understanding you gained by writing about the facts. This double-checking of rule-based and narrative reasoning against each other is a perfect example of why both are critical to good analysis.

Announcing an outcome without explaining the reasoning.   This common weakness usually results from thinking that the application of the rule to the client's facts is obvious. That's probably not the case, but even if the application is clear, *some* explanation of the supporting reasoning is necessary. State the specific facts that made you predict the outcome the way you did, and say why they point to that prediction. You can use the express facts to draw inferences about what might have happened.

For example, assume that Sonya has died. Her lawyer says that several years ago, Sonya executed a will, which she took home with her upon leaving the lawyer's office. Now the will can't be found. You recall from your wills class that a person can revoke his or her will by destroying it. Also, Sonya's possible beneficiaries are feuding, and some of them have had access to Sonya's house. What different inferences can you draw about what might have happened to the will? Your rule application section would need to account for all of these possible inferences.

Not accounting for other possible interpretations of the facts.   Sometimes this weakness results from forgetting to think independently and realistically about the facts. Don't just accept the inferences that someone else—like the client or the requesting attorney—has drawn from the facts. Most sets of facts support diverse inferences and interpretations.

For example, in our antique quilt example at the end of Chapter 7, recall that Stewart winked several times. What might Ryan have thought that meant? You should be able to think of at least two possible interpretations.

It's hard to imagine multiple interpretations simultaneously. Look at Figure 8-1. You might have seen a graphic like this before. Do you see the old woman? Do you see a young woman as well? Your brain can organize the black and white lines into a picture of either, but most of us can only see one at a time. More pointed for our purposes, once your brain has organized the sections to display one figure, it's hard to find the other figure at all. Imagining diverse interpretations of facts is just as hard as imagining diverse interpretations of these black and white lines.

Not "seeing" these diverse interpretations of the facts is difficult to diagnose and cure. If your assignment permits, ask others to help you imagine possible interpretations of the facts. Taking care not to breach your duty of confidentiality, describe the facts objectively to a friend or colleague. Your goal is to learn what story someone else might see in the facts, especially someone who has not first seen the story through your or your client's eyes.

If you must work alone, try to think both critically and creatively about the facts. How might the various other parties to the situation describe it? How

Figure 8-1
How Old Is This Woman?

would you describe it if you were representing those parties? How might the facts appear to someone who disliked your client and was therefore looking for a negative interpretation? It might not be easy, but each year of law practice will improve your ability to see diverse interpretations of a set of facts. Take the opportunity presented by your first few writing assignments to begin practicing fact interpretation.

PYLE/GAVIN EXAMPLE—RULE APPLICATION ADDED

I. Did Howard Gavin commit legal malpractice in his representation of Linda Pyle?	ISSUE
A lawyer has a duty to provide a client with representation that meets or exceeds the standard of professional skill and diligence *commonly possessed and exercised by a reasonably prudent lawyer in this jurisdiction. Jacobson v. Kamerinsky* [citation].	RULE

[See the end of Chapter 7 for rule explanation.]

RULE
EXPLANATION

RULE
APPLICATION

A judge would probably find that a reasonably prudent lawyer representing any purchaser in a real estate transaction would check the title to the property for easements. Receipt of title is, after all, the heart of the transaction, and carefully checking the title would be critical to evaluating the title the purchaser would receive from the seller.

Thesis sentence stating general conclusion

Reasoning from general facts

The duty to check the title carefully would be particularly clear in a situation like Gavin's where the client has asked specifically whether there would be any problem with using the land for a particular purpose. A prudent lawyer would know that the use of real property can be limited either by law (such as by a zoning regulation) or by private agreement (such as an easement or a restrictive covenant recorded against the title). The client's specific question should have flagged the issue for Gavin, making Gavin's error even less excusable than the error in *Jacobson*. In *Jacobson*, the client did not ask a question that should have reminded the lawyer of the possible problem; yet the lawyer's error constituted professional malpractice anyway. [citation]

Thesis sentence applying Gavin's particular facts

Reasoning from facts

Comparing facts (counter-analogy)

Further, both of the *Jacobson* gauges point toward liability. Representing a party to a real estate transaction probably falls within the group of tasks a general practitioner is familiar with doing. Basic real estate transactions are as common in the general practice of law as filing lawsuits. Nor was Gavin's omission a mere error in the exercise of professional judgment. The need to look for an easement would have been apparent if Gavin had done adequate *legal* research, and the easement itself would have been apparent if he had done adequate *factual* research. Just as in *Jacobson*, Gavin's error could have been prevented by proper research.

Thesis: an aspect of rule explanation

Apply 1st gauge

Compare facts

Apply 2nd gauge

Reasoning from facts

Compare facts

Since the standard is not reduced by virtue of facts particular to the lawyer's experience, Gavin's long absence from law school and his practice limitation will not affect the legal result. Nor will his status in the bar or his usual skill and diligence. However, these facts do add to the equities of his case, especially since a judge in this jurisdiction would probably be aware of them. Although those facts should not change the ultimate result, they probably mean that the judge will not be happy about having to rule against Gavin. The evidence at trial will have to establish the cause of action clearly.

Thesis sentences dealing with another aspect of facts

Flagging the human impact

Finally, this evaluation that Gavin's representation fell below the prudent lawyer standard is based on an assumption that the standard can be judged without expert testimony. Additional research would be necessary to check this assumption. If the standard must be evaluated by reference to expert testimony, it will be necessary to consult with an expert.

Pointing out a necessary qualification

The claim that Gavin breached the applicable standard of care is strong. The subject matter of the representation is common to general practitioners. The problem could have been prevented with proper research. If Pyle is interested in pursuing the matter further, our next step should be the completion of our research on the need for expert testimony.

CONCLUSION Statement

Summary of most important points

CHECKLIST FOR RULE APPLICATION[4]

Apply the Rule to Your Client's Facts
- ☐ Be sure the content of the explanation and application sections are consistent and that you applied the rule you explained.
- ☐ Compare the key facts from the case authorities to the key facts of your client's situation, noting the legally significant similarities and differences.
- ☐ Explain the inferences and factual conclusions that a judge or jury could draw from your client's facts.
- ☐ In the draft of an office memo, identify any unknown facts that would be important to a resolution of the legal issue.
- ☐ Evaluate the appropriateness of the factual discussion's depth.

State Your Conclusion
- ☐ If the analysis has been long and complex, include a short summary of the primary reasons supporting the conclusion.

———————

Overall Evaluation
- ☐ Have you cited a source for each statement of a rule, a holding, the court's reasoning, or the facts of a case?
- ☐ Have you used thesis sentences where possible?
- ☐ Have you limited each paragraph to a single thesis?
- ☐ Have you signaled each transition to a new thesis?
- ☐ Have you kept paragraphs to less than half a double-spaced page?

———————

4. See the end of Chapter 7 for a rule explanation checklist.

☐ In each section, have you read all the thesis sentences to check for a logical internal organization and to spot any gaps in reasoning?
☐ For an office memo, have you remained as objective as possible?

EXERCISE 8-1

Recognizing Analogies and Counter-Analogies
In the sample office memo in Appendix A, identify each example of analogical and counter-analogical reasoning.

EXERCISE 8-2

Practicing Analogies and Counter-Analogies
Formulate the rule of law from *Goldman v. Kane*, reprinted in Appendix G. Then read Karen Berry's facts set out in Chapter 13, Exercise 13-2. Make a list of the similarities between Berry's facts and the facts in *Goldman v. Kane*. Make a list of the differences. Identify which are legally significant for Berry's case and explain why.

EXERCISE 8-3

Writing the Rule Application, Using Analogies and Counter-Analogies
Write a working draft of your analysis of the issue set out in Chapter 7, Exercise 7-2. If you already wrote out an answer for that exercise, simply complete the working draft by adding the rule application half of the paradigm. Pay special attention to using analogical and counter-analogical reasoning.

CHAPTER 9

ANALYZING A SINGLE ISSUE: USING MULTIPLE AUTHORITIES

Chapters 7 and 8 explained the organizational paradigm and how to use a case within that organization, but only rarely will you be using just one case. The next step is learning how to order and work with multiple authorities. When you have multiple cases and other sources, which should come first and where should the others go?

I. INVESTIGATING THE OPTIONS

Organizing a sprawling batch of multiple authorities can seem daunting. Usually the key is the explanation section, since most of the discussion of the authorities will be located there. To work out an organizational plan, start by gathering some information. Here's what to do:

- Check the rule's historical development.
- Look for commonly recurring kinds of factual situations.
- Notice cases that focus on specific key points about the rule.
- Evaluate precedential values.

This information will tell you what you need to know to organize the explanation section, but like most other parts of the writing process, it will also deepen your understanding of the rule.

Check the rule's historical development.   Make a list arranging the authorities in chronological order and try to understand the historical development of the rule. What did each case add or change? How has the rule evolved over time? Do you see a trend? What refinements do you see? Sketch out a few notes about the rule's development.

Look for recurring factual situations.   Make another list of the cases based on their facts. Do you see certain recurring types of situations? If so, list these recurring situations and note which cases fall into which category. How does the rule seem to be applied in each situation? Do you see any patterns or signals for predicting how the rule is applied in each? Even if you don't see any factual categories, make a list of cases in the order of their similarity to your client's facts. Put the most similar cases at the top of the list.

Notice cases that focus on key points about the rule.   Do some of the cases discuss the rule in general while some discuss different legal aspects of the rule? Maybe some cases talk mostly about some subparts. For example, in our "competent representation" issue, some of the cases might give you a generalized description of what a client has a right to expect from a lawyer. Other cases might tell you whether the lawyer's representation must meet the standard created by a generalist or by a specialist in that area of law. Others might tell you whether the standard is different depending on whether the client was a paying client or a pro bono client.[1] List these key points and note each case that deals with each point. Include "discussion of the rule in general" as one of the categories. If a case deals with more than one topic, be sure to list the case under each.

Evaluate precedential values.   Finally, make a list ordering the authorities by their precedential value (see Chapter 6). Do you see significant differences? Maybe you have a statute and the cases that interpret it. Maybe you have several opinions from the highest appellate court in your jurisdiction, several opinions from the intermediate-level appellate court, and the rest are opinions from another jurisdiction. List the authorities in that order.

II. ORGANIZATIONAL OPTIONS: RULE EXPLANATION

Now you have the information you need to choose an order for the authorities. *Ideally, the order you select should help you make one or more substantive points about the rule.* Consider what you've learned by making your four lists. Which set of notes shows you relevant substantive information about the rule? Do you see any historical turning points or several relevant points about how the rule functions? Do you see some cases especially like your client's facts? Or maybe all the cases are quite different from your client's facts, which might make you wonder whether the rule would apply differently in your client's case. Do you see important differences among the precedential values?

---

1. The full phrase is *"pro bono publico,"* meaning "for the public good." In common usage, the phrase refers to representing a client without charging a fee. The standard of competent representation is the same even without a fee.

Next, with your notes in mind, consider these common organizational approaches:

- importance-to-analysis approach
- topical approach
- historical development approach
- a combination

These common formats are simply ideas to get you started. Here are descriptions of each:

Importance-to-Analysis Approach

This organizational choice is the workhorse of legal analysis. Think of it as your default choice, at least for your working draft.

Begin generally, by *stating the rule and supporting it with its most important source*. If the rule comes from a statute, cite first to the statute. If the rule depends primarily on case law, the most important source is the most important binding case in your jurisdiction.[2]

After you've set out the rule and its most important source, what you do next will depend on the kind of assignment you have. One kind of assignment is primarily about what the rule is in your jurisdiction (either a statutory issue or a court-controlled issue). The other kind of assignment is primarily about how that rule would apply to your client's situation. The dividing line usually isn't clean, but ask yourself where the real action is for your assignment. Is it mostly about what the rule is or mostly about how it would apply to your client. Then consider these approaches:

> **To Sum Up**
> Three Common Kinds of Assignments
> - what is the rule (statutory)?
> - what is the rule (case law)?
> - how does the rule apply to my facts?

A question primarily about what a statute means:

Use the statutory tools set out in Chapter 4. Discuss them in the rough order of their importance, supplementing each with any cases that discuss the point:

- the text itself, including the canons of construction
- any cases from your jurisdiction interpreting the statute
- the intent of the legislature
- the policies implicated by possible interpretations

---

2. You can add one or two other important cases, policies, or secondary sources here, to explain the rule generally, but only if they add something to the analysis. If no cases in your jurisdiction have addressed your question, say so and use the most important case from another jurisdiction.

- the interpretation of any governmental agencies charged with enforcement of the statute
- the opinions of courts from other jurisdictions or respected commentators

After you've explained the way these points support your predicted interpretation, include any counter-analysis (any points that support some other interpretation). Then explain why you think your interpretation is more likely.

A question primarily about what approach your jurisdiction's courts have taken:

Use the case reading tools from Chapter 5 and the tools for evaluating authority from Chapter 6. Discuss the cases roughly in the order of their importance, usually beginning with any cases from your jurisdiction's highest appellate court and any cases that discuss the rule most broadly.

As you decide what to write about each case, review again the suggestions in Chapter 7, section IV. Remember that when you're dealing with a rule based primarily on a case, the most important tools for "proving" the rule are:

- describing what the court said about the rule
- describing how the court applied the rule
- pointing out any relevant information about how the court did *not* apply the rule
- pointing out any relevant facts the courts emphasized
- describing the policy considerations that support the rule

Don't just report this information. Write a thesis sentence, using the case to make a point about the rule.

A question primarily asking how a rule would apply to your client's facts:

After stating the rule and supporting it with its most important case, explain how the courts have applied the rule *in situations like your client's facts.* Focus on the cases with the most similar facts (maybe one to three), but *don't mention your client's facts yet.* You'll do that when you make analogies in the rule application section. When you discuss the cases, *point out any standards, guidelines, or signals the courts seem to be using.*

Next, discuss any cases that are *unlike* your client's facts (maybe one or two), but only if those cases add something relevant to your client's question.[3] Conclude with any relevant information from a secondary source or with any policies relevant to how the rule might apply to scenarios like yours.

---

3. For instance, a case might apply the rule to a scenario different from your client's facts, but it might include dicta saying that the result would have been different if the facts had been thus-and-so (a scenario more like your client's).

Some of your cases might be useful in more than one way. Maybe one case provides both an important general explanation and facts like

> Don't use unimportant authorities just to prove you've read them.

yours. You can use the case twice, first in the generalized explanation and then when you're discussing cases with similar facts. But don't use unimportant authorities just to fill up space or to prove that you've read them. Instead, show your reader that you have the lawyerly skill of identifying the *key* authorities and analyzing them thoroughly.

After you've explained the way these points support your predicted interpretation, include any counter-analysis (any points that support some other interpretation). Then explain why you think your interpretation is more likely.

If the explanation section has been long and complex, end with a *short summary* of its key points. That summary will be your jumping-off point for rule application.[4]

Topical Approach

A topical approach orders authorities by reference to the list identifying topics about the rule. The topics might be subparts of the rule (such as factors or guidelines)[5] or other discrete points of relevant information about the way the rule functions.

Begin with an explanation by stating the rule and using the most important authorities to explain the rule *in general*, just as described above. Then discuss each relevant separate legal topic. Order those topics by their importance, and discuss the most important authorities for each topic.

Don't include points that won't be relevant to your client's situation. Your reader wants a concise explanation of the points that will matter, not an academic treatise explaining everything there is to know about the rule.

If the discussion has been long and complicated, end the rule explanation with a short summary (several sentences) of the general rule and the points you've discussed.

Historical Development Approach

The historical development approach is less common, but it's the best choice if:

- the rule's development is important for understanding the rule and the authorities that articulate it; or
- the rule's current form doesn't decisively answer your client's question but the rule's history shows a trend that can help predict the answer.

The order in the historical development approach will vary depending on the rule's individual history and the reason the history is helpful. Here is an

---

4. Look again at the sample office memo in Appendix A (subsection A) for an example of organizing the explanation section this way.

5. See Appendix B for an example of an explanation section for a factors test.

example of a historical development approach when a historical trend can help predict the answer to a new question.

SUMMARY OF AN HISTORICAL DEVELOPMENT APPROACH

- State and explain the rule in its current form. Use the current authorities to set out the parts of the legal question the current rule *does* answer.
- Identify and explain the parts of the legal question that the authorities *don't* answer.
- Trace the historical development (inside or outside the jurisdiction, or both) to explain the trend of the rule's development on that point.
- Use that trend to explain your prediction for the unanswered parts of the legal question.

The point you make from the rule's history will differ from situation to situation. Organize by the logical steps leading to the point you want to make.

Combination Approach

The organization you choose should help you make one or more substantive points, so as you pondered your four lists, you might have noticed several kinds of important information—perhaps a case remarkably on point factually; an important historical turning point; and several relevant discrete topics of legal information. If so, combine the three approaches. While the combination approach defies reduction to a standard format, two principles usually apply: (1) Begin with a general explanation of the current rule and the several most important authorities establishing it. (2) Discuss together all the authorities that pertain to each point.

III. FORMATS FOR USING CASES TO EXPLAIN THE RULE

No matter which organizational approach you choose, you'll be using cases to help you explain what the rule means, what policies underlie it, and how it might or might not apply in certain kinds of situations. You'll need to match how much you say about each case to the point you want to make. Choose the level of detail necessary for making that point.

Professor Michael Smith has identified three basic ways to use cases in a rule explanation section:

- using a case only as a cite for a proposition;
- adding a parenthetical illustration to the cite; or
- providing an in-text illustration.[6]

---

6. Michael R. Smith, 1991 Course Handouts, "Techniques for Using Authority in a Memo," on file with the author.

Using a case only as a cite for a proposition. This technique provides the most limited use of a case. Simply state the point you found in the case and place the case name and citation immediately after your sentence. For example:

> One who is a minor at the time of making a contract can disaffirm the contract within a reasonable time after reaching the age of majority. *Woodall v. Grant*, 9 S.E.2d 95 (Ga. Ct. App. 1940). The rationale for the rule is the recognition that minors have not yet attained sufficient maturity to be responsible for the decisions they make, so they should be protected from at least some of the consequences of their bad decisions. *White v. Sikes*, 59 S.E. 228 (Ga. 1907).

Adding a parenthetical illustration. This technique adds a parenthetical to the case citation. The parenthetical contains a phrase that helps the reader understand how the case supports the proposition. You can use a parenthetical when a concrete illustration of just a few words would help to explain the general proposition. Here are examples:

> *Ways to Use Cases:*
> - citation only
> - citation plus parenthetical
> - in-text illustration

> A minor is estopped from disaffirming a contract if the minor knowingly misrepresented his age at the time he made the contract. *Woodall v. Grant*, 9 S.E.2d 95 (Ga. Ct. App. 1940) (minor did not knowingly misrepresent his age when he signed but did not read a contract representing that he was an adult); *Carney v. Southland Loan Co.*, 88 S.E.2d 805 (Ga. 1955) (minor knowingly misrepresented his age when he affirmatively told the agent that he was 22).

Providing an in-text illustration. For this technique, the illustration is explained in the text itself. The added information gives the reader a more complete understanding of what happened in the cited case and why that case supports the proposition, including a summary of the relevant facts, rationale, and holding. Here is an example:

> A minor is estopped from disaffirming a contract if the minor knowingly misrepresented his age at the time he made the contract. *Woodall v. Grant*, 9 S.E.2d 95 (Ga. Ct. App. 1940). In *Woodall*, the minor had signed a brokerage contract to purchase stock options, and the contract contained a representation that the purchaser had attained the age of majority. However, the minor had signed the contract without reading it. The court reasoned that the law does not require a minor to read a contract and does not enforce the same consequences on a minor as it would on an adult in the same circumstance. The court held that the minor had not knowingly misrepresented his age and, therefore, that he was not estopped from disaffirming the contract.

Each time you use a case to help you explain the rule, you'll need to decide which technique to use. What is your purpose for using the case? How much information will your reader need? If the point is undisputed and requires no explanation, you can use the first technique (case citation only). If the point could benefit from a short concrete example, you can use the second technique (case citation plus a parenthetical illustration). For important cases, though, use the third technique, an in-text illustration, including as much relevant information as is helpful.

This chapter has covered how to organize a discussion of multiple authorities for a single issue. Chapter 10 will cover our last working draft topic—writing an analysis of multiple issues.

ANALYZING MULTIPLE ISSUES

Chapters 7 through 9 explained how to write an analysis governed by a single rule with no subparts (no subissues). This chapter moves to the next and last level—how to deal with multiple issues. The basic principle is still to explain the law and then apply it. But because each issue and subissue will be governed by a separate rule, the analysis is a bit more complicated.

Chapter 7 explained how to tell whether your rule raises multiple issues. We'll look first at how to write the analysis of a single rule with subparts, like the Shaffer burglary example from Chapter 3.

I. WRITING THE ANALYSIS OF AN UMBRELLA RULE WITH SUBPARTS[1]

Recall our basic premise—that the structure of the rule will form the large-scale outline of the analysis. For the Shaffer issue, here is the structure of the rule:

> I. To obtain a burglary conviction, the state must prove *all* the following elements:
>
> A. breaking
> B. entering
> C. dwelling house
> D. of another
> E. in the nighttime
> F. intent to commit a felony therein.

---

1. Recall from Chapter 3 that the *umbrella rule* is the larger rule that establishes the relationships among the subrules.

An analysis of the burglary rule requires analyzing the subissues one by one — stating, explaining, and applying the rule governing that *sub*issue before proceeding to the next one. The paradigm you learned in Chapters 7 through 9 will serve nicely for each of these separate discussions, but first you'll need to write an "umbrella" section to introduce these separate discussions and place them in context. Then, after discussing each element, you'll write a conclusion that pulls them all together and predicts a result. We look first at the umbrella section.

A. The Umbrella Section

Assume that you've stated the question, using it as your Roman numeral heading, just as Chapters 7–9 explained. The *umbrella section* is the material you place between this heading and the first subsection.

The umbrella section has two functions: (1) It states the umbrella rule (citing to the main authority establishing the rule), and (2) it begins rule explanation by explaining any information that applies to the entire rule, not just one subpart. Here are some examples of general information that applies to the entire rule:

- who has the *burden* of proof[2]
- what *level* of proof is required[3]
- whether there is a relevant presumption[4] or a policy leaning[5]
- whether the procedural posture of a case favors one party[6]
- whether a canon of statutory construction calls for a strict reading of a statute.[7]

Often the umbrella section is simple. For instance, in the Shaffer example, the umbrella section would state the rule defining burglary (and cite to the statute establishing it). The statement of the rule already includes the relationship of the elements (all are necessary). Two items apply to all elements: the burden and level of proof. Because the rest of the rule explanation consists of explaining each element, one by one, the umbrella section of your working analysis doesn't need to contain anything else. It might look like this:

---

2. The burden of proof places on one party the responsibility of proving the necessary facts.

3. Proof levels are preponderance of the evidence, clear and convincing proof, or beyond a reasonable doubt.

4. A presumption assumes that something is true unless evidence shows otherwise.

5. For example, case law might hold that, as between the criminal defendant and the prosecution, doubts are to be resolved in favor of the criminal defendant.

6. For example, on a motion to dismiss the complaint, the court must assume that all allegations in the complaint are true. On a motion for summary judgment, the court must draw all factual inferences in favor of the nonmoving party.

7. See pp. 42-43.

I. Do the Shaffer facts establish the elements of burglary?

[UMBRELLA SECTION:]
To obtain a burglary conviction, the state must prove that Shaffer's conduct constituted a breaking and entering of the dwelling house of another in the nighttime with the intent to commit a felony therein. The state must prove each of these elements beyond a reasonable doubt. **[Cite to the applicable authority.]**

[Proceed with the discussion of each element, using for each the paradigm from Chapters 7 and 8.]

A. breaking
B. entering
C. dwelling house
D. of another
E. in the nighttime
F. intent to commit a felony therein.

B. The Discussion of Each Subissue

After you've written the umbrella section, write each subsection. Use the basic paradigm discussed in Chapters 7 through 9. In each subsection, state the rule governing that subpart, citing to the main authority establishing it.[8] Next *explain* the rule governing that element, using all the tools discussed in Chapter 7. Then *apply* it to your client's facts, just as Chapter 8 described.
End each subsection by stating your conclusion on that element, including a short summary of your key reasons, if helpful. This intermediate conclusion — the conclusion for just this subissue — is important. You can call it the "landing." It's the spot where your analysis returns to the firm ground of the rule structure before it jumps off again into the analysis of the next subissue.

C. The Overall Conclusion

When you've written the analysis of each subsection, write a conclusion pulling together the results for each subissue and setting out the overall conclusion for the question you've been asked. Include a summary of the primary reasons for the overall conclusion.

---

8. The "rule" might not always be announced as a rule. You're looking for what the authorities identify as the way to decide that element. The authorities might state the rule expressly ("nighttime" is the time between thirty minutes after sunset and thirty minutes before sunrise). Or you might have to deduce the rule yourself, by noticing how the courts decide that element.

BASIC MULTI-ISSUE PARADIGM

I. **Question Presented**
Umbrella section setting out all rule explanation that applies to all subparts
  A. **First element**
   - Rule statement and explanation unique to this element
   - Rule application
   - Landing
  B. **Second element**
   - Rule statement and explanation unique to this element
   - Rule application
   - Landing
  [Any other elements]

Conclusion

II. WRITING THE ANALYSIS WITHOUT AN UMBRELLA RULE

Your assignment might not be structured around an umbrella rule. For example, you might be asked to analyze several separate rules or decide which of several rules a court might apply. If you don't have an umbrella rule, just introduce the subsections by identifying them, explaining briefly what part they play in the analysis, and if helpful, explaining the order for each discussion. Here is an example:

I.   Does the law impose a warranty on the Foster car sale?

   In this jurisdiction, warranties governing transactions covered by U.C.C. warranty provisions are set out in [citation to statute]. Warranties governing other transactions are set out in [citation to statute]. Because these warranty provisions differ in relevant ways, this memo first discusses whether U.C.C. warranty provisions would apply to this transaction.

   The first section concludes that U.C.C. warranty provisions probably will govern this question, so the second section discusses how those provisions would apply here. However, because the application of U.C.C. warranties is a close question, the final section discusses the possible application of non-U.C.C. warranties.

A. Do U.C.C. warranty provisions apply to this transaction?
   [rule, rule explanation, rule application, landing]

B. If U.C.C. warranty provisions apply, is this one of the kinds of transactions upon which those provisions impose a warranty?
[rule, rule explanation, rule application, landing]
C. If non-U.C.C. law controls, does it impose a warranty on this transaction?
[rule, rule explanation, rule application, landing]

Conclusion

III. VARIATIONS

Like the paradigm for a single-issue analysis (Chapters 7–9), the multi-issue paradigm gives you the basic format for a multi-issue analysis. But you'll still have decisions to make. In addition to deciding *depth*, you also might need to make these decisions:

A. Order of Elements

When you convert your working analysis to a document designed for a reader, the order of your discussion of the elements will be significant. We'll explore those reader-centered decisions in Chapter 12. At the working draft stage, though, the order of your discussion matters less. You might discuss the elements in the order stated in the rule, or begin with those explained most thoroughly by the authorities, or begin with the element(s) you think will resolve the question. (See the next section.) For now you can use any order that makes logical sense.

B. Whether to Cut Short the Analysis

Sometimes one element of the rule will resolve the question, eliminating the need to analyze the rest. For instance, if Mr. Shaffer's conduct occurred at 2:30 in the afternoon, you wouldn't need to analyze whether it was a "breaking" or an "entering." Because all elements are necessary to establish burglary, the clear absence of the "nighttime" element would answer the question.

Deciding whether to cut the analysis short like this can be tricky. How sure are you of the conclusion on the seemingly decisive element? If you have no doubt, such as in the Shaffer example, you can discuss the decisive element first and stop right there. But answers to legal issues usually aren't so clear. Lawyers abridge an analysis at their own risk. If another conclusion on the seemingly decisive element is possible, even if unlikely, complete the analysis.

C. Whether to Combine Rule Explanation and Rule Application for All Elements

As we've seen, the paradigm for a multi-issue analysis separates each subissue into separate rule explanations and applications, like this:

I. Question Presented
[Umbrella section setting out all rule explanation common to the elements.]
A. First element
   • Rule statement and explanation unique to this element
   • Rule application and landing
B. Second element
   • Rule statement and explanation unique to this element
   • Rule application and landing

Conclusion

You might wonder whether you can state and explain the rules for *both* elements and then combine the rule application sections for both elements. An outline for that approach would look like this:

I. Question Presented
[Umbrella section setting out all rule explanation common to the elements.]
A. Rule statement and explanation
   1. First element
   2. Second element
B. Rule application
   1. First element
   2. Second element

Conclusion

In *some* situations, you might explain all elements before you apply any of them, as this outline does. The rules and rule explanations for each element might be particularly interrelated in the authorities. The distinctions between them might be minor. Separating the rule explanation sections might require you to repeat material. If your careful evaluation of the rule convinces you that these descriptions apply to your assignment, you can opt for this variation of the multi-issue paradigm. Remember, though, that the virtue of the basic paradigm is that its structure forces you to think precisely about each element. Don't discard the advantages of that structure lightly.

EXERCISE 10-1

Identifying the Parts of a Multi-Issue Discussion
Read the discussion section of the office memo in Appendix A (a multi-issue discussion). Identify and label each part of the multi-issue discussion. Include the parts of the basic paradigm within each subsection of the discussion. Keep in mind that the sample memo is in final form, so the statements of the issues have been converted into statements of the conclusions about those issues, as we'll discuss in Chapter 12. Otherwise, the parts of the discussion are the same.

EXERCISE 10-2

Writing a Multi-Issue Discussion
Write a working draft of an answer to the *Question Presented* below using as your only authority the case summaries in Chapter 6, Exercise 6-3.

Facts

Mr. and Mrs. Carillo, each 64 years old, live in a neighborhood that includes older people, middle-aged people with teenagers, and people with young children. The elementary school is about two blocks away. Most children walk to school down the next street over. The closest neighbors who have children living at home are the Lupinos, three houses away from the Carillos.

About a year ago, the Carillos bought a trampoline for the use of their grandchildren who visit from time to time. They put the trampoline in their backyard. The yard isn't fenced, but it is surrounded by a hedge and other shrubbery that effectively shield the backyard from view. The neighborhood children know the trampoline is there, however, because they sometimes play with the Carillos' grandchildren. All the children know that they are not permitted to jump on the trampoline unless an adult is present.

One day last spring, nine-year-old Jimmy Lupino was playing outside with a group of friends. One of the friends remembered the trampoline and suggested to the group that they ask the Carillos if they could play on the trampoline. They knocked, but the Carillos were not home. They huddled about what to do and decided they would each take just one turn on the trampoline. They went around to the Carillos' backyard and began to take their turns. When Jimmy was taking his turn, he got too close to the edge, hit the metal side of the trampoline, and broke his spine. He is now partially paralyzed.

The Lupinos have asked if your firm will represent them on a contingency basis in a lawsuit against the Carillos. To decide whether to accept the case, you need an idea of what claims the Lupinos might be able to bring. One possible claim you need to evaluate is an attractive nuisance claim.

Question Presented

Do the Lupinos have a reasonable chance of recovery on an attractive nuisance claim?

CONVERTING YOUR WORKING DRAFT TO AN OFFICE MEMO

CHAPTER 11

THE OFFICE MEMO AND THE LAW-TRAINED READER

Now that you've done a solid legal analysis, it's time to turn your attention to the document you're going to write and to the reader for whom you'll write it.

I. OBSERVATIONS ABOUT READERS

A. Focus on the Reader

We'll think first about the characteristics of law-trained readers. After all, the goal of writing is to communicate with a reader. When you write a legal document, you might not know your reader well—maybe not at all. But you can still write with a fairly accurate focus on this unfamiliar reader because readers, particularly law-trained readers, tend to share certain characteristics. Even in large cities, lawyers and judges live in a legal community that shares certain values, customs, and forms of expression. You'll need to present your message in a way that makes sense in the context of that legal community.

B. Attention Levels

Before you can communicate, your audience must be listening. Here is some information about the attention levels of law-trained readers:

- A reader's attention is finite. Even the most diligent reader will run low or run out.
- Law-trained readers are extraordinarily busy. The judge has many other cases. The senior partner has many other obligations and depends on

you—the memo writer—to analyze thoroughly but communicate succinctly.

- A reader's attention isn't consistent. It is greatest in the first several pages and decreases rapidly. But see the next point.
- Readers often save some attention for the Conclusion. They are willing
to invest attention there, but only if they can locate the Conclusion easily and if the Conclusion is clear and compelling enough to warrant the
investment.
- Attention levels usually revive a bit at internal beginnings and endings,
like the start of a new issue or the last few paragraphs of a statement of
facts. This revival is more likely if the new issue is marked by a heading
or subheading.
- Stories, especially real-life stories, are engrossing. Some readers pay
more attention to facts than to abstract legal concepts. So, attention levels are probably higher in the middle of an effective Statement of Facts
than in the middle of an Argument or Discussion section. Also, even in
the middle of a Discussion or Argument section, a reader's attention
level will rise a bit when the material begins to discuss the facts.
- A reader's attention level is lowest about three-fourths of the way through
the Discussion section of an office memo or the Argument section of a
brief.

What does all this mean? It means that *placement of material* is one of the
important decisions you'll need to make. While a reader wants the analysis to
be complete, she'll also want the most important parts of the analysis placed
where she can find them quickly and give them priority for her attention.

C. Road Maps

Most nonfiction readers want a road map—some sense of where they are
and where they are headed. But law-trained readers have an even greater need
for an organizational structure. Here's why:

A reader's highest priority is to understand the law, and as you learned in
Stage One, a law-trained reader's first step in the process of understanding the
law is an "outline." It's how most lawyers and judges studied law, and it's basic
to the way they think. It might even be the primary component of that vague
phrase "thinking like a lawyer."

And thinking like a lawyer means solving problems. Lawyers and judges
don't read the law out of intellectual curiosity. They have a problem to solve,
and they hope your memo or brief can help them solve it. So your discussion
of the law must be clearly and closely tied to the facts and issues of the case,
and your organizational structure shows that connection.

What's more, a law-trained reader reads skeptically, constantly assessing
the strength and accuracy of the analysis and the ability and credibility of you,

the writer. The most visible part of the analysis, the part the skeptical reader first evaluates, is its organization. A reader who doubts the organization will doubt both the writer and the analysis itself. Law-trained readers aren't comfortable with unexplained organizational surprises, and an uncomfortable reader is an unreceptive reader.

D. Law Professors as Readers

The two primary kinds of writing you'll do in law school course work will be the documents you write for your legal writing assignments and your answers to law school exams. Your primary readers for these documents will be the law professors who drafted the assignments and exam questions. Of course, these professors already understand a great deal about the law, the authorities, and the facts for your analysis.

Ordinarily a writer should tailor the document to the reader's preexisting knowledge. If the reader knows some of the relevant information, the writer would only refer to it generally when necessary to put new information in context. But law school writing is different. Unlike most readers, your professor isn't reading to learn information, but instead to evaluate what information *you* have learned and how well you can communicate it. If the information isn't in your document, your professor won't know whether and how well you understand it.

So, in law school, pretend to be writing to someone else—to a lawyer with no particular expertise. Then you can strike the right balance between including the information your professor wants to evaluate without explaining more than the assignment requires.

II. AN OVERVIEW OF THE OFFICE MEMO

In addition to considering your reader, you'll need to know four more things: (1) your document's function, (2) its format, (3) its degree of formality, and (4) the rules of ethics that apply to memo writing.

A. Function

As you'll recall from Chapter 1, an office memo is an internal working document of the firm. It isn't designed for outside readers. Its function is to answer a legal question, usually for a certain client in a certain situation. It will probably be the primary basis for deciding a question with both legal and nonlegal consequences.

But it might need to do even more. The firm might have a "form file" in which it keeps legal memos for future use. The idea is to eliminate the need to reinvent the wheel for topics that might recur. So your document might have a long life, might impact many clients, and might create impressions about you in the minds of many future readers.

Remember also that your job is to predict, not persuade. You must take an objective view, not advocate for a certain result. It can be easy to forget this role. When your client's situation would be better served by a certain answer, it's easy to slip into advocating for that answer instead of taking a balanced view. But if the answer will be bad news, the client and requesting lawyer need to learn that news now and from you. Learning it later could be costly for everyone.

B. Format

A memo's format is designed to fit its function and its reader's needs. Because a memo is an internal document, law firms are likely to have a preferred memo format. That format might use different words for the section titles, it might place the sections in an order different from that described here, or it might include other sections. If your reader (your teacher or law firm) has a format preference, use it. If not, you can use this standard memo format:

1. The **Heading** identifies the requesting attorney, the writer, the date, and the legal matter.[1]
2. The **Question Presented** identifies the question you've been asked. It allows your reader to confirm that you've understood the question, and it also might remind a busy reader of the question she asked you to analyze.[2]
3. The **Brief Answer** comes next, and if you remember what we've learned about law-trained readers, you'll understand why. Law-trained readers are nearly always in a hurry. They want answers quickly and right up front. Then they can decide how much attention to invest in what follows. As the writer, you had to go through the analysis reflected in the discussion section before you could decide the answer, but in the document designed for this busy reader, provide the answer first.[3]
4. The **Fact Statement** comes next.[4] You probably received the facts from your reader (the requesting attorney) in the first place, so why repeat them? Repeat them to assure the attorney that you've understood them and to help your busy reader have them freshly in mind. And remember that the requesting attorney might not be the only reader. Other attorneys working on this case might need the analysis, and if your memo is placed in the firm's memo file, attorneys working on future cases might need it too.

---

1. See Chapter 13, section I.
2. See Chapter 13, section II.
3. See Chapter 13, section III.
4. See Chapter 13, section IV.

As the writer, you, too, have an interest in writing out the facts. Your legal analysis is based on the facts as you understand them. If the facts were to change, the result might change. If you memorialize the facts you have been given—the facts on which your answer is based—you ensure that your work will be evaluated with reference to those facts. No future reader will think you had access to other, different facts and therefore expect you to have reached a different answer.

5. The **Discussion** section explains to your reader the analysis that led to your answer. Your working draft, with some alterations, will become the Discussion section. Chapter 12 will explain how to convert your working draft into the memo's Discussion section.

6. A **Conclusion** section (when appropriate) summarizes the main points of your analysis.[5] Why include a Conclusion when your Brief Answer has already stated the answer and the Discussion has already explained the analysis in detail? If the analysis has been complex, a Conclusion can tie together and summarize the analysis. And a Conclusion can increase your reader's options. A Conclusion typically goes into more detail than the Brief Answer but not as much as the Discussion, so a law-trained reader can read your Brief Answer first, then proceed to your Conclusion for somewhat more depth, and finally read your Discussion for even more depth.

Look at the sample memo in Appendix A to find and review each component.

C. Degree of Formality

In practice, you'll find wide variations in the degree of formality a reader expects in an office memo. Choose the level of formality your reader desires. If you have no specific instructions, look at examples of memos done by others in the firm. Resolve doubts in favor of formality. In law school, unless your teacher tells you otherwise, use traditional professional formality such as that demonstrated in the sample memo in Appendix A.

D. Ethical Requirements

Finally, remember your professional responsibilities:

1. A lawyer must provide competent representation, including legal knowledge, skill, thoroughness, and preparation.[6]
2. A lawyer must act with diligence and promptness.[7]

---

5. See Chapter 13, section V.
6. ABA Model R. Prof. Conduct 1.1.
7. ABA Model R. Prof. Conduct 1.3.

3. Generally, a lawyer must not reveal a client's confidences.[8]
4. A lawyer's advice must be candid and unbiased, not adversely influenced by conflicting loyalties to another client, to a third party, or to the lawyer's own interests.[9]
5. While a lawyer's advice must provide an accurate assessment of the law, it also can refer to moral, economic, social, and political factors relevant to the client's situation.[10] However, the lawyer's representation of a client does not constitute a personal endorsement of the client's activities or views.[11]
6. A lawyer must not advise or assist a client to commit a crime or a fraud.[12] When the client expects unethical assistance, the lawyer must explain to the client the ethical limitations on the lawyer's conduct.[13]

Although promulgated rules of professional responsibility cover only licensed lawyers, practically speaking they govern law clerks and other support personnel as well. First, your work will affect a real client. Second, the lawyers for whom you work are responsible for the work you do. Further, you might be held accountable for your work when you apply for membership in the bar yourself, not because the rules covered you at the time you did the work but because your prior work could be evidence of the kind of lawyer you would be, if admitted.

But the best reason to adhere to the rules is more personal, however. Your first legal work will be the raw material for developing your *own* professional standards. Begin now to expect yourself to meet or exceed the professional responsibilities of a lawyer. Do it for the sake of yourself and your craft.

Now that you have an introduction to your reader, to the office memo's function and format, to your choices about the appropriate degree of formality, and to your ethical responsibilities, it's time to begin creating your document. Chapter 12 explains how to convert your working draft into the Discussion section. Chapter 13 explains how to draft the remaining sections of the memo.

---

8. ABA Model R. Prof. Conduct 1.6.
9. ABA Model R. Prof. Conduct 1.7.
10. ABA Model R. Prof. Conduct 2.1.
11. ABA Model R. Prof. Conduct 1.2(b).
12. ABA Model R. Prof. Conduct 1.2.
13. ABA Model R. Prof. Conduct 1.2(e).

ORGANIZING FOR YOUR READER: THE DISCUSSION SECTION

The rule's structure gave you the organization for the working draft. That organization has been your analytical tool. It helped you work out how the parts of the rule fit together. It helped you decide which elements are in question and which are not. It was a helpful disciplinarian as you wrote. Now you're ready to revise that organization with your reader's needs in mind.

When you convert your working draft into a Discussion section, your *structure* will probably remain the same, but you might need to reorder the subparts by moving some of the sections around. The reason relates to the different functions of the drafts. The function of the working draft structure is primarily to help *you,* the writer, analyze the law and its application to the facts, so it must track the rule's structure to keep the analysis from missing any steps. Chapters 1 through 6 explained how this works.

But an office memo should serve the *reader's* needs. Your reader will want the most important parts of the analysis to be right up front, so be ready to adjust the working draft's organization. You'll have several organizational options, but no matter which you choose, introduce that choice in the umbrella section.

I. THE UMBRELLA SECTION

Your working draft probably already contains an umbrella section, so your task now is to revise it with your reader's needs in mind. The revised umbrella section should serve your reader in these four ways:

- by summarizing the rule, setting out all subparts and clarifying how they relate to each other;

- by identifying any undisputed issues and explaining briefly why they aren't in dispute;
- by previewing the order of the remaining issues, explaining your choice of that order; and
- if necessary to prevent confusion, by identifying any related legal issues *not* covered by the memo.[1]

You're now ready to decide whether any issues are undisputed. For any possibly undisputed issues, ask yourself whether your conclusion will be readily apparent to your reader or whether the reader will need some analysis to be satisfied on the point. Assess your reader's existing knowledge of the law, the degree of your reader's faith in you as a legal thinker and writer, and your reader's need for certainty. Decide conservatively. If in doubt, treat the issue as meriting discussion.

If an issue is undisputed and you think your reader will be satisfied without a separate discussion, use the umbrella section to dispose of the issue. Give the reader a cursory explanation of why the issue is undisputed—just enough to reassure your reader that your reasons for this conclusion are consistent with the reader's understanding. A reader who understands and accepts your reasons will appreciate your decision to target the issues that matter.

Then identify the remaining issues and explain the order you've chosen for them. Explaining your choice of structures is particularly important if your structure is different from the one your reader might be expecting. An umbrella section gives the reader the context for what will follow, and it clears away the underbrush—the issues the reader can ignore. It meets the reader where she is, deals with her immediate needs, and leads her to the starting point of the analysis.

II. ORGANIZATIONAL CHOICES

After the umbrella section, proceed to the issues at the heart of the analysis. Choose an order that fits both the analysis and your reader's needs. You'll have at least four organizational plans to choose from:

- dispositive issues;
- important issues;
- threshold issues; and
- familiar order.

---

1. For example, the attorney might have asked you to analyze claims under one statute, but claims might exist under other statutes as well. If so, clarify that your memo covers only the identified statute. Your reader will appreciate the clarity, and you'll be protected from later misunderstandings.

A. Dispositive Issues

If the rule has several elements or other subheadings, usually some are more dispositive than others. If so, consider starting with the issue most likely to decide the question. Be sure to explain your decision. Your reader will welcome this structure, but only if she understands the reasons for it. For example, assume that to enforce a covenant not to compete, the plaintiff must prove that the duration, geographic scope, and nature of the activity restrained are all reasonable. Because all three terms must be reasonable, the most dispositive term (that is, the term most likely to decide the issue) will be the term most likely to be found *un*reasonable. The dispositive issues organization would place it first, followed by the term next most likely to be dispositive.

B. Important Issues

This kind of organization prioritizes the issues most important to the reader and to the analysis. It can be a good choice when a rule contains a list of factors the decision-maker must consider. Usually, no one factor is dispositive, but some will be more important than others.

For example, consider a child custody case in which the statute defines the standard as the best interests of the child. The statute sets out a set of factors to consider in deciding best interests. No doubt, some will be more important in some cases than in others. Your discussion probably should organize according to importance in your case. Begin with the most important and end with the least important.

C. Threshold Issues

As we've already seen, the analysis might require two or more steps, and the first step might be a threshold issue. A *threshold issue* is one that determines the direction of the analysis from that point on. For example, assume that a rule of law tells you that if a business is a lending institution, it may not do certain things. The issue of whether your client is a lending institution within the meaning of that rule determines the direction of the analysis from that point on. If your client is *not* a lending institution, the rule prohibiting certain conduct does not apply to your client, and the analysis can move on to any other rules that might apply. But if your client *is* a lending institution, the rule does apply, and the analysis must continue to determine whether your client's proposed action falls within the prohibited conduct. The question of whether your client is a lending institution is a threshold issue. The best organizational choice usually is to place the threshold issue first. Your reader is likely to expect the analysis to begin there.

D. Familiar Order

Many legal rules are familiar to law-trained readers, and the elements are often listed in a certain familiar order, usually the order the rule uses. Common law burglary is a good example. The definition of burglary is traditionally stated as "the breaking and entering of the dwelling house of another in the nighttime with the intent to commit a felony therein." On a burglary issue, your reader will be accustomed to thinking of the elements in that order, and your first draft probably would have analyzed them in that order.

Unless other considerations are more important, choose an order your reader is expecting. You don't want to add unnecessarily to the reader's natural skepticism by imposing an unfamiliar organization. Familiar order organization can serve as a default position—your choice unless there is a reason to prefer a different plan. And of course, if another plan is preferable, use the umbrella section to explain your choice.

You can see that the underlying *structure* of the analysis remains the same. It's still structured according to the rule's structure. But now your assessment of your reader's needs has governed the *order* of the discussion. Some sections may move into the umbrella section (uncontested issues). Some may move up to the beginning of the Discussion section (the most dispositive or important issues or a threshold issue). After you've selected and implemented your organizational plan, your draft of the Discussion section is nearly done. All that remains is to check your subsection lengths, revise your section headings, and smooth out the transitions between the sections.

III. CHECK SUBSECTION LENGTHS

Now that you have your organization in place, check the length and complexity of each of the subsections. If several subsections are short and this troubles you, you could consider combining them. Rewrite the original subheading to cover them all. Within that new and larger section, use clear transitional phrases or sentences to mark the beginning and end of your discussion of each of these smaller issues. Don't be too hasty to obscure the rule's structure, though. Law-trained readers are less troubled by short sections than by confusion about content or rule structure.

If a subsection strikes you as particularly long and complex, consider further subdivisions with smaller subheadings. These subdivisions can reflect different lines of authority, different tests set out in case law, rule explanation versus rule application, or any other points of division that would be helpful to your reader. For length, use three pages as a rough outside limit. Headings and subheadings are your reader's road map. Most busy readers want to orient themselves in the text at least every three pages or so. Also remember that reader attention wanes within large sections and can be renewed with a subheading.

IV. REVISE HEADINGS

A reader cares about headings because they make the large-scale organization visible at a glance. They mark her progress through the analysis, so she always knows where she has been and where she is headed. They allow her to find the conclusion on an issue by locating the heading for the next issue and then reading the paragraph immediately before it. They mark the spots where she might choose to invest a bit more attention.

They also help a reader evaluate the analysis itself, and through it, your ability and credibility. They prevent possible impatience with preliminary issues, since she knows that anticipated sections are coming. They allow her to jump immediately to the section she wants to review.

Your working draft headings (those marked by Roman numerals) might have been phrased as questions, and for subheadings, you might have used phrases instead of complete sentences. Questions and phrases were fine for the working draft because they helped you work out your analysis, but now it's time to write to a reader. Consider revising the headings and major subheadings into complete thesis sentences asserting your conclusions.[2] Your busy reader will probably prefer to see your *answer* in the heading rather than a question.

V. INSERT A THESIS SENTENCE OR PARAGRAPH

Insert a thesis sentence or paragraph immediately after each heading or subheading. This sentence or paragraph should state both your conclusion and a short summary of your reasons. A busy reader will appreciate a summary of what the section will set out. Here is an example of such a thesis sentence:

> I. The court will probably grant primary custody of Bonnie to Ms. Hutchinson.
>
> Because Ms. Hutchinson maintains a stable home, works only part time, and is not required to travel, the court will probably grant her primary custody of Bonnie.

---

2. An example of a subheading that states the conclusion is: "The defendant's conduct constituted a 'breaking' pursuant to the burglary statute."

So now you've converted your working draft to a discussion designed for a reader. With experience, the first stage (the working draft) might become so easy for you that it seems like second nature. If so, you'll be able to combine the processes of creating the working draft and of creating a reader-centered document. Even if you are new to legal thinking and writing, you might be able to collapse the two stages if your issues are few and simple. But most of us, in our first legal writing tasks, need to keep these two stages separate to be sure that each is serving its special writing function. Remember the adage: Two hands while learning.

CHAPTER 13

COMPLETING THE DRAFT OF THE OFFICE MEMO

Now that a draft of the Discussion section is in place, it is time to add the remaining sections.[1]

I. THE HEADING

Draft a Heading in the format of standard business interoffice communications. Here's an example:

TO:	Ramon Caldez
FROM:	Marcia Willingham
DATE:	August 17, 2018
RE:	Sharon Watson (file #96-24795); covenant not to compete against Carrolton; enforceability of the covenant.

The date is important to both you and your readers. Your readers need the date because the law is subject to change. They might look back at your memo months or even years later. The memo's date tells them how much updating is needed. And you want your work to be evaluated on the law at the time of your research, not on later developments you couldn't have known without a crystal ball.

---

1. Because a memo is an internal document, law firms are likely to have a preferred format. That format might use different words for the section titles, or place the sections in a different order, or include other sections. If your reader (your teacher or law firm) has a format preference, use it. If not, you can use this standard memo format.

The "RE" section identifies the client and the file number, both for your current reader and so the memo can be returned in case it's later separated from the file. It identifies the *legal matter* because your firm could be handling other matters for this same client. It identifies the issue you've been asked to analyze because this legal matter might raise other issues that will be the subject of other memos.

II. THE QUESTION PRESENTED[2]

The Question Presented states the question you've been asked to answer. It helps your reader confirm that you've understood the question. It reminds a busy reader of the question she asked. It allows lawyers working on other cases in the future to decide whether the analysis in your memo will be relevant to these other cases.

A. Content and Format

If you've only been asked to research the governing law, not how it would apply to a certain case, the Question Presented simply states that legal question. Here is an example of that kind of question:

> Under what circumstances does Iowa law allow recovery on a claim for the wrongful death of a fetus?

But if you've been asked to apply a rule to a set of facts and predict a result, drafting a readable Question Presented can be more challenging. Here are three format options:

Option 1: State the *legal* question and a concise statement of the major relevant fact(s).

Can . . . [state the legal question] . . . when . . . [state the major facts]?

This format doesn't state the rule as part of the Question. Here's an example:

Can Carrolton enforce the Watson covenant not to compete when the covenant prohibits Watson from making sales contacts for three years and applies to the three counties closest to Carrolton's headquarters?	Legal issue Major facts

---

2. Some law firm formats title this section the "Issue."

Common verbs for beginning a Question Presented in this format are "Can . . . ?" "Did . . . ?" "Was . . . ?" "May . . . ?" and "Is . . . ?" Common transitions into the factual description are "when . . . ?" and "where. . . ?"

Option 2: An even simpler format does the same thing (states the rule and the key facts) but in only a clause beginning with "whether." Here's an example:

Whether Carrolton can enforce the Watson covenant not to compete when the covenant prohibits Watson from making sales contacts for three years and applies to the three counties closest to Carrolton's headquarters.	Legal issue Major facts

Customarily, the "whether" format is followed by a period and treated as if it were a complete sentence although it's not.

Option 3: You can use the "under/does/when" format. This one usually includes the rule within the Question, so it results in the longest and most complex Question Presented. But it usually shortens the Brief Answer (the next section), which otherwise would have had to include the rule. Here's an example:

Under the Georgia rule that enforces covenants not to compete only when the terms are reasonable, can a covenant not to compete be enforced when the covenant prohibits the promisor from making sales contacts for three years and applies to the three counties closest to the company's headquarters?	The rule Legal issue Major facts

Notice that the middle verb can vary, using the same common verbs identified above: "can," "did," "was," "may," or "is."

Use the format your teacher or supervisor prefers. Otherwise, consider using the first format, because it results in a simpler, more understandable sentence and because identifying the applicable rule of law is usually part of the question you are asked to answer.

B. Generic Versus Specific References

No matter which format you use, you'll need to decide whether to use general or specific references. For example, the first two examples above refer specifically to Watson and Carrolton, but the third example does not. That one is phrased as a generic legal question without direct reference to Watson or Carrolton. Here's an example of a generic Question Presented drafted in format 1:

Can a covenant not to compete be enforced where the covenant prohibits the promisor from making sales contacts for three years and applies to the three counties closest to the company's headquarters?	Legal issue Major facts

You'll find proponents of both the generic and the specific Question Presented. The specific Question Presented directly states the question the requesting attorney wants to know. The senior attorney isn't asking an academic legal question. She wants to know the fate of Sharon Watson. The memo might someday be placed in the firm's memo file for use in another case, but its primary function is to answer a question about Watson. Also, a Question Presented using the parties' names is usually shorter and more readable than a generic Question. Some Questions Presented must include a great deal of information, so finding ways to shorten and simplify the sentence structure can be helpful. As with all writing decisions, choose the format your teacher or supervisor prefers.

C. Degree of Detail

Try to limit the Question Presented to one readable sentence. Packing the legal issue, the rule, and the major facts into one readable sentence can be quite a challenge. If your draft of the Question Presented is unwieldy, first use the editing techniques described in Chapter 15. If you still can't achieve a readable sentence, consider shortening the facts you include. If all else fails, use two sentences. Two easy-to-read sentences are better than one monster of a sentence.

D. Role

Finally, remember your role. As you wrote the analysis, you convinced yourself of a certain conclusion. You'll probably tend to state the Question Presented (especially the facts) as an advocate for the conclusion you reached instead of as an objective legal analyst. Resist. Stick to your objective role.

EXERCISE 13-1

Drafting a Question Presented
Draft a Question Presented for an office memo addressing Ms. Ryan's question from Chapter 7, Exercise 7-2.

III. THE BRIEF ANSWER

A. Content and Format

The Brief Answer gives your busy reader the answer quickly and right up front. State the answer forthrightly ("yes," "probably yes," "no," or "probably not"). Then, if the Question Presented used Format 1 or 2 (one that doesn't include the rule), set out the rule and a summary of your reasoning. For example, assume that you've decided that Carrolton will be able to enforce the Watson covenant. Your Brief Answer might be:

Probably yes **[forthright statement of the answer]**. A covenant not to compete is enforceable under Georgia law if the activity restrained, the geographic area of the restraint, and the duration of the restraint are all reasonable **[statement of the rule]**. Several Georgia courts have held that covenants restraining sales contacts are nearly always reasonable as to the activity restrained. Georgia courts have also held covenants reasonable when the duration of the restraint was up to three years and when the area restrained included up to ten counties **[summary of reasoning]**.

If the Question Presented used Format 3 (one that includes the rule), you don't need to repeat the rule. Just provide a summary of your reasoning:

Probably yes **[forthright statement of the answer]**. Several Georgia courts have held that covenants restraining sales contacts are nearly always reasonable as to the activity restrained. Georgia courts have also held covenants reasonable when the duration of the restraint was up to three years and when the area restrained included up to ten counties **[summary of reasoning]**.

B. Generic Versus Specific References

Use references that match those in the Question Presented. If you used the parties' names in the Question, use them in the Brief Answer. If you didn't, don't use them here.

C. Degree of Detail

An average length for a Brief Answer is one readable paragraph (about one-third to one-half of a double-spaced page). The function of the Brief Answer is compromised when the Answer is longer. Try to limit this section to a maximum of five clear, readable sentences.

D. Degree of Certainty

This might be the hardest decision you'll have to make. Maybe the answer seems clear. Did you just happen to receive a straightforward, easy assignment? How can you be sure you're not missing something? Or maybe you think the answer could go either way, and you can't decide which is more likely. Yet the requesting attorney wants an answer, not a coin toss.

Sadly, there isn't an easy solution to this discomfort. You're just beginning a lifelong project of developing your good legal judgment. You'll get better and better at making these judgments.[3] For the time being, though, research and analyze thoroughly and then make the best judgment you can. Keep in mind the possible spectrum:

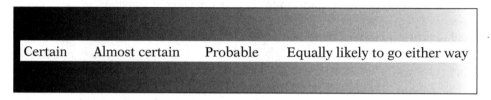

Certain   Almost certain   Probable   Equally likely to go either way

Be suspicious of an answer on either end of the spectrum. Some issues do have undisputed answers, but before you decide that yours is one of them, think twice. Some issues are truly a coin toss, but before you decide that yours is one of them, ask whether you're simply resisting the discomfort of having to make an uncertain prediction.

So, here is how our office memo looks so far:

TO:	Ramon Caldez
FROM:	Marcia Willingham
DATE:	August 17, 2018
RE:	Sharon Watson (file #96-24795); covenant not to compete against Carrolton; enforceability of the covenant.

QUESTION PRESENTED

Can Carrolton enforce the Watson covenant not to compete where the covenant prohibits Watson from making sales contacts for three years and applies to the three counties closest to Carrolton's headquarters?

BRIEF ANSWER

Probably yes. Carrolton should be able to enforce the Watson covenant. A covenant not to compete is enforceable under Georgia law if the activity restrained,

---

3. In practice (and in a law school class, if your teacher permits it), you often can discuss the law and the facts with other more experienced lawyers.

the geographic area of the restraint, and the duration of the restraint are all reasonable. Several Georgia courts have held that covenants restraining sales contacts are nearly always reasonable as to the activity restrained. Georgia courts have also held covenants reasonable when the duration of the restraint was up to three years and when the area restrained included up to ten counties.

IV. THE FACT STATEMENT

The fact section usually includes only facts, not discussion of the law or conclusions about how it would apply to your client. In the fact section, you have three tasks: selecting which facts to include; organizing those facts in an effective way; and remembering your predictive role.

A. Fact Selection

Your busy law-trained reader will want to know only facts relevant to the question presented and background facts that provide necessary context. Contextual facts will come to you naturally as you write, so we'll focus on identifying the legally relevant facts.

Relevant facts are those that help you decide how the rule of law applies to your client's situation. For instance, for the rule we devised from the *Fox* case in Chapter 5, the relevant facts include those that tell you about the kind of activity restrained, the geographic scope, and the duration of the restraint.

Also, include any facts that might have a powerful emotional impact on the decision maker, even if those facts aren't technically relevant to the legal issues. Judges are human. Few of us can completely ignore our reaction to a compelling story. For example, in a divorce case, a judge deciding property issues might be influenced by knowing that one spouse abused the other, even if the applicable law doesn't make fault relevant to property division. If your case includes emotionally powerful facts, don't ignore them.

B. Organization

Once you've identified the facts, think about how you want to organize them. The most common choices are these:

1. Chronological.   This choice is usually the best for a simple set of facts. For instance, the Ryan/Kaplan facts at the end of Chapter 7 are organized chronologically. Recall that the legal issue there is whether a reasonable person would have thought that Kaplan was serious. Another example is the fact statement in the sample trial-level brief[4] (Appendix D). The chronology

---

4. This example is a brief instead of an office memo, but the principle is the same.

is important for that procedural issue, so a chronological organization works well.

2. Topical.   A topical organization might work best when the facts are complicated, cover multiple topics, or include more description than just a series of discrete events. For example, look back at the Tobin/Carletta facts in Chapter 3, Exercise 3-2. There chronology isn't important. The facts simply describe topics: Carletta's statement, the circumstances surrounding it, the possible consequences of it, and Tobin's reaction to it. If we had more detailed facts about each of those topics, perhaps each topic might become one or more paragraphs. This would be an example of a topical organization.

3. Combination of chronological and topical.   It's common for facts to have characteristics of both patterns. Look at the Carillo facts in Chapter 10, Exercise 10-2. Some of the facts have chronological importance, but many are descriptive. Notice how they fall roughly into four topics: (1) an introduction of the Carillos and a description of their neighborhood; (2) facts surrounding the purchase of the trampoline, its placement in their yard, and the rules for its use; (3) the events on the day of the accident; and (4) the present status of the matter. The overall organization of that fact statement is topical, devoting a paragraph to each factual topic, but the topics themselves are chronological and the facts in Topic 3 are presented in a chronology.

C. Remembering Your Role

As you begin to write the Fact Statement, remind yourself that your factual description should be as objective as possible. Watch for the tendency to try to "prove" something by the way you tell the story. Here are three techniques to help prevent this role confusion:

1. Use neutral language and objective characterizations when possible.

Instead of this:	Write this:
The defendant roared through the school zone at 50 miles per hour.	The defendant drove through the school zone at 50 miles per hour.
Wade brutally beat the plaintiff.	Wade struck the plaintiff in the face, resulting in bruising, abrasions, and a cut requiring 15 stitches.

2. Check to be sure you've included the facts that run counter to your prediction.[5]

---

5. For example, notice that the Buckley facts in Appendix A include Buckley's potentially problematic answer to the agent's question.

3. Consider mentioning any important but unknown facts. Looking for unknown facts can help you resist the unconscious tendency to think the facts are more certain than they are. And as an added benefit, the requesting attorney will appreciate the heads-up.[6]

EXERCISE 13-2

Critiquing Fact Statements
You've been asked whether Karen Berry, a lawyer, violated the ethical limitations on doing business with a client. To prove that she did not, she must show (1) that she conducted the transaction fairly and equitably; (2) that she did not misrepresent or conceal any material fact; (3) that she made sure her client was fully informed of the nature of the transaction and his own rights and interests; and (4) that she made sure her client had competent legal advice in the matter.

Evaluate the following Fact Statement, using the criteria above and any others you noticed.

Fact Statement

On March 1, 1996, our client Karen Berry, a lawyer, loaned $50,000 to her client, Morgan Cox. Cox was to use the money to purchase a lot on which he planned to build a warehouse for his wholesale distribution company, ABC Distributing. The loan was to be repaid over ten years. As security for the loan, Berry took a mortgage on the lot and assumed a 51 percent partnership status in ABC. The partnership documents give Berry both control over ABC and joint ownership with Cox of all company assets.

ABC had been operating out of leased space, but their lease was due to expire, and the owner had served notice that the lease would not be renewed. ABC had only four months to vacate the leased premises. Berry had learned this fact during her representation of Cox and ABC in the negotiations to renew the lease. Upon learning that the owner had decided not to renew the lease, Berry suggested to Cox that he buy a certain lot in the heart of the industrial district and build a warehouse there. Cox replied that he did not think he could come up with the necessary funds. Berry offered to loan him the $50,000 purchase price at an interest rate of 8 percent. She said that as security she would take a mortgage on the lot and assume 51 percent partnership status in ABC.

The law requires that Berry refrain from misrepresenting or concealing any material fact. Berry knew that the lot was close to one of the routes proposed for a planned interstate connector. She knew that the value of the

---

6. For example, look at the last line of the Buckley facts in Appendix A.

lot would increase if that route was chosen for the highway. Berry says that she told Cox about this possibility. Whether Cox will confirm Berry on this point is presently unknown.

On the matter of the $50,000 loan, Berry says that she explained the transaction to Cox. However, she says that Cox already understood the proposed transaction clearly since he has over twenty years of business experience. Cox has a Masters degree in Business Administration, and he was at one time a licensed real estate broker. Clearly, with this kind of background, Cox should have been aware of the nature and effect of the proposed transaction. Being sure that the client is aware of the nature and effect of the proposed transaction is one of the key elements required by *Goldman v. Kane*.

Shortly after completing the transaction Berry discovered that Cox had a gambling problem and was draining ABC of its cash. The business was in serious trouble. Fortunately for Berry, she dissolved the partnership agreement before she incurred significant liabilities. Since Cox was in default on the loan payments, Berry foreclosed on the lot. She did not claim an interest in any other company asset.

Within a month after Berry took title to the lot, the proposed connector route nearest the lot was selected for the new highway. Two months later Berry sold the lot for $80,000. Cox has filed a disciplinary grievance against Berry, alleging that Berry violated the ethical rule governing a lawyer's business transactions with a client.

V. THE CONCLUSION

If your Discussion is relatively short and clear *and* if your teacher or requesting attorney does not have a preference, you need not add a separate Conclusion section. But if your analysis has been complicated, a Conclusion section can tie together and summarize the Discussion. It also can increase your reader's options for deciding how much attention to invest in understanding the details. A Conclusion should go into more detail than the Brief Answer but not as much as the Discussion. This allows a reader to read your Brief Answer first, then proceed to your Conclusion for somewhat more depth, and finally read your Discussion for even more depth.

CHECKLIST FOR AN OFFICE MEMO

Heading

1. Have you included the attorney's name, your name, the date, the client's name, the file number, and a phrase identifying the legal issue?

Question Presented

2. Have you chosen an effective format?
3. For format option 1 (legal issue and major facts in a complete sentence), did you state the legal question in the first half of the sentence and the significant facts in the second half?
4. For format option 2 (the "whether" format), did you state the legal question first and the significant facts second, all in a clause that begins with "whether" and ends with a period?
5. For format option 3 (the "under/does/when" format), did you state the rule, then the legal question, and then the significant facts?
6. Have you chosen whether to use generic or specific references?
7. Have you edited to achieve one readable sentence, if possible?
8. Have you maintained an objective perspective?

Brief Answer

9. Have you clearly stated the answer in the first several words?
10. Have you included a statement of the rule if the Question Presented didn't already state it?
11. Have you summarized the reasoning?
12. Have you chosen either generic or specific references to match the Question Presented?
13. Have you kept the Brief Answer to a maximum of one-half of a double-spaced page?
14. Have you taken a position, even if you're not sure?
15. Have you avoided sending your reader mixed signals about how sure you are of your answer?

Fact Statement

16. Have you included all legally significant facts?
17. Have you included sufficient contextual facts?
18. Have you included any major emotional facts?
19. Have you avoided including discussion of legal authority?
20. Have you avoided "arguing" the facts or drawing legal or factual conclusions?
21. Have you pointed out any important unknown information?

Organization

22. Have you identified the client and the client's situation at the beginning of the Fact Statement?
23. Have you selected an appropriate organization (chronological, topical, or combination)?
24. If helpful, does your last paragraph transition into the Discussion section by explaining the procedural posture and legal issue?

Have you used neutral language and objective characterizations?
Have you included both favorable and unfavorable facts?

Discussion (Umbrella Section)

27. Have you summarized the rule, setting out all subparts and clarifying how they relate to each other?
28. Have you included any important information about how the rule functions generally, such as the burden of proof or a relevant presumption?
29. Have you identified any genuinely undisputed issues and provided a cursory explanation for why they aren't in dispute?
30. Have you stated the order of the remaining issues, explaining the reason for that organizational choice?
31. If necessary to prevent confusion, have you identified any related legal issues not covered by the memo?

Discussion of Issues

32. Have you selected an appropriate organization for the issues (dispositive, important, threshold, or familiar)?
33. Have you checked section lengths, combining or dividing subsections where appropriate?
34. Have you revised your headings into complete thesis sentences?
35. Have you stated your conclusion on each issue at the beginning of the discussion of that issue and again at the end?

Conclusion

36. Have you added a Conclusion section if the Discussion has been long and complex?
37. Is your Conclusion more detailed than the Brief Answer but significantly less detailed than the Discussion?

Revising to Achieve a Final Draft

CHAPTER 14

CITATIONS AND QUOTATIONS

After you have a completed draft, it's time to edit cites and quotes.

I. CITATION IN LEGAL WRITING

In legal writing, as in other writing, you must cite to the sources for both ideas and quoted words. Citing to authority has twin purposes:

- to show your reader the authority that supports what *you* say, and
- to identify the ideas and words that *someone else* said.

In legal writing, it's essential to show support for your points. Your cites should prove that the law is what you say it is and means what you say it means.

A cite is also your attribution to another writer, recognizing that the ideas (and the words, if you are quoting) came from that writer. Remember the discussion of plagiarism in the Introduction to this book. Because a reader will assume that you are the source for uncited material, a cite is your way of disclaiming credit for the words and ideas you didn't create. So, cite when you quote and when you paraphrase someone else's point.

> USE CITATIONS
>
> 1. When you state a legal principle.
>
>   *Example:* Intent is a required element of a plaintiff's claim. *Peterson v. Taylor,* [citation.]

2. When you refer to or describe the content of an authority.

   Example: In an earlier opinion, the court had held that intent was irrelevant. *Crenshaw v. Baldwin*, [citation.]

3. When you quote.

   Example: The court reasoned that "the state of mind of the defendant had no impact on the extent of damages suffered." *Crenshaw v. Baldwin*, [citation.]

EXERCISE 14-1

Recognizing Ideas That Need Citations

Read the following passage.[1] Identify the statements for which a citation is either necessary or desirable. Be prepared to explain your answers.

The lawyer has a fiduciary relationship with his or her client. The fiduciary aspect of the relationship is said to arise after the formation of the attorney-client relationship, and it applies to a fee agreement reached after the attorney-client relationship has been entered.

There are at least three reasons for imposing fiduciary obligations on a lawyer. Once the relationship is established, the client will likely have begun to depend on the attorney's integrity, fairness, and judgment. Second, the attorney might have acquired information about the client that gives the attorney an unfair advantage in negotiations between them. Finally, the client will generally not be in a position where he or she is free to change attorneys, but will rather be economically or personally dependent on the attorney's continued representation.

Several cases illustrate the contours of the attorney's fiduciary duty. In *Benson v. State Bar,* the attorney borrowed money from a current client. He "was heavily in debt, and insolvent, at the time he approached [the client] for these loans." In return for the loans, he gave the client unsecured promissory notes. In disbarring the lawyer, the court described the client's trust in the lawyer's judgment and wrote:

> The gravamen of the charge is abuse of that trust, and regardless of petitioner's contention that he never specifically recommended the unsecured loans to [the client], it is undisputed that in soliciting them he failed to reveal the extent of his preexisting indebtedness and financial distress.

In *People v. Smith,* James Smith, an attorney, was under investigation for drug use. He offered to cooperate with Colorado police as an undercover informant. He secretly recorded a telephone conversation with a former client in

---

1. Modified from Stephen Gillers, *Regulation of Lawyers: Problems of Law and Ethics* 61–62 (4th ed., Aspen 1995).

which he asked the former client to sell him cocaine. He then met with the former client wearing a body microphone. The recorded conversations were ultimately used to convict the former client of three felony charges. The Colorado Supreme Court held that although Smith

> no longer represented the [former client], the conduct in all probability would not have occurred had [Smith] not relied upon the trust and confidence placed in him by the [former client] as a result of the recently completed attorney-client relationship between the two. The undisclosed use of a recording device necessarily involves elements of deception and trickery which do not comport with the high standards of candor and fairness to which all attorneys are bound.

For these and other offenses, Smith was suspended from the practice of law.

II. CITATION FORM

A citation is your promise to your reader that the cited material says what you say it says. It also helps your reader find the source and gives some basic information about precedential weight. Several commercially published citation authorities exist, and some courts have adopted their own citation rules. The two most often used citation guides are the *ALWD* (pronounced "ALL-wid") *Guide to Legal Citation*[2] ("*ALWD Guide*" or "*ALWD*") and *The Bluebook: A Uniform System of Citation* ("the *Bluebook*").[3]

Learning to use one of the citation systems is unavoidable. As much as you might like to, you can't just copy the citations you find in the authorities. Many of those citations don't conform to current citation requirements. This chapter covers both the *ALWD Guide* and the *Bluebook*. We'll begin by becoming familiar with the overall layout of each book.

A. Using The *ALWD Guide to Legal Citation*

1. Sections of the ALWD Guide

The *ALWD Guide* contains the following sections and features:

1. *Part 1—Introductory Material: ALWD* begins with a short section expressly designed to introduce you to the book and show you how to use it. This section explains the book's organization and helps you

---

2. ALWD & Coleen Barger, *ALWD Guide to Legal Citation* (6th ed., 2017).
3. *The Bluebook: A Uniform System of Citation* (Columbia Law Review Ass'n et al., eds., 20th ed., 2016).

find quick answers to common questions. A particularly helpful feature of this section is the discussion of how word processing software can affect citation formats. The section gives suggestions for handling margin settings, spacing, default settings, and quick-correct features, all of which can alter your citations in ways you didn't expect or intend. Reading these five pages will help you understand how to use the guide and how to manage your word processor.

2. *Part 2—Citation Basics:* This section gives you key general information, such as when to italicize or underline, how to abbreviate, what to capitalize, and how to decide spacing. Familiarize yourself with the foundational points in this section before you look up citation rules in later sections.

3. *Part 3—Citing Specific Sources:* The citation rules specific to all printed legal authorities are found in Part 3. The most commonly used are cases (Rule 12), statutes (Rule 14), books (Rule 20), and periodicals (Rule 21). One of the best features of the *ALWD Guide* is the use of Fast Formats at the beginning of each rule covering kinds of sources. The Fast Format gives you, on a single page, examples of how to cite to that kind of authority in all the most common circumstances.

4. *Part 4—Online Sources:* This section tells you how to cite to electronic legal sources such as a website or cases from Westlaw and Lexis.

5. *Part 5—Incorporating Citations into Documents:* You'll find more basic information here about how to use citations, covering such common questions as how many and which citations to include, where to put them, in what order, how to use signals, and how to use explanatory parentheticals.

6. *Part 6—Quotations:* Pesky questions about handling quotations are answered here. This section covers use of quotations as they appear in the original source, alteration of quotations, and trimming quotations down to size.

7. *Appendices:* The appendices contain a wealth of important information. Appendix 1 tells you exactly how to cite all the primary authority (like statutes and cases) from your particular jurisdiction. Appendix 2 gives you all the court citation rules from each jurisdiction. Appendices 3-4 show you how to abbreviate almost all the words you'll need to abbreviate as you cite.

2. How to Locate the Rules You Need

Finding the rules you need in the *ALWD Guide* isn't hard. Here are the best strategies for locating rules and finding out how to cite a certain kind of source:

WAYS TO FIND THE RULES YOU NEED

1. For the quickest way to check basic form, *use the Fast Format Locator on the inside front cover*. This handy list will take you immediately to the Fast Format for the source you're citing. For example, if you want to see how to cite to a case, the Locator will refer you to the Fast Format found at the beginning of Rule 12, the rule covering cases. There, on a single page, you'll find examples of how to use all the major varieties of case cites. Then, if you need more, you're already at the beginning of the section covering cases, so you can simply go further into the following pages to find a more specific answer.
2. If you can't find what you need by using a Fast Format, use the index, which is excellent.
3. To find larger sections of the *ALWD Guide*, such as the whole section covering electronic sources, use the Table of Contents.

B. Using the *Bluebook*

The *Bluebook* will intimidate you if you let it. The best way to approach the *Bluebook* is to cut it down to size mentally by identifying the primary parts you'll use. Notice the larger sections of the *Bluebook* as they are set out in the Table of Contents.

1. Sections of the Bluebook

1. *Introduction and Inside Covers.* The *Bluebook* begins with an Introduction expressly designed for new users. The Introduction describes the parts of the *Bluebook*. Also, notice the reference guides on the inside front and back covers.
2. *The "Bluepages."* This section is necessary because the rest of the *Bluebook* focuses on citation form for law review publishing. The Bluepages section adapts the rules in the rest of the *Bluebook* to practitioner writing—the kind you'll be doing in your legal writing class and in practice. This section also includes a table for suggested abbreviations to use in court documents and a table identifying jurisdiction-specific citation rules.
3. *Rules.* The rules themselves come next. Rules 1–9 are general rules that apply broadly to many situations. They are followed by rules dealing with citing kinds of sources. You'll use Rules 10, 12, 15, and 16 (cases, statutes, books, and periodicals) most often.
4. *Tables.* After the rules comes a second set of tables. These are reference sources for basic information about court and reporter systems and

statutory compilations for each jurisdiction as well as standard abbreviations for courts, case names, publications, and other commonly used terms.

2. How to Find the Rules You Need

Here are the best strategies for finding information in the rules:

WAYS TO LOCATE THE *BLUEBOOK* RULES YOU NEED

1. Use the *Bluebook*'s index, which is quite good.
2. Use the Table of Contents.
3. When reading a rule, look at the listed cross-references.
4. Use the Quick Reference [for] Court Documents and Legal Memoranda found on the last page and the *back* inside cover. (The one on the front inside cover and first page is for law review citations.)

C. Several Key Concepts

Before you dive into either citation guide, you'll want to know these two general concepts:

1. Typeface requirements. The *Bluebook*'s rules (the white pages) are designed primarily for law review writing, not practitioner writing. For law review writing, the *Bluebook* requires, on different occasions, large and small capitals, regular typeface, and italics. The examples and explanations in the rules section (the white pages) use those typeface distinctions. Practitioner writing is simpler, using only regular type such as courier and *either* italics or underscoring. Simply type everything else in regular typeface, and don't worry about the more complicated distinctions in the rules section of the *Bluebook*.

The *ALWD Guide* follows the commonly accepted approach for practitioner writing, so selecting the correct typeface is easy. Most material in a citation is presented in ordinary type, italics, or underlined type. The *ALWD* rule covering a certain kind of source will tell you (and show you) which information, if any, to italicize.

Notice, though, that for practitioner writing, both the *ALWD Guide* and the *Bluebook* use the word "italics" to include either slanted type or underscoring.[4] You can use either, but don't use both in the same document.

2. Citing in text versus citing in a footnote. Law review articles are notorious for footnotes, and the rules section of the *Bluebook* provides special requirements for citations in law review footnotes. But footnotes should be the exception rather than the rule for practitioner writing. When practitioners

---

4. ALWD R. 1.3(a); Bluebook B2.

do use a footnote, they usually use the same citation principles they have been using in the text.

D. Introduction to Citation Form

Although the applicable rules are more detailed, an overview will help you put the more detailed rules into a context. Here are the basic components of a citation to a case, a statute, a book, and a law review article:

BASIC COMPONENTS OF A CITATION TO A CASE

1. Case name
2. Case's location:
   a. Volume
   b. Abbreviation for name of reporter
   c. Page where the case begins
   d. Page where the cited material appears
3. Court abbreviation
4. Year

STATE COURT EXAMPLE

Watzek v. Walker, 485 P.2d 3, 6 (Ariz. Ct. App. 1971).

    1   2a 2b 2c 2d   3   4

FEDERAL COURT EXAMPLE

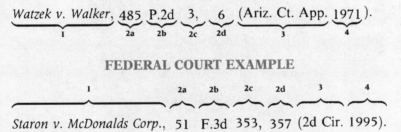

    1   2a 2b 2c 2d 3 4

Staron v. McDonalds Corp., 51 F.3d 353, 357 (2d Cir. 1995).

BASIC COMPONENTS OF A CITATION TO A STATUTE

1. Title number (if the code uses title numbers)
2. Abbreviation for name of code
3. Section number
4. Year the code was published

EXAMPLE

   1 2 3 4

11 U.S.C. 523 (1994).

BASIC COMPONENTS OF A CITATION TO A BOOK

1. Author's name(s)
2. Title of book
3. Volume number, if any
4. Section, paragraph, or page number
5. Edition number, if more than one
6. Year

EXAMPLE

Richard H. Chused, *A Property Anthology* 149 (2d ed. 1997).

BASIC COMPONENTS OF A CITATION TO A LAW REVIEW ARTICLE

1. Author's name
2. Title of article
3. Location of article:
   a. Volume number
   b. Abbreviation for name of law review
   c. Page where article begins
   d. Page where cited material appears
4. Year

EXAMPLE

Murray M. Schwartz, *The Exercise of Supervisory Power By the Third Circuit Court of Appeals,* 27 Vill L. Rev. 506, 508 (1982)

E. Matching the Citation to the Text

A writer tells a reader which point the cite supports by where she puts the cite. If the cite is put outside the textual sentence, the reader knows that the cite supports all the material in the preceding sentence. For example:

To prove a claim for sexual harassment without showing an adverse employment action, a plaintiff must show that the harassment created a "hostile or abusive work environment" and that the plaintiff indicated that the harassment was unwelcome. *Meritor Sav. Bank v. Vinson*, 477 U.S. 57, 66 (1986).

This sentence says two things: that the plaintiff must show a hostile environment and that the plaintiff must show that he or she communicated that the conduct was unwelcome. The placement of the citation to *Meritor* outside the textual sentence (as a *citation sentence* of its own) tells the reader that *Meritor* establishes both points.

But if *Meritor* supported only the first of these points, the cite would go inside the textual sentence, immediately after the point it supports (as a *citation clause*). The writer would cite another authority for the other proposition, like this:

To prove a claim for sexual harassment without showing an adverse employment action, a plaintiff must show that the harassment created a "hostile or abusive work environment," *Meritor Sav. Bank v. Vinson*, 477 U.S. 57, 66 (1986), and that the plaintiff indicated that the harassment was unwelcome [cite to the other case].

If the writer has authority for one part of the sentence but no authority for the other part, the cite still goes immediately after the proposition it supports, like this:

Though a plaintiff can prove a claim by showing that the harassment created a "hostile or abusive work environment," *Meritor Sav. Bank v. Vinson*, 477 U.S. 57, 66 (1986), Willingham has made no such showing in this case.

Sometimes a writer points out an aspect of an authority and then uses that aspect of the authority to reason her way to another point about that authority. The first point came from the authority but the second point didn't, so the cite goes immediately after the point that came from the authority, like this:

The court has allowed recovery on an attractive nuisance claim by a child who came into the defendants' yard to hide from her friends and fell into a swimming pool while there. [The citation to *Newcomb v. Roberts* goes here.] Though *Newcomb* made no mention of the issue, the court's allowance of recovery on these facts shows that recovery no longer requires that the child be drawn to the property by the artificial condition. [The citation to *Newcomb* does *not* go here because *Newcomb* doesn't say that actual attraction is no longer required.]

EXERCISE 14-2

Identifying the Text the Citation Supports

Identify the proposition(s) each of the following citations supports.

A malpractice action can be based on conduct other than a failure to exercise the proper standard of care. It also can be based on violation of a duty the lawyer owes the client as a fiduciary. For example, a fiduciary's duty of loyalty requires her to avoid conflicts of interest. *Simpson v. James*, 903 F.2d 372 (5th Cir. 1990). Ethics rules require the same, ABA Model R. Prof. Conduct 1.7-1.9 (1998), and a violation of a rule of ethics is considered evidence of malpractice, *Beattie v. Firnschild*, 394 N.W.2d 107, 109 (Mich. 1986). If a client suffers a loss as a result of a lawyer's conflict of interest, the client will be able to recover in malpractice. *Simpson*, 903 F.2d at 377; *Miami Int'l Realty Co. v. Paynter*, 841 F.2d 348, 353 (10th Cir. 1988).

Similarly, except in limited circumstances, a fiduciary may not reveal a client's confidential information to the client's disadvantage. Not only is this an ethical rule, ABA Model R. Prof. Conduct 1.6 (1998), but if a lawyer improperly reveals confidential information, a malpractice action will lie. *Tri-Growth Centre City, Ltd. v. Silldorf, Burdman, Duignan & Eisenberg*, 216 Cal. App. 3d 1139, 265 Cal. Rptr. 330 (Div. 1, 4th Dist. 1990).

Breach of fiduciary duty also can occur if a lawyer helps another agent of a client violate the agent's fiduciary duties to the client. *Avianca, Inc. v. Corriea*, 705 F. Supp. 666 (D.D.C. 1989).

F. Citing with Style and Grace

Citations can make the text hard to read. A reader must jump over all the names, numbers, and parentheticals; find the spot where the text begins again; and then pick back up on the message. Granted, law-trained readers become good at these mental and visual gymnastics, but even law-trained readers can use all the help a writer can give them. Here are some suggestions for minimizing the disruption caused by citations:

1. Move the cite out of the middle of the sentence.   Cites in the middle of the sentence make it hard to find the key parts of the sentence and combine them into a coherent thought. For example, notice how you have to hop through this sentence:

A majority of the Court in *General Electric Company v. Gilbert*, 429 U.S. 125, 136 (1976), followed *Geduldig v. Aiello*, 417 U.S. 484 (1974), and held that pregnancy classifications were not gender classifications.

These techniques can help clear the reader's path from subject to verb to object:

a. Move the cite outside the sentence and into its own citation sentence.
b. Move the cite to the beginning of the sentence, in an introductory phrase.

c. When the sentence contains two propositions, each requiring its own authority, consider dividing the sentence into two sentences. Then each citation can be moved outside the textual sentences.

d. Consider moving less important material into a parenthetical in the citation.

Notice how techniques *a* and *d* have made the sentence more readable:

In 1974, a majority of the Court held that pregnancy classifications were not gender classifications. *General Electric Company v. Gilbert,* 429 U.S. 125, 136 (1976) (following *Geduldig v. Aiello,* 417 U.S. 484 (1974)).

2. **Avoid beginning a sentence with a hard-to-read cite.** Here is an example of a sentence with this problem and a better version:

Change	Public Law 95-555, 92 Stat. 2076, October 31, 1978, included a new § 701(k).
To	Congress added a new version of § 701(k) when it enacted Public Law 95-555, 92 Stat. 2076, October 31, 1978.

3. **Avoid string citations.** A s*tring citation* "strings" together many authorities to support the same point. Lawyers often cite several authorities for an important proposition, but the longer the "string," the more the citations impair readability and frustrate a reader. And since citations alone are devoid of discussion, the long list seldom adds much to the analysis. Generally, it's better to cite and discuss the several most important authorities and omit the others.[5]

EXERCISE 14-3

Editing the Placement of Citations

Use the techniques described in Section D to make the following passage more readable and to be sure that the placement of the citation accurately identifies the textual material it supports:

42 U.S.C. § 2000e-2(a) prohibits employers from discriminating against applicants or employees based on the individual's race or sex. The act, titled the "Civil Rights Act of 1964," protects individuals of all races and both genders, not just minorities and women. *McDonald v. Santa Fe Trail Transp. Co.,* 427 U.S. 273, 280 (1976); *Hannon v. Chater,* 887 F. Supp. 1303, 1312 (N.D. Cal.

---

5. String cites can be helpful when your reader needs every relevant authority or in the unusual situation when you want to demonstrate, graphically on the page, the overwhelming strength of support for the point. If you do cite to multiple authorities, place them in the order set out by ALWD Rule 36 or Bluebook Rules 1.3 and 1.4.

1995); *Hall v. City of Brawley,* 887 F. Supp. 1333, 1342 (S.D. Cal. 1995); *Curler v. City of Fort Wayne,* 591 F. Supp. 327, 333 (N.D. Ind. 1984).

However, the Court has never been comfortable with the issues raised by the application of Title VII to the racial majority or to men. In *United Steelworkers of America v. Weber,* 443 U.S. 193, 215 (1979), the Supreme Court upheld a voluntary race-conscious affirmative action plan, but several years later the Court held that, to be permissible, a voluntary affirmative action plan had to benefit only "actual victims of the discriminatory practice." *Firefighters Local 1784 v. Stotts,* 467 U.S. 561, 579 (1984).

Just three years later, the Court, in *Johnson v. Transportation Agency of Santa Clara County,* 480 U.S. 616 (1987), seemed to reaffirm its holding in *Weber* when it expressly followed the *Weber* holding. The Court wrote that the *Johnson* issues "must be guided by our decision in *Weber." Id.* at 627. *Johnson* dealt with a voluntary affirmative action plan designed to improve the representation of racial minorities and of women in traditionally male jobs. *Johnson v. Transp. Agency of Santa Clara County. Id.* at 627.

G. Editing Citation Form

This section assumes that you've looked up the relevant citation rules in your citation manual. What follows is an editing checklist to help you find the most common citation errors.

CHECKLIST FOR EDITING CITATIONS

GENERAL PRINCIPLES

		ALWD	*BB*
1.	Where possible, have you cited legal authority for each point you have made about the law or the authority?	pp. 2-3	B1
2.	Have you placed each citation immediately after the proposition it supports?	34.1	1.1
3.	Have you placed your citations at the end or the beginning of your sentences whenever possible?	34.1	—
4.	Have you avoided unnecessary string citations?	34.3	—
5.	Have you minimized the number of sentences beginning with a citation?	—	—

		ALWD	BB
6.	Have you italicized or underscored using an unbroken line:	1.3	B2
	• Case names, titles of books, and articles?		
	• Signals (such as *e.g.* or *see*)?		
	• Phrases giving prior or subsequent history (such as *aff'd* or *cert. denied*)?		
	• Terms used in short citation forms to indicate a cross-reference (such as *id.*)?		
7.	For citing all authorities other than names of periodicals, have you closed up all adjacent single capitals, individual numerals, and ordinals (for example, "3d"), and initials in personal names?	2.2 4.3	6.1(a)
8.	Have you left a space between single capitals and multiple-letter abbreviations (for example "F. Supp.")?	2.2(a)	6.1(a)
9.	When you put the citation outside the sentence, have you placed a period at the end of the citation?	34.1(a)	B1
10.	When you put the citation inside a sentence, have you set off the citation with commas?	34.1(b)	B1
11.	When you have cited to several authorities together, have you separated them with semicolons?	36.2	B1
12.	In a title, have you capitalized according to the relevant rule?	3	8
13.	Have you placed multiple authorities in the order set out by the relevant rule?	36	1.4

QUOTATIONS

		ALWD	BB
14.	For all cites to the quotation, including parallel citations, have you included the pinpoint cite to the page where the quoted material appears?	5.2	3.2(a)
15.	When you have used a block quote, have you placed the citation at the normal left margin on the line immediately following the block quote?	38.5(e)	5.1(a)(ii)
16.	When the source to which you are citing has quoted the material from another source, have you used an explanatory parenthetical?	38.4(c) 38.5(b)	5.2(e)
17.	When you have added or deleted citations or indications of emphasis, have you used an explanatory parenthetical?	39.4 40.3(c)	5.2
18.	Where you have altered a quote, such as by changing a lowercase letter to an uppercase letter, have you signaled the alteration by using brackets?	39.1	5.2(a)
19.	Have you indicated an omission with an ellipsis?	40.1	5.3

CASES
Long Form

	ALWD	BB
20. Have you used only the last names of the individual parties?	12.2(d)	10.2.1(g) B10.1.1(ii)
21. Have you omitted all parties other than the first party listed on each side?	12.2(c)	10.2.1(a) B10.1.1(i)
22. Have you avoided using "et al." to signal that you have omitted the names of additional parties?	12.2(c)	10.2.1(a) B10.1.1(iii)
23. Have you used "v." (rather than "vs." or "v" or "V")?	12.2(c)	B10.1.1(i)
24. Have you abbreviated case names in citations according to the relevant rule?	12.2(d) & (e)	10.2.1 & 2 T.6
25. Have you placed a comma after the case name and refrained from underlining or italicizing the comma?	1.3	10 B10.1
26. For federal district court and circuit court cases, have you closed up the spaces in "F.3d" but left a space in "F. Supp."?	2.2(a)	6.1(a)
27. Have you included a pinpoint cite to the page(s) of the opinion where the referenced material is located?	5.2	3.2 B10.1.2
28. Have you refrained from placing any punctuation between the page number of the case and the parenthetical?	12.1	10
29. Have you included the opinion's date in parentheses?	12.7	10.5
30. For cases from a state's highest court, where the state is not unambiguously conveyed by the reporter title, have you included the name of the state in the parentheses?	12.6	10.4(b)
31. For state cases where the court deciding the case is not the highest court of the state, have you included the court's name and district or division in the parenthetical?	12.6(c)(1)	10.4(b)
32. For cases from federal circuit courts, have you identified the circuit in the parenthetical and used the correct abbreviation for it (1st Cir., 2d Cir., 3d Cir., 4th Cir., 5th Cir., 6th Cir., 7th Cir., 8th Cir., 9th Cir., 10th Cir., 11th Cir., D.C. Cir., Fed. Cir.)?	12.6(c)(2)	10.4(a) T. 7
33. For federal district courts, have you identified the district in the parenthetical (for example, "S.D. Cal.")?	12.6(c)(1)	10.4(a)

34.	Have you refrained from putting a comma between the date and any other information within the parenthetical?	12.7	10
35.	For the circumstances set out in the relevant rule, have you included the subsequent history in a full citation to a case?	12.8	10.7 B10.1.6
36.	Have you used a comma to separate the subsequent history of the case?	12.8(c)	10.7.1 B10.1.6
37.	Have you included an explanatory phrase in a second parenthetical (and before any subsequent history) when additional information would be helpful for evaluating the weight properly given to the authority?	12.8(g)	10.7.1 B10.1.5
38.	Where a phrase of information would help the reader understand the significance of the cited authority, have you included that information in an explanatory parenthetical?	12.10	1.5 B10.1.5
39.	Have you complied with the relevant rule by using the appropriate signal to introduce cited authorities that:	35	1.2

- represent one example of many authorities standing for the same proposition? (*E.g.*)
- support the stated proposition implicitly (rather than explicitly) or in dicta? (*See*)
- support the stated proposition by analogy only? (*Cf.*)
- are compared to each other to show different results? (*Compare . . . with*)
- directly contradict the stated proposition? (*Contra*)
- contradict the stated proposition by analogy? (*But cf.*)
- provide background information? (*See generally*)

40.	Have you underscored or italicized all signals?	35.4	1.2 & B2
41.	Have you refrained from using a signal when the authority directly supports the stated proposition?	35.2	1.2(a)
42.	When you are citing to a concurring or dissenting opinion, have you disclosed in a parenthetical this potential limitation on the weight of the cited material?	12.10(a)	10.6

43. Have you indicated by parenthetical any other limitations on the weight of the cited material (for example that the cited language is dictum or that your proposition is contained in the cited material only by implication)?	12.10(b)	10.6
44. For cases available only on an electronic database, have you followed the format provided in the relevant rule?	30.2	10.8.1
45. When more than one source is available, have you cited to the appropriate source?	12.4(b)	10.3.1 B10.1.3(v)
46. When citing United States Supreme Court cases, have you cited to the official reporter (U.S.) where possible?	12.4(b)(2)	10.3.1 T.1 B10.1.3(i)

SHORT FORMS

	ALWD	*BB*
47. Have you used a full citation the first time you cite to a particular authority?	11.1(a)	—
48. Have you chosen to use a short citation form with the reader's needs in mind?	11.2	B4
49. When you have used *id.*, have you been referring to the case cited immediately prior to the *id.* cite?	11.3(a)	4.1 B4
50. Have you refrained from using *supra* to refer to a case?	11.4(b)	4.2 B4

STATUTES AND RULES

	ALWD	*BB*
51. Have you abbreviated the statutory compilation as provided in the relevant table?	App. 1	T. 1
52. If the information would be helpful, have you given the statute's name (official or popular)?	14.2(a)	12.3.1(a)
53. If possible, have you cited to the official code rather than to an unofficial code?	14.1 App. 1	12.2.1 T. 1
54. Have you included in parentheses the year of the code you are citing (*not* the year the statute was enacted)?	14.2(f)	12.3.2
55. Have you identified the title, chapter, or volume number, if any, according to the relevant rule?	14.2(b) App. 1	12.3.1(b) T. 1
56. Have you refrained from using "*et seq.*," but rather designated the exact sections you are citing?	14.2(d)	3.3(b)

57. Have you left a space after the section symbol?	6.2 14.2	6.2(c)
58. If you have cited a privately published version of the code, have you identified the publisher in the parenthetical that contains the year?	14.2(f)(1) 14.4 App. 1	12.3.1(d) T. 1
59. If you are citing material contained in a supplement, either alone or in addition to material contained in the main volume, have you followed the format shown in the relevant rule?	8.1 8.3	3.1(c) 12.3.1(e)
60. If you are citing a statute that has been repealed or superseded, have you followed the format shown in the relevant rule?	14.3	12.7
61. If you are citing rules of evidence or procedure, have you followed the format provided in the relevant rule?	16.1	12.9.3
62. Have you used a full citation the first time you cite to the statute?	11.1(a)	B12.2
63. If you used a short form of citation, have you followed the format set out in the relevant rule?	14.5	12.10 B12.2

BOOKS

	ALWD	BB
64. For the first citation to the book, have you used the author's full name followed by a comma?	20.1(b)	15.1
65. If the book has more than one author, have you followed the relevant rule?	20.1(b)(2)	15.1
66. If the book has an editor or translator, have you followed the relevant rule?	20.1(e)	15.2
67. Have you italicized the name of the book?	20.1(c)(1)	B15
68. Have you capitalized the name of the book as set out in the relevant rule?	3.2	8 15.3
69. Have you cited to the latest edition and identified the edition in the parenthetical?	20.1(e)(3)	15.4
70. In the parenthetical, have you identified the year of publication?	20.1(e)(5)	15.4
71. If the cited material appears in a supplement, have you followed the format set out in the relevant rule?	8	3.1
72. If you have used a short form for later citations to the same book, have you complied with the relevant rule?	20.6	15.10 15.2
73. Have you used a pinpoint cite to identify the page(s) on which the cited material appears?	5.2 20.1(d)	3.2(a) B15.1 & 2

PERIODICALS

		ALWD	BB
74.	Have you provided the author's full name (including student authors) followed by a comma?	21.2(a)	16.2
75.	Have you italicized the title of the article and followed the title with a comma?	21.2(c)	16.3 B1
76.	Have you capitalized the title in accordance with the relevant rule?	3.2	8
77.	Have you abbreviated the periodical as set out in the relevant table? If your periodical is not included in the list, have you used the relevant rules as your guides for constructing the periodical's abbreviation?	21.2(e) App. 3 App. 5	T.13
78.	Have you followed the relevant rule for spacing between the letters abbreviating the periodical name?	2.2	6.1(a)
79.	Have you included the volume number of the periodical (before the abbreviated title of the periodical)?	21.2(d)	16.4
80.	Have you identified the page on which the article begins, placing it after the abbreviated title of the periodical and refraining from using a "p." or "pp."?	21.2(f)	16.4 16.5
81.	Have you included a pinpoint cite to the page(s) where the cited material is found?	5.2 21.2(f)	16.4 16.5 B16.1
82.	Have you refrained from putting a comma between the page number and the parenthetical?	21.2(g)	16
83.	Unless the periodical uses the date for the volume number, have you included the date of the volume in the parenthetical?	21.3(d)	16.4 16.5

EXERCISE 14-4

Editing for Citation Form
Edit the following citations for correct citation form. Use the checklist in section G. If you spot an error that you cannot correct without additional information, simply note the error and identify the information you would need to correct it.

1. *Leibel vs. Raynor Manufacturing Co.*, 571 S.W. 2nd 640 (1978).
2. Brown v. New Haven Civil Service Comm., 474 F.Supp. 1256, 1263, (1979).
3. *Equal Pay Act of 1963*, 29 USC § 206(d), *et seq.*
4. *Connecticut v. Winnie Teal, et al.*, supra at 444.
5. Harold S. Lewis, Jr., Litigating Civil rights and Employment Discrimination cases, 1996. (This is a book.)
6. *Humphrey v. McLaren*, 402 N.W.2d 535 (Minn, 1987). [cited in a brief filed before a trial court in Minnesota]
7. *Prandini v. National Tea Co., Id.* at 49.
8. Jack Lee Sammons, *The Professionalism Movement: the Problems Defined*, 7 Notre Dame Journ. of Law, Ethics & Public Pol. 269, 1993.
9. e.g., *U.S. Dept. of Labor v. Triplett*, 494 US 715, 716 (1990).
10. *Laffey v. Northwest Airlines, Inc.*, 567 F.2d 429, 431 (1978).

III. QUOTATIONS

The most common quotation problems are (1) not using quotation marks for borrowed language; (2) using too many quotes; (3) not editing a quote down to its nub; and (4) making errors in quotation mechanics. The rest of this chapter deals with these common quotation problems.

A. When Quotation Marks Are Required

Use quotation marks to show that the words themselves came from someone else.[6] Quotation marks tell a reader the source of the language, and they give the creator the credit (or blame) for the creation.

Quotation marks are necessary when you quote the words of another but unnecessary when you paraphrase. Sometimes it's hard to tell the two apart. When are the words yours and when are they "the words of another"?

Start with the proposition that usually you should rephrase the thoughts of others into your own words and sentence structures. But even if you aren't looking at the source while you write, you might find that your text turns out to be similar to your source's text. Maybe the source uses common words or sentence structures to express the idea, or maybe, without realizing it, you've been thinking of the topic in the source's words.

If the original text used the word "table" and you use it too, no one would argue that you should put quotation marks around "table" in your document. But if your draft shares a whole paragraph in common with the original text,

---

6. *Ideas* that come from another author must always be attributed to the other author. This section assumes that you're already attributing the *ideas* to their source. Here we're dealing only with deciding when to attribute the *words*, too.

everyone understands that the paragraph must be presented as a quotation. Somewhere between these two extremes lies the point at which the words qualify as someone else's (and quotation marks become necessary), but no bright-line test will tell you precisely where.

The absence of a clear test is particularly unfortunate in legal writing. Legal writers rely heavily on sources, and most legal writing texts advise writers to paraphrase most sources. If you follow this good advice, you'll be doing a lot of paraphrasing. How can you know whether your paraphrase is different enough from the original text that it doesn't need quotation marks?

To decide whether you need quotation marks, consider the *combined effect* of these factors:

- the length of the common unit of text;
- the number of units in common;
- whether the sentence structure is the same or similar; and
- whether the common units include particularly striking language.

Some writers use a seven-word benchmark as a starting point for measuring the length of a common unit. If seven or more words used together in your text match the text of the source, use quotation marks for those words. The benchmark recognizes the unlikelihood of a common seven-word unit appearing inadvertently in texts by different authors. So to be safe, use quotation marks *at least* for any unit of seven or more words.

But you can't avoid quotation marks just by changing every seventh word. The seven-word benchmark is only an approximate measure, and it applies only when the texts aren't similar in other ways, so consider also whether there are other common units of text and whether the sentence structure is similar. Would an objective reader think that this passage is fundamentally someone else's, with just a few surface changes?

Finally, use quotation marks for language another author has used in a particularly vivid, creative, or unusual way. For example, in *Griggs v. Duke Power Company*, Chief Justice Burger condemned employer practices that function as "built-in headwinds" impeding employment for minority groups.[7] In *Watson v. Fort Worth Bank and Trust*, Justice O'Connor described the positions argued by the parties as "stark and uninviting alternatives."[8] In his dissent in *Wards Cove Packing Company v. Atonio*, Justice Stevens described the living and working conditions at the defendant's canneries as "a plantation economy."[9]

These are examples of words and phrases used in distinctive ways. In each case, the author was especially effective in selecting the words to express the idea. In each case, the author's effective use of language merits recognition,

---

7. 401 U.S. 424, 432 (1971).
8. 487 U.S. 977, 989 (1988).
9. 490 U.S. 642, 662 n.4 (1989).

and other writers who use these phrases should give credit to the original author by using quotation marks.

Make your decisions conservatively. It's far better to use quotation marks or to paraphrase the passage more thoroughly than to risk questions about whose writing your document really reflects.

B. Choosing to Use Quotation Marks

Even if quotation marks aren't required, you might choose to use them anyway, for example, when the analysis applies a particular legal test or interprets the words of a statute. Here are examples:

PARTICULAR LEGAL TEST
A lawyer must use the degree of skill commonly exercised by a "reasonable, careful and prudent lawyer." *Cook, Flanagan Berst v. Clausing*, 438 P.2d 865, 867 (Wash. 1968).

PARTICULAR WORDS OF STATUTE
Title VII makes it unlawful for a labor organization "to exclude or expel" an individual because of religion. 42 U.S.C. § 2000e-2(c)(1) (1994).

Quotation marks wouldn't be required for these words, but you should use them anyway to let the reader know that these are the key words at issue in the analysis.

C. Overquoting

Chapter 7 warned against using too many quotations.[10] There, in the working draft stage, the danger was confusing quoting the authorities with analyzing them. The editing stage raises two more reasons to minimize quotes. First, busy readers are tempted to skip quoted material entirely. Maybe they assume that the quoted material simply supports the points the writer has already stated. Maybe busy readers are discouraged by the single-spacing of a block quote. Whatever the reason, readers do tend to skim or skip quoted material.

Second, a quotation seldom communicates your point as clearly, directly, and succinctly as you could. After all, the original writer wasn't writing about *your* case. Your paraphrase can do what quotations can't, that is, tie the substance of the precedential source directly to the issues of *your* case.

---

10. ALWD Rule 38.1 contains the same caution.

Generally, quote only in these circumstances:

1. Quote when the issue will turn on the interpretation of key words of a statute, rule, or case, as described above. Limit the quotation to *those words* so your reader will understand the issue and your analysis of it. Here is an example:

    > A lawyer must use great care in deciding whether to undertake representation of a new client when that representation might be directly adverse to an existing client. The existing client must consent to the lawyer's representation of the new client. ABA Model R. Prof. Conduct 1.7(a)(2) (1998). However, even if the client consents, the lawyer must not undertake the new representation unless the lawyer "reasonably believes" that the new representation will not "adversely affect the relationship" with the existing client. *Id.* at § 1.7(a)(1).

2. Quote *key* language from an authority with a great deal of precedential value. This could be mandatory authority or highly respected persuasive authority such as an opinion of the United States Supreme Court, a provision of a Restatement of Law, or an opinion written by a respected judge, for example:

    > To prevail, the plaintiff must prove that the injuries would not have happened but for the defendant's unlawful actions. That causation standard requires the court to imagine a scenario that did not, in fact, occur. As Justice Brennan has observed,
    >
    > > But-for causation is a hypothetical construct. In determining whether a particular factor was a but-for cause of a given event, we begin by assuming that that factor was present at the time of the event and then ask whether, even if that factor had been absent, the event nevertheless would have transpired in the same way.
    >
    > *Price Waterhouse v. Hopkins*, 490 U.S. 228, 240 (1989).

3. Quote *key* language when the author has found a particularly effective way to express the idea you want to convey, for example:

    > Under Rule 60(b) the court possesses "a grand reservoir of equitable power" to accomplish justice. *Thompson v. Kerr-McGee Ref. Corp.*, 660 F.2d 1380, 1385 (10th Cir. 1981).

D. The Mechanics of Quoting

Here is an editing checklist to help you flag the most common quotation errors:

1. Indent quotations of 50 or more words from both side margins. The indentation indicates that the material is quoted, so don't use quotation

marks. Indented quotations should be single-spaced. *ALWD* R. 38.5; *Bluebook* R. 5.1(a).

2. Don't indent or single-space quotations shorter than 50 words. Use quotation marks. *ALWD* R. 38.4; *Bluebook* R. 5.1(b).

3. Put end punctuation inside the quotation marks if it is part of the quoted material. For punctuation you add, put commas and periods inside the quotation marks, but put other added punctuation outside the quotation marks. *ALWD* R. 38.4(b); *Bluebook* R. 5.1(b).

> "Discriminatory employment practices are prohibited."
> [The period is part of the quoted material.]

> The statute prohibits "discriminatory employment practices."
> [The period is not part of the quoted material.]

> Does the statute prohibit "discriminatory employment practices"?
> [The question mark is not part of the quoted material.]

4. Show changes in the quotation by using brackets and ellipses. Use brackets when you replace letters or words or when you add material to the quotation:

> "[R]egulations [of employee appearance] making distinctions on the basis of sex will not support allegations of discrimination unless [the regulations] are unreasonable or unevenly enforced."

In the first bracket, the uppercase *R* replaces a lowercase *r* because in the original the quoted language did not begin a sentence. The second and third brackets identify material added or substituted to clarify, simplify, or shorten the quoted material. *ALWD* R. 39; *Bluebook* R. 5.2 & 5.3.

5. To show that you've omitted letters, use empty brackets. For instance, write "draft[]" when omitting the "ing" from "drafting." *ALWD* R. 39.2; *Bluebook* R. 5.2(b).

6. To show that you've omitted words, use ellipses. An ellipsis is a series of three dots with a space before, between, and after. *ALWD* R. 40.1 & 40.2; *Bluebook* R. 5.3.

> "The evidence included a communication . . . suggesting that the employee should wear clothing of a more feminine style."

7. Don't use an ellipsis at the beginning of a quotation. A reader will know that the original source might include material ahead of the quote. *ALWD* R. 40.3(b); *Bluebook* R. 5.3(b)(i).

8. Don't use an ellipsis at the end of a quotation if the quoted material ends with a complete sentence. A reader will know that the original source might contain material after the quoted sentence. *ALWD* R. 40.3(c); *Bluebook* R. 5.3(b)(iv).

9. When you use material that was a *part* of a sentence in the original but you are using it as a complete sentence in your text, show the omitted

material at the end of the quotation with an ellipsis after the end of the quote.

> "The mere existence of a grievance procedure does not insulate an employer from liability . . . ."

The ellipsis tells the reader that in the original, the sentence contained additional material. *ALWD* R. 40.2(b); *Bluebook* R. 5.3(b)(iii).

10. Use a parenthetical at the end of the cite to signal that you've omitted citations or footnotes or to signal added or deleted emphasis. *ALWD* R. 40.3(c); *Bluebook* R. 5.3(c). For example:

> The court observed that a partner's interest in partnership property "is a derivative interest subject to significant limitations. [A partner] has *no right to use this property for other than partnership purposes* without the consent of the other partners." *Bellis v. U.S.*, 417 U.S. 85, 98 (1974) (citations omitted; emphasis added).

Here, the original material contained citations after "limitations" and before the next sentence. The italicized phrase was not italicized in the original.

11. If you find an error in the quoted material, either alter the quotation to correct the error or signal the error by following it with "sic" enclosed in brackets. *ALWD* R. 39; *Bluebook* R. 5.2(c). For example:

> "The party least anxious to settle was her [sic]."

E. Editing Quotations

Edit quotations down to their key words so your reader doesn't have to sift through unnecessary material to find your point. Editing must not change the meaning, but within that constraint you have great latitude to clear away the underbrush. Often the most effective quotation has been edited down to a short phrase or even a single word. Restrained use of italics and underlining in quoted material can encourage busy readers not to skim or skip quotations.

For example, assume that you represent the defendant in a sexual harassment claim. The plaintiff alleges that her supervisor pressured her into going to dinner with him and kissing him. You are writing a brief to the trial court on the issue of what the plaintiff must prove. Compare the following examples:

Example 1:

The Supreme Court has held that "the District Court in this case erroneously focused on the 'voluntariness' of respondent's participation in the claimed sexual episodes. The correct inquiry is whether respondent by her conduct indicated that the alleged sexual advances were unwelcome, not whether her actual participation in sexual intercourse was involuntary." *Meritor Sav. Bank v. Vinson*, 477 U.S. 57, 68 (1986).

Example 2:

The Supreme Court has held that a plaintiff cannot prove a sexual harassment claim merely by showing that she participated in the sexual conduct involuntarily. She must prove that "by her conduct [she] *indicated* that the alleged sexual advances were unwelcome." *Meritor Sav. Bank v. Vinson*, 477 U.S. 57, 68 (1986) (emphasis added).

Which manner of quoting distills the key distinction and highlights it for your reader? Which states the legal principle as it would apply to the procedural posture of your case? Which states the legal principle in language that would apply to the facts of your case? Which is more readable?

Now that your citations and quotations are in good shape, we're ready for the last step: editing the rest of the document.

CHAPTER 15

REVISING FOR USAGE AND STYLE

The last step in the writing process is editing. Good editing requires reading the document as if you've never seen it before and that's hard to do if you've been working on it intensely. Try to arrive at the editing stage with enough time to put the document down for at least a day. Even if you don't have that luxury, let a couple of hours pass. Then try to read as if you were a stranger to the document.

Use the sections of this chapter as a checklist. These sections identify many of the most common trouble areas. Also, check your draft against the material on paragraphing and transitions in Chapters 7 and 8. Confirm that your paragraphs aren't too long and that they don't wander. Be sure that the transitions are clear.

Watch for other errors not highlighted here and for typographical errors. Have a good composition handbook or style manual handy to check grammar or punctuation questions. You can use computer programs for checking grammar, punctuation, style, and cite form, but remember that no computer program can replace your own careful proofreading.

I. PROFESSIONAL TONE AND LEVEL OF FORMALITY

Most legal writing calls for the degree of formality appropriate for traditional business and professional writing. *For office memos,* the practice in your firm may be as formal as that for a brief or slightly less formal.

| *More formal* | Before filing the complaint, it will be necessary to confirm the defendant's correct corporate name. |
| *Less formal* | Before filing the complaint, we'll need to confirm the defendant's correct corporate name. |

If you're unsure, use traditional formality. Unlike this book (which has a different purpose), don't use contractions, colloquialisms, slash constructions ("and/or"), and abbreviations appropriate only for note taking or citations:

The plaintiff *will not* [rather than "won't"] be able to argue that . . . .

Clayton's *children* [rather than "kids"] were visiting their grandmother.

The corporate president, vice president, *and* [rather than "&"] secretary all testified.

The stockholders can sue the corporate president or vice president *or both* [rather than "president and/or vice president"].

The defendant's employment policy prohibits sexual harassment such as unwanted touching, verbal intimidation, displaying pornography, *and other sexually offensive conduct* [rather than "etc."].

Here are some other things to avoid in your tone:

- Unnecessary references to yourself, your firm, or opposing counsel. Keep the focus on the parties and the issues.
- Sarcasm and anger. In the rough and tumble arena of litigation, other parties (or even judges) will sometimes make you angry. Allowing your own emotional response to color your writing is both unprofessional and counterproductive.
- Humor. Unfortunately, humor is rarely appropriate. Legal matters and the parties involved in them deserve to be taken seriously.
- Rhetorical questions (questions asked merely for effect).[1]

II. LEGAL USAGE AND CUSTOMS

Legal *usage* refers to the accepted way lawyers use legal language. Citation manuals cover some legal usage questions such as capitalization, quotations, and titles of judges, officials, and court terms. For other legal usage questions, you can consult a legal usage dictionary.[2] The items that follow answer some of the most common usage questions for new legal writers:

---

1. Here is an example of a rhetorical question: "How can the plaintiff argue that her claims are just?"
2. Two good references are Bryan A. Garner, *Garner's Dictionary of Legal Usage* (3d ed., Oxford U. Press 2011), and David Mellinkoff, *Mellinkoff's Dictionary of American Legal Usage* (West 2009).

1. Courts "find" facts and "hold" legal conclusions. Use "find" when referring to decisions the court made about facts. Use "hold" when referring
   to decisions the court made about the law and the outcome of the case.

Compare	The evidence supported the court's *finding* that the car was traveling fifty miles per hour.
With	The court *held* that driving 50 miles per hour constituted negligence.

Compare	The court *found* that the officer had not advised the defendant of his right to remain silent.
With	The court *held* that the failure to advise the defendant of his right to remain silent violated the defendant's Constitutional rights.

2. Reserve the verb "held" for the court's holding and use verbs like
   "observed" or "stated" for dicta.
3. Courts don't have to persuade anyone of anything, so courts don't
   "argue" ("The court argued that the rule's policy supports its holding.")
   Courts don't "stipulate" because courts don't negotiate with parties.
4. Capitalize "Court" only when naming a certain court with its full name
   ("the United States District Court for the District of Idaho") or when
   referring to the United States Supreme Court ("In *Brown v. Board of
   Education* the Court held . . . ").
5. Capitalize a party's procedural designation (plaintiff, defendant, appellant) when referring to the parties of your case ("The Appellant did not
   file its motion within the statutorily required time."), but not when
   referring to a party in another case ("In *Bell v. Burson* the plaintiff . . . .").
6. Capitalize the actual titles of court documents filed with the court in
   your case ("Plaintiff's Motion for Summary Judgment was filed within
   the required time limit"), but not the generic name for a kind of document ("The parties must file all motions for summary judgment by
   April 27").
7. If a court issued an opinion ten years ago, or even ten minutes ago, the
   court's action is a *past* legal event; therefore, refer to that event using a
   past tense verb. But a rule of law is a current reality and calls for a verb
   in the present tense.

Court opinion (past tense)	The court *held* (or "observed," "stated," "applied," "rejected," "adopted") [rather than "holds," "observes," "states," "applies," "rejects," "adopts"] . . .
Rule of law (present tense)	The court adopt*ed* (past tense) the rule that a covenant not to compete *is* [rather than "was"] enforceable if . . .

8. Although the human beings who decide cases are called "judges," it's customary to refer to them as "the court."

> In *Bell v. Burson* the *court* [rather than "judge" or "judges"] held . . .

9. A "court" (even a court with more than one judge) is an entity rather than a group of several judges. Therefore, "court" takes a singular pronoun:

> The appellate court overruled *Janace v. Harbison. It* [rather than "they"] held that . . .

10. A criminal defendant may "be found guilty" or may "be convicted" of a crime. In civil litigation, the comparable term is "held liable":

> Shaffer was *convicted of* burglary.

> After the criminal prosecution, Shaffer's former wife sued him for damages resulting from the assault. He was *held liable* for $50,000.

11. When you refer more than once to a party or an entity with a long name, use a shorter form of reference for those later references. Use the full name for the first reference, but introduce the shorter reference in parentheses.

> The Department of Human Services (DHS) denied the claim.

12. Avoid footnotes if possible. If something is important enough to say, it's probably important enough to put in the text.

III. GENDER-NEUTRAL WRITING

Although the use of only masculine nouns and pronouns for general reference is technically correct, most of today's good writers avoid or minimize it. If your writing reflects modern standards of style, your readers will notice. They'll suspect that you are skilled and careful in performing other lawyering tasks as well.

Before exploring technique, we need to clarify what *gender-neutral writing* is and is not. Gender-neutral writing doesn't mean not referring to gender when writing about a specific person. That person has a gender, and there is nothing wrong with recognizing it. Gender-neutral language simply means that you try to avoid using masculine nouns and pronouns for *general* reference. For example:

Change A person cannot recover damages for injuries sustained primarily due to *his* own negligence.

To A person cannot recover damages for injuries sustained primarily due to *that person's* own negligence.

Here are some strategies for gender-neutral writing:

A. Nouns: Eliminate or Substitute

1. Where possible without loss of clarity, eliminate the noun entirely. For example, you could probably eliminate the term "bat boys" from the following sentence without altering the meaning, especially if your legal issue isn't specifically about "bat boys."

   > . . . to all players, coaches, [bat boys,] ticket takers, concession workers, or other employees whose jobs are related to the sport of baseball.

2. Substitute gender-neutral synonyms where the noun is necessary.

Use	Instead of
worker	workman
mail carrier	mailman
chairperson	chairman
supervisor	foreman
server	waitress
reporter	newsman
housekeeper	maid
spouse	husband/wife
sibling	brother/sister
firefighter	fireman
police officer	policeman
flight attendant	stewardess
supplier	materialman
humans, persons, individuals	man, men, mankind
humanity, humankind	mankind
staffing	manning

B. Pronouns (He, She, His, Hers)

1. Where showing possession is not necessary to the meaning, substitute "the" or "an" for the pronoun:

   > A plaintiff may petition the court for relief, attaching to *the* [rather than "his"] complaint a copy of . . .

2. Repeat the antecedent. The antecedent is the noun to which the pronoun refers. In the following example, "doctor" is the antecedent:

   > a doctor and the nurses, secretaries, and receptionists in *the doctor's* [rather than "his"] office . . .

3. Make the antecedent plural so you can use the plural (nongendered) pronoun "their."

> The license fee applies to *taxi drivers* [rather than "a taxi driver"] driving *their* [rather than "his"] own taxi*s*.

Avoid using the plural pronoun ("they" or "their") without pluralizing the antecedent. Here is an example of this error:

> *Anyone* who rides a roller coaster must assume the risk, and cannot recover for *their* injuries.

4. Rephrase to use a clause beginning with "who."

Change	A person must assume the risk of injury if he rides a roller coaster.
To	A person who rides a roller coaster must assume the risk of injury.

5. Eliminate the pronoun by using a passive construction.

> If the examining physician knows that the person *being examined* [rather than "he is examining"] has been under treatment . . .

Warning: Use this technique sparingly. As section IV explains, overusing the passive voice is not good style.

6. Rephrase the clause entirely.

Change	For each speaker, enclosed is an outline of his presentation, a copy of the exercise he has prepared, and a memorandum explaining his exercise.
To	Each speaker has prepared a presentation outline, an exercise, and an explanatory memorandum. Copies are enclosed.

8. If these strategies fail, use both pronouns separated by a conjunction, such as "and" or "or."

> A parent may enroll his or her child . . .

9. You'll sometimes see the following techniques. Avoid them in formal professional writing:

> his/her
> he/she
> s/he
> "her" in place of "his"
> alternating between "his" and "her"

C. Proper Names and Titles

Refer to a client in the way the client prefers. If the client doesn't have a preference, use these guidelines:

1. Be consistent with courtesy titles. If you don't use "Mr." for men, don't use "Miss," "Mrs.," or "Ms." for women.
2. Unless you have a good reason, use "Ms." rather than "Mrs." or "Miss." The object is to treat men and women the same. The courtesy title for men ("Mr.") doesn't indicate a marital status, so the title for women shouldn't either.[3]
3. Be consistent in the use of first names and last names. You can use last names only, first and last names together, or (rarely) first names only. However, unless you have a good reason, apply your decision equally to both genders.

IV. CLEAR SUBJECTS AND STRONG VERBS

The best tip for improving your writing style is probably using clear subjects and strong verbs. Here are some of the best techniques for this goal:

1. Passive voice.   Mediocre legal writing is filled with unnecessary passive verbs. Learn to spot them, evaluate whether they serve a purpose, and get rid of them if they don't. Recognize passive verbs by checking the subject of the sentence. Identify the subject and ask yourself whether the subject performed the action described by the verb. If it did, then the verb is in the *active* voice. If it didn't, but instead was acted *upon*, the verb is in the *passive* voice.

Active	Ms. Watson signed a covenant not to compete.
Passive	A covenant not to compete was signed by Ms. Watson.

Sentences overloaded with passive verbs are usually longer. You can see this on a small scale in the example above, and the effect can compound:

Passive	It was insisted by Carrolton that the covenant had been breached by Ms. Watson.
Active	Carrolton insisted that Ms. Watson had breached the covenant.

The first sentence contains fourteen words, and the second sentence contains nine words, a reduction of 36 percent.

Second, sentences in the active voice are often clearer. The passive voice may omit the identity of the actor, a fact that is usually (although not always) important. These versions of our earlier examples reflect this problem of ambiguity (or complete mystery):

---

3. You can use "Mrs." or "Miss" when a reader or client prefers it, when the issue makes marital status relevant, or when it will prevent confusion.

A covenant not to compete was signed. [Who signed?]

It was insisted that the covenant had been breached. [Who insisted? Who breached?]

Finally, writing in the active voice is more forceful. A sentence in the active voice drives forward in a straight line; the subject "does" the action to the object. But a sentence in the passive voice moves in reverse, backing in stops and starts toward the subject. Like a car, a sentence driving forward moves more smoothly and forcefully than a sentence in reverse.

Although writing in the active voice is generally preferable, an occasional passive-voiced verb can serve a function. For example, Section III explained that a passive verb can sometimes eliminate the need for using a masculine noun or pronoun. In persuasive writing, as Chapter 22 will explain, other strategic considerations may call for a passive verb. Also, sometimes the identity of the "actor" really is unimportant, and a passive verb can appropriately focus the attention on the object or the action.

However, most legal writing, including the case law you spend so much time reading, relies far too much on verbs in the passive voice. Because so much of what you are reading everyday is infected with passivitis, you'll have to struggle against developing the habit yourself.

2. Nominalizations.   The second technique for clear subjects and strong verbs is avoiding nominalizations. Nominalizations are nouns that began life as a verb and should have been content with their lot in life. When a verb aspires to upward social mobility (becoming a noun), it soon finds that it needs a crowd around it. Suddenly, your sentence has several more words than it used to.

No nominalization	The sellers decided to accept the buyer's offer.
One nominalization	The sellers *made a decision* to accept the buyer's offer.

If your sentence contains several nominalizations, the party can get out of hand.

No nominalizations	The sellers decided to accept the buyer's offer, so they authorized their broker to announce their decision.
Three nominalizations	The sellers *made a decision* to accept the buyer's offer, so they *issued an authorization to* their broker to *make an announcement of* their decision.

Wordiness isn't the only problem nominalizations cause. Sentences using nominalizations are both weaker and less clear than sentences in which the verbs stay where they belong. Because nominalizations are still verbs at heart, they don't do a very good job of being nouns. They are by nature more vague than "real" nouns. Worse yet, when the hole left by the departed verb is filled, the substitute verb is usually weaker than the departed verb.[4] Altogether, these consequences weaken the sentence and obscure the meaning.

Here are examples of common nominalizations and the verb forms to which they should return.

Change	To
enter into an agreement	agree
contains a provision	provides
have a collision	collide
file a motion	move
give consideration to	consider
had knowledge that	knew
effect a termination	terminate
make an assumption	assume
make a decision	decide
places emphasis on	emphasizes
it is a requirement of the contract that	the contract requires that
commencement of discovery will occur	discovery will commence

3. Throat-clearing.   Another major obstacle to strong subjects and verbs is "throat-clearing" —using introductory phrases that communicate little more than "I'm getting ready to say something here." You'll notice an abundance of it in law practice. Often throat-clearing phrases begin with "it is" and end with "that." Here are some examples:

It is interesting to note that . . .
It is important to remember that . . .
It seems that . . .
It is clear (or obvious) that . . .
It is widely understood that . . .
As noted above . . .
As to . . .
With respect (or regard) to . . .

Other examples introduce an assertion by unnecessarily assigning responsibility for it, such as "The defendant [your client] submits (or believes, argues, or contends) that . . . ."

---

4. Verbs like "make," "issue," "is," and "had" are much weaker than action verbs like "agree," "announce," "object," "collide," and "revise."

We can guess why these phrases slip into our writing. Maybe they reflect a natural human insecurity about the material that is to follow. Maybe they reflect an inaccurate perception that these phrases elevate the tone or convey an objective perspective. Maybe they are simply habits born of reading the legal writing of others. Whatever the reason, unnecessary throat-clearing impedes good writing. If some of these phrases slip into your writing in the working draft stage, edit them out in revision.

4. Keeping the subject and verb close together.   A reader tackles a sentence by looking for its basic components: the subject, the verb, and the object. First, a reader looks for the subject. Once the subject is found, the reader's urge to find the verb is strong. The primary meaning of a sentence is communicated by the *combination* of the subject and the verb. A reader who can't find and mentally combine them quickly will be frustrated and confused.

A reader has a hard time finding the subject and verb when they are separated by a long modifying phrase or clause. Move long modifying phrases to the beginning or end of the sentence or into a new sentence. Consider this example:

> In the first month of his marriage, the defendant, who was only nineteen at the time and who had not completed high school or developed a trade and who had just lost his part-time job, was charged with robbing a convenience store at the corner of Bayside and Tenth Avenue.

This writer has a lot to say about the defendant — a heavier load than one sentence should carry. The result is the placement of several modifying phrases or clauses between the subject and the verb. The solution is to remove those interrupting phrases and clauses. The sentence really has no other place for them, so use another sentence:

> In the first month of his marriage, the defendant was charged with robbing a convenience store at the corner of Bayside and Tenth Avenue. He was only nineteen at the time. He had not completed high school or developed a trade, and he had just lost his part-time job.

Not only is the second version easier to read, but it helps the reader organize the information.

5. Keep modifiers close to the word(s) they modify.   Separating the modifier and the word it modifies jeopardizes clarity and makes for difficult reading.

6. Break up long sentences.   Remember that the more complex the message, the simpler the medium should be. Break up sentences that are longer than roughly 25 words.

V. AVOIDING WORDINESS

1. Watch for phrases that can be replaced by a single word.   Unnecessary phrases abound in poor legal writing. Phrases beginning with "the fact that" are nearly always culprits, but many other phrases constitute clutter as well. Here are examples of common unnecessary phrases and their single-word synonyms.

Change	*To*
at the time when	when
at the point in time when	when
as a result of	because
by reason of the fact that	because
due to the fact that	because
for a period of one week	for one week
for the purpose of	to
for these reasons	therefore
inasmuch as	since
in many cases	often
in order to	to
it was formerly the case that	formerly
previous to	before
that was a case where	there

Also watch for ideas that take up more than their fair share of space.

Change	the contract between Wigby and Matthews
To	the Wigby-Matthews contract
Change	The buyer discovered six violations of code requirements. The violations dealt with plumbing.
To	The buyer discovered six plumbing code violations.
Change	. . . for the purpose for which it was intended . . .
To	. . . for the intended purpose . . .

2. Avoid matched pairs. Legal language has developed the habit of *matched pairs,* two words commonly used together but having the same meaning. Here are some examples:

adjudged and decreed	full and complete
alter and change	good and sufficient
attorney and counselor	null and void
bind and obligate	stipulate and agree
by and through	true and correct
cease and desist	use and benefit
covenant and agree	will and testament
each and every	

Matched pairs clutter good writing, and they can cloud meaning as well. Avoid them. When the two terms mean the same thing, choose the shorter or more familiar of the two and delete the other.

3. Avoid legalese.   For the same reasons, purge your writing of unnecessary legalese. Here are examples of unnecessary legalese:

assuming *arguendo*
the *instant* case
the *above-captioned* case
the *said* defendant
the *aforementioned* contract
the items *hereinafter* described
to remove *therefrom*
to wit
whereas
the party of the first part
supra (except when properly used in a legal citation)
all Latin words except those few that have become true terms of art (such
    as "pro se," "res ipsa," "pro bono," "prima facie")

4. Avoid redundancies.   Redundancies can slip into language easily. Here are examples to avoid:

advance planning	past experience
final outcome	point in time
first and foremost	reason is because
honest truth	whether or not
old adage	

5. Unnecessary variations.   Use terms consistently. Once you pick a term, use the same term for each reference. Otherwise your reader wonders whether you mean something different from the prior term. Professor Wydick uses this example:

> The first case was settled for $200,000, and the second piece of litigation was disposed of out of court for $300,000, while the price of the amicable accord reached in the third suit was $500,000.[5]

In legal writing, consistency is important. Don't worry about repetition. It's far more important to be understood.

6. Avoid most intensifiers.   Because generations of writers have overused words like "clearly" or "very," these and other common intensifiers have become nearly meaningless. As a matter of fact, for some readers, they've even

---

5. Richard C. Wydick, *Plain English for Lawyers* 70 (5th ed., Carolina Academic Press 2005).

begun to develop a connotation exactly the opposite of their original meaning. Generations of writers have used those labels in place of well-reasoned analysis, so some readers see these intensifiers as signaling a weak analysis. Avoid these words:

clearly	quite
extremely	very
obviously	

VI. MISCELLANEOUS

Tabulate.   When your document deals with several items (elements of a rule, factors, guidelines, categories of facts), tabulating helps a reader navigate the text.

> The plaintiff must prove (1) that the defendant owed a duty to the plaintiff, (2) that the defendant breached that duty, (3) that the plaintiff suffered compensable damages, and (4) that the defendant's breach proximately caused those damages.

Not only will a tabulated list be easier for your reader to understand, but the process of listing and tabulating gives you another chance to double-check your analysis, and demonstrates to the reader that you are controlling the content rather than the other way around.

Names of parties.   You have three basic choices for referring to people:

- use some form of the person's name, such as last name only, first and last name, or last name with a courtesy title;
- use a procedural designation, such as "plaintiff" or "appellee"; or
- use a characterization based on the person's role in the factual story, such as "landlord" or "tenant."

Choose the reference that will be easiest for your reader.[6] You can easily use names or procedural titles if your document refers only to a few people. Consider using a reference based on the person's role ("landlords") if you're referring to more people or to a group or if the litigation has several parties with the same procedural title. For example, you might refer to Fitzpatrick, Cramer, Burns, and Wells (who are joint venturers in a business) as "the joint venturers." Or you might refer to Baldwin and Sammons (the buyer and seller, respectively, of real property) as "the buyer" and "the seller" and to both together as "the contracting parties." Whichever you choose, be consistent.

---

6. When writing a brief, you might have strategic reasons for certain choices. We'll cover that subject in Chapter 22.

Readers are easily confused by encountering several different references for the same person.

Names of things. If the document refers to only one of a certain thing, the generic name will be the best form of reference. For instance, if the document refers to only one contract, "the contract" is the clearest and easiest reference. If the document refers to several contracts, find an easy identifying characteristic and use the same characteristic to distinguish between the contracts. For instance, common distinguishing characteristics for several contracts are the dates or the parties' names: "the September 5 contract" and "the December 23 contract," or "the Owens contract" and "the Guzman contract." Just as with references to people, be consistent.

CHECKLIST FOR LANGUAGE AND USAGE ERRORS

Have you:

1. avoided slang and note-taking abbreviations?
2. avoided unnecessary personal references?
3. avoided contractions?
4. used "found guilty" or "convicted" for a criminal matter and "held liable" for a civil matter?
5. used short-form references to parties with long names, introducing the shortened references in a parenthetical?
6. avoided footnotes?
7. used a past tense verb when referring to something the court did ("the court held")?
8. used "find" for a court's decision about facts and "hold" for a court's decision about law?
9. used a present tense verb for the rule set out in an authority ("the court held that a covenant *is* enforceable")?
10. avoided saying that the court "argued" or "stipulated"?
11. capitalized documents that were filed, but avoided capitalizing generic kinds of documents?
13. capitalized "Court" only when appropriate?
14. capitalized the procedural titles of the parties in your case but not the procedural titles of parties in legal authorities?
15. purged your document of sarcasm, anger, humor, and rhetorical questions?
16. avoided gendered writing?
17. avoided overusing passive verbs?
18. avoided nominalizations?
19. edited out throat-clearing phrases?
20. kept your subjects and verbs close together?
21. broken up long sentences?

22. kept modifiers close to the words they modify?
23. edited wordy phrases, replacing them with shorter synonyms?
24. avoided matched pairs?
25. avoided legalese?
26. checked for redundancies and unnecessary variations?
27. deleted unnecessary intensifiers?
28. tabulated lists?
29. used generic references for people and things?

———————————

At last you are done. You've been through a long and difficult process. The process required you to (1) formulate a rule of law; (2) articulate it in a rule structure; (3) use that structure to create the large-scale organization of your analysis; (4) write out a working draft of the analysis for each subpart of the rule; (5) convert the working draft to the Discussion section of a memo; (6) add the other components of an office memo; (7) edit for proper and effective citation form and quotations; and (8) edit the draft for tone, formality, usage, gender-neutral writing, grammar, punctuation, and style.

Working through this process is among the hardest but most important of all lawyering tasks. Congratulations for making it through each stage. If you continue to use this process consciously and carefully, it will dramatically improve your skills of both analysis and expression for many years to come.

PART II

PROFESSIONAL LETTER WRITING

CHAPTER 16

WRITING PROFESSIONAL LETTERS

Letters and e-mail messages are critical to a lawyer's reputation. Lawyers write far more letters and e-mail messages than office memos or briefs. These less formal communications are seen by many people—people with whom the lawyer must maintain key professional relationships and people the lawyer will never meet. Letters create impressions about the writer's skill, character, and personality. These opinions might not be true, but they become part of the lawyer's reputation anyway.

Of course, letters and e-mail messages are important substantively as well. Key information is conveyed. Clients make decisions based on their lawyers' letters and e-mails, and lawyers are exposed to malpractice liability when a letter or e-mail is inaccurate or misleading.

> **Consider your reader's**
> - Current knowledge and understanding
> - Mental and emotional status
> - Personality

This chapter introduces professional letter writing.[1] The first section discusses the general characteristics of professional letters. Later sections introduce the most common kinds of letters lawyers write. For each, we'll explore the three most important considerations in letter writing: the reader, the purposes, and the content.

I. GENERAL CHARACTERISTICS OF PROFESSIONAL LETTER WRITING

Readers. Because letters are personal, it's especially important to consider the needs and characteristics of the reader. Lawyers write letters to

---

1. For easier reference, we'll include both electronic and paper communications in the term "letters."

diverse people in diverse emotionally charged circumstances. Often the lawyer has delicate purposes for the communication, so it's especially important to sharpen the focus on the reader.

Consider three kinds of facts about your reader. First, what does your reader already know and understand? Your reader might be a lawyer, a judge, or a well-educated and experienced business person who knows nearly as much about the legal environment of her business as you do. Or your reader might be uneducated or developmentally disabled or not fluent in English. You'll communicate the same information to these readers in very different ways.

Second, what is your reader's current mental and emotional status? All emotions, especially anxiety, fear, grief, and anger, affect the way people receive and process information. You'll need to be sensitive not only to which emotions your reader might be feeling but also to their causes. The letter's content might touch on some of those causes, and you'll need to decide how to handle those subjects appropriately.

Third, if you're writing to your client, what do you know about her personality? Does she prefer to be treated formally or informally? Does she want a calm, wise counselor or an impassioned advocate? Does she want an empathetic lawyer or one who is businesslike and efficient? You might not always choose the persona your client seems to want.[2] You'll choose the persona that will serve your client best in the present situation. But knowing the client is the first step toward making that decision.

Substantive purposes.   Every letter has at least one substantive purpose. You'll use letters (1) to convey information or advice, (2) to document information for the protection of your client and yourself, and (3) to persuade someone to do something. For these purposes, you'll need the same analytical skills you have already been learning: accurate content, good organization, and clarity of expression.

Relational purposes.   Every letter also has at least one relational purpose. Relationally, letters are used primarily

- to establish and maintain a good relationship
- to communicate the writer's competence
- to establish professional boundaries.

For these relational purposes, you'll need one more important writing skill—the careful use of tone.

Tone.   Tone establishes relationship. It communicates two important kinds of information: (1) your personality and character, and (2) your opinion

---

2. The answers won't prompt you to become someone you're not. Every good lawyer possesses all these traits and more.

of your reader. Tone implies personality and character traits. Some traits are appropriate in nearly all situations: trustworthiness, knowledge, skill, experience, reliability, and diligence. Other traits are appropriate in some but not all situations: warmth, empathy, passionate advocacy, detachment, coolness, efficiency, and measured rationality. Some traits are inappropriate: sarcasm, contempt, and anger.

Tone is created primarily by:

- content choices
- attention to detail
- word choices
- placement choices
- sentence formats.

Content choices and attention to detail help establish many of the most important traits of the lawyer: trustworthiness, knowledge, experience, skill, reliability, and diligence. Traits relating to more personal aspects of the relationship are more subtle. Here are some examples of methods for creating a warm tone (friendly, kind, empathetic, encouraging) or a cool tone (detached, efficient, rational, stern).

Warmer Tone	*Cooler Tone*
Beginning and ending the letter with content establishing a personal connection	No content establishing a personal connection
Word choices without connotations of blame, fault, criticism	Word choices that are sharp, blunt, or biting
Words with more syllables and soft initial sounds; sentences with longer phrases	Shorter words with hard consonant sounds; shorter sentences with powerful verbs and vivid nouns but fewer adjectives and adverbs
Contractions (only when informality is appropriate)	No contractions
Mutual references using the pronoun "we" to underline the relationship	Liberal use of the pronoun "you" to separate the writer and the reader
Tempering any uncomfortable subjects with offsetting indirect assurances that the writer likes and respects the reader	Discussing uncomfortable subjects without reassurances
Using the passive voice for uncomfortable subjects	Using the active voice for uncomfortable subjects
Placing uncomfortable subjects in the middle of the letter or in the middle of a paragraph	Placing uncomfortable subjects early in the letter or at the beginning of a paragraph

Letters as public documents.   One word of caution: Because letters are addressed to identified readers and aren't usually filed in court, it's easy to think of them as private documents. But any document that goes outside your office is, or could one day become, a public document. You might find your letter appended as "Exhibit A" to a motion or presented against you or your client in a future dispute or settlement negotiation. Never write a letter that you would cringe to see again in another context. If you're angry, don't mail a letter until you either have calmed down or asked another lawyer to review what you've written. Don't click the "send" icon in the heat of the moment.

II. LETTERS TO CLIENTS

A. General Considerations

Purposes.   Letters to clients are used for all three substantive purposes. Lawyers write client letters to communicate information and advice. For example, they update clients on their cases. They write opinion letters to explain the results of research the firm has conducted. They convey the lawyer's professional judgment and advise clients about pending decisions.

Lawyers also write to clients to document information in case an issue arises in the future. For example, a lawyer should write a letter confirming the oral transmission to a client of any important information, such as a settlement offer, a deposition date, a trial date, or the fee agreement. The letter will help the client remember the information and help the lawyer demonstrate that she met her professional duty to inform her client of that information.

Finally, lawyers write to persuade their clients to do (or not to do) something. For example, lawyers persuade their clients of the wisdom of certain legal and extralegal decisions. Sometimes lawyers must try to persuade their clients to act within the law or within moral boundaries.

Client letters are also used for all three relational purposes. The lawyer surely intends that a client letter will help establish and maintain a good relationship. Letters can be effective for this purpose because they carry relationship messages and because clients typically reread their lawyers' letters many times. Carefully written letters also effectively communicate the writer's competence. Nearly all clients can distinguish sloppy letters from careful letters. The letter itself is powerful proof of the lawyer's ability and diligence.

Finally, lawyers sometimes must write to establish professional boundaries with clients. A client might disregard a fee agreement or other policies of the firm; might be overdependent on the lawyer in inappropriate ways; or might desire an unprofessional relationship. In any of these situations, the lawyer's letters would include a boundary-setting purpose.

B. Retainer Letters

Retainer letters, sometimes called "engagement letters," are written to document the beginning of a representation. A good retainer letter achieves a delicate balance between establishing a positive relationship and setting boundaries. On the one hand, the lawyer hopes the letter will leave the client glad to have selected the lawyer. The client should feel confident that the lawyer's loyalties are grounded in the client's needs, not the lawyer's profit-making purposes. The client should sense that she and her lawyer will function well, as a team working toward the same goal.

On the other hand, the letter informs the client about uncomfortable but necessary subjects such as fees, costs, allocation of decision-making authority, and conditions under which the firm can withdraw. Achieving this balance can be a daunting task requiring wise selection of coverage and careful attention to tone. You can find a sample retainer letter in Appendix C.

C. Advice Letters

Lawyers write two kinds of advice letters: formal advice letters (usually called "opinion letters") and informal advice letters. Opinion letters are formal documents communicating a lawyer's legal opinion. They are commonly required for certain kinds of transactions, providing assurance to the parties about their legal situation. Formal opinion letters are less common, and their requirements can be highly specialized. Informal advice letters, however, are common, important, and well within your present ability. Here is a summary of the content and organization of an informal advice letter. Use your understanding of your reader to help you choose an appropriate level of formality. Refer to the advice letter in Appendix C for an example of each of the following components:

Opening paragraphs. Begin with any personal material that is appropriate for your relationship with this client. For example, imagine that you are probating the estate of your client's deceased wife and that during your last conversation with your client, he told you that his children were having difficulty adjusting to their mother's death. You might begin with an expression of hope that the children are doing better. Don't manufacture a stilted opener. Just respond genuinely to your client, as one human being to another.

Then set out a summary of the question you've analyzed. Usually you can summarize the question in one paragraph or less. If you think your reader is ready, provide a summary of your conclusion here as well. If you think your reader will be more receptive to your conclusion after reading your reasoning, postpone the conclusion.

Fact summary. Usually you should include a fact summary to be sure that your client understands the facts on which you're basing your conclusion.

If your understanding is incorrect or incomplete, the client can let you know. Your responsibility for your conclusion is limited to the facts you know. If different circumstances develop in the future, you won't be held accountable for a conclusion not meant to apply to those other circumstances.

Legal analysis.   Explain the results of your research and the legal conclusions you've reached. Use your understanding of your reader to help you decide the appropriate level of detail for this explanation and the degree to which you can use legal terms. Follow roughly the paradigm for legal analysis; that is, explain the governing law and then apply it to your client's situation. If the analysis must cover several separate topics, use headings to help you mark the transition from one topic to the next. Clear organizational markers help readers manage new, frightening, or complex material.

Advice.   You might have been asked simply to provide a legal conclusion, such as whether certain conduct would be legal. If so, your analysis in the prior section will have answered that question. But you might have been asked a broader question, such as, "Should I sue my employer for salary discrimination?" The answer to that question includes legal questions aimed at learning whether your client has a legally viable claim. But the question also asks you to help the client think about the personal and professional consequences of bringing a claim against a current employer—an extraordinarily difficult decision. If the answer to the broader question is complex or sensitive, you might prefer to discuss it in a personal meeting with your client, summarizing your advice in writing after the meeting. If the answer to the broader question is more straightforward, you can communicate it here, at the end of your legal analysis. Feel free to organize the components of your advice according to topics, such as advantages, disadvantages, likelihood of success, and time frame.

D. Status Letters

Not only do ethical rules require lawyers to keep clients informed, but good relations with clients demand frequent communication. This need is even greater if the fee arrangement requires monthly billing. Clients hate to receive nothing but bills from their lawyers. If you are billing your client monthly, include with the bill a status letter explaining what has happened on the case that month. Knowing that you'll have to report to your client also prompts you to attend to the case.

If you aren't billing monthly, report to your client at the intervals your client prefers, within reason. If the case is in litigation, monthly reports are appropriate. Your goal is to keep the client informed and reassured of your attention to the matter, but not to cause the client to think that you are billing him for too many unnecessary letters.

Report the developments in the case at a level of detail appropriate for your client. You don't need to explain the intricacies of a discovery dispute unless the client will need to know the precise legal grounds for the dispute. To the extent that you explain procedural developments to lay clients, try to use clear, simple language. See the sample status letter in Appendix C.

One final word about status letters: Don't avoid telling your client bad news. Many a lawyer has gotten into disciplinary trouble for pretending that a case was proceeding well instead of disclosing unfavorable results. Ultimately, your client will learn the truth, and the consequences will be worse if you have tried to hide the situation.

III. LETTERS TO OTHER LAWYERS

A. General Considerations

Lawyers write many letters to other lawyers. These letters might convey straightforward procedural information, like the time and place of a deposition, or substantive material, like a demand letter or a settlement offer. Two important considerations apply to all these letters: the importance of careful writing and the importance of tone.

Careful writing (including careful legal analysis) is important for obvious reasons: Lawyers have a professional obligation to do good work on behalf of a client. Also, a lawyer's reputation among other lawyers and judges is critical to a successful career. A reputation is formed largely by the quality of the work other lawyers observe. Among the most visible work products are the letters lawyers write to each other. So, take care with your letters to other lawyers. Be sure your analysis is complete and your writing is free of errors.

Tone is important because representing your client well while simultaneously enjoying your job depends on establishing good relationships with other lawyers. If your working relationships are good, you'll offer professional courtesies to other lawyers and receive them in return. These courtesies will benefit you and your clients alike. Other lawyers with whom you are on good terms will be willing to accommodate your scheduling conflicts and will hesitate to treat you as they do not wish to be treated in return. The tone of your letters will help establish and maintain these positive relationships.

Always maintain a professional tone, even if you are frustrated with the recipient of your letter. Don't descend into sarcasm or angry rhetoric. It won't advance your client's cause, and it doesn't wear well in the long term. Generally, acting out of anger is a sign of weakness rather than strength. Before you write, wait until you regain your emotional equilibrium.

Formalities. Use a customary business letter format. One added suggestion is helpful for letters to other lawyers. Often, it's appropriate to provide other people with copies of your letters to counsel. Copying your client is a good way to keep your client informed. When you send copies to other people, note the fact in one of two ways: If you want your primary recipient to know that you sent the copies and to whom, use the standard "cc" notation ("courtesy copy") along the lower left margin and include the names of your secondary recipients. If you don't want your primary recipient to know of the copies, use "bcc" ("blind courtesy copy") *on the copies themselves and on your file copy, but not on the original.* This way your file will reflect the fact that you sent the copies. Here is an example of a letter with each kind of copying choice:

[date, recipient's name and address, and "re" line]

Dear Mr. James:

. . . . [the body of the letter] . . . .

Very truly yours,

Karen Kelly
Attorney at Law

cc: Benjamin Ahmad Home Care, Inc.
bcc: Sarah Lancaster

B. Demand Letters and Responses

Before proceeding to litigation or other enforcement mechanisms on behalf of a client, a lawyer usually sends a demand letter setting out the claims and the damages the client incurred. A demand letter can have three purposes;

- It invites an early, inexpensive resolution.
- It sets up a claim for attorney's fees if you prevail.
- In some kinds of cases, a demand letter is a legal prerequisite for filing suit.

If the opposing party is represented, the demand letter goes to the lawyer, not the party. It can be as short as a one- to two-paragraph statement of the client's claim, the damages she has sustained, and the recovery she seeks. If you think that early settlement is unlikely, you might send such a conclusory demand letter. But if you think that settlement is possible, you might send a more thorough demand letter—one that presents the claim as thoroughly and persuasively as possible. Even if you doubt the chances of early settlement, you might want to send a message to the opposing lawyer—the message that you are a diligent and skilled lawyer who intends to take this case seriously. A more thorough demand letter might set out the results of your legal and factual research and might include exhibits like photographs or key documents. Demand letters of this second kind can be long and can even accompany a specifically prepared settlement brochure.

For a more detailed demand letter, begin by identifying your client and summarizing the claim. Then set out the facts of the case, truthfully but phrased favorably for your client. Emphasize the culpable conduct of the other party and minimize any culpable conduct of your client. Include a description of your client's damages in sufficient detail to justify the claim. Next, explain the results of your legal research, again framing it in the light most favorable for your client's claim.

Finally, make a demand for a certain sum and any nonmonetary relief your client seeks. Express your hope that the matter can be settled short of litigation. Invite a response from the lawyer to whom you are writing, set a deadline, and indicate what action you will take if the deadline isn't met.

An example of a relatively simple demand letter is found in Appendix C.

C. Confirming Letters

In practice, lawyers often reach agreements orally. In litigation, these agreements can range from relatively unimportant procedural matters to settlement of the case. In transactional matters, oral agreements can range from setting meeting times to major terms of a transaction. All these agreements should be promptly confirmed in writing. Confirming the agreement will help you clarify your understanding of its terms, and your recipient will go through a similar process when reading the letter. Then, any misunderstandings can be resolved before the parties rely on the agreement. Also, if memories fade, the confirming letter will be there in both files to clear up the confusion.

In a confirming letter, recite the terms of the agreement. Take care to get the details right. If the other lawyer has extended you a courtesy, do not forget to thank her. Here is an example of a simple confirming letter:

[date, recipient's name and address, and "re" line]

Dear Ms. Keller:

This letter confirms the rescheduling of Mr. Burston's deposition until 10:00 on April 12, 2018. I understand that the location has been moved to your office. Mr. Burston will make every effort to bring with him the documents you requested. Thank you for agreeing to the later date.

Very truly yours,

Keith Salter
Attorney at Law

cc: David Burston

IV. TRANSMITTAL LETTERS

Transmittal letters ("cover letters") accompany documents or other enclosures provided to clients, other lawyers, or the court. Sometimes the letters include an explanation of the enclosures or instructions about what to do with them.

The letters provide a record of the transmission for your file, and they allow you to provide explanation or instruction in a form the recipient can keep and review as necessary.

Transmittal documents are notorious for stilted, obtuse language. Some lawyers still write "Enclosed please find . . . " followed by a parade of "herewiths" and "saids," strung together in long, nearly indecipherable sentences. Instead, use normal twenty-first-century English words and syntax, for example:

[date, recipient's name and address, and "re" line]

Dear Ms. Cantrell,

I have enclosed drafts of your will and the trust agreement for your son. Please read these drafts, and let me know if you have any questions or concerns. You can sign the final versions of both documents in my office when we meet on Monday. By law, you will need two witnesses not related to you. Members of our staff can serve as your witnesses, or you can bring witnesses of your own choosing as long as they are not beneficiaries under the documents. I look forward to seeing you next week.

Very truly yours,

Keith Salter
Attorney at Law

Clearly set out any explanations or instructions your reader will need. If there are more than two enclosures, tabulate or format the list in a way that will help your reader tell at a glance what is enclosed. Here is a sample letter to a lay person familiar with the litigation process:

[date, recipient's name and address, and "re" line]

Dear Mr. Gomez,

I am enclosing for your review the following discovery documents received today from Air Mart, Inc.:

First Set of Interrogatories
Requests for Production of Documents
Requests for Admission
Notice of Deposition (Francis Hawley)
Notice of Deposition (James Bainbridge)

Please calendar the dates of the depositions and let me know if any schedule conflicts arise. Our response to the written discovery is due on May 5. We can discuss those responses when we meet next week.

Very truly yours,

Keith Salter
Attorney at Law

If the transmittal letter accompanies documents mailed to the court, don't forget to send a copy to all other parties (through their lawyers). Indicate that you have done so by using a "cc" as explained above. Ethical rules prohibit any ex parte (private) communication with a judge about a pending matter,[3] so you'll need to demonstrate to the judge that you've included all parties in this communication. The "cc" format shows the judge that you've complied with your ethical duty.

---

3. ABA Model R. Prof. Conduct 3.5.

PART III

THE PROCESS OF WRITING PERSUASIVELY: THE BRIEF

STRUCTURING FOR PERSUASION: OUTLINING THE WORKING DRAFT

CHAPTER 17

ETHICS, JUDGES,
AND BRIEFS

In Part I, we saw that the process of writing an office memo divides into four stages. Brief writing does, too, but with the added goal of persuasion. In the two working draft stages (Chapters 17 through 22), you'll do more than structure a rule from the authorities. You'll structure the most favorable rule you reasonably can. In the third stage, converting your working draft into a brief, you'll do more than organize logically. You'll organize to persuade. Finally, in the fourth stage, editing the brief (Chapter 24), you'll edit not only for style and compliance with technical rules, but also for persuasion.

> **Three Cardinal Rules:**
> - Be honest
> - Be accurate
> - Be clear

The briefs you write will be vital to your clients. The outcome of most cases depends on the court's rulings on many legal questions arising during the litigation. Most of these issues are decided primarily by briefing. Judges are usually more influenced by briefs than by any other form of argument, so your clients will need your brief to be thorough, well written, accurate, honest, free of technical errors, and in compliance with court rules.

Your brief writing will be important to you as well. Your reputation will be built, in significant part, by the care you take in brief writing. And reputation is more than just a personal matter. It's an integral part of your professional effectiveness. Over the course of her career, a lawyer with a reputation for honest, careful work will be able to accomplish much more for her clients than a lawyer with a reputation for dishonesty or slipshod work. Thus, every brief you write is a document with persuasive impact, for good or for ill, not only on the pending case, but on all future cases you'll handle.

Your firm's reputation hangs in the balance, too. A firm's reputation is built by the quality of the work its lawyers produce, and especially by the quality of the writing the firm allows to pass through its doors. Your firm's reputation will affect its ability to attract clients and its ability to represent them effectively. So, write as if your practice depends on it, because it does.

We begin our study of brief writing with these three cardinal rules: Be honest. Be accurate. Be clear. The honesty, accuracy, and clarity of your arguments will affect a judge's decision far more than any strategy or rhetoric you could employ. The starting points for thinking about these cardinal rules are the ethical duties that govern lawyers as advocates, the characteristics of judges as readers, and an overview of the document that must comply with these rules—the brief.

I. THE ETHICS OF BRIEF WRITING

Language and its relationship to justice are distinctive attributes of humanity. Human beings don't growl and gesticulate naked aggression or craving. We use language to reason toward resolutions that are just, compassionate, and practical. This connection between language and justice made rhetoric an honored study and practice in antiquity. In writing a brief, today's lawyer takes her place within the tradition of ancients such as Socrates, Aristotle, and Cicero. Reasoned argument in the quest for justice is not a mere trade performed for pay, but a craft in the full Aristotelian sense, and its right practice helps sustain and advance our common humanity. This is no small thing.
The starting point of this "right practice" is ethical compliance, governed primarily by the rules of professional responsibility. In addition to the ethical duties set out in the Introduction (competence, diligence, loyalty, promptness, confidentiality), persuasion brings with it other professional duties:

1. Don't knowingly make a false statement of law.[1]   This means, for example, not saying that a case stands for a proposition when it clearly doesn't and not "forgetting" to mention that a case has been reversed or overruled. Also, many lawyers and judges believe that citing an authority implicitly represents that you've read it. Whether it does or not, citing an authority you haven't read and updated is unprofessional and extraordinarily risky. Never do it.

2. Don't knowingly fail to disclose directly adverse legal authority in the controlling jurisdiction.[2]   Disclosure is not only ethically required, but it's strategically wise as well. If you wait for the opposing lawyer to raise the adverse authority, you'll miss the chance to be the first to interpret it and explain its impact. You'll start out behind, running to make up lost analytical ground.

What kind of adverse authority must be disclosed? In a pre-Model Rules Formal Opinion, the ABA Ethics Committee described this test:

---

1. ABA Model R. Prof. Conduct 3.3(a)(1).
2. ABA Model R. Prof. Conduct 3.3(a)(3).

The test in every case should be: Is the decision which opposing counsel has overlooked one which the court should clearly consider in deciding the case? Would a reasonable judge properly feel that a lawyer who advanced, as the law, a proposition adverse to the undisclosed decision, was lacking in candor and fairness to him? Might the judge consider himself misled by an implied representation that the lawyer knew of no adverse authority?[3]

The ABA Model Rule requires disclosure only if the authority is in the controlling jurisdiction, but some jurisdictions require more. For example, the New Jersey Supreme Court has required, on federal questions, disclosure of adverse decisions of any federal court.[4]

    3. Don't knowingly make a false statement of fact or fail to disclose a material fact if nondisclosure would assist a client with a criminal or fraudulent act.[5]   Not only must you avoid *knowingly* making such a statement, but if you've *unknowingly* done so, you must correct the statement promptly when you learn that it was false.[6]

    4. Don't assert a frivolous legal argument.[7]   What's frivolous? We'll start with what's not frivolous. A position that argues for an extension, modification, or reversal of existing law isn't frivolous. In criminal defense, it's not frivolous to test the government's argument on each element of the case.

A claim isn't frivolous merely because you believe it will ultimately fail.[8] But if you can't "make a good faith argument on the merits of the action," the claim is frivolous.[9] Your subjective belief isn't enough. The test is whether a reasonable, competent attorney would believe that the argument could have merit.[10]

The meaning of "frivolous" is subject to debate, even among experienced lawyers. While you're still learning which kinds of arguments might have merit, you might feel at sea with this standard. When in doubt, consult a more experienced lawyer.[11] Also, ask yourself (and the more experienced lawyer) whether making such a marginal argument is good strategy, even if the argument is permissible. If you're wondering whether the argument is so weak that it might be considered frivolous, your position might be stronger without it.[12]

---

3. ABA Committee on Ethics & Prof. Resp., Formal Op. 280 (1949).
4. *In re Greenberg,* 104 A.2d 46 (N.J. 1954).
5. ABA Model R. Prof. Conduct 3.3(a)(1) and (2).
6. ABA Model R. Prof. Conduct 3.3.
7. ABA Model R. Prof. Conduct 3.1; Fed. R. Civ. P. 11 (establishing an affirmative duty to investigate the law and the facts).
8. ABA Model R. Prof. Conduct 3.1 cmt. 2.
9. *Id.*
10. *See, e.g., Beeman v. Fiester,* 852 F.2d 206, 211 (7th Cir. 1988).
11. Take care not to violate any honor code regulations pertaining to your law school assignment or your duty of confidentiality to a client.
12. See Chapter 18.

5. Don't communicate ex parte[13] with a judge about the merits of a pending case.[14]   In the context of brief writing, this means that you must provide each party (through counsel, if any) with a copy of your brief. Court rules require certification that you've done so.[15]

6. Don't intentionally disregard filing requirements or court rules.[16]   Most courts operate under rules of procedure that set out time deadlines and format requirements for your brief. Courts impose page limits, and some prescribe the margins and number of permissible characters per inch. You can guess the purpose behind these rules. It might be tempting to change the font or ignore the margin requirements, but it's neither ethical nor wise. Resist the temptation, both in practice *and* in your legal writing course.

II. JUDGES AS READERS

Judges are much like other law-trained readers.[17] Their attention is finite. They are busy and impatient to get to the bottom line. They generally focus more attention on the beginning and end of a document or a section than on the middle. They find facts interesting. They want a road map. They value clear organization structured by the rule. But judges tend to have some additional characteristics too. Here are some of them:

1. *Testing ideas.* Any law-trained reader is a skeptical reader, testing the analysis at each step, but a judge is particularly so. This skepticism and testing is the heart of a judge's job. Girvan Peck described judges as "professional buyers of ideas."[18] Imagine them kicking the tires and looking carefully under the hood.
2. *Reputation.* Even skeptical judges will be less skeptical of a brief by a lawyer known for careful and honest work than by a lawyer with a poor reputation for either competency or candor.
3. *Equities.* Because judges are human, a judge who is already convinced of the equities will be more receptive to your legal arguments. The judge will *want* you to be right on the law. This human desire can help to overcome a little of the judge's natural skepticism.
4. *Relationship.* Most of us are more willing to accept the analysis of someone who has been respectful and considerate of our needs. So, too, for

---

13. *"Ex parte,"* in this context, means without notice to other parties in the litigation.
14. An exception is created for those unusual situations in which governing law allows ex parte communications. ABA Model R. Prof. Conduct 3.5(b).
15. See p. 203.
16. ABA Model R. Prof. Conduct 3.4(c) and 3.2.
17. See Section I of Chapter 11.
18. Girvan Peck, *Writing Persuasive Briefs* 77 (Little, Brown & Co., 1984).

judges. A lawyer who treats the judge professionally, with respect and consideration, is a more effective advocate than the lawyer who doesn't.

5. *Policy.* As public servants, judges care about the social policy implications of their decisions. This is especially true for a jurisdiction's highest appellate court, so policy arguments are more persuasive there. Trial and intermediate appellate court judges view their role primarily as applying the law the way the jurisdiction's highest court would, but on the margins, even those judges can be persuaded by policy rationales.

6. *In it for the long haul.* Most judges plan to spend many years on the bench, so they take a long-term view of each legal issue. They are concerned about how an individual ruling could constrain or empower them in future cases.

7. *Whose idea?* All of us are attached to our own conclusions, and judges are no different. Effective legal arguments don't push a judge down a path. They place the judge at a vantage point that allows the *judge* to see and choose the best path.

8. *Behaving like grown-ups.* Judges often relate to the lawyers who practice in their courts much like parents relate to children. All parents know that there is nothing quite as tiresome and irritating as constant fighting and bickering among children. Most judges have little tolerance for bickering and blustering lawyers. Judges much prefer to focus on legal issues, not the personalities of the lawyers in the case.

III. OVERVIEW OF A BRIEF

No standardized format applies to all briefs, but the following sections describe the components you might be asked to include. Include those required by the applicable court rule,[19] local or firm custom, your professor's instructions, or the circumstances and legal issues of the case. The trial- and appellate-level briefs in Appendices D, E, and F can serve as examples.

Component	*Trial-Level Brief*	*Appellate Brief*
Caption	Yes	Yes
Table of Contents	Only if the brief is long and complex	Yes
Table of Authorities	Only if the brief cites many sources	Yes

---

19. *See, e.g.,* Fed. R. App. P. 28 (2009).

Component	Trial-Level Brief	Appellate Brief
Statutes Involved	Usually not. Instead, quote the statute early in the argument section.	Yes, or you might provide the statute in an appendix
Opinion Below	No	Optional
Jurisdiction	No	Optional unless court rules require it
Standard of Review	Only if the trial court is reviewing a matter decided in another forum	Yes[20]
Preliminary Statement (Introduction)	Optional	Optional
Questions Presented (Statement of Issues)	Only if the brief covers several issues	Yes
Statement of Facts (Statement of the Case)	Yes	Yes
Summary of Argument	Only if the brief is long and complex	Yes
Argument	Yes	Yes
Conclusion	Yes	Yes
Certificate of Service	Yes	Yes

We'll say more about drafting the major components in later chapters, but here is an overview:

1. Caption. The caption identifies the case and the document. See Appendices D, E, and F for examples of customary formatting. In cases with multiple parties, the caption need only list the first plaintiff and the first defendant followed by "et al."[21] The Caption includes the title of the document and the case number assigned by the court. Court rules might require additional information such as the name and address of the attorney or the name of the assigned judge.

2. Table of Contents. A Table of Contents includes each section and designates the page number on which that section begins. For the Argument

---

20. Some court rules require the standard of review to constitute its own section. If the court rules are silent, you can cover the standard of review early in the Argument section instead of in its own separate section.

21. "*Et al.*" is an abbreviation for "*et alii*", meaning literally "and others." *See* Fed. R. Civ. P. 10(a).

section, include each point heading and subheading, using the same font/print style as is used for that heading in the body of the argument.

3. Table of Authorities. This table lists the authorities cited in the brief and the page(s) on which each is cited. If the authority is cited so frequently that listing individual page numbers would be unwieldy, use the term *"passim"* (meaning "throughout") instead. List the authorities in separate categories, such as cases, statutes, treatises, articles, and miscellaneous. If the brief cites many cases, consider organizing the cases by issuing court, starting with the highest level and going to the lowest level. Within each list of cases, order the entries alphabetically.

4. Statutes Involved. This section sets out the text of the relevant part(s) of applicable statutes.

5. Opinion Below. This section of an appellate brief tells the reader where to find the opinion from the court below. Provide the page numbers within the court record and, for a reported opinion, the citation.

6. Jurisdiction. This section provides the citation to the statute conferring on the court the jurisdiction to hear this type of case.

7. Standard of Review. This section sets out the appropriate standard for the court's review of the legal issue(s) raised by the brief. Include citations to relevant authority establishing the standard.[22] If the brief addresses more than one issue, remember that the standard of review might be different for each.

8. Preliminary Statement (or Introduction). The Preliminary Statement summarizes the procedural history leading up to this issue.

9. Question(s) Presented (or Statement of Issues). The Question(s) Presented section identifies the legal issues and their factual context.

10. Statement of Facts (or Statement of the Case). This section sets out the relevant facts and the factual context.

11. Summary of Argument. The Summary of the Argument is exactly that—a concise statement of the nub of your argument on each issue. It's often the first place a reader looks to answer the question, "OK, so what is this case about?"

12. Argument. The Argument contains the fully articulated argument on the legal issues. Just as your working draft became the Discussion section of the office memo, your working draft will become the Argument section of the brief.

---

22. See Chapter 19 for a discussion of standards of review.

13. Conclusion.   Two schools of thought exist on Conclusions. The more traditional approach limits the Conclusion to a *pro forma* statement of the precise relief sought.

> For the foregoing reasons, the Court should reverse the trial court's opinion and remand this case for trial.

But if court rules and local customs permit, consider a Conclusion that gives you one last opportunity for advocacy. This sort of Conclusion should still be short—no more than half a double-spaced page—but it could gather together the most compelling arguments on each issue. Here's an example:

> Therefore, as this brief has demonstrated, the circumstances of this case render the covenant's terms unreasonable. The covenant would protect Carrolton to a degree far greater than necessary, while devastating both Ms. Watson's fledgling business and her personal finances. Further, it would significantly infringe upon the public's interest in reasonably priced health care equipment, merchandise vital to the community's well-being. For these reasons, Carrolton's Motion for Summary Judgment should be denied.

14. Certificate of Service.   Court rules require copies of all filings to be served upon all parties, via their attorneys.[23] Also, ethical rules prohibit direct contact with a party represented by an attorney,[24] so a copy of the brief must be served on the party's attorney rather than directly on the party. The Certificate of Service demonstrates compliance with these rules.

Now that you know your ethical responsibilities, the general characteristics of judges as readers, and the components of a brief, you're ready to begin work on the brief you've been assigned.

---

23. *See, e.g.,* Fed. R. Civ. P. 5(a) (2010).
24. ABA Model R. Prof. Conduct 4.2.

CHAPTER 18

STRUCTURING THE ARGUMENT: FIRST STEPS

Creating the working draft of a brief is much like creating the working draft of an office memo, but a brief must also persuade. Ideally, it meets its reader—the judge—wherever she is and moves her to the spot where the client needs her to be. In addition to presenting an honest, accurate, and clear legal discussion, you'll also need to

- formulate the most favorable rule you can;
- choose an organization that maximizes persuasion;
- write out compelling arguments under each section; and
- use the facts to tell a compelling story.

These tasks are among the most interesting parts of a lawyer's job. In some ways, they complicate the writing process, since they add the goal of persuasion. But in some ways, they simplify the process. For an office memo, you had to figure out your answer, but for a brief, you already know what position to take. Your job is to make the best argument you can for that position.

Fortunately, the first few steps are much like those you already learned as you wrote your office memo. This chapter explains how to begin to organize what will become the argument. Remember that the function of the working draft is to help you work out those arguments. That's an important function, but it doesn't require a strict format. Don't worry about complying with hard and fast formatting rules in this stage. Later, when you convert this working draft to the brief's Argument section, you'll edit your working headings into headings designed for your reader.

I. FORMULATING AND STRUCTURING A RULE: REVIEW

Just as we saw in Chapters 2 through 6, the first step in brief writing is to formulate a rule from the authorities and write it out using one of the basic rule structures. Then you'll use that structure to identify the issues you'll argue and to organize those arguments. Recall the basic rules structures from Chapter 2[1]:

1. Mandatory-elements structure (a conjunctive test).   This kind of rule lists a set of elements, all required. The burglary rule was our example:

> To establish a burglary, the state must prove *all* the following elements:
>
> - breaking
> - entering
> - dwelling
> - of another
> - in the nighttime
> - with the intent to commit a felony therein

2. Either/or structure (a disjunctive test).   This kind of rule sets out two or more subparts, either of which is enough to answer the question. We used an easement example:

> An easement can be created in any of the following ways:
>
> 1. by deed;
> 2. by an exception to the statute of frauds;
> 3. by implication; or
> 4. by prescription.

3. Factors (aggregative) test.   This kind of rule gives us a flexible standard guided by a list of criteria. Factors tests give discretion to the judge but provide a set of suggested criteria for exercising that discretion wisely. We used a child custody rule as our example:

---

1. It's possible that the rule you're working with might be a simple declarative statement with no subparts (e.g., to be valid, a will must be signed). If so, the working draft's organization is as simple as that rule. You'd have only one issue (the signature), and your brief would analyze what the requirement of a signature means. For instance, what about initials? A nickname? The mark of an "X"? A first name only? A signature begun but interrupted before completion?

Child custody shall be decided in accordance with the best interests of the child. Factors to consider are:

1. the fitness of each possible custodian;
2. the appropriateness for parenting of the lifestyle of each possible custodian;
3. the relationship between the child and each possible custodian;
4. the placement of the child's siblings, if any;
5. living accommodations;
6. the district lines of the child's school;
7. the proximity of extended family and friends;
8. religious issues; and
9. any other factors relevant to the child's best interests.

Remember the difference between factors and mandatory elements. Mandatory elements are just that—they all must be met. But factors are a set of criteria to be considered together, all as part of the same mix. One or more can be absent entirely. The judge gauges the importance of each and decides the issue by considering them all together.

4. Balancing test. This kind of rule balances opposing considerations against each other. Because a balancing test is also inherently flexible, it often includes factors or guidelines to help the judge weigh each side of the balance. Here's an example:

A party must respond to interrogatories unless the burden of responding substantially outweighs the questioning party's legitimate need for the information.

A. The burden of answering:
   1. the time and effort necessary to answer
   2. the cost of compiling the information
   3. any privacy concerns of the objecting party
   4. any other circumstances raised by that party's situation
B. The questioning party's need for the information:
   1. how important the information would be to the issues of the trial
   2. whether it would be available from another source or in another form
   3. any other circumstances relating to the party's need for the information

5. Rule with exception(s) (a defeasible rule). Any of these rule structures also might include exceptions. Here is an example of a rule with two exceptions:

> A lawyer shall not prepare any document giving the lawyer a gift from a client except:
>
> A. where the gift is insubstantial, or
> B. where the client is related to the lawyer.

Again, notice the difference between this structure and the others. The introductory language defines the subparts as exceptions to a general principle.

6. Rules combining several structures. A rule might combine more than one rule structure. The larger structure will fit one of our examples, but within a subpart, the rule might use a different structure. For example, notice that in our balancing test example, the larger structure balanced burden with need. But we evaluated both burden and need by using a factors test.

Remember, too, these hints about rule outlining: Follow traditional outlining principles, noticing the relationships among the subparts. Notice whether all listed factors are meant to be exclusive or whether they are just examples of criteria to consider. If you're struggling, ask yourself what someone would have to prove to show that the rule is met.

At the working draft stage, don't forget to separate each point that must be decided. Consider again our example: If a valid offer requires that the recipient had a reasonable belief that an offer was intended, the words "reasonable belief" require proving two distinct things—(1) that the listener believed that the speaker intended to make an offer, and (2) that this belief was reasonable. Finally, remember that you can change the tabulation (the numbering and lettering scheme used by the statute or case) if it helps you express the rule more simply and clearly.

Stop now and take your first run at formulating and structuring the rule for your assignment.

II. USING THE RULE TO BEGIN TO ORGANIZE THE DRAFT

As you can already guess, the rule will create the argument's working draft organization. We'll use the burglary rule as an example, this time from the perspective of the prosecutor. We'll reserve the Roman numeral for the overall conclusion. Then, because a prosecutor must prove all the elements,[2] we'll include sections for each.

---

2. For the purposes of this example, we'll assume that the prosecutor is responding to a post-trial motion challenging the sufficiency of the evidence on each element.

For the office memo, you used the early writing stages to figure out your answer, so initially you put that question in the place of the Roman numeral. Then, later in the writing process, you changed the headings to statements of the conclusion. For a brief, though, you already know which side you're taking, so you can personalize all the headings now and express them as a conclusion—the answer you hope the judge will reach.

If it's helpful at this stage, you can add the overall rule statement between the Roman numeral and the subheadings. If you're ready, you can also add the rule that applies to each subheading. Here's how the outline looks now:

I. Mr. Shaffer's acts constituted burglary.

To prove burglary, the state must prove that the defendant broke and entered the dwelling of another in the nighttime with the intent to commit a felony therein.

A. Shaffer's acts constituted a breaking.
   [state the rule on what constitutes a breaking]

B. Shaffer's acts constituted an entry.
   [state the rule on what constitutes an entry]

C. The premises was a dwelling.
   [state the rule on what constitutes a dwelling]

D. The premises belonged to another.
   [state the rule on what it means to belong "to another"]

E. Shaffer's acts occurred in the nighttime.
   [state the rule on what constitutes nighttime]

F. When he committed these acts, Shaffer intended to commit a felony inside the premises.
   [state the rule on how to determine intent to commit a felony]

The rule's outline has structured the working draft, just as it did for the office memo. The argument will address each element separately, explaining and applying the rule on that element.

III. IDENTIFYING ISSUES

In our example, the prosecutor doesn't have to identify which issues to argue because she knows that, ultimately, she must prove them all. But what if you're representing the defendant, Shaffer? Most likely, some of the elements will be conclusively met and some will be contestable. You'll need to decide which is which. If you have any doubt, treat an element as contested at the working draft stage. After you've done your best to construct a persuasive argument on each possible issue, you can decide whether the argument is strong enough to include in the brief.

Remember how a rule statement helps you identify issues. Look back at Chapter 4, where we used the statute on cemeteries to identify issues:

> **THE STATUTE**
> No cemetery shall be hereafter established within the corporate limits of any city or town; nor shall any cemetery be established within two hundred and fifty yards of any residence without the consent of the owner of the legal and equitable title of such residence.[3]

We identified the key terms and found that each one raised a potential issue:

> **KEY TERMS**
>
> | | | | | |
> |---|---|---|---|---|
> | cemetery | hereafter | established | within | corporate limits |
> | city | town | 250 yards | residence | |
> | consent | owner | legal title | equitable title | |

The rule statement is how you find the issues. Your research on both the facts and the law will tell you which issues are potentially in contest. Argue those and concede the rest.

IV. IDENTIFYING AND DRAFTING WORKING POINT HEADINGS

Now that you've formulated a rule and identified the possible issues, you're ready to draft working headings. The working headings will guide you as you use the writing process to work out the best arguments. In the next stage (converting the working draft into a brief), you'll convert these working headings into the brief's point headings and subheadings. You can fine tune the headings then. For now, all you need is a set of headings that will organize and guide your thinking and writing process.

---

3. Va. Code, § 56 (Michie 1942), construed in *Temple v. Petersburg*, 29 S.E.2d 357 (Sup. Ct. Apps. Va. 1944).

A. Identifying Working Point Headings

Once you've decided which issues to argue, decide which of these issues will become point headings (the highest level of headings, usually identified with Roman numerals).

Usually, *a point heading* is the statement of your argument on a *dispositive* legal issue—that is, an independent and freestanding ground that entitles your client to the relief you seek. Ask yourself this question: If the judge agrees with me on *only* this one point—this one component of the rule—is that enough to get the ruling I want? If so, then your argument on that part of the rule will be a point heading.

This definition will be clearer if we look again at the burglary case. The prosecutor must prove *all* the elements to show that Shaffer committed burglary. The state can't win just by winning on any *one* element. In the prosecutor's brief, then, each challenged element will be a subpoint. The prosecutor's brief will have only one *point* heading—a point arguing that all elements are proven.[4] Look back to the working draft outline above and notice that the prosecutor's brief has only one point heading, which includes arguments on all the elements.

But the defense attorney's brief would be different. That brief can succeed if it wins on any single element. In the defense attorney's brief, then, each challenged element will be an independent basis for winning. If the defense attorney challenges the state's proof on two elements (for example, "of another" and "intent"), that brief will have two independent, freestanding ways to win—thus, two point headings. The argument on each contested element will constitute its own separate point heading. Here's how the defense attorney's working organization would look, with a roughed-out version of an introduction before the first point heading:

To prove burglary, the state must prove that the defendant's acts constituted a breaking and entering of the dwelling of another in the nighttime with the intent to commit a felony therein. As this brief will show, the house Shaffer entered was his own dwelling, and he did not enter with the intent to commit a felony. Thus, Shaffer did not commit a burglary.

I. The house was Shaffer's own dwelling.
   [state the rule on what it means to belong "to another"]

II. Shaffer did not enter with the intent to commit a felony.
   [state the rule on how to determine intent to commit a felony]

---

4. Having only one Roman numeral is fine. Let the Roman numerals identify for your reader the freestanding arguments that entitle your client to the result you seek.

B. Variations on Identifying Point Headings

As explained above, in brief writing, the normative approach is to reserve point headings for arguments that, if proven, mean that you prevail. But this idea of a point heading isn't a rigid rule. It's a custom and a general principle of persuasion. In most situations, your case will be more persuasively presented if you follow it. Rarely will you have multiple freestanding grounds for relief that would be more persuasively argued under a single point heading. Instead, you'll want to emphasize each by giving each its own point heading. You'll want the judge to know at a glance that you win for two or more independent reasons, not just one.

Sometimes, though, you might choose to treat an issue as a point heading even if it isn't a freestanding ground for relief. Here are two common situations for using point headings this way: (1) when you have a major threshold issue; and (2) when you must win on two weighty issues, especially if they are very different from each other.

1. Arguing an Important Threshold Issue

Recall from Chapter 12 that a threshold issue is one that determines the direction of the analysis from that point on. For example, the question of which state's law will apply to your legal issue (State *A* or State *B*) would be a threshold issue. Or maybe your client's legal duty would be different depending on whether a certain statute applies to your client. For example, under Title VII, an "employer" must not discriminate based on religion.[5] The question of whether the statute applies to your client (whether your client is an "employer" as defined by the act) would be a threshold question. As we'll soon see, the applicable standard of review might be a threshold issue on appeal.

An evidentiary or procedural issue might be a threshold issue. For example, the court might have to consider whether a document was properly admitted into evidence before considering whether the (properly admitted) evidence was sufficient to support the trial court's opinion.

If you have a threshold issue like one of these and if you don't have much to say about it, you can simply include it in the umbrella section or as a sub-heading of another point heading. But if you have a great deal to say about it, you might want to give it a point heading of its own.

2. Arguing Two Major Issues

Occasionally you'll have to win on two weighty issues and the analyses of these weighty issues will be quite different in nature. For example, you might have to argue both that the relevant statute is constitutional and that the opposing party breached the statute's terms. While you'll have to win on both issues, you might find that each issue is very large and the arguments and authorities

---

5. 42 U.S.C. § 2000e-2(b)(2000).

will be quite different for each (constitutional principles for one and statutory construction principles for the other). If so, you might choose to give each of those weighty issues its own point heading. Don't worry overmuch about this decision at this stage. Your goal now is just to have a structure to guide you when you think and write. You can re-evaluate your choice later, after the writing process has taught you all you need to know about these issues.

C. Drafting Working Point Headings

Now that you know which points will be marked by Roman numerals, you're ready to draft *working point headings* for each of those points. For now, you don't need to follow any certain format. You can use the writing process to figure out your arguments. Then, when you convert the working draft to the brief's Argument section, you can finalize the format of the point headings. But if you already have a sense of what your arguments will be on each point, you can rough out a heading in a more complete format. Here are the characteristics of a good working point heading:

- It's a single, complete sentence.
- It identifies the ruling you want.
- It asserts that your argument is correct.
- It states how your client's facts fit the rule, showing that you should win.

A good way to draft working point headings is to think of the point heading in halves, using this basic formula:

BASIC FORMULA FOR POINT HEADING

[First Half: Identify the ruling you seek and assert its correctness.]

because

**[Second Half: State the facts that fit the rule, entitling
your client to the result you seek.]**

For example, assume that the defendant is challenging the "nighttime" element and that "nighttime" means any time between thirty minutes after sunset and thirty minutes before sunrise. The defendant's working point heading might look like this:

The burglary charge should be dismissed

[Identifying the ruling you seek and asserting its correctness.]

because

the alleged breaking and entering occurred at 5:30 p.m., an hour earlier than thirty minutes after sunset.

[Stating the facts that fit the rule, entitling your client to the result you seek.]

Don't try to state the rule simply with a legal citation ("The motion to dismiss should be granted because the contract complies with the rule in *Smith v. Jones*."). Stating the key part of the rule in the heading will help keep your thinking focused, and later, your reader will need to know that rule right up front.

EXERCISE 18-1

Identifying Working Point Headings

Facts

Several years ago Clifford Foodman defended Raymond Carson on hit-and-run charges (*State v. Carson*). Now Foodman represents Alice Janoff, the defendant in a contract dispute. Carson is the plaintiff in that case.

Hit-and-run case:	Contract dispute case:
State v. Carson	*Carson v. Janoff*
|	|
(Foodman)	Foodman)

Before Foodman agreed to represent Janoff, Foodman wrote to Carson. In the letter, Foodman explained that Janoff had asked Foodman to represent her in *Carson v. Janoff*. The letter said that if Carson didn't reply within ten days, Foodman would assume that Carson was consenting to the proposed representation. Carson did not reply, so Foodman wrote to Carson again. This letter said that since Carson hadn't replied, Foodman would proceed with representing Janoff. Again, no reply.

Now, eight months later and well into the case, Carson has filed a motion in *Carson v. Janoff* seeking Foodman's disqualification from representing

Janoff. The judge has asked both parties to submit simultaneous briefs on the issue. Assume that this is the applicable rule:

> A lawyer who has formerly represented a client in a matter shall not thereafter represent another person in the same or a substantially related matter in which that person's interests are materially adverse to the interests of the former client unless the former client gives informed consent, confirmed in writing.[6]

Assuming that reasonable support exists for each, which of the following arguments would qualify as a *point* heading for Carson, arguing that Foodman should be disqualified? Which would qualify as a *point* heading for Janoff (Foodman), arguing that Foodman should not be disqualified?

a. *Carson v. Janoff* [is] [is not] substantially related to *State v. Carson*.

b. Janoff's and Carson's interests in *Carson v. Janoff* [are] [are not] materially adverse to each other.

c. Carson [did] [did not] consent to Foodman's representation of Janoff.

EXERCISE 18-2

Evaluating Working Point Headings

Using the facts and the rule from Exercise 18-1, assume that you work for Foodman. Choose the best working point heading, that is, the one that will best focus your thinking on the arguments you'll make. Why is it the best?

a. *State v. Carson and Carson v. Janoff* are not substantially related matters.

b. The motion to disqualify should be denied because a hit-and-run charge is not substantially related to a business dispute alleging a contract breach.

c. The motion to disqualify should be denied because *State v. Carson and Carson v. Janoff* are not substantially related matters.

d. The motion to disqualify should be denied.

V. IDENTIFYING AND DRAFTING WORKING SUBHEADINGS

After you've identified and drafted working point headings for your assignment (the Roman numerals), identify working subheadings. Reserve the first level of subheadings for any separate single issues for your argument.[7] Remember

---

6. ABA Model R. Prof. Conduct 1.9(a).

7. If the issue includes only one single issue, it will already be covered by the point heading.

from Chapter 7 how to identify a "single issue." Find the parts of the rule that must be considered together and the parts that will be decided separately. The parts that will be decided separately are single issues. For example, if the rule is a list of elements, all required (like the burglary rule), each element is a single issue. If the rule is a factors test, the factors will all be decided in relation to each other, so the single issue includes them all.

Use as many levels of subheadings as you need to cover these single issues. Then, within each, you can further subdivide into other logical sections if you like. For example, you can subdivide according to the factors in a factors test. Or you can subdivide according to the various kinds of arguments you'll make on that single issue (for example, factual, analogical, policy, statutory, historical, current trend).

The content of a working subheading can be simple. A working subheading can just identify the argument (the point to be made) for that subsection. You can edit subheadings later, when you convert the argument to the format for a brief. For now, just use these subheadings to organize and focus your arguments. In Chapter 23, we'll consider what order to use for headings and how to edit them for maximum persuasion.

CHAPTER 19

FINDING AND STRUCTURING A MORE FAVORABLE RULE

Chapter 18 covered the first draft of rule formulation and structure, but a brief should do more than present a justifiable version of the rule. It should present the most favorable version of the rule you can support. As we saw in Chapter 5, formulating a rule—especially a rule derived primarily from case law—can be a slippery task. Judges try to do a good job of writing opinions, but the constraints of the job can get in the way. Opinions aren't always crystal clear and don't always explain how they fit with other authorities. This chapter explains how contestable case law can help you write a better brief—in other words, how to formulate and structure the most favorable rule you can.

I. FORMULATING A MORE FAVORABLE RULE

As you continue to put together the working draft, you might notice a problem. The rule you first formulated could be well reasoned and faithful to the sources, but it might not be especially helpful to your client. You'll want the rule to give maximum legal significance to your client's strongest facts and to limit the legal significance of your client's weakest facts. How well does your rule measure up? Will your formulation of the rule help or hurt your client?

If the rule comes primarily from a statute, with little interpretive case law, you might not have much flexibility in how you formulate it. For example, the burglary rule is what it is. It is set out in a statute, and you can't express it differently.

But if the rule comes primarily from case law, you might have some flexibility. If so, see if you can formulate a more favorable rule. You'll have two primary methods for dealing with case law that seems to set out a troublesome rule:

- Discount or reinterpret the troublesome cases.
- Synthesize the cases into a more favorable rule.

A. Discounting Troublesome Cases

Here, roughly in the order of their strength, are reminders from Chapters 5 and 6 of some ways to discount a case:

1. **Appeal to stronger authority.**   You might be able to discount the opinion by trumping it with stronger authority. There is no rigid formula for deciding which rule is stronger precedent. You can argue for the greater merit of the rule you prefer. Remember these tools:

- Mandatory authority controls over persuasive authority.
- Opinions from higher courts control over those from lower courts.
- On questions of state law, opinions from a state's highest court control over an opinion of a federal court.
- Statements that are part of the holding carry more authority than dicta.[1]
- The more prestigious the court (or the judge), the stronger the authority.
- Opinions that have earned favorable comment by other authorities carry more weight than opinions seldom discussed.
- Thoroughly explained, well-reasoned opinions carry more weight than cursory opinions.
- The more subscribing justices, the stronger the opinion.
- A more recent opinion usually carries more weight than an older opinion.[2]
- Opinions that adopt the majority view carry more weight than those adopting a minority view.
- Well-settled rules carry more weight than brand new ideas.
- But once a new idea has gathered momentum, it becomes a modern trend, which can carry more weight than older approaches.

2. **Distinguish the facts and policies.**   As you know by now, the strength of precedent cases is measured, in part, by their factual similarity to your client's situation. The more similar, the stronger the authority. Strength is also affected by policy—the goals to be served or the problems to be avoided by the rule. What if you find a troublesome case that seems factually similar to yours

---

1. See Chapter 5.
2. Always check to be sure that the opinion has not been reversed or overruled, either expressly or by implication.

but reaches an unhelpful result? Maybe the court stated a rule that would be fatal to your case if the court's language were applied literally?

You might be able to distance your case from that troublesome case by showing that the court's statements weren't really intended to apply to a situation like yours. You'll need to show that your client's facts are different *and* that the difference is legally significant. Look for language that might imply that the court was thinking only of the sort of situation before it. If you can't find express support for this argument in the opinion, you still might be able to use reason, common sense, and justice to argue that the factual difference should matter.

For example, assume that you represent someone who was injured when he knowingly entered a burning building to save his child. You are suing those who caused the fire. What if you find a case that refused recovery to a plaintiff who had knowingly entered a burning building, as your client did? The court in that case held that someone who knowingly subjects himself to danger can't recover. But you know that the doctrine of assumption of the risk is built on a policy to protect a defendant from liability when the injured party freely chose to subject himself to the danger. The troublesome case mentioned only the "knowingly" aspect of the facts. But maybe the court didn't mention voluntariness because the facts of that case didn't raise an issue of voluntariness. You can distance your case from the troublesome case by showing the factual difference and arguing that the difference is legally significant. You'd point to the policy behind the rule and argue that the court didn't intend its rule statement to cover all possible situations. It didn't mention voluntariness because it wasn't an issue raised in the facts before the court.

3. Reinterpret the opinion. Carefully reread the opinion and all other authority from the jurisdiction asking yourself whether you misinterpreted the troublesome language. Look particularly at the terms the opinion uses. Did the court actually mean what you first thought it meant? Did the court really mean to be saying that the troublesome sentences are part of the legal test (the rule)? Read any cases the court said it was following. Those cases might not contain the troublesome language.

One of the best ways to check the court's articulation of the law is to measure what the court *said* against what it *did*. The court might have stated a rule carelessly or unclearly, but rendered a result consistent with your client's needs. Look at the section of the opinion where the court applied its rule to the facts of the case before it. Maybe the court used some troublesome language while describing the rule but then didn't seem to be looking for facts relevant to that troublesome language. All these things can yield good clues about what the court really meant. You might be able to interpret the case to find a way around that troublesome language.

B. Synthesize the Authorities into a More Favorable Rule

The second way to deal with troublesome cases is to reconcile them to more favorable authority. You might be able to combine the language from multiple cases into one rule of law. This process is often called "synthesizing" or "harmonizing" or "reconciling" opinions. Maybe the troublesome opinion didn't explain how its statements would relate to other authorities.

Look for clues that might point to a possibly more favorable rule statement. Reread all the opinions. Look for later cases that might help solve the mystery in a favorable way. Even if the later cases don't mention the inconsistency, they'll probably state and apply a rule, giving you important clues about whether reconciliation is possible.[3]

When it comes to reconciling opinions, there is no handy checklist. Each situation is different. So we'll look at an example of how to work with cases to reconcile them into a more favorable rule.

We'll use the Watson covenant-not-to-compete example, which first appeared in Chapter 5. You'll recall that Sharon Watson was a sales employee of Carrolton Company. She was interested in leaving Carrolton to form her own company that would compete with Carrolton. She had come to you asking whether Carrolton could enforce the covenant. Recall that we found *Coffee System of Atlanta v. Fox* (see Appendix G) and from that case, we formulated this rule:

A covenant is enforceable if all the following elements are reasonable:

1. the kind of activity that is restrained;
2. the geographic area where it is restrained; and
3. the time period of the restraint.

But then, in Chapter 6, we also found *Clein v. Kapiloff* (Appendix G). The rule from that case seemed more like this one:

To be enforceable, a covenant not to compete:

1. must be supported by sufficient consideration, and
2. must be reasonable. The test for determining reasonableness is:
   a. whether the covenant is reasonably necessary to protect the interests of the party who benefits by it;
   b. whether it unduly prejudices the interests of the public; and
   c. whether it imposes greater restrictions than are necessary.

---

3. Judges seldom *mean* to maintain two inconsistent rules in a single jurisdiction, but an inconsistency might have developed nonetheless. For example, two courts of equal rank in the same jurisdiction might adopt differing rules until a higher court resolves the question.

Fox and *Clein* are from the same jurisdiction, but they seem to lay out different rules. This looks like a problem, since the judge will need to know *Georgia's* rule on enforcing covenants not to compete. So, in Chapter 6, we worked out a third possible rule formulation that reconciled the two cases:

To be enforceable, a covenant not to compete must meet these requirements:

A. It must be valid in all other essentials, including sufficiency of consideration.
   [Discuss cases pertaining to contract essentials including *Fox* and *Clein*.]

B. The kind of activity restrained must be reasonable.
   [Discuss cases about the nature of the restrained activity, including *Fox* and *Clein*.]

C. The geographic scope must be reasonable.
   [Discuss cases about geographical limits, including *Fox* and *Clein*.]

D. The duration of the restraint must be reasonable.
   [Discuss cases about the duration of a restraint, including *Fox* and *Clein*.]

Now we'll add some more facts. Watson has now left Carrolton and begun her own competing business (Acme Health Care Equipment). Here is the history of her decision:

Originally Watson owned Carrolton. Carrolton has been and still is the only retailer of in-home health care equipment in the area, so it does a large volume of business each year and is quite profitable.

One year ago, Watson sold Carrolton to its present owners. She stayed on, accepting employment in a sales position for the company, and she agreed to the covenant not to compete as one of the terms of the sale. The covenant applies only to making sales contacts, not to any other aspect of the business. The covenant restricts Watson only in the three counties closest to the company headquarters and only for three years after leaving Carrolton's employ.

When Watson owned Carrolton, she used a reasonable markup so that customers paid fair prices. She tried to be responsive to customer needs in other ways as well. She saw the business as a responsible commercial citizen of the community. But the new owners of Carrolton have taken a different approach. Given the lack of competition in the area, they have substantially raised prices. They aren't concerned about customer requests and complaints, knowing that customers have nowhere else to go for the health care equipment they need. Watson became increasingly frustrated as she watched the slow destruction of the business reputation she had built over many years. She became more and more concerned about the welfare of her customers. She also recognized a business opportunity.

For these reasons, Watson left Carrolton and formed Acme. Acme has begun to compete with Carrolton, and Watson has begun to make sales contacts for Acme. Start-up costs for a health care equipment retailer are high. Ms. Watson is dealing with those costs in two ways: She has incurred substantial personal debt to pay some of the costs, and she has postponed some of the costs by planning to start small, selling equipment in only several of the categories of products currently sold by Carrolton. In the first two years of business, Acme will do well to break even. Acme can't expect to garner more than 20 percent of Carrolton's business in the products it will sell and none of Carrolton's business in the other categories. The loss of that much business would still leave Carrolton with healthy profits.

Carrolton has sued Watson, seeking to enforce the covenant not to compete. You represent Watson. You must write a brief setting out the law the court should apply and arguing that the covenant isn't enforceable. Therefore, you'd like to set out a rule of law that Carrolton would find harder to meet.

Where does that leave you? You quickly notice that under even the third version of the rule statement (the reconciled rule), Sharon Watson's case doesn't look very good. Many Georgia cases upheld restrictions of the same kind, geographic scope, and duration as the Watson-Carrolton covenant, and the rule seems to focus primarily on those three features.

But Watson's case might look different (and better) under some of the language from the rule we originally formulated from *Clein*. If the judge could assess Carrolton's need for the covenant, the judge might find that Watson's competition during the period of the restraint would do little harm to Carrolton. If the judge could consider the interests of the public, the judge might decide that the public has a significant interest in the benefits of more competition, especially reasonable prices on vital home health care equipment. If the judge could consider Watson's needs for just this little bit of commercial freedom, the judge might be less willing to enforce the covenant.

Equally important, a brief should present a sympathetic and compelling personal story, a set of *facts* that will make the judge want to agree with your argument on the *law*.[4] Generally, though, a brief presents only the facts that have *legal* significance—that is, only the facts the judge needs to know to apply the relevant rule of law. If the Georgia rule only compares the kind of activity, the duration, and the geographic scope (ignoring the needs of the public and the parties), then you won't be able to present Watson's full story. She started the new company for some good reasons, and you'd like to be able to present them to the judge.

What to do?

The answer is easy, but the solution might take some work. You need to find a way to articulate the Georgia rule in a form that includes *Clein's*

---

4. See Chapter 22.

concerns for the needs of the public and both parties. Yet you can't ignore the way the *Fox* opinion seemed to set out the Georgia test. *Fox* is mandatory authority, it's a more recent opinion than *Clein*. Its holding hasn't been overturned.

The only possible factual difference you notice between *Fox* and *Clein* is that the *Fox* covenant was part of an employment contract, while the *Clein* covenant, like Watson's, was part of the sale of a business. But that won't help, because a covenant that is part of the sale of a business should be *more* easily enforced than a covenant that is merely part of an employment contract. If the covenant is part of a sale, the seller (here, Watson) has bargained for a price that includes the covenant. The buyer has paid good money for it. So, this factual distinction won't help.

Back to the opinion in *Fox*. It's true that *Fox* primarily focuses on duration, geographic scope, and activities restrained, but *Fox* does mention the concerns of the public and the parties. The opinion never rejected those considerations expressly. How likely is it that the court really meant to exclude the parts of *Clein* you want to use? In other words, did the court in *Fox* really *mean* to be saying that a judge is *not supposed to* consider the interests of the public or the situation of the parties?

This is your clue. Maybe what first seemed to be a *complete* statement of a test is just a part of the test. Maybe the *Fox* opinion was identifying of the key terms that the court should examine. You read the *Fox* language again and this time you notice that the opinion introduces the list as "elements" the court has considered in determining whether a covenant is "reasonable."

Now you're onto something. Maybe the *Fox* list of three (time, geography, activity) only identifies the *elements* (the terms) of the covenant that the court should examine. Maybe the *standard* that each of those terms must meet is "reasonableness." Then maybe the *Fox* opinion doesn't mean to be setting out the complete, exclusive statement of how to decide enforceability of a covenant. After all, wouldn't we still need to know *how* a court is to judge whether the covenant's terms (time, geography, activity) are reasonable? *Fox* itself implicitly supports this understanding: After *Fox* sets out the list of three elements, the opinion goes on to consider each element. In the process of examining the reasonableness of the time, geography, and activity restricted, *Fox* discusses "reasonableness" in part by reference to the interests of the public and the needs of the restraining party.

In other words, in *Fox* the Georgia Supreme Court listed the three key *terms* a court should test for reasonableness. When it mentioned the needs of the public and the parties, it gave us clues about *how to decide the reasonableness* of those key terms.

So, it looks as if you can formulate a rule that harmonizes the *Fox* and *Clein* opinions more favorably for Watson's case. You might come up with something like this:

A covenant not to compete is enforceable only if it is reasonable. [*Fox* and *Clein*]

The terms of the covenant that must be reasonable are (1) the kind of activity restrained, (2) the geographic scope of the restraint, and (3) the duration of the restraint. [*Fox*]

The way a court judges "reasonableness" is by considering (1) the needs of the restraining party [*Fox* and *Clein*], (2) interests of the public [*Fox* and *Clein*], (3) the needs of the restrained party [*Clein*], and (4) all other circumstances [*Clein*].

Notice how much stronger Watson's legal arguments will be under this rule formulation. You can argue that the covenant is unreasonable in *Watson's* case because of the needs of the parties and interests of the public. You won't have to just compare the terms of her covenant with the terms of the covenants enforced in other cases. Because you looked for ways to salvage good language from the authorities and reconcile it with more troublesome language, you've formulated a rule more favorable than the one you initially thought *Fox* and *Clein* set out.

Notice also how this formulation of the rule will let you to put Watson's whole story before the judge. Because you were paying attention to your client's story, you formulated a rule that gives legal significance to Watson's best facts. The combination of narrative and rule-based reasoning has made this result possible.

II. STRUCTURING A FAVORABLE RULE

A. Subparts

After you have *formulated* a favorable rule, you'll want to *structure* it in the way most helpful to your client. In other words, if the authorities leave you some latitude you'll want to choose a rule structure that maximizes your best arguments. Keep in mind that the subparts you identify will probably become the organizational groupings for your discussion, either formally, as subheadings, or informally, as the organizational scheme within rule explanation and rule application. So, you want to look for subparts that emphasize helpful material and deemphasize unhelpful material.

Pay attention to the parts of the rule that will become subheadings in the final draft. Recall these two ways that subheadings function: (1) They emphasize their own content and obscure other content. (2) They often serve as a reader's mechanism for keeping score.

1. Choosing Subheadings for Emphasis

Subheadings emphasize their own content and deemphasize other content, so choose subheadings strategically. Look for a way to stress favorable points by making them subheadings. By providing visibility, repetition, and substantive focus, a subheading ensures emphasis of that part of the analysis. Further, emphasizing a certain part of the rule necessarily draws attention *from*, and therefore deemphasizes, parts not used as subheadings. What parts of the rule do you want to emphasize? The answer will depend on the facts of your case and on the characteristics of judges, especially their concern for the equities and social policy.

2. Subheadings as a Tallying Mechanism

Subheadings provide the judge with a handy tallying mechanism, and readers do tend to keep score, especially when the discussion identifies categories like subheadings. A judge may stop at the end of a subsection and mentally label that subsection as either weak or strong. So try to maximize the *number* of strong subsections and minimize the *number* of weak subsections. Look for ways to break the stronger part of your case into several strong arguments with separate subheadings. Look for ways to lump the weaker parts of your case into fewer subheadings. Not only does this minimize the number of weaker points, but sometimes several weaker points, combined, can become one stronger point. A judge will be more convinced by one strong argument than by a series of weak ones.

B. Example: Structuring a Favorable Rule from *Fox* and *Clein*

We'll use the Watson case as an example to see how this process works. Here is the rule we formulated above:

A covenant not to compete is enforceable only if it is reasonable. [*Fox* and *Clein*]

The terms of the covenant that must be reasonable are (1) the kind of activity restrained, (2) the geographic scope of the restraint, and (3) the duration of the restraint. [*Fox*]

The way a court judges "reasonableness" is by considering (1) the needs of the restraining party [*Fox* and *Clein*], (2) interests of the public [*Fox* and *Clein*], (3) the needs of the restrained party [*Clein*], and (4) all other circumstances [*Clein*].

Notice that this formulation of the rule gives you two options for structuring the rule: You can organize the rule by the terms of the covenant to be judged *or* by the interests used to judge them.

Terms of Covenant	*Interests*
I. REASONABLENESS OF COVENANT	I. REASONABLENESS OF COVENANT
A. Activity restrained **[Discuss interests of parties and public.]**	A. Needs of restraining party **[Discuss activity, territory, and time.]**
B. Territory restrained **[Discuss interests of parties and public.]**	B. Needs of public **[Discuss activity, territory, and time.]**
C. Time restrained **[Discuss interests of parties and public.]**	C. Needs of restrained party **[Discuss activity, territory, and time.]**
	D. Any other circumstances **[Discuss activity, territory, and time.]**

Both structures are accurate representations of the rule, but notice the difference in emphasis. How well does each set of subheadings accomplish your goal of emphasizing and deemphasizing in a strategically helpful way? Which structure would focus more attention on Watson's most helpful arguments? The structure on the left (organized by the *terms* of the covenant) would focus the judge's attention on what is restrained, where it is restrained, and how long it is restrained. Watson's facts on those comparisons aren't strong. Her covenant restrains only limited activities in a limited geographical area for a limited time.

But the structure on the right (organized by the *standards* for judging reasonableness) would focus the judge's attention on how little Carrolton needs the restraint, on how the public's interests are hurt by it, and on how much Watson herself would be hurt by it. Watson's facts on these standards are stronger.

The second structure would also be more interesting to the judge and therefore would maximize the judge's attention. The set of subheadings on the left emphasizes uninteresting facts (categories of jobs and numbers of counties and years), but the set on the right emphasizes compelling facts about people. The set on the right also emphasizes equities and social policy. It also emphasizes the breadth of factors the judge may consider, thus appealing to a judge's concern about the effect of this ruling on deciding future cases.

Your decision here is easy; the rule structure on the right is the better choice. This rule structure will form the organization of your legal discussion.

———————

You've now taken your first run at *organizing* your working draft. Next you'll *write* the working draft, filling in content beneath each heading and subheading. The next chapters tell you how to organize each part of the analysis. But remember that if you find yourself struggling with which authorities go where, return to those authorities and revisit your organization. You might rethink the rule and your organization several times before your analysis is accurate and complete.

Notice, too, how much you can massage some legal rules. In Chapter 5 we formulated a rule directly from *Fox*. In Chapter 6 we formulated a rule from *Clein*. Then we formulated another rule from *Fox* by harmonizing it with *Clein*. Now we've formulated a fourth rule from these two cases. Further, we've structured this fourth rule in two ways—ways so different that they seem like two completely different rules instead of merely two ways of structuring the same rule. Each of these rule statements and structures is supportable from the two cases we have worked with. Let this example of the diversity of rule formulations be another reminder of the pliability of many rules of law and of your power to advocate for the rule that best serves your client.

DRAFTING FOR PERSUASION: WRITING THE WORKING DRAFT

CHAPTER 20

WRITING THE WORKING DRAFT: FIRST STEPS

With your working organization in place, it's time to start writing. As you begin to fill in the content beneath your headings and subheadings, you'll use the same organizational paradigm you already know: first explaining the rule and then applying the rule. Of course, you'll set out and explain the most favorable version of the rule you can justify from the authorities. You'll apply the rule to persuade the judge to rule in your favor. You'll make all the arguments you can support from the authorities, from the policy rationales, and from your own logic and common sense.

One suggestion before we continue: You might find it helpful to rough out a draft of the facts before you begin writing about the law. Many people find that starting with a rough draft of the fact statement helps them focus as they write about the law. It can also help to overcome writer's block.

If you choose this approach, write out a draft of the legally significant facts now, before you begin writing out your arguments. The draft of the facts doesn't need to follow any special format since you'll revise it later. But if you want to see what the fact statement will look like in the completed brief, review the fact statements in the briefs in Appendices D, E, and F.

I. GETTING READY TO WRITE

Start with your working outline. As you'll recall, there will be a short introductory section (probably one paragraph or so) before the heart of the argument begins. This introductory section usually appears in one of two places: either between the Roman numeral and the first subheading or ahead of the first

Roman numeral. This is often called the Umbrella section. Here is where you state the overall rule (the umbrella rule)[1] and any information that will apply to the entire rule. You'll also state your overall conclusion and perhaps the most important facts about how that rule should be applied in your case.

Recall Chapter 18's example of how this roughed out Umbrella section might look. There we used the example of a brief on behalf of the defendant in the burglary case. Because all the defendant's arguments were separate point headings, the Umbrella section came ahead of the first point heading. Here is how the umbrella paragraph might look at this point:

> To prove burglary, the state must prove that the defendant's acts constituted a breaking and entering of the dwelling of another in the nighttime with the intent to commit a felony therein. As this brief will show, the house Shaffer entered was his own dwelling, and he did not enter with the intent to commit a felony. Thus, while Shaffer did commit assault and battery, he did not commit a burglary.
>
> I. The house was Shaffer's own dwelling.
>   [state the rule on what it means to belong "to another"]
>
> II. Shaffer did not enter with the intent to commit a felony.
>   [state the rule on how to determine intent to commit a felony]

For the prosecutor's brief, the Umbrella section would come between the point heading and the subheadings. It might look like this:

> I. Mr. Shaffer's acts constituted burglary.
>
>   A burglary charge is proven when the evidence shows a breaking and entering of the dwelling of another in the nighttime with the intent to commit a felony therein. As this brief will show, the trial evidence established all the burglary elements. Shaffer broke down the door and entered his wife's dwelling. He was there for the purpose of assaulting his wife. Upon entering, he promptly carried out that purpose. He struck her multiple times, causing cuts and bruises and a broken rib. All these events occurred at 6:30 p.m., more than thirty minutes after sunset. Thus, in addition to the assault and battery, Shaffer's acts constituted a burglary.
>
>   A. Shaffer's acts constituted a breaking.
>   [state the rule on what constitutes a breaking]
>
>   B. Shaffer's acts constituted an entry
>   [state the rule on what constitutes an entry]

---

1. See Chapter 3, section III.

C. The premises was a dwelling.
   [state the rule on what constitutes a dwelling]

D. The premises belonged to another.
   [state the rule on what it means to belong "to another"]

E. Shaffer's acts occurred in the nighttime.
   [state the rule on what constitutes nighttime]

F. When he committed these acts, Shaffer intended to commit a felony inside the premises.
   [state the rule on how to determine intent to commit a felony]

You might have already added a draft of this section and also the rule statements for each point or subpoint when you worked through Chapter 18. If you didn't add them there, add them now.

II. REVIEW OF THE PARADIGM

As you'll recall, explaining comes before applying. You've already stated your conclusion on each element and stated the rule for that element. Next, for each section, explain each rule and apply it to the facts:

PARADIGM FOR A WORKING DRAFT

RULE EXPLANATION

1. State your conclusion.
2. State the most favorable rule you can support from the authorities.
3. Explain what the rule means and use cases to illustrate it.

RULE APPLICATION

4. Explain how the rule applies to your client's facts, using factual inferences and favorable analogies if possible.
5. State your conclusion.

Remember to keep the two halves (explanation and application) separate, at least at this stage. Of course, you don't have to finish writing the explanation section before you can work on the application section. For early versions of the working draft you can write more freely. Using the paradigm just means that when you finish the draft, it should explain the rule fully before applying it to the facts.

Identifying and Labeling the Parts of the Paradigm
Read the "Facts" section of the brief in Appendix D. Then read the Argument through subsection A (a single-issue discussion). Identify and label each part of the paradigm for a single-issue argument.

III. USING CASES TO EXPLAIN THE RULE

Rule explanation is much the same for an office memo and a brief except that, for a brief, your goal is to persuade instead of to predict. You'll use the authorities to argue for the best version of the rule the authorities will support.

Thinking of points to make by using the cases.   So, you've found a batch of cases. What points can you use them to make? Start by remembering Chapter 5's tools for finding information from a case:

- Notice what the court *said* about the rule.
- Notice how the court *applied* the rule.
- Notice how the court did *not* apply the rule.
- Notice the *facts* the court emphasized.
- Notice the *policy* considerations the court discussed.

Once you've mined the cases for what they're worth, jot down a list of the points you want to make about the rule. You can organize the points into categories starting with general information and proceeding to more specific information. For example, here are three common categories: (1) how the rule functions generally; (2) what you want the judge to know about each possible topic (factors or guidelines), if any; and (3) what you want the judge to know about how the rule applies in specific kinds of situations.

Which cases?   To help you get started, you can use these three categories as your basic order for the explanation, beginning with how the rule functions *generally*. After you've stated the rule, start with the most important authority (or perhaps two) to prove that the rule is what you say it is and means what you want it to mean. You can include the policy rationale here, using cases to support it if possible.

Then discuss the authorities in the order that helps you make your persuasive points. If there is a favorable trend or shift in approach, use the cases to show that trend or shift. If certain cases focus on specific favorable points about the rule, discuss them here.

If you notice particularly relevant topics about the rule, you can organize the authorities by those topics. For example, look again at the brief in Appendix D, section A. The Tenth Circuit case had announced four factors for deciding excusable neglect. Notice that the argument organizes the cases around those four factors.

As you write, you'll probably think of additional points. Simply add them in an appropriate place. Don't worry if you don't have information in one of the categories. For example, your rule might not have factors or guidelines, so you wouldn't have a second category. Sometimes the case doesn't tell you any relevant information about how the rule applies in certain situations, so you might not have a third category. But intentionally looking for information in each category will help you notice points you might have missed.

What to say about the cases.   For each case (and to the extent the information is both relevant and favorable), provide roughly the same information as when you were using cases to predict:

- Describe what the court said about the rule.
- Describe how the court applied the rule.
- Point out any relevant information about how the court did *not* apply the rule.
- Point out any relevant facts the courts emphasized.
- Describe the policy considerations that support the rule.

This time, of course, you're providing the information to help support an argument.

What about cases with facts similar to your client's facts?   If you've found favorable cases with facts similar to yours, feature them when you explain the rule. But don't make the analogy to your facts just yet. Wait to do that in the rule application section, where you'll discuss the case again. A principle of persuasion teaches us that a reader is more persuaded when she thinks of the conclusion herself than when someone has told her what to think. You can use the factually similar cases here, in rule explanation, to lead the judge to the analogy. Remember that the judge will have already read the fact statement, so when you set out the facts of the precedent case in rule explanation, she'll jump to make the analogy for herself. Then, where you make it expressly in the application section, you'll be restating what the judge has already thought. Your point will just confirm what the judge already knew.

Always start with thesis sentences.   When you're using cases to persuade, start with a thesis sentence that explains what point the case makes, and what argument it supports. A thesis sentence asserts a position. It tells the judge why the case matters. Then the rest of the discussion of that case will prove that point. Remember our comparison of topic and thesis sentences. Which of these is a thesis sentence?

| *Cantwell v. Denton* [citation] dealt with the issue of when a choice is sufficiently voluntary to constitute assumption of the risk. . . . | A choice is not sufficiently voluntary to constitute assumption of the risk if the defendant's negligence has forced the plaintiff to choose between the threatened harm and another equal or greater harm. *Cantwell v. Denton* [citation]. . . . |

IV. ARGUMENTS ABOUT STATUTES

When you're arguing about what a statute means, remember the tools for statutory interpretation, and discuss them in roughly this order:

- the text itself, including the canons of construction;
- any cases from your jurisdiction interpreting the statute;
- the intent of the legislature;
- the policies implicated by possible interpretations;
- the interpretation of any governmental agencies charged with enforcement of the statute; and
- the opinions of courts from other jurisdictions or respected commentators.

Thinking of points to make about a statute. Use Chapter 4's "Five W's" to get you started on identifying points to make. Whose actions are covered? What kinds of actions are required, prohibited, or permitted? When did the statute become effective? Where must the actions have taken place to be covered? What consequences follow? If you want the statute to apply to your client, you'll want to explain the answers to these questions in a favorable way. If you don't want the statute to apply to your client, look for one or more of these questions that will help you argue that the statute doesn't apply.

Remember that you might need to read more than the specific provision at issue in your case. If your statute is part of an act with multiple parts, you'll need to carefully read at least these additional parts:

- any other provisions expressly cross-referenced by your provisions;
- the titles of all the provisions of the entire act;
- any definitions of terms used in the relevant provisions;
- any statement of purpose and preamble to the act;
- if length is not prohibitive, read the entire act;
- the dates of enactment and effective dates of the act and its relevant provisions;
- all this information for any amendments to relevant provisions; and

- if available, read the same information for any prior versions of relevant provisions (to understand what changes the legislature intended to make when it enacted the current version).

Read these parts of the statute word by word and phrase by phrase, paying attention to every detail. Even the internal tabulation (numbering or lettering) can be significant. Notice especially whether any list set out in the statute is meant to be exclusive.[2] As you read, keep a list of all the things you'll want to prove or disprove about how the statute applies to your client (or doesn't).

What to say about statutes. If binding case authority has already told you what the statute means, you can rely on that case law. But if case law hasn't resolved the statute's interpretation, you'll have to use other tools. Reread Chapter 4's discussion of these important tools:

- the text itself, including any definitions and sections that explain the act's purpose;
- the legislature's probable intent, including any relevant legislative history;
- the policies the statute tries to accomplish, especially if set out in the statute or in cases;
- general policies that apply to statutes of that kind (e.g., criminal statutes should be construed narrowly to protect the rights of the accused; or statutes should be construed, if possible, to render them constitutional);
- relevant interpretation by an enforcing agency; and
- what cases and commentators have said.

Remember, too, the canons of statutory construction. When a statute contains a drafting ambiguity, courts will sometimes look to these commonly accepted maxims of interpretation. Here are some of the most generally applicable:

- Give effect to rules of grammar and punctuation.
- Use the technical meaning of technical terms and the ordinary (person on the street) meaning for nontechnical terms.
- If the same words appear in various parts of an act, we presume that the words have the same meaning throughout.
- If the statute sets out a list that ends with a phrase like "and any other," those "other" items should refer only to things that are relevantly similar to the items in the list.[3]

---

2. The statute might tell you expressly, by using language like "and any other factors relevant to the child's best interests." Or the statute might merely imply whether the list is exclusive, for instance, by introducing the list with a word like "including."

3. This principle is sometimes called the principle of "ejusdem generis," meaning literally "of the same genus."

- Modifying words generally modify the first possible referent immediately prior to the modifier.[4]
- Where a statute from state X is adopted in state Y, the interpretation by the courts of state X should be followed in state Y.
- If the statute doesn't contain an exception for a certain situation, the courts shouldn't create one.
- Absent clear indication, the court should presume that the legislature didn't intend to enact a statute that contravenes fundamental shared societal values.
- Specific description of one or more situations in the text of a statute implies the exclusion of other kinds of situations not mentioned.
- Different statutes on the same legal issue (statutes "in pari materia") should be read consistently, especially where the legislature intended to create a consistent statutory scheme.
- Sometimes the courts of state X will have interpreted a word in a certain way. If the legislature of that state later enacts a different statute that uses that same word and doesn't define it, we should presume that the legislature meant to use the court's preexisting meaning for that word.
- Although not technically part of the statute's text, such items as titles, preambles, and section headings provide evidence of legislative intent.
- If a court has interpreted a statute in a certain way and the legislature later amends the statute but doesn't change that language, we might conclude that the legislature was satisfied with the court's interpretation.

Canons of construction may be treated as legal principles in and of themselves, so if you use one or more of them, you should try to cite to a case that applied that canon. But even if you can't find case authority that adopts the maxim, a court still might be persuaded by the canon's logic.

Always start with thesis sentences. Just as when you're using cases to persuade (explained above), start a point with a thesis sentence telling the judge what point you're about to make. The rest of that paragraph (and perhaps additional paragraphs) will prove that point. Sometimes you'll need to write a draft of the paragraph before you understand your own point. Then go back and add the thesis sentence.

---

4. For example, consider a statute that uses the phrase "relating to aggravated sexual abuse, sexual abuse, or sexual conduct involving a minor or ward." Does an offense relating to aggravated sexual abuse have to involve a minor or ward? Probably not. The modifying phrase ("involving a minor or ward") should refer only to the possible referent immediately prior ("sexual conduct"). *See Lockhart v. United States*, 136 S. Ct. 958 (2016).

V. COUNTERANALYSIS OF THE RULE

You've explained why you think the rule is what you want it to be, but what will the opposing brief say about the rule? Will it argue for a different understanding of the rule? Do you expect the heart of the dispute to be, at least in part, about what the rule means? If so, you might need to address the opposing view of the rule here.[5] That will be especially true if you don't expect to have the chance to file a reply brief after you receive the opposing brief. See if you can preempt the opposing arguments about the rule by being the first to raise and address them. Explain the other possible interpretation of the rule, and then explain why that interpretation is incorrect and your interpretation is correct.

Match the depth of your discussion to your assessment of the strength of the opposing argument. If it's possible but unlikely that a court would adopt it, cover it less thoroughly. But if it's a closer call, discuss the counteranalysis in more depth so you can be sure you haven't underestimated its support. Either way, conclude your counteranalysis with the reasons that your interpretation should prevail.

VI. WRITING THE RULE APPLICATION: TWO APPROACHES

As you know, the point of the paradigm is to apply the favorable rule you've just explained, so the application section should roughly track the explanation section. You could begin by applying each point you discussed in the explanation section, knowing that you'll supplement those points with analogies and other forms of reasoning. This way you're sure to apply the rule you just explained instead of allowing your application section to wander.

You might find, though, that a slightly different approach works better for you. While your analysis ultimately should be framed in tightly reasoned logic, it should also embrace a flowing narrative, and plugging into the narrative first can give you arguments that rule-based reasoning misses.

So, many writers find it more natural to begin writing rule application by focusing on the narrative (the facts), without looking back to the rule explanation section. As they write the first draft of the application section, they have the rule explanation in mind, but more impressionistically so. This strategy frees them to think like a storyteller thinks, and thus be more tuned in to the facts of their case.

If you choose this approach, you might need to revise your initial draft of the application section so the rule explained in the first half matches the rule applied in the second half. But just as often, maybe more often, you'll return

---

5. Your large-scale organization might have already provided a place for discussing the counteranalysis. See, for example, the large-scale organization of the warranty issue in Chapter 10. But if not, consider addressing it here.

to the explanation section to add or edit the discussion of a point you hadn't noticed until you began to write about your client's facts. No matter which way you approach the writing process, the result should be the same—a logical explanation of a favorable rule applied to your client's persuasive narrative.

VII. OVERALL CONTENT OF RULE APPLICATION

The organization of each rule application section will be unique, but the most important parts of application sections are usually made up of two key kinds of reasoning: (1) making analogies (case comparisons); and (2) drawing inferences from facts. The next two sections will cover analogies and inferences in more detail. Meanwhile, here are some general principles to get you started as you rough out your working draft:

- For each relevant point you made about the rule, *write a thesis sentence stating how you think that point will apply to your client's facts*.
- In one or more paragraphs following the thesis sentence, *use your client's facts to argue for a favorable application*. Explain the inferences and factual conclusions you want the judge to draw.
- *Try to support your thesis with direct fact-to-fact comparisons*. For favorable cases, show that your client's situation is as similar as possible to the facts of that case. For unfavorable cases, show the opposite. If possible, show that your case is even stronger than a favorable case by showing that your facts are even stronger than the facts in that case.
- *If it would be helpful, apply the rule's underlying policies to your client's situation*. Try to show that your client's situation does (or doesn't) raise the concerns the rule was designed to address.
- *Include any necessary counterapplication*. If you expect the opposing brief to argue a different interpretation of the facts and if you think you can preempt that argument, address it in your brief. Show that your factual interpretation is stronger than the interpretation you expect to see in the opposing brief.
- *State your conclusion*. After you've explained how the rule applies to your client's facts, end by restating your conclusion. If the discussion has been long and has covered multiple points, summarize your strongest factual arguments as part of the conclusion.

VIII. MAKING FACTUAL INFERENCES

For a brief, factual inferences are among the most effective of all strategies for persuasion. Your fact statement has set out all the relevant facts about who did what, when, and to whom. Those evidentiary facts are susceptible to actual proof. But often, the most important factual points are those the judge will *infer* from the evidentiary facts. Learning to make those inferences—and to help the judge make them—is critically important for every advocate.

So, what is a factual inference? A simple example might help. Assume that Michael Green, a car salesman, sold a car to Sonya Garcia, a minor. Sonya's parents, who did not know about the transaction, have sued to set it aside. On the day of the transaction, Green had asked Garcia whether she was "old enough to buy a car." Garcia had answered that she was. One of the elements in dispute is whether it was reasonable for Green to rely on Garcia's answer without checking further. He might be expected to check further, for instance, if he thought she looked too young.

Michael Green is not likely to admit in his testimony that he thought Garcia looked too young to buy a car. But you can create an inference if you can show that he questioned her about her age. The inference is even stronger if you can show that he did not routinely question his customers about their ages. The argument would go like this:

> Green did not routinely question his customers about their ages, but he did question Sonya Garcia. The only reason he would have added that question to his routine sales strategy is that he observed Garcia and suspected her of being too young. Thus, Green's reliance on Garcia's ambiguous answer to his vague question was not reasonable. He should have checked her driver's license.

Notice that the argument states the evidentiary facts (that is, that Green questioned Garcia and that he did not usually question his customers). Those are the facts you'll prove at trial by testimony and by documents. But the argument goes on to state the inference those facts support: that the only reason Green would question Garcia was that he suspected her of being too young. It also connects the inference to the legal conclusion: that his reliance on her answer was not reasonable.

Look for factual inferences you can draw in your argument. Use your common sense. Imagine the situation. What would it have looked like? Seemed like to each party? What would each party have done next, depending on how they interpreted the situation? Did they do those things? What other things might have been true if these are the facts?

IX. USING CASE COMPARISONS

In a rule application section, the other critically important persuasive strategy is the skill of using case comparisons to make a point. Case comparisons include analogies (pointing out similarities between cases) and distinguishing cases (pointing out differences between cases). For favorable cases, you'll probably want to show that your case is like that case and therefore the result in your case should be the same. For unfavorable cases, you'll want to show that your case is different from that case, so the result in your case should be different.

Chapter 8 introduced you to making analogies and distinguishing cases. Look back at what we learned there. Now you're ready to hone your skills even further. Here are suggestions:

Know exactly why you are making the comparison. Don't discuss the case simply to show that you've read it. Check your reasons. Can you explain to yourself or to someone else exactly what point you're going to make with the case comparison? Can you explain exactly what it is about that case that points toward the same (or a different) result in your case?

State your point in a clear thesis sentence right up front. Now that you know exactly why you are making the comparison, lead with it. Don't make the judge read a long description of the cited case without knowing what your point will be. For example, in the Buckley short-form example in Chapter 8, the case comparison began like this: "Buckley's representation that she was old enough to buy a car is significantly different from the representations in *Carney*." After reading that sentence, the judge would know exactly what to be looking for as you begin to explain what happened in *Carney*. Then in the next several sentences, we find the exact factual comparison and what it should mean about the case.

Choose whether to use a long-form comparison or a short-form comparison. For each case comparison, you'll need to decide how much to say about it. Look back at Chapter 8's discussion of long-form and short-form comparisons. Use the long form for important or complicated comparisons and the short form for all other circumstances. In either format, though, be sure to give direct, fact-to-fact comparisons.

Use parallel structure to make the similarities and differences clear. The parallel structure will let you put the key facts right beside each other so the judge can compare them up close. For instance, in the Frimberger example in Chapter 8, the comparison begins with the key thesis (that the *Fahmie* case is remarkably similar to Frimberger's situation) and then lays out the comparisons like this:

> Just as in *Fahmie*, [states a similarity]. In both cases, [states another similarity]. In both cases, [states a third similarity]. In neither case [states a fourth similarity]. In both cases, [states a fifth similarity].

Use as many key similarities (but only *key* similarities) as you can.

Use mostly your own words. If there is key language in the cited case, quote only those key words. If the judge wanted to read long passages from the cited case, the judge would just read that case and not bother with your brief. Your purpose in the brief is to write primarily about your own case and make the comparison easy to read. The best way to do that is to minimize quoting. That way, when you *do* quote a word or a phrase, it takes on added importance. For instance, notice how the Buckley example in Chapter 11 uses a single quoted word to bring the key comparison into focus:

> Buckley's statement is much closer to the situation *Woodall*, in which the minor made the representation "unknowingly." In *Woodall*, the minor did not realize that he was making a representation of majority because he did not read the contract he was signing. Similarly, Buckley did not realize that she might be making a representation of majority because she misunderstood the agent's question. In both cases, the requisite intent to deceive is absent. Therefore, the result in Buckley's situation should be the same as the result in *Woodall*—an order permitting disaffirmance.

Don't be afraid to say your case is different from a cited case with a result you like. What you are looking for is a key difference that makes your client's case even more compelling than the cited case. For instance, in the Frimberger example in Chapter 8, after pointing out relevant similarities, the comparison points out a key difference[6]:

> The only relevant difference between the two situations shows, even more clearly, that in the present case, Jenkins did not breach the covenant. In *Fahmie*, the state agency actually required the plaintiff to replace the inadequate culvert. . . . Here, however, the state agency has taken no action to require abatement of the violation. As a matter of fact, the agency has invited Frimberger to apply for an exception to the relevant requirement, a procedure that Frimberger has thus far declined to pursue. Therefore, the result in *Fahmie* is even more appropriate here, in the present case.

Consider other effective formats. If you have mastered the basic formats explained in Chapter 8 and if your professor agrees, you can adapt the basic formats to suit your purpose and situation. Remember, though, that effective comparisons nearly always begin with a clear thesis sentence stating the point you want to make and nearly always put the points to be compared up close to each other.

X. COMMON TROUBLE SPOTS IN RULE APPLICATION

For predictive writing, we saw that the three most common weaknesses in rule application sections are these:

---

6. This example is slightly edited to show how it might be phrased in a brief.

- not applying the rule as the first half of the paradigm explained it;
- announcing an outcome without sufficiently explaining the supporting reasoning; and
- not accounting for different possible interpretations of the facts.

These same weaknesses can affect the application section in a brief as well. Understanding them will help you avoid falling victim to them.

Not applying the rule as the explanation section described it.   The explanation section has included only relevant information, so match the application section to that coverage and approach. Equally important, revise the explanation section to reflect any new arguments you've thought of as you wrote about the facts. This double-checking of rule-based and narrative reasoning against each other is a perfect example of why both are critical to a good argument.

Announcing an outcome without explaining the reasoning.   Remember that you can't just announce a factual conclusion, even if you think the reasoning should be obvious. Especially remember to state and explain the factual inferences you want the judge to draw. Use the evidentiary facts to draw inferences about conclusions you can't prove directly.

For example, assume that Martha Gerring has died. Her lawyer says that several years ago, Martha executed a will, which she took home with her upon leaving the lawyer's office. Now the will can't be found. You recall from your wills class that a person can revoke her will by destroying it. Also, you know that Martha's possible beneficiaries are feuding, and some of them have had access to her house. What inferences might explain what happened to the will? Identify the inference you'd like the judge to draw and use as many evidentiary facts as possible to argue for that inference.

Not accounting for other possible interpretations of the facts.   Remember the picture of the old/young woman from Chapter 8. Ask yourself what the facts might look like to your opponent or to a skeptical judge. If there is another possible factual interpretation, consider dealing with it as counterapplication, as the next section explains.

XI. COUNTERAPPLICATION

Just as you might need to discuss and refute other reasonable interpretations of the rule (in the explanation section), you might need to discuss and refute other possible interpretations of the facts in the application section. Ideally, you can and should do that as you make your own arguments, so the refutation comes hand in glove with your own interpretation. But if, for any reason, you haven't been able to cover the counterapplication already, you can put it here in a section at the end. Just remember to conclude with a persuasive statement of why your interpretation is the better choice.

Now that you have a very rough draft of your argument section, you can look back at what you've written to find ways to deepen the analysis and make it more persuasive. Don't just write it and turn it in. Remember the adage: There is no good writing. There is only good rewriting.

CHAPTER 21

REFINING THE ARGUMENTS: THE STANDARD OF REVIEW AND THE QUESTION PRESENTED

Once you have a relatively solid working draft of your arguments, it's time to refine them. For an appellate brief, you'll need to identify the appropriate standard of review. For most briefs, appellate or not, you'll deepen them by identifying the nub of your argument and stating it in a Question Presented.

I. IDENTIFYING THE STANDARD OF REVIEW

For an appellate brief, you'll be required to identify the relevant standard of review. Court rules might require that the standard be identified in its own labeled section, or the standard may simply be set out early in the Argument section. More relevant for our purposes in this chapter, the point headings and subheadings should ordinarily reflect the standard of review.

The *standard of review* defines the level of deference the appellate court must give to the trial court's decision on the question appealed. Can the appellate court freely decide the question on its own, without any regard for the decision of the trial court? This standard would be good news for the *appellant*, who objects to the trial court's decision. It would be like starting over, as if the trial court had never decided the question.

Or must the appellate court give some level of deference to the trial court's decision? This more limited standard would be good news for the *appellee*, who agrees with the trial court's decision. This standard increases the odds that the appellate court will agree with the trial court's decision. The question of which party will have the good news and just how good the news will be depends on the kind of trial court decision being appealed.

A. Categories of Trial Court Decisions

In a bench trial, the judge must decide both the law and the facts. The judge also must decide many discretionary questions, often procedural in nature. Errors in making any of these kinds of decisions can lead to an appeal. Here are the relevant categories of questions on appeal and the standard of review and policy rationale for each.

1. Questions of Law

A pure question of law can be decided without any reference to the facts of the case. Does this jurisdiction recognize a claim for the wrongful death of a fetus? Within what time period must a notice of appeal be filed? Must a contingent fee agreement be put in writing? Must a will be signed? These are all purely questions of law. They can be researched and answered without reference to any set of facts.

A trial court's decision on a pure question of law is subject to *"de novo"* review by an appellate court. *De novo* review means that the appellate court doesn't have to give any deference to the trial court's opinion. The appellate court is free to substitute its own opinion on the question of what the jurisdiction's law provides. The principle of stare decisis encourages the appellate court to pay some deference to the existing law, but this deference is unrelated to whether the lower court adopted and applied that law.

Therefore, an appellate court need not give any deference even to a trial court ruling that is *correct* — correct in the sense that it accurately states the rule of law at the time of the lower court's decision. Depending on the level of the appellate court and on the nature of the issue being appealed, the appellate court may decide that the trial judge was right in concluding what the law *was*, but that the law *ought* to be something else. The appellate court might take the opportunity presented by this case to announce a change in the law. As a matter of fact, the primary rationale for the *de novo* standard is the role of appellate courts to make new law.

2. Questions of Fact

A pure question of fact is a question that can be decided only on the evidence. What the law is or is not has absolutely nothing to do with the question. What speed limit was posted? Did the defendant enter the building? Is the signature on the contract that of the plaintiff? These are all purely questions of fact. They can be decided without reference to any rule of law. You could have decided such questions long before you came to law school.

A trial *judge's* decision on a pure question of fact is reviewed using a "clearly erroneous" standard. To overturn a trial judge's decision on a pure question of fact, an appellate court would have to decide that, while the trial record might include *some* evidence supporting the decision, the appellate court "is left with the definite and firm conviction that a mistake has been committed."[1] It's not enough that the appellate court would have made a different decision. If the trial court's decision is plausible, the opinion must be upheld. On pure questions of fact, the trial court has the primary responsibility, in part because the trial court could observe the witnesses and judge credibility.

A *jury's* decision of a pure question of fact usually is subject to an even more narrow standard of review—a "competent evidence" standard. If the jury was properly instructed and if the record contains some modicum of evidence supporting the decision, the appellate court must allow the jury's decision to stand.[2] In other words, the appellate court's only function in reviewing a jury verdict is to be sure that the jury's verdict is not irrational.[3] An additional rationale for this "competent evidence" standard—the most limited of reviews—is a party's constitutional right to a trial by jury.

3. Mixed Questions of Law and Fact

Identifying purely factual or purely legal questions and the corresponding standards of review is straightforward. But it's more confusing when the question mixes law and fact. For example, assume that a plaintiff is suing a defendant for damages arising from a car accident. Here are some questions of fact and the trial court's decisions on them:

Questions of Fact	*Trial Court's Answers*
What speed limit was posted?	55 mph
What speed was the defendant traveling?	65 mph
Was it raining?	Yes
Did the driver signal an intention to turn?	No

Here is a question of law and the trial court's answer to it:

Question of Law	*Trial Court's Answer*
What is the duty of care owed by an automobile driver to other drivers?	A driver must exercise the degree of care that would be exercised by a reasonable person under those same circumstances.

Having decided the *facts* and decided the relevant *law,* the trial court now decides *how the law applies to the facts of the case.*

---

1. *Anderson v. City of Bessemer,* 470 U.S. 564, 573 (1985).

2. *See, e.g., I.M.A. v. Rocky Mountain Airways, Inc.,* 713 P.2d 882 (Colo. 1986).

3. Robert J. Martineau, *Fundamentals of Modern Appellate Advocacy* 133–134 (Lawyer's Co-op 1985).

Question of Mixed Law and Fact	*Trial Court's Answer*
Is driving 65 mph in the rain when the speed limit is 55 and not signaling the intention to turn **[Facts]**	No
consistent with	
the degree of care that would be exercised by a reasonable person under those same circumstances? **[Law]**	

Now, assume that the defendant appeals. She doesn't disagree with the trial court's answers about the speed limit, her own speed, whether it was raining, or whether she signaled (the facts). Nor does she disagree with the trial court's answer defining the duty of care owed to other drivers (the applicable state law). But she does disagree with the trial court's decision that driving at that speed under those conditions and turning without signaling *was inconsistent with* the way a reasonable person would drive. In other words, she disagrees with the way the trial court applied the law to the facts. This is a disagreement about a mixed question of law and fact.

What is the standard of review for a mixed question of law and fact? The appellate court must decide whether to use a *de novo* standard or a "clearly erroneous" standard. Usually the court chooses the standard on a case-by-case basis, deciding whether factual questions or legal questions will predominate. Most mixed questions turn out to be subject to *de novo* review, and mixed questions of constitutional law are nearly always subject to *de novo* review.[4] Questions of negligence generally are subject to "clearly erroneous" review.[5]

4. Questions Within the Trial Court's Discretion

We need to cover one other category of trial court decisions: decisions within the trial court's discretion. A trial judge has no discretion about whether to apply the relevant rule of law. But during litigation, a trial judge decides other questions, questions that the applicable rule of law leaves within the judge's discretion. The applicable rule might provide the judge with factors or guidelines to help the judge know *how* to make the decision, but the applicable rule doesn't tell the judge *what* to decide. Instead, the rule recognizes that the best answer will differ from situation to situation and will depend on circumstances that no single rule of law could anticipate, describe, and evaluate.

Questions left in the trial court's discretion are usually either matters of equity or matters of procedure and case management. For example, after the initial stages of litigation, a party who has filed an answer usually must obtain the judge's permission to amend that answer.[6] Case law construing the

---

4. *See, e.g., United States v. McConney,* 728 F.2d 1195 (9th Cir. 1984) (en banc).
5. *Id.*
6. *See, e.g.,* Fed. R. Civ. P. 15(a).

applicable rule might give the judge some guidelines about when to give permission, but under most court rules, the decision is left to the trial judge's discretion. The trial judge's duty in making such decisions is simply to refrain from acting unreasonably or arbitrarily.

This scope of authority gives a trial judge broad latitude. Correspondingly, then, it gives appellate courts only a narrow role in reviewing such trial court decisions. An appellate court is not free to overturn a trial judge's decision just because the appellate court would have made a different decision. To overturn a decision left to the trial court's discretion, the appellate court must decide that the decision was an abuse of discretion.[7] If the trial court's decision was not unreasonable or arbitrary, the appellate court must affirm it.

B. Advocating a More Favorable Standard of Review

Section A sets out the general rules that usually determine the appropriate standard. But courts don't always follow the general rule. The best way to identify the appropriate standard of review for your case is to look for opinions issued by the court that will be deciding your case. Search for cases deciding issues like yours, and see what standard of review the court used in those cases.

Look for authority, including policy arguments, supporting the most favorable standard of review possible. Where doubt exists as to the proper standard, an appellant should argue for the *least* restrictive standard—a standard that maximizes the appellate court's authority to overturn the challenged decision. An appellee should argue for the *most* restrictive standard—a standard that limits the appellate court's authority to overturn the trial court's ruling.

C. Editing Headings to Conform to the Standard of Review

Once you have identified the applicable standard of review, edit your point headings and subheadings to conform to the relevant standard. Here are examples of headings phrased according to the appropriate standard:

No competent evidence	The burglary conviction should be overturned because the record contains no competent evidence that the breaking and entering occurred later than thirty minutes after sunset.
Clearly erroneous	The judgment should be overturned because the trial court's finding of intent to discriminate was clearly erroneous.

---

7. *See, e.g., Napolitano v. Compania Sud Americana De Vapores*, 421 F.2d 382 (2d Cir. 1970); *Kern v. TXO Production Corp.*, 738 F.2d 968 (8th Cir. 1984).

De novo The trial court should have denied the defendant's motion to dismiss because this jurisdiction allows parents to bring a claim for the wrongful death of a fetus.

Abuse of discretion The trial court did not abuse its discretion when it issued a preliminary injunction prohibiting the defendant from concealing or disposing of his assets.

Notice that the *de novo* standard doesn't change the phrasing of the argument because that standard puts no gloss whatsoever on the question. That standard imposes no limitations on the appellate court's decision.

EXERCISE 21-1

Identifying Categories of Trial Court Decisions

For each of the following issues on appeal, decide whether the issue is a question of law, a question of fact, a mixed question, or a question of the trial court's exercise of discretion. Here are the facts:

You represent Sophia Guzman. Ms. Guzman's husband died three years ago, and she has had to resort to public assistance to support herself and her five children.

Guzman and her children rent a two-bedroom apartment in a dilapidated building owned by A-1 Realty Co. Neither Guzman nor the other tenants have a lease. The tenants can move anytime they choose, and the landlord can evict them anytime it chooses. However, Guzman and her neighbors live there because they can't afford to pay higher rent or moving costs. They don't think they could find another apartment at this price. But the building is in terrible shape and may be a health risk. The water and sewer system work sporadically, the power surges and wanes, and the rat population is increasing.

Guzman and a group of her neighbors have been complaining to their landlord for over a year. A-1 Realty's president admitted that the building needed work and promised to fix these problems, but nothing has been done. The tenant group then complained to a city agency, but to no avail. Their next strategy was to sue the landlord, alleging constructive eviction.

a. Assume that the trial court ruled against Guzman and in favor of A-1 Realty. The trial court held that, to prevail on a claim for constructive eviction, the plaintiff must prove that the property was unsuitable for occupancy for the purposes for which the occupancy was intended. The court decided that the building does not contain rats. Guzman has appealed the court's decision that the building does not contain rats.

b. Assume that the trial court ruled against Guzman and in favor of A-1 Realty. The trial court held that, to prevail on a claim for constructive eviction, the plaintiff must prove that the property was unsuitable for occupancy for the purposes for which the occupancy was intended. The court decided that the apartment had been leased as a residence and that the condition of the apartment was suitable for occupancy as a residence. Guzman has appealed the court's decision that the apartment was suitable for occupancy as a residence.

c. Assume that the trial court ruled against Guzman and in favor of A-1 Realty. The trial court decided that, to prevail on a claim for constructive eviction, the landlord must have intended to force the tenant to move. Guzman appeals the trial court's decision that intent is an element of a claim for constructive eviction.

d. When A-1 Realty filed its Answer to Guzman's Complaint, it added a series of allegations detailing Guzman's rental payment history and showing that over the years, Guzman had sometimes been late in paying her rent. Guzman filed a motion to strike these allegations from A-1 Realty's Answer, arguing that this information is irrelevant to a claim for constructive eviction. Rule 12(f) of the Federal Rules of Civil Procedure provides that a court "may" order any immaterial allegations stricken. The trial court refused to strike the allegations and Guzman has appealed.

II. DRAFTING THE QUESTION PRESENTED

The Question Presented (or Statement of Issues) is your chance to distill the issues down to their very heart and to phrase them in a way that suggests a favorable answer. To begin to get a sense of what you're after, read the Questions Presented in Appendices E and F.

A. Purpose and Function

In the Argument section, you molded the authorities, facts, and policy rationales to make the best argument you could. The Question Presented distills the heart of that Argument section to its purest form. The Question Presented has twin functions: It presents the judge with the legal issue and it begins persuading the judge to decide the issue in your client's favor. To accomplish both goals, you'll need to walk a fine line between neutrality and overzealous advocacy. The goal is to draft a Question that accurately states the issue *and* suggests a favorable answer. Here are examples of Questions Presented from opposing briefs:

BRIEF ON BEHALF OF CARROLTON

Is a covenant not to compete enforceable where the covenant was a bargained-for term of the sale of a business, where the term was negotiated as part of the agreement to allow the seller to continue working for the business, and where the sales price specifically included the company's customer lists and good will?

BRIEF ON BEHALF OF WATSON

May a large, established business enforce a covenant not to compete against a small start-up, where the covenant would eliminate all competition for providing health care products within the market area and where the prohibited activity would affect, at most, only 4 percent of the larger, established company's annual profits?

Notice how each Question Presented accurately recites the legal issue and several key facts while suggesting an answer favorable to that client.

B. Traditional Content and Format

1. Traditional format for a pure question of law.   A pure question of law asks only what the law of that jurisdiction requires. It doesn't apply that law to any set of facts. For example, you'd have a pure question of law if you are arguing that your state should begin to impose a duty to disclose all material facts in the sale of real estate.

A Question Presented that deals only with an issue of law is a straightforward statement of the legal issue, perhaps with some supporting policy rationale. It should identify the legal issue, rather than simply asking who should win. If feasible, it should also include supporting rationale. Here are examples of a Question Presented for a pure question of law. Which is best and why? Which suggests the desired answer? How is that suggestion made?

Can Dole bring a claim for malicious prosecution?

Can a criminal defendant bring a civil action for malicious prosecution prior to the resolution of the criminal proceeding on which the claim is based?

2. Traditional format for a question involving facts.   The easiest way to draft a Question Presented that requires the application of law to fact is to think of the Question in two parts. The first part states the legal issue and the second part states the key facts.

Can [state the legal question] . . . when . . . [state the major facts]?

Can a large, established business enforce a covenant not to compete against a small start-up when the covenant would eliminate all competition for providing health care products within the market area and when the prohibited activity would affect, at most, only 4 percent of the established company's annual profits?

Here are the most common verbs for beginning the Question Presented:

- "May . . . ?"
- "Does . . . ?"
- "Is . . . ?"
- "Did . . . ?"

The Question Presented can also be stated as a phrase beginning with "whether" and ending with a period:

> Whether a large, established business can enforce a covenant not to compete against a small start-up where the covenant would eliminate all competition for providing health care products within the market area and where the prohibited activity would affect, at most, only 4 percent of the established company's annual profits.

3. Standard of review. The Question Presented for an appellate brief should focus on the alleged error of the trial court. Lawyers disagree about whether the Question Presented must always be phrased in the terms of the relevant standard of review. Here is an example of an appellate brief that phrases the Question Presented in terms of the standard of review:

> Did the trial court abuse its discretion to allow the plaintiff to reopen his case when . . . ?

Follow the directions of your professor or supervising attorney. If you haven't received directions, consider these guidelines: Omit the standard when you are dealing with a pure question of law. The judge will already know that the relevant standard of review is de novo. Include the standard when the court must decide whether the lower court abused its discretion. When the standard is "clearly erroneous" and the standard is favorable for your argument, be sure to include it. If the "clearly erroneous" standard is unfavorable to your argument, leave it out if you can phrase the Question Presented accurately without emphasizing the unfavorable standard.

4. References to parties. A Question Presented often refers to the parties, so you'll need to choose a way to make those references. Will you use the parties' names? Generic descriptions (property owner, retailer, buyer, lessor)? Procedural titles (plaintiff, defendant, appellant, respondent)? You'll find proponents of all three. As always, follow the directions of your professor or your supervising attorney. If you haven't received directions, consider these thoughts:

You might choose generic descriptions so the judge won't have to remember the parties' names or remember which name goes with which party. Also, the judge's decision shouldn't rest on who the parties are, but rather on the situations and activities at issue. Generic descriptions let you emphasize the characteristics you want the judge to remember. For instance, in the Carrolton example above, the generic description "a larger, established business" is longer than the name "Carrolton" would have been, but it conveys helpful information about the larger business.

On the other hand, if the facts are simple and the parties are few, the actual names would be the most direct form of reference. And sometimes using the parties' names, especially with first names included, can serve the strategic function of humanizing the parties and the legal issues.

Avoid using procedural titles.[8] They force the judge to stop, trying to remember who the parties are in this case—in other words, who filed suit first (and is therefore the plaintiff) or who appealed first (and is therefore the appellant). That distraction makes the Question harder to understand and weakens its persuasive force.[9]

5. Don't avoid the actual question the judge must decide. Some writers are tempted to assume the answer to the question the judge must decide, like this:

> May Carrolton enforce the terms of the covenant not to compete where the terms are unreasonable?

Neither party argues that Carrolton can enforce a covenant with unreasonable terms. Rather, the question the judge must decide is *whether the terms are reasonable.* Perhaps the drafter of this Question Presented was hoping that the assumption would slip past the judge, but it won't. Don't avoid the real issue and thus miss the opportunity to state it in the most persuasive way you can.

6. Don't overdo the advocacy. Some court rules require that Questions Presented not be argumentative. Even in the absence of court rules, overzealous advocacy is counterproductive. It causes the skeptical reader to discount the material because the writer's agenda is too obvious. The goal is to state the Question Presented in a way that allows the *facts* to speak for themselves. Facts persuade more effectively than rhetoric ever can. Here is a Question Presented that has crossed the line into argumentativeness:

> Can a reckless defendant, whose callous conduct caused the death of a precious new life, escape liability for wrongful death just because the baby's guardians had not yet completed an adoption proceeding?

---

8. One situation calls for using procedural titles: when the legal issue concerns the law that applies to a party in that procedural posture. Here is an example:

> Can a criminal defendant bring a civil action for malicious prosecution prior to the resolution of the criminal proceedings that give rise to the claim?

For such a legal issue, the procedural title is actually the generic description of the situation and kind of party at issue.

9. The Federal Rules of Appellate Procedure provide that counsel should avoid using procedural titles ("appellant" and "appellee") and should use generic designations ("the employee," "the taxpayer") or the parties' actual names. *See* Fed. R. App. P. 28(d).

To avoid argumentative Questions Presented, limit adjectives and adverbs. Use facts instead of characterizations. Edit out heated rhetoric or language that smacks of name calling. Stick to facts the opposing party can't dispute.

> Can legal guardians recover for the wrongful death of a child when the guardians had raised the child as their own for four years, had instituted adoption proceedings two years prior to the child's death, and had believed, reasonably and in good faith, that a final adoption decree had been issued?

7. Do try to phrase the question in a way that suggests a favorable answer. Generally, a question that suggests an affirmative answer is more persuasive than a question that suggests a negative answer. But sometimes the rhetorical impact of a negative structure can outweigh the advantage of calling for an affirmative response. For example, a structure that asks, "Can X require Y to do Z?" implies that X is being oppressive to Y, simply by virtue of the structure of the question. The structure might invite the reader to respond with a resounding "No." For example, consider this Question Presented:

> Can an employer, in order to collect urine samples, require employees to urinate in the plain view of a supervisor?

8. Multiple questions presented. A brief can raise several issues and thus have several Questions Presented. Simply draft a separately numbered Question Presented for each legal question. Put the Questions Presented in the same order in which the issues appear in the Argument.

C. "Deep" Issue Statements[10]

If court rules permit some variation, you might not be limited to the traditional one-sentence format. If so, consider using two or even three sentences so you can add context while maintaining clarity. The Question Presented should still be short—usually no more that about 70 to 80 words—but the multiple-sentence structure will allow you to tell a tiny story, to clarify the legal standard, or to frame the issue more effectively. Here is an example of a "deep" issue:

> To maintain a cause of action for fraud under California law, a plaintiff must show that the defendant made a false representation. In his deposition, Jones concedes that neither Continental nor its agents or employees made a false representation. Is Continental entitled to summary judgment on Jones's fraud claim? [49 words.][11]

---

10. Bryan A. Garner, *The Deep Issue: A New Approach to Framing Legal Questions*, 5 Scribes J. Leg. Writing 1 (1994–1995).

11. *Id*. at 4.

This issue statement uses three sentences. The first clarifies the applicable legal standard. The second presents the key facts. With both the legal standard and the applicable facts clearly stated, the third sentence asks the question.

A "deep" issue format can state the facts first, essentially telling a ministory, for example:

> At 7:30 one morning last spring, Father Michael Prynne, a Roman Catholic priest, was on his way to buy food for himself at the grocery store when his car collided with Ed Grimley's truck. The Catholic Church neither owned Michael Prynne's car nor required its priests to buy groceries as part of their priestly functions. Was Michael Prynne acting as an agent for the Church at the time of the accident?[12]

Once in a while you might even use more sentences while keeping them short enough to remain within the seventy- to eighty-word range. Here is such an example:

> Fiver's insurance policy required it to give Barndt Insurance notice of a claim "immediately." In May 1994, one of Fiver's offices was damaged by smoke from a fire in another tenant's space. Ten months later, Fiver gave notice. Barndt investigated the claim for [six] months before denying coverage and did not raise a late-notice claim until [eighteen] months after the claim was filed. Can Barndt now deny coverage because of late notice? [73 words][13]

D. Drafting Hints

Creating a Question Presented is like creating a haiku. Each of these literary forms requires meticulous attention to word selection and placement, sentence structure, and theme. Unlike poetry, however, no one would argue that obscurity of message is desirable for a Question Presented. Rather, a Question Presented should be a powerful statement that is *easily understandable on first reading.*

Keep reworking the Question Presented for readability and subtle persuasiveness. Use the techniques covered in Chapter 15. Try to achieve a concise, clear, and direct style, and a persuasive framing of the Question.

EXERCISE 21-2

Critiquing Questions Presented

  a. Review the Carillo facts in Chapter 10. Assume that the matter is now in litigation. Critique these two versions of the Question Presented in a brief for Jimmy Lupino. Write a better version.

---

12. *Id.* at 13.
13. *Id.* at 35.

VERSION 1

Can the Carillos maintain an attractive nuisance in their backyard?

VERSION 2

Does a trampoline constitute an attractive nuisance?

   b. Review the Guzman facts in this chapter. Critique these two versions of the Question Presented in a brief for Guzman. Write an improved version. The issue is whether the premises have become unsuitable for the purposes for which they were leased.

VERSION 1

Has an apartment become unsuitable for use as a dwelling when the utility services are unreliable?

VERSION 2

Has a slum lord constructively evicted poor tenants who cannot afford to move elsewhere when he callously forces children to live with rats and without heat, water, and toilet facilities?

III. PERSUADING USING POLICY

As you are deepening your arguments, do one last check to see if you can add any policy rationales. Courts will almost always consider them as part of their reasoning process. The best sources for identifying relevant policies are the authorities themselves, but you can also think of some by using your own common sense. To help you get started, consider these:

1. As between two parties, the law should place the risk of liability on the party most able to prevent a loss.
2. As between two parties, the law should place the risk of liability on the party most able to insure against it.
3. As between two parties, the law should place the risk on the party who already bears similar risks and therefore whose legal and practical situation will be least affected by the risk.
4. Where the bargaining positions of certain kinds of parties are grossly disparate, the governing rule should protect the weaker party.
5. The law shouldn't impose a liability that might limit the ability of people to engage in a particular business in the future, especially if the business provides a socially desirable service.
6. The rule should place the burden of proof on the party with the easiest access to the evidence.

7. The governing rule should be workable in light of the practical realities of day-to-day life. It should incorporate a realistic view of human psychology and business custom.

8. The governing rule shouldn't create a legal test that is easily subverted by crafty individuals and businesses.

9. Stability in the law is desirable. The law shouldn't change unless the need for the change is clear.

10. The realities of modern life have changed significantly (explain how). The law must be willing and able to change and adapt to changing circumstances.

11. A governing rule should encourage moral behavior in society, such as honesty, fair dealing, and altruism. It should discourage morally questionable behavior, such as greed, scheming, and taking advantage of others who are vulnerable.

12. The law should resist the temptation to rush to the rescue when a refusal to intervene will encourage people to be diligent and responsible in handling their economic and legal affairs.

13. A rule shouldn't create additional costs for a person or an industry unless the harm to be prevented justifies the imposition of those costs.

14. A rule shouldn't add impediments to the free transfer of assets and the ease of doing business.

15. A rule should preserve individual freedom.

16. A rule should be concrete enough to allow people to predict whether the conduct they contemplate will be considered lawful and, therefore, to conform their conduct to the law.

17. A governing rule should be flexible enough to allow future courts to achieve a fair result in individual circumstances.

18. A governing rule should be concrete enough to ensure that future adjudications will be based on objective criteria rather than on prejudices of the decision maker.

19. The rule should defer to the expertise of decision makers most able to decide wisely.

20. A court should choose a rule that is as consistent with established custom as possible. Customs exist because people have discovered that they work well.

Naturally, you'll want to focus on policy rationales that support your client's desired result. In the rule explanation section of your argument, explain these rationales and show why they are desirable. Then in the rule application section, apply them to your client's situation. Explain why your client's desired result would best serve the relevant policy rationales and wouldn't unduly impinge on competing policy concerns.

IV. RULE APPLICATION WITH FACTORS OR GUIDELINES: ADVANCED TECHNIQUES

You'll have several options for organizing factors or guidelines. After you've written a draft, check to see if the organization you chose worked well, especially in the rule application. If not, you have some options:

A. First Organizational Option: By Factor

You might have organized rule *application* by factors, making your case on each of them, one by one. For example, consider this statute governing a judge's decision on child custody in a divorce.

> As between the parents, custody is to be decided according to the best interests of the child. The court may consider the following factors in deciding the best interests of the child:
>
> 1. the fitness of each parent;
> 2. the appropriateness for parenting of the lifestyle of each parent;
> 3. the relationship of the child to each parent;
> 4. the placement of other children;
> 5. the child's living accommodations;
> 6. the district lines of the child's school;
> 7. the proximity of extended family and friends;
> 8. religious issues; and
> 9. any other factors relevant to the child's best interests.

In rule application, the writer *could* simply apply each factor, one by one, just as the rule explanation explained each factor.

Did you discuss each factor, one by one, in rule application? If so, how did it work? First, remember that readers keep score. Keeping score, factor by factor, implicitly tends to equalize the importance of the factors. Thus, organizing according to the statute's list of factors tends to equalize the emphasis on favorable and unfavorable factors. Does that help or hurt your client?

If this organization might not be your best choice, consider the next two.

B. Second Organizational Option: By Party

Another option is to organize the rule application by party. That organization might look like this:

I. BEST INTERESTS OF THE CHILD
    Rule explanation [explaining the factors one by one]

Rule application:

- Interests served by awarding custody to mother:
  [Discuss, in the best light possible, the statute's identified factors that favor the mother. Since the statute allows consideration of other factors, discuss also any unidentified factors that favor the mother.]

- Interests served by awarding custody to father:
  [Discuss, in a less favorable light, the factors that favor the father. Compare these to the interests served by awarding custody to mother, showing that the latter outweighs the former.]

Depending on your case, this plan might offer several advantages. It would be flexible, allowing you to combine factors, to emphasize and deemphasize, and to advance a theme within each subsection. The writer could argue a primary theme about the advantages of placement with the mother and could argue a different primary theme about the disadvantages of placement with the father.

Second, this organization has the appearance of objectivity. It is the classic "on the one hand this; on the other hand that" structure. Because its *structure* appears neutral, it might reduce the reader's skepticism.

Third, it seems to equalize the score, at least initially. If the majority of the statute's identified factors would favor the opposing party, using this "balancing" format lets you deemphasize the imbalance.

Finally, it might be most like the judge's natural thought process. If you use this organization, the judge might choose to use your brief (not the opposing brief) as the starting point for the judge's own reasoning.

C. Third Organizational Option: By Theme

One other possibility invites you to organize directly by themes. Step back and ask yourself why, in the final analysis, this child should be placed with the mother? Why not the father? What is the real heart of your argument? For example, maybe the court-appointed social worker has identified this child's two greatest present needs as stability and a sense of control over his own fate in the midst of this frightening process of divorcing parents. Many of the statute's listed factors would fit under these two categories (and probably some others too). You could organize the statute's factors (and any others you want to add) beneath categories defined by these two identified needs. The application section might look like this:

I. BEST INTERESTS OF THE CHILD
    Rule explanation [explaining the factors one by one]

Rule application:
Child's need for stability [Discuss each factor that impacts stability]:

- Personal fitness of each parent to provide stability [Placement with the mother would provide more stability because she has a more stable personality, keeps daily activities on a predictable schedule, etc.]
- Personal lifestyle of each parent as it affects stability [The father travels sometimes and would need either to take the child with him or leave him in the care of a babysitter, who would be a new person in the child's life.]
- Relationship of the child to each parent as it affects stability [While the child cares deeply for each parent, the child has spent more time with his mother than with his father.]
- Living accommodations as they affect stability [While the father's new home is nicer, the mother will be living in the former family home and the child would not have to move.]
- District lines of the child's school as they affect stability [While the father's new house is closer to the child's school, stability counsels for having the child continue to ride the same school bus with the same group of children.]
- Any other factors relevant to stability

Child's need for sense of control over his own fate

- Personal fitness of each parent as it affects the child's sense of control [While both are fit parents, the mother is more likely than the father to allow the child to make decisions in appropriate areas of the child's life.]
- Other factors affecting the child's sense of control [The child has decided that he wants to operate a paper route and placement with the father would prevent him from having the paper route.]
- Any other factors relevant to sense of control

This plan organizes by *theme*. It's the most flexible. It allows the most room for combining the discussions of factors, so that the stronger ones strengthen the weaker ones.

Second, this plan lets you mold the statute to suit your client's needs. You can identify this particular child's greatest needs. After these needs are identified—and who could argue that the child does *not* need stability and some sense of control?—you can show how the factors work for those goals.

Third, this plan lets you emphasize larger and more compelling categories than the factors listed in the statute. You can pit these larger needs against the smaller individual factors that favor the other party. For example, assume that the father has moved close to the child's grandparents, and placement with the father would have the advantage of proximity to the grandparents. Under this organization, you could weigh the child's need for stability against the advantage of proximity to the grandparents rather than weighing the child's need to avoid changing schools against the advantage of proximity to the grandparents. The judge is more likely to agree that, although proximity to grandparents is nice, the need for stability in a child's life is vital.

CHAPTER 22

THE STATEMENT
OF FACTS

There is an adage among trial lawyers: If you have to choose between the law and the facts, take the facts. The adage reflects the experience of many lawyers that a judge or jury convinced of the justice of your cause will try hard to find a way around unfavorable law. Conversely, if the judge or jury perceives that justice is on the other side, favorable law might not be enough.

The Statement of Facts is the primary place where a judge forms her sense of justice about the case. When it comes to creating attitudes about justice, narrative is more effective than heady analysis. Upton Sinclair's *The Jungle* (1908) persuaded countless readers of the inhumanity of the meat-packing industry. *Cry, the Beloved Country (1948), by Alan Paton,* persuaded people around the world of the injustice of apartheid.

Consider your own reactions. Imagine reading a well-reasoned analysis arguing that Hitler should not have imprisoned and killed German Jews. The analysis uses moral reasoning, explaining and applying moral principles from various philosophers. Imagine your response. Now compare it to your response to *The Diary of Anne Frank* or *Schindler's List* or *Sophie's Choice.* Which would you find more powerful—the analysis or the stories of the people who lived the facts? Which would you remember longer? Which would persuade you more?

Stories grab us, persuade us, motivate us. Your client's story can persuade a judge, just as a movie or book can persuade you. But to be persuasive, your client's story must be told skillfully. Many lawyers believe that the brief that tells the most effective story is the most likely to prevail, so the stakes are high.

Not only does the fact statement matter, but in at least one important way, it takes more skill than writing fiction. Writing a fact statement is harder because you can't make up the facts. You have to persuade using the facts fate handed you. What's more, you have to persuade without appearing to manipulate those facts. You'll need to state the facts in a way that is objective enough to be fair and also persuasive enough to be compelling. As Professors Ray and Cox put it:

> If briefs to the court were gymnastics events, the statement of facts would occur on the balance beam. Writing a persuasive statement is accomplished not by following one set of rules, but by balancing your use of various techniques to maintain credibility while achieving the stance needed to highlight favorable facts. It does not require the brute force of emphatic language so much as a subtle blend of strength and control of structure and detail. It involves much thought, consideration of alternatives, and monitoring the interactions of various techniques. Yet an excellent statement of facts looks natural and effortless, just as a complex routine looks easy when completed by a skilled gymnast.[1]

It takes years to master the art of legal storytelling. This chapter will give you some techniques to practice as you begin your career.

I. ETHICS, READERS, AND THE CONVENTIONS OF FACT STATEMENTS

Before beginning, remember the general principles that apply to Fact Statements and their readers.

A. Reminders About Ethics

Remember from Chapter 17 that a lawyer must not misrepresent facts.[2] Misrepresentation includes both stating facts untruthfully and omitting material facts when the result is to create a false inference. In virtually every case, you'll find some facts you wish weren't there. The more important those facts are, the more you wish they didn't exist. But they do exist, and leaving them out of your Fact Statement won't make them go away. They'll certainly appear in the opposing brief. Omitting them from your brief will only damage your credibility, causing the judge to wonder how much she can rely on the other facts you assert and even on the law your argue. Few things make a judge angrier than feeling misled by a lawyer.

Omissions cause another problem as well. They send the judge to the opposing party's Fact Statement, not yours, as the court's primary factual reference. These consequences are serious for both you and your client. Therefore,

---

1. Mary Barnard Ray & Barbara J. Cox, *Beyond the Basics: A Text for Advanced Legal Writing* 167 (2d ed., West 2003) (footnotes omitted).
2. A lawyer shall not knowingly make a false statement of fact. ABA Model R. Prof. Conduct 3.3(a)(1).

both ethics and good strategy require including all material facts, whether favorable or not.[3]

B. Reminders About Readers

Review the sections in Chapters 11 and 17 about law-trained readers in general and judges in particular. Remember especially that:

- judges want to do justice;
- stories, especially stories about people, are compelling;
- readers invest more attention at the beginning of the document (which is where the Fact Statement appears) than to any other part; and
- readers devote more attention to the beginning and end of a section than to the middle.

C. The Conventions of a Statement of Facts

Certain formal requirements and generally accepted conventions apply to the Statement of Facts. Take a look at the Statements of Facts in Appendices D, E, and F for examples of these conventions:

1. A Statement of Facts shouldn't refer to evidentiary facts not in the court record. For trial-level briefs, the record includes the pleadings and the information gleaned from discovery.[4] For appellate briefs, the record includes all relevant proceedings from the trial court. Because the point of an appeal is to decide whether the lower court's decision on a certain point was supported by the facts *before that court,* the appellate court considers only the factual record that was before the lower court at the time of the decision.[5]

When a fact statement states a fact, it should provide the location of that fact in the record. The record cite lets the judge confirm that the fact is in the record and double-check the writer's description and characterization.[6] Judges *do* check the facts. For an appellate brief, you can provide record cites in either of these ways:

R. 34
R. at 34

---

3. Later sections in this chapter identify ways to neutralize or deemphasize unfavorable facts.

4. You might also be able to supplement the record by filing a witness affidavit simultaneously with the brief. The affidavit can include a document (like a contract, deed, will, or letter) as an exhibit. The affidavit sets out the sworn facts necessary to add the document to the record. You'll learn more about these requirements when you take Evidence.

5. Evidentiary facts are the facts that explain what happened in the case—what happened to the parties and others who participated in the events being litigated. Policy facts (sometimes called legislative facts) are different, however. Policy facts provide the court with information relevant to a policy argument. For example, if the brief argues that marriage equality does not harm children, a brief might cite a social science study supporting that conclusion.

6. Fed. R. App. P. 28(e).

2. As part of a legal document, the fact statement retains the formal style of the rest of the brief.   Although a Statement of Facts tells the story of the legal dispute, its style is not informal. You don't want the judge to wonder if she is reading fiction. Avoid obvious appeals to emotion, grand description, dramatic literary devices, and other obvious attempts to manipulate the reader. The style should be dignified and courteous, never sarcastic or angry.

3. Generally, a fact statement doesn't discuss law.   A fact statement sets out all the facts that the rule makes important, but it usually doesn't explain the rule or the rule's relationship to the facts. Rule explanation and application come in the Argument section. An exception to this convention is that the last paragraph of the fact statement can segue into the legal argument by stating the legal issue the Argument will address.[7]

4. A Statement of Facts doesn't include overt argument, whether legal or factual.   For example, for a case alleging medical malpractice, the fact statement might relate the patient's vital signs, the medical test results, the patient's medical history, and the nurse's observations, but you wouldn't state that the doctor acted carelessly.

But here's an important clarification: This restriction applies to conclusions *you* state yourself. It doesn't apply to *someone else's conclusions*. For example, although you wouldn't state your conclusion that the doctor acted negligently, you can report the testimony of an expert witness who concluded that the doctor acted carelessly. The testimony of the witness is a *fact* that occurred at a deposition or at trial. Quotations are appropriate in a Statement of Facts and often are effective, as section IV explains.

5. A Statement of Facts can point out the *absence* of certain facts from the record.   The absence of a fact from the record *is itself a fact*. Thus a fact's absence is fair game.

> At trial, three officers testified that they were stationed at the building's entrance between 5:00 and 6:00. However, no witness testified to seeing the janitor enter or leave the building.

Pointing out a fact's absence lets you make a point about the evidence while remaining within the legitimate bounds of fact reporting. Don't forget to notice important *absent* facts.

---

7. Experienced practitioners sometimes do include some law in their fact statement, but only in certain kinds of very specific situations. Those situations won't apply to your legal writing assignments.

II. DEVELOPING A THEORY OF THE CASE AND SELECTING FACTS

You'll include the primary facts no matter what the theme, but some other fact-selection decisions are tied directly to the choice of theme. This section explores selecting facts of both kinds.

A. Developing a Theory of the Case

Lawyers use the term "theory of the case" to refer to the theme they weave throughout the facts, the theme that will explain the facts from their client's perspective. The theme should be sympathetic to the client. It should help the judge understand who the client is, why the client acted in the way he did, feels the way he does, and needs the things he needs. At the least, a good theory of the case assures the judge that a ruling in favor of your client won't be unjust. At best, the theory convinces the judge that justice requires that ruling.

Of course, the theory of the case will have to be consistent with the key facts. Creating a theory is easy when the facts are generally favorable and much more difficult when they are not. For troublesome facts, you'll have to work even harder to *see and feel* the story from your client's perspective. Look again at the sample Questions Presented for Carrolton and for Watson on page 266. Can you see what Carrolton's theory of the case will be? How about Watson's?

You've already been working with the facts as you've been working on the brief. You might have found a number of themes playing out. Finding an effective theory of the case starts with talking to your client, but your client might not be good at communicating the heart of his position and might not even be consciously aware of it himself, so you'll also need to use your imagination. Try to put yourself in his position. Imagine what it must have been like, what it must be like now. Try to understand who this person is and who the other key characters are. Mull it over in the shower, on your morning run, and on your way to the grocery store. Try to fill in the blanks of the following statement: "This is a story about a (man)(woman) who (is)(was) . . . [describe client] . . . and who is struggling to. . . ."

If you can do so without breaching client confidentiality, try telling the story orally. Go to lunch with another lawyer from your firm and tell her your client's story. Telling the story and then talking about it with another person can give you a fresh perspective. After you've developed a clearer sense of your client and the situation, what helps you understand your client's behavior? What moves you about the story? What might move the judge? Once you have an idea, try articulating it in a few sentences, like so:

> Carrolton bought Watson's company, the only provider of health care products in the area, and immediately began to take advantage of the company's customers by raising prices, limiting product lines, and allowing long delays

for special-order items. Since the customers had nowhere else to go for their health care products, they had no choice but to pay the prices and put up with the limited service. Watson, who had continued to work at the business, had to sit by and watch as Carrolton took advantage of her neighbors and long-time customers. Many of them even thought that Watson was intentionally profiting at their expense, since she was still the customer contact person in the office—the only face her old customers saw. Not only was this situation personally distressing to Watson, but she became increasingly convinced that it just wasn't right.

A good theory of the case should be consistent with the facts and with a commonsense notion of fairness. It should explain as many of the unfavorable facts as possible, and it should cast your client in a sympathetic light.

B. Selecting Facts

Once you've developed your theory of the case, select the facts you'll include in the Statement of Facts. Generally, include facts falling into any of these categories:

- facts that fit the theory of the case;
- facts mentioned in the Argument section of the brief;
- all legally significant facts, whether favorable or unfavorable;
- significant background facts; and
- emotionally significant facts.

Like the process of *legal* analysis, the process of writing the fact statement is recursive. You'll find that your understanding of the possible significance of each fact will develop as you work through each step. This developing under-standing will send you back to earlier steps to add, delete, or amend your draft. Don't resist the need for these revisions; your best work will come from them.

III. ORGANIZATION

A. Formats

Chapter 13 identified the most common organizational formats for Fact Statements: chronological, topical, and a combination of the two. This chapter reviews these formats and discusses another: organizing by theories of the case.

1. Chronological.   For simple facts, a chronological presentation is often best. For instance, in a simple collection matter, the facts will usually set out the events giving rise to the debt, the default, the plaintiff's demand that the defendant cure the default, and the amount owed. These simple facts are best presented chronologically.

2. Topical or combined approach. For more complex facts, the topical or combination formats work best. As you know from Chapter 13, these formats organize facts into topics. For example, in an employment discrimination case, the plaintiff's facts might be organized in topics like these: the nature of the defendant's business; the defendant's usual hiring process; the defendant's usual employee evaluation procedure; the procedures used in selecting employees for layoffs; the hiring process for the plaintiff's position; the hiring decision; the terms of the plaintiff's employment; the plaintiff's employee evaluations; the business conditions that necessitated layoffs; the selection of the plaintiff and others for layoff; and the defendant's efforts to assist the laid-off employees. Both the topics themselves and the individual facts within each topic should be ordered logically. Logical order might or might not be chronological, depending on the situation.

3. Theory of the case. You might want to consider another organizational format: organizing by theories of the case. This format might be effective when the opposing party has some powerful facts that seem to support her position, but you have some key facts or a compelling theory of the case that could explain those opposing facts.

Surprisingly, this format begins with the bad facts—the facts that create your opponent's theory of the case. Bad facts can't be ignored, so the question is how best to deal with them. Try setting them out first and then neutralizing them with the good facts that create your own theory of the case.

Organizing by theory of the case is a more daring choice for several reasons. First some believe that the beginning of a section soaks up more reader attention than does later material. Second, a busy judge might not finish reading the Fact Statement. Third, this choice bets a large stake that the supporting facts can neutralize the opposing facts. After setting up such a direct juxtaposition of the facts, that's a bet you'll need to win.

When this organizational format works, however, it's extraordinarily effective. Having seen the worst facts and then seen them neutralized, the judge is far less likely to be impressed on reading them again in the opposing brief or on hearing them at oral argument. So, be aware that this organizational format is an option, but choose it only after careful evaluation.

B. Subheadings

Whatever organizational format you choose, consider using subheadings. For lengthy fact statements, subheadings can help you organize effectively and help the judge follow the facts. Subheadings are particularly effective for topical or combination formats. Even if your final draft won't need subheadings, you might use them to help you organize as you write. You can always delete them when you edit the draft.

C. Procedural History

Whichever format you choose, you'll need to decide where to put the procedural history. Court rules or the instructions for your assignment might make this decision for you.[8] If the rules or instructions might require a Preliminary Statement (or Introduction), the procedural history goes there, in its own section. If court rules or your instructions haven't specified a location, the two most common choices are at the beginning or the end of the Fact Statement. At the beginning, it can help to establish the context for the facts that follow. At the end, it can serve as a natural segue into the Argument section.

IV. TECHNIQUES FOR PERSUASION[9]

Before you choose an organization, keep in mind these principles for persuading with facts:

A. General Principles

1. Clarity is more important than using sophisticated techniques for persuasion. Judges won't be persuaded by something they can't understand. If any of the following techniques conflict with the goal of clarity, ignore the technique.
2. Don't use a technique that the judge is likely to notice. A persuasive technique should be invisible, or nearly so. Once the judge recognizes the technique, it loses its power. The judge's attention is on the technique and not the fact. For example, you might have used repetition to emphasize a favorable fact. But if the judge thinks, "Ah, look, the writer is repeating this fact to try to get me to notice it," then the judge is thinking about how you're trying to manipulate her. The fact statement would have been more persuasive without the technique.
3. Don't overuse any technique. Overuse creates monotony and distraction and it increases the odds that the judge will notice the strategy.
4. Any technique for emphasizing one fact or group of facts automatically deemphasizes the other facts, so don't try to emphasize too many facts. Pick the few facts you want most to emphasize and allow the others to serve as the background.
5. Some of the techniques described below are inconsistent with each other. That doesn't mean that one is right and the other wrong—only

---

8. *See, e.g.,* Fed. R. App. P. 28(a)(6).
9. Lawyers must not misrepresent facts, so persuasive techniques must always remain within the bounds of reasonable and fair argument. All the techniques described in this section must be used in ways that comport with ethical duties.

that each has its own advantages and disadvantages. Your job is to select the one that will work best for your client's situation.

B. Large-Scale Organization

The Beginning

6. Assume that the judge is not already familiar with the case. The beginning of the fact statement should establish the context for the facts that follow. Otherwise, the judge might find herself reading a chronological account of a series of events without knowing why these events are important. You can provide context with a procedural history or a short summary of what the case is about, written consistently with your theory of the case. Here is an example written on behalf of Carrolton:

> This is an action to enforce the terms of a covenant not to compete. As part of the sale of her business to Carrolton Company, the defendant promised that for the three years immediately following the sale she would not compete with Carrolton in the three counties closest to Carrolton's headquarters.
>
> Eighteen months after the sale was completed, the defendant opened a competing business just one mile from Carrolton's office. She has been competing directly with Carrolton in the three prohibited counties ever since. This action seeks to enjoin her continued breach of the covenant not to compete.

See how these two short paragraphs provide context for everything that will follow.

7. The reader's attention level is greatest in the first few paragraphs. If possible, capitalize on the increased attention level with an organization that lets you put favorable material there. For example, a summary of the case like the one above would use this technique.

8. Aim for a beginning that sparks the judge's interest. Journalists call this "the lead." The conventions of a legal document don't allow for some of the more dramatic forms of attention grabbing, but do try to draw the judge into the story. For example, a prosecutor's brief would begin with the facts of the crime rather than with the procedural history of the appeal.

The Middle

9. Here is a possible place for the facts you want to deemphasize. Normally, a reader's attention level is at its lowest about three-fourths of the way through the section.

The End

10. Readers might pay more attention to the material at the beginning, but they remember longest the material at the end. At the end of the fact statement, readers tend to take a momentary mental break to let the story sink in, so the last sentence still lingers in their minds. Try to select an organization that allows you to end with material you want the reader to remember.

11. The last paragraph should have the feel of a concluding paragraph. One way to accomplish this is to close with a transition into the legal argument by identifying the legal positions staked out by the parties. Don't state the opposing position any more favorably than you have to. Since the last sentence will linger in the judge's mind, end with your legal position, not your opponent's. Here is an example:

> The bank has admitted that it did not disclose the effective interest rate to the Turners. However, it claims that disclosure was not required, arguing that the transaction was not a "consumer loan" under the Consumer Protection Act. This brief will show that the transaction was, indeed, a "consumer loan" and that the bank's failure to disclose the interest rate violated the Act.

C. Paragraph Organization

12. A reader invests more attention to the beginning and the end of a paragraph than to the middle. You can put facts you want to emphasize in the first sentence or in the last clause or phrase of the last sentence. You can deemphasize unfavorable facts by putting them in the middle.

13. Notice paragraph length. In sections where you want to emphasize the facts, keep paragraphs relatively short. Where you want to deemphasize facts, let the paragraphs get longer and put the facts you want to deemphasize deep in the paragraph.

D. Techniques with Sentences

14. As a general rule, reduce clutter by using the techniques in Chapter 15. Clutter reduces clarity, irritates the judge, and deemphasizes important facts. Occasionally, you can allow just a bit of clutter to surround an unfavorable fact, using the clutter to reduce emphasis by lengthening the sentence and by making it less striking. Use this technique sparingly.

15. Use active verbs to emphasize and passive verbs to deemphasize or to avoid focus on the identity of the person who took the action. Here are examples:

a. *To encourage focus on the person taking the action:*

> Shaffer kicked in the front door of the house and attacked his estranged wife, breaking her forearm.

[Here the prosecutor wants all attention on Shaffer as he takes these violent actions.]

b. *To avoid focus on the person taking the action:*

> Acme Health Equipment was formed and began operation on April 22, 1995.

[Here the writer seeks to deflect attention away from the person who formed and ran Acme—Watson.]

c. *To focus on a person other than the one taking the action:*

> In the early morning of January 1, 1995, after attending several New Year's Eve parties, the defendant was stopped for a routine sobriety test.

[Here the writer is not so much trying to keep attention *away from* the police officer who stopped the defendant as to keep the focus *on* the defendant who was stopped.]

16. Consider placing favorable facts in main clauses and unfavorable facts in dependent clauses. Here is an example in a brief for Watson:

> Although Acme's business does compete with Carrolton [dependent clause], the competition extends to only three small product lines and impacts, at most, only 4 percent of Carrolton's profits [main clause].

If an unfavorable fact *must* go in the first or last sentence of a paragraph, place the dependent clause carrying the unfavorable fact toward the interior of the paragraph. So, for the first sentence of the paragraph, a dependent clause carrying an unfavorable fact should go at the end of the sentence. Which party's brief would contain this opening sentence?

> Acme competes directly with Carrolton in the three prohibited counties [main clause], although the competition extends to only three product lines [dependent clause]. [paragraph continues by setting out the facts of the competition].

For the last sentence of the paragraph, try putting the dependent clause at the beginning:

> [paragraph has set out the facts establishing the competition] Thus, while the competition extends only to three product lines [dependent clause], Acme directly and openly competes presently with Carrolton in the three prohibited counties [main clause].

17. Occasionally, when you want the reader to slow down and take in the significance of the material in all parts of the sentence, place a phrase

or dependent clause in the middle of the sentence, interrupting the reader's direct path from the subject directly to the verb.

> Watson, who admits that she is intentionally violating the terms of her covenant, asks this Court to use its equitable powers to relieve her of the consequences of her own actions.

Use this technique sparingly because it makes sentences less readable.

18. Use shorter sentences for material you want to emphasize and longer sentences for material you want to deemphasize.

> **LONGER SENTENCES FOR LESS EMPHASIS**
> On July 1, when Mr. and Mrs. Emilio and their daughter Ashley were driving south on Interstate 75 toward Valdosta, a car swerved across the median and hit the Emilio car. Mr. and Mrs. Emilio survived, although they were seriously injured. Their daughter, who had been riding in the back seat, died as a result of the injuries she sustained in the accident.

> **SHORTER SENTENCES FOR GREATER EMPHASIS**
> On July 1, Mr. and Mrs. Emilio were driving south on Interstate 75 toward Valdosta. Their daughter Ashley was riding in the back seat. A car swerved across the median and hit the Emilio car. Mr. and Mrs. Emilio survived, though seriously injured. Ashley, however, died.

E. Other Small-Scale Techniques

19. Compress the space you devote to unfavorable facts and expand the space you devote to favorable facts. The more material you provide about the favorable facts, the more emphasis they soak up.

20. Use detail to describe the material you want to emphasize. Limit the detail about unfavorable facts.

21. Use *visual* facts to describe favorable facts but avoid them for unfavorable facts. Visual images carry particular power for placing the reader, mentally, at the scene.

> On July 1, Mr. and Mrs. Emilio were driving south on Interstate 75 toward Valdosta. Their daughter Ashley was riding in the back seat. A car swerved across the median and slammed into the side of the Emilio car. The front of the other car hit the Emilio car at the left rear door, precisely where Ashley was sitting, strapped in by her seat belt.
>
> The force of the impact carried the other car's engine well into the passenger cabin of the Emilio car. It ripped Ashley from her seat belt, pinned her against the opposite door, and crushed her thoracic cavity.
>
> Mr. and Mrs. Emilio survived, though seriously injured. Ashley, however, died at the scene.

22. Short quotations (a sentence or two) or snippet quotations (just a word or a phrase) can be powerful. If the words of the witness or document are particularly helpful, quote them.

> Shaffer left the bar, declaring "I'm going to go talk to my wife, and she'll need a doctor before I'm through."

But avoid overquoting. Quoting too much results in a disjointed story and causes the most effective quotes to fade into the pack with the rest of the quotes.

23. When you can repeat key facts *unobtrusively*, the repetition serves to emphasize those facts. For example, the first sentence of the paragraph might summarize the facts and the remaining sentences could set out the facts in more detail. Or the beginning of a sentence might refer to the facts of the prior sentence as a transition.

> Marie Claxton, the expert witness who testified on behalf of Pyle, concluded that a reasonable and prudent lawyer would have checked the deed for easements. Claxton explained that deeds often contain restrictions that significantly affect the use of the property. She testified that any prudent lawyer would know that such restrictions are common. According to Claxton, Gavin's failure to check the deed fell below the standard of professional skill and diligence of a reasonable and prudent lawyer.

But don't just repeat particular facts, seemingly for no reason. That would bore and irritate the judge. Remember that the Argument section gives you a natural opportunity to repeat key facts.

24. Place unfavorable facts in a favorable or mitigating context. You can juxtapose the unfavorable fact with favorable facts or you can position the unfavorable fact in a context that negates some of the unfavorable inferences the fact might otherwise invite.

> JUXTAPOSING AN UNFAVORABLE FACT WITH FAVORABLE FACTS
> Although Acme does compete with Carrolton, the competition extends to only three small product lines and could impact, at the most, only 4 percent of Carrolton's profits.

> PLACING THE UNFAVORABLE FACT IN A MORE FAVORABLE CONTEXT
> While the demonstrations against the abortion clinic are disruptive to the family practice office, the McSwains cannot prevent the demonstrations; nor can they force the clinic to move until the clinic's lease term expires.

25. Humanize your client. The most important way to do this is by telling the story from the client's perspective, as your theory of the case will already accomplish. Include, where possible, hints of the client's feelings, responses, and motivations. Also, refer to your client by name, with honorary titles that communicate respect, like "Mr.," "Ms.," "Dr.," or "Officer."

Humanizing corporate clients is especially important. Remember that every story about a corporation is really a story about people. Identify the people who took the actions, and humanize those people. Portray them in a sympathetic light by putting their actions in context.

26. Generally, don't go out of your way to humanize opposing parties. Where there is no need to use the names of opposing individuals, consider using generic descriptions instead ("the officer," "the insurance agent," "the electrician"). Generic descriptions can be especially helpful where the description has unsympathetic connotations, such as "the finance company," "the insurance company," or "the corporate purchaser."

It's often best to avoid unnecessarily humanizing opposing parties, but the strategy might be different if you need to show outrageously bad behavior of one or more of the opposing parties. If so, humanize opposing parties so you can show their outrageous behavior.

27. Use graphic words, especially verbs, for facts you want to emphasize.

> The van *slammed into* [instead of "hit"] the taxi, and the force of the impact *splintered* [instead of "broke"] the driver's spine.

28. Avoid name calling. Name calling tells your reader that you don't have good facts, so you're resorting to derogatory characterizations.

29. Where possible, delete adverbs in favor of additional facts and more vivid verbs. Vivid verbs, alone, are much more powerful than a ho-hum verb ramped up with an adverb. Avoid such artificial intensifiers as "very" or "extremely."

Compare: "The defendant drove very fast" or "drove rapidly"
With: "The defendant careened through the intersection at 78 m.p.h."

30. Pay careful attention to common connotations of words. Choose helpful connotations and avoid unhelpful connotations.

> **A WORD WITH POTENTIALLY TROUBLING CONNOTATIONS**
> Mr. and Mrs. McMann were *anxiously* awaiting the birth of their first child.

["Anxiously" carries the connotation of worry. Use it if the connotation helps your theory, but avoid it if the connotation either impedes the theory or may distract the reader into wondering what they were worried about.]

> **AN OPTION WITH A BETTER CONNOTATION**
>
> Mr. and Mrs. McMann were *anticipating* the birth of their first child.

Finally, put the draft aside for a bit and then read it afresh. Read openly, as you hope the judge will do. Notice your reactions and fix anything that troubles you.

CHECKLIST FOR STATEMENT OF FACTS

LARGE-SCALE ORGANIZATION

1. Does the draft present the facts clearly? Is it easy to follow?
2. Does the organizational format let you put most of the unfavorable facts in the middle and put some of the favorable facts at the beginning and the end?[10]
3. Does the material at the beginning catch the judge's interest?
4. If the judge needs context, does the material at the beginning provide it?
5. Does the draft communicate your theory of the case?
6. Does the draft include all significant facts and all facts mentioned in your argument?
7. Does the draft include context, so the judge will understand the dispute and your theory of the case?
8. Does the draft put the procedural history at an appropriate spot?
9. Does the last paragraph have the feel of an ending?
10. Does the draft end with a sentence you want the judge to remember?

PARAGRAPH ORGANIZATION

11. Are your best facts on the outside ends of the paragraph and your least favorable facts in the middle?
12. Does the last phrase or clause of the paragraph include favorable information?
13. For facts you want to emphasize, are the paragraphs relatively short? For facts you want to neutralize, are the paragraphs longer?

TECHNIQUES WITH SENTENCES

14. Are the sentences (except one or two carrying unfavorable facts) free of clutter?
15. Do the passive-voiced verbs serve a purpose? Are there any actions you'd like to deemphasize by changing to passive?
16. Where appropriate, are unfavorable facts in dependent clauses juxtaposed with more favorable facts or explanatory context or vice versa?
17. Do the shorter sentences carry favorable facts? Where appropriate, are the unfavorable facts in longer sentences?
18. Using different colored pens, circle the text of favorable topics and the text of unfavorable topics. How does the total allocation of space to each compare?
19. Notice where you've used detail and visual images. Notice where you haven't.
20. Does each quotation really help?
21. If you've used the technique of repetition, is it too obvious?

---

10. The theory-of-the-case format is an intentional exception to this principle.

22. How have you referred to your client? To the opposing parties?
23. At spots where you're presenting favorable material, can you replace ho-hum words (especially verbs) with more powerful or graphic synonyms?

EXERCISE 22-1

Critiquing a Statement of Facts
Here are two basic Statements of Facts on the Watson covenant not to compete issue. Each fact statement has strengths. Neither is perfect. Evaluate each, identifying what works well and what could be improved.[11]

Recall from Chapter 19 that one formulation of the governing rule of law is:

A covenant not to compete is enforceable if all of the following elements are reasonable:

A. the kind of activity that is restrained;
B. the geographic area where it is restrained; and
C. the time period of the restraint.

Another formulation of the rule is:

To be enforceable, a covenant not to compete must be reasonable. Factors for deciding reasonableness are:

A. the needs of the restraining party;
B. the needs of the public;
C. the needs of the restrained party; and
D. any other relevant circumstances.

Which rule formulation does the drafter of each Statement of Facts seem to have in mind?

Statement of Facts on Behalf of Carrolton

STATEMENT OF FACTS

This is an action to enforce the terms of a covenant not to compete. On Dec. 1, 2015, the Defendant sold Carrolton Company to Richard Meyers, Andrea McPhane, and James Rey ("Purchasers") for $220,000. The sale included not only Carrolton's inventory and accounts receivable, but also the company's good will in the community. As part of the contract of sale, the Defendant promised that she would not compete with Carrolton for the three years immediately following the sale. The covenant covers only Quincy, Herring, and Gawin Counties, the three counties closest to Carrolton's office.

---

11. For purposes of this exercise, record citations have been omitted.

The covenant not to compete was an integral part of the Defendant's sale of Carrolton to the Purchasers. Carrolton retails in-home health care products in the Kinston, Georgia, area. Through her ownership of Carrolton, the Defendant had been engaged in the retail sales of health care products in the Kinston area for fifteen years. On behalf of Carrolton, she had made and maintained the sales contacts necessary to a successful retailer of those products. Her contacts and ongoing relationships with physicians and customers were part of the good will for which the Purchasers paid. Thus, these contacts and relationships were a critical part of the sale of the business. The covenant prohibits the defendant from making sales contacts for in-home health care products in the three counties that comprise the heart of Carrolton's marketing area.

After the Defendant sold Carrolton to the Purchasers, the Defendant remained with the company, employed as Carrolton's General Manager. She held that position of trust for fourteen months after the sale. On February 21, 2017, the Defendant left her position as Carrolton's General Manager and immediately opened a competing business one mile from Carrolton's office. Since that date, the Defendant has been making sales contacts for health care products in the three prohibited counties, in direct competition with Carrolton. The Purchasers have filed this action seeking to enjoin the Defendant's continued breach of the covenant not to compete.

Statement of Facts on Behalf of Watson

STATEMENT OF FACTS

In 2000, Sharon Watson founded Carrolton Company, a retailer of in-home health care equipment in Kinston, Georgia. Before Carrolton opened, residents of Kinston and the surrounding area had to travel seventy-five miles to the nearest retailer of health care equipment. The lack of a nearby health care equipment retailer was particularly problematic for the Kinston community because people needing in-home health care equipment are among those least able to make a seventy-five-mile trip to purchase that equipment. With Carrolton's opening, area residents had local access to the health care equipment they needed.

As the only retailer of in-home health care equipment in the area, Carrolton did a large volume of business. Ms. Watson believed that Carrolton's virtual monopoly brought with it an obligation not to take advantage of her customers. Thus, she used a markup of only 35 percent to ensure that her customers paid fair prices. She kept the business responsive to customer needs, making diligent efforts to fill special orders and maintaining close communication with local physicians. She made certain that Carrolton was a concerned and responsible commercial citizen of the community.

In early 2015, a group of Atlanta investors approached Ms. Watson about the possibility of buying Carrolton. Over the next few months the parties discussed the terms of a possible sale. During these conversations, Ms. Watson expressed concern about how the business, still a virtual monopoly, would be run.

In response to these concerns, the investors suggested that Ms. Watson remain with the company as General Manager and continue to manage the operation. The investors explained that they would not want Carrolton's fundamental operating policies to change, and Ms. Watson's continued management would be a way to continue the company's successful marketing approach. They explained that Ms. Watson's approach was so important to them that they would like the transaction to include the covenant that Ms. Watson would not leave Carrolton to compete in the local market for at least three years. Ms. Watson agreed, and on Dec. 1, 2015, after fifteen years of building the business, Ms. Watson sold Carrolton to its present owners. The terms of the sale placed Ms. Watson in the position of General Manager. While the contract did not expressly state the reason for the terms, the parties had always discussed Ms. Watson's continued service and noncompetition covenant as a method to maintain continuity of management philosophy. The covenant prohibited Ms. Watson from competing with Carrolton's new owners in the three counties that make up Carrolton's virtual monopoly.

Within a month after the sale, Carrolton's new owners began implementing management changes. They issued new pricing policies, raising the company's markup on its product lines. They ordered Ms. Watson to lay off one of Carrolton's only two other employees, and they eliminated most special orders. Eliminating these special orders effectively blocked the access of area customers to any health care products not a part of Carrolton's regular inventory.

In response to Ms. Watson's protests, the owners argued that these new policies maximized efficiency and company profits. They maintained that customer complaints were not important since without Carrolton, customers would have no local access to health care equipment at all.

On Feb. 21, 2017, after repeated attempts to persuade Carrolton's new owners to rescind their new policies, Ms. Watson left her position at Carrolton. Believing that Carrolton's owners had breached their assurances that Carrolton would continue being responsive to its customer's needs, Ms. Watson formed Acme Health Care. Ms. Watson incurred $75,000 in personal debt to open Acme, mortgaging her home to secure the loan. In the first two years of business Acme will do well to break even. During that time, Ms. Watson will have to make loan payments from her personal savings.

Although Ms. Watson hopes that one day Acme will represent a viable customer alternative to Carrolton, presently Acme competes with Carrolton in only three product lines: respiratory equipment, diabetic monitoring equipment, and wheelchairs. Even in these lines, Acme's business is just beginning. Presently, Acme carries only the products of the two leading manufacturers in these product lines. During the next nineteen months (the remaining term of the covenant not to compete), Acme cannot expect to attract more than 30 percent of Carrolton's business in these product lines. Acme will have no impact on Carrolton's virtual monopoly over the twenty-two other product lines Carrolton sells.

Even if Acme meets with phenomenal success during the next nineteen months, Carrolton will still make healthy profits. During the remaining covenant term, Acme poses no realistic threat to Carrolton's business. Acme's potential threat to Carrolton is the potential end to Carrolton's virtual monopoly over the in-home health care market in the Kinston area. That threat to Carrolton's market position would arise, if at all, long after the covenant has expired.

CONVERTING THE WORKING DRAFT TO A BRIEF

CHAPTER 23

CONVERTING THE DRAFT TO A BRIEF

Once you have a solid working draft of the facts and your arguments, it's time to put together the brief itself. That means it's time to do these things:

- finalize Umbrella sections
- double-check the order of the arguments
- finalize the point headings and subheadings
- add the brief's remaining components

We'll begin with finalizing the Umbrella sections. You might have roughed out your Umbrella section(s) as you worked on your early draft (see Chapter 18). If so, use this next section to revise. If not, use it to insert them now.

I. UMBRELLA SECTION

For a single-issue brief where the judge needs no context, you might not need an Umbrella section. But for most briefs, an Umbrella section can serve important functions. It can explain your organizational choices so the judge will have a road map. Also, by providing context, the Umbrella section can be another tool for persuasion. Ideally, the brief should *teach* the judge your argument. Most of us learn best when we have a context for new information. An Umbrella section can provide that context.

An Umbrella section should be concise—no more than one or two paragraphs. It introduces the sections that follow, so you can use an Umbrella section at the beginning of the Argument section (before the first Roman numeral) and to introduce subparts within a Roman numeral. Here's what an Umbrella section usually does:

- summarizes the umbrella rule of law
- explains the status of any relevant elements you *won't* discuss
- asserts the ruling you seek on the elements you *will* discuss
- identifies the relevant standard of review, if any
- explains the order in which the points will be presented, if helpful

1. Summarize the rule and cite the controlling authority defining the rule. The summary should be complete enough to give the judge a quick, clear overview of the relevant parts of the rule. Include any other principles that favorably affect the functioning of the rule, such as presumptions, burdens of proof, or policy leanings.

2. Explain the status of any elements *not* discussed in the brief. Your argument might omit some of the elements either because those elements are undisputed or not at issue at this stage in the litigation. If the status of these undiscussed elements might be initially unclear to the judge, clarify their status here. If the uncontested elements favor your client, say so here.

What if the element favors the opposing party, and *you* don't contest it? In other words, what if the rule contains elements on which you have no reasonable argument? Consider conceding those elements here, at the outset of the argument, so you can earn valuable credibility points. A concession implies that your argument on the *contested* elements is legitimate, because you've been straightforward enough to concede the *uncontested* elements.

3. For the elements your brief *will* discuss, assert the correctness of the ruling you seek. You can add a one- or two-sentence persuasive summary of your argument on each element.

4. For an appellate brief, identify the relevant standard of review, especially if it's favorable. If the standard of review doesn't have its own labeled section, you can put it here. But if you expect the standard to be disputed, consider making it a subheading unto itself.

5. If helpful, explain the order of the arguments. If you think the judge may resist your chosen order, explain the choice.

EXERCISE 23-1

Labeling the Components of the Umbrella Section
Here is an example of a prosecutor's Umbrella section. Some of the information is placed before the first point heading and some is placed before the first subheading. Notice the information included in these paragraphs.

ARGUMENT

To convict the defendant of burglary, the jury must find that the defendant (1) broke and (2) entered (3) the dwelling (4) of another (5) in the nighttime (6) with the intent to commit a felony therein. [citation] The defendant has conceded the first four of these elements. The defendant challenges only whether the breaking and entering occurred in the night-time and whether the defendant had formed the requisite intent when he entered the dwelling. This brief will show that the expected trial evidence establishes these final two elements as well.

I. THE BURGLARY INDICTMENT SHOULD NOT BE QUASHED BECAUSE THE EVIDENCE WILL PROVE THE NIGHTTIME AND INTENT ELEMENTS.

To defeat a motion to quash the indictment, the state need only show that, after considering the expected trial evidence, a reasonable jury could find each challenged element proven. [citation] The state's expected trial evidence more than meets this standard.

A. The Evidence Will Show That the Crime Occurred in the Nighttime.
[rule explanation and rule application on nighttime element]

B. The Evidence Will Show That the Defendant Intended to Commit a Felony When He Entered the House.
[rule explanation and rule application on intent element]

II. CHOOSING AN ORDER FOR THE ARGUMENTS

A. Ordering Point Headings

Your draft already has working point headings, but now consider the *order* in which they appear. The working draft might already have them in an order that works perfectly well, but just take a few moments to double-check. While no one right order exists, the most common choices for ordering point headings are (1) by strength on the law, (2) by strength on the equities, and (3) by the reader's priorities.

1. Strength on the Law

If one or two points are stronger on the law than the others, you'll nearly always want to put the strongest points first. You already have a good idea why. The judge's attention is greatest at the beginning and begins to drop off as the argument proceeds. Judges are busy and want to see the strongest arguments first. What's more, judges usually presume that the strongest argument is first, so they assume, before they even read further, that the later arguments are weaker.

2. Strength on the Equities

Some arguments rely primarily on rules of *law* and some rely primarily on the equities, that is, on *facts* that speak to the judge's sense of justice. If your points are of relatively equal legal strength, you might choose to order them according to their equitable (factual) strength. Identify which is which by asking yourself, "Which of these points really sounds like an appeal to justice? Which convinces me that my client *should* win, not just that she is *supposed* to win on the law?"

If you have a point that relies heavily on the equities, you'll want to capitalize on those equities. You can do that in two ways: by putting the point strongest on the equities first or by putting it last.

Putting it first wouldn't be a mistake. The reasons are obvious. But strange as this might sound, sometimes you can capitalize more effectively on a justice argument by putting it last. This makes more sense when you remember that the judge will read the fact statement before reading the argument section. In Chapter 22 we saw that a brief can make an argument implicitly (especially an equitable one) with a well-written fact statement. That section tells the story of the events that led to the pending issues. It makes no express legal argument. Yet it might well be the section with the most persuasive potential. A well-written fact statement could let you present the judge with the equities even earlier than the first legal argument.

If so, putting the justice argument last has advantages. It lets the favorable facts convince the judge before you make the express argument. Because the fact statement doesn't seem like a legal argument, the judge's level of skepticism isn't as high there. And implying the justice argument in the fact statement invites the judge to think of the justice argument herself, before you make it. As you'll recall from Chapter 17, a reader is more persuaded by a position she thinks she reached herself than by a position first argued by someone else. Then, when the judge reads the justice argument at the end of the Argument section, it will just seem to confirm what she already thought. And of course, placing the equitable argument last capitalizes on the principle of recency—the idea that we remember best what we've encountered most recently.

3. Your Reader's Priorities

Occasionally your brief will have a point heading with priority in the judge's mind, perhaps because of a judicial preference for basing a decision on some kinds of legal rulings rather than on others. For instance, courts normally decide issues on jurisdictional grounds first, on procedural grounds second, and on substantive grounds last. Judges often prefer to decide issues on narrow grounds rather than on broad grounds. When both a constitutional ground and a nonconstitutional ground are dispositive, constitutional jurisprudence requires courts to decide as many of the issues as possible on the nonconstitutional ground.

Take these judicial preferences seriously. If the issues with priority for the judge also happen to be your strongest arguments, your decision is easy. If your argument on the judge's priority issue is weak, you'll have to decide whether you can afford to lead with it. Usually your best choice will be to place your strongest points first, but to use an Umbrella section to assure the judge that your argument will address the other point as well. Of course, you won't announce that you've placed that point last because your argument on it is weak. Instead, explain that the argument on the first point is so dispositive that it might not be necessary to consider the remaining point.

B. Ordering Subheadings

In addition to express persuasion, subheadings have three primary functions. They provide the judge with an easily identifiable road map. They let the judge pause for a moment, and thus invite increased attention levels. They make visible the persuasive rule structure you formulated.

The working draft has already identified the primary subheadings. Now, as you convert the working draft to the Argument section, order subheadings of equal rank according to the organizational principles described above for point headings. If the discussion under a subheading is long or complex, consider subdividing further to help the judge follow the argument.

III. CONVERTING WORKING HEADINGS TO THE BRIEF'S POINT HEADINGS

In the working draft, the headings guided you in drafting the argument. In the brief, they also serve as a persuasive tool. Headings persuade if they state your position in compelling language. The judge is likely to read the point headings and subheadings first, either in a Table of Contents or by paging through the body of the Argument itself. If so, the headings provide a quick, persuasive summary of your entire argument.

Converting your working headings to the final headings takes two steps: adding the key facts and law and editing for readability and persuasion.

A. Adding the Key Facts

The final version of the point headings ideally should refer to the key facts entitling your client to the desired result. Think of the point heading in halves, as you began to do in Chapter 18. The first half asserts the ruling you want, in terms that state its correctness. The second half identifies your best facts on that issue. The second half of the point heading implicitly identifies the part of the rule at issue. Here is an example:

The burglary charge should be dismissed

[Identifying the ruling you seek and asserting its correctness.]

because

the testimony of the bartender and other bar patrons establishes that Mr. Shaffer arrived at the house earlier than thirty minutes after sunset.

[Identifying the key facts and how they establish the correctness of the ruling.]

If the point heading must cover more than one element, adding the key facts for all the elements in one sentence along with the other required information can be unworkable. If so, you can move the facts for each element into the subheading dealing with that element. For example, here are the prosecutor's revised headings in a brief that must argue three elements. Because the prosecutor must win on all three, the point heading covers all three, with separate *sub*headings for each:

I. THE INDICTMENT'S BURGLARY CHARGE SHOULD BE AFFIRMED BECAUSE THE EVIDENCE AT TRIAL WILL ESTABLISH ALL ELEMENTS OF BURGLARY.

    A. The evidence will show that the crime occurred in the nighttime because it occurred at 6:45 P.M., more than thirty minutes after sunset.

    B. The evidence will show that the defendant intended to commit a felony when he entered the house because he alluded to his intent to batter Mrs. Shaffer before he left the bar for her home.

    C. The evidence will show that the house was not the defendant's dwelling because he had waived his claim to the premises and did not retain any right of access.

In summary, try to include in the final version of the point heading (or the combination of the point heading and its subheadings) the following information:

- that your client should win on the issue
- some reference to the legal rule
- the key facts

After you try to pack all this information into one sentence, you'll probably need to edit for readability and persuasion. The next two sections will tell you how to tame unmanageable point headings.

EXERCISE 23-2

Evaluating the Content of Point Headings

Review the facts set out in Chapter 18, Exercise 18-1. Then read the following versions of the "consent" point heading for Foodman's brief. Identify the point heading that contains each component for a complete point heading. Identify the best point heading and explain why.

> a. Carson consented to Foodman's representation of Janoff when he did not respond to Foodman's letter.
> b. The motion to disqualify should be denied because Carson did not respond to Foodman's letter.
> c. The motion to disqualify should be denied because Carson consented to the representation.
> d. The motion to disqualify should be denied because Carson's failure to respond to Foodman's letter constituted consent to the representation.

B. Editing For Persuasion

Before you make your final edits, consider these rhetorical strategies:

1. Affirmative language versus negative language.   Most briefs focus on certain conduct: Was it lawful? Proper? Desirable? You'll articulate the client's position either by using affirmative language or negative language. In addition to being more readable, affirmative language often is more persuasive and appealing than negative language. Here are examples of two point headings, one using affirmative language and one using negative language.

Negative: Carrolton's Motion for Summary Judgment should be granted because Watson is unable to show that the terms are unreasonable or that she has not breached those terms.

Affirmative: Carrolton's Motion for Summary Judgment should be granted because the terms of the covenant not to compete are reasonable and the uncontested facts establish Watson's breach.

Notice how much better the second version is—how easy to read and understand.

2. Varying the structure of the point heading.   The point heading structure described in this chapter is the easiest structure for learning to draft a readable point heading. It begins with the relief you want and follows with the supporting facts and law. After you've had a little practice with drafting point headings, however, you can vary the formula and sometimes achieve a more persuasive version. For example, consider these versions of the Shaffer heading. What differences in effectiveness do you notice?

VERSION 1

The burglary charge against Mr. Shaffer should be dismissed because the alleged breaking and entering occurred at 6:15 P.M., which was earlier than thirty minutes after sunset.

VERSION 2

Because the alleged breaking and entering occurred at 6:15 P.M., which was earlier than thirty minutes after sunset, the burglary charge against Mr. Shaffer should be dismissed.

VERSION 3

The alleged breaking and entering occurred at 6:15 P.M., which was less than thirty minutes after sunset, and therefore the burglary charge against Mr. Shaffer should be dismissed.

Tinker with the structure of the point heading until you are satisfied that it is as persuasive as it can be.

3. Phrasing alternative arguments.   When you have more than a single point heading, one or more might be an alternative argument—an argument presented in case the judge doesn't agree with the first argument. The trick here is to avoid reducing the credibility of the first argument by making the alternative argument. Here is an example that falls into this trap. Can you see why the second point heading undercuts the first?

I. THE LAW OF THIS STATE DOES NOT ALLOW RECOVERY FOR THE WRONGFUL DEATH OF A FETUS, EVEN IF THE FETUS IS VIABLE AT THE TIME OF THE INJURY.

II. THE LAW OF THIS STATE ALLOWS RECOVERY FOR THE WRONGFUL DEATH OF ONLY A *VIABLE* FETUS.

Rather than following a strong argument with a second argument that seems to undercut it, state alternative arguments in terms that *assume the correctness* of the first argument. One way to do this is to reaffirm the first argument expressly, like this:

I. THE LAW OF THIS STATE DOES NOT ALLOW RECOVERY FOR THE WRONGFUL DEATH OF A FETUS, EVEN IF THE FETUS IS VIABLE AT THE TIME OF THE INJURY.

II. EVEN IF CASE LAW COULD BE READ TO PERMIT A CLAIM FOR THE DEATH OF A FETUS, THE FETUS WOULD HAVE TO HAVE BEEN VIABLE.

Can you see how the second point heading strengthens the first rather than weakening it? The second point heading uses the subjunctive form of the verb ("could" instead of "can"). The subjunctive form implies that the proposition it's describing *isn't true*. When the judge reads the first clause of this point heading ("Even if case law could be read to permit a claim") a little voice seems to add "but it can't." For example, if someone says "if I were you," it's clear that the speaker is *not* the listener. The speaker is simply imagining an untrue scenario. After the phrase "If I were you," a little implied voice says "but I'm not." For an even easier example, consider this familiar phrase:

If I were a rich man . . .

The verb "were" is telling the reader that the writer is *not* a rich man. The writer is imagining a hypothetical situation *other than reality*. Here are some examples of subjunctive verb forms:

If the plaintiff's argument were true, . . .
Even if the defendant had been drunk, . . .
Even if the employer could have anticipated the problem . . .

Notice that each of these examples implies that the postulated hypothetical isn't correct. The plaintiff's arguments aren't true. The defendant wasn't drunk. The employer couldn't have anticipated the problem.

C. Editing For Readability

The most important quality of a persuasive point heading is readability. Adding all the information we've discussed can produce a long, complex, and obtuse sentence. But the judge can't agree with a proposition she can't understand. And readability is especially important for point headings because the traditional format for point headings (all caps) already hinders readability.[1]

The best editing techniques for simplifying and clarifying a monster point heading are already set out in Chapter 15. Here are some of the most important:

1. *Keep the subject and the verb close together.* In other words, avoid intrusive phrases and clauses interrupting the flow of the sentence. Either eliminate them or move them to the beginning or the end.

2. *Avoid nominalizations.* Remember that nominalizations are verbs pretending to be nouns. "Investigate" is a verb, but "investigation" is a nominalization. Nominalizations often require more words and make sentences less clear.

3. *Avoid unnecessary passive-voiced verbs.* Passive-voiced verbs make the sentence's subject something other than the actor. Like nominalizations, passive verbs often require more words and make sentences less clear.

4. *Keep the facts and reasoning at the end of the sentence.* Placing the desired result first and the facts and reasoning second generally produces a more readable point heading.

5. *Avoid negatives.* Negatives, especially multiple negatives, can make a sentence harder to understand.

6. *Use other techniques from Chapter 15 for reducing the number of words.*

---

1. If your court rules, professor, or supervising attorney agree, don't use all-caps for point headings. This book uses them only because that's the traditional format.

Sometimes it's just not possible to include everything and still have a readable point heading. If you've tried all these editing techniques and still have a problematic point heading, you might have to remove one of the items of information (generally either the key facts or the relief requested). Decide which to sacrifice based on persuasiveness. If the key facts are particularly persuasive, remove the relief requested. Usually the judge can find the requested relief elsewhere, including in earlier sections. As a last resort (and only then), remove the facts. An easily readable point heading that asserts the party's legal argument but lacks supporting facts is more persuasive than a point heading that includes the facts but can't be understood.

EXERCISE 23-3

Editing Headings for Readability

Edit these headings to make them more readable. Use the techniques identified in the prior section and in Chapter 15.

1. It is clear that Crawford's actions of sitting peacefully in the parking lot of an open store, entering the store and leaving therefrom without incident, and driving lawfully out of the parking lot do not give rise to a reasonable, articulable suspicion of criminal activity to make a valid stop of said defendant.

2. The Defendant's Motion to Dismiss should be granted in as much as the contract involved provided that the escrow account under consideration could be closed by the escrow agent at the point in time when at least three days have passed from the date the notice of default was issued by the lender.

3. The Motion to Attach Assets should be denied because the Court should take into consideration the defendant's reduced line of credit and the unavailability of other sources for cash for the purpose of operating the business during the litigation in this matter.

4. The Motion for Summary Judgment filed by the Defendants, Mr. and Mrs. Carillo, should not be denied due to the fact that the evidence will show that the injured child understood the danger involved in a trampoline.

5. There is no reasonable, articulable suspicion to justify a stop of Salavar where the testimony of the officer is contradicted on virtually every point, where the officer has no facts to support a claim of criminal activity, and where the officer only witnessed Salavar's car in an area of criminal activity and therefore the Defendant's Motion to Dismiss should be granted.

6. The leased premises, which are subject to the constant threat of very disruptive demonstrations, are not suitable with regard to the purpose for which they were leased, and therefore the lessees have been constructively evicted.

7. A minor who induces another to enter into a contract with him by making a false representation of his age is estopped from a disaffirmance of the contract if the other party demonstrated reasonable and justifiable reliance on the minor's representation.

IV. FORMATTING THE BRIEF

At long last, it's time to add the remaining sections. Refer to the instructions you received with your assignment, to section III of Chapter 17, and to the sample briefs in Appendices D, E, and F. Draft all the components your finished brief will contain. For formatting information, follow first the applicable court rules and your law firm's or professor's instructions. To whatever extent they don't contradict your other instructions, follow these guidelines:

1. Caption. Use all caps for the court's name, the parties' names, and the document title. Use initial caps for the parties' procedural titles (Plaintiff, Appellant, Defendant, Appellee).

2. Components. Center and underline the titles of the components of the brief (for example, Question Presented, Statement of the Case, Argument, Conclusion). Use all caps. Some court rules require the Question Presented to appear on a page by itself.

3. Point headings. If you're using traditional formatting, you'll use all caps for the point headings (those marked by Roman numerals). If you have some flexibility, avoid all caps, which are hard to read. In either event, single-space the point headings. Some writers center them, but that can make a long point heading even harder to read. A better choice might be to use the full width of the line so the reader isn't confronted with a block of capital letters resembling a ten-story building.

4. Subheadings. Subheadings should be indented one tab space and single-spaced, using initial caps.

5. Table of Contents. Include section titles (such as Question Presented, Statement of the Case, Argument, Conclusion), point headings, and all subheadings.

6. Text. Briefs should be double-spaced except where otherwise indicated (for example, in a block quote). Use one space between sentences. Don't justify

the right margin. Use a proportional font. Page numbers should be centered at the bottom of the page.

———————————

Now, with all the brief's components in place, you're almost done. Take just one last look for final editing, as the next chapter describes.

REVISING TO ACHIEVE A FINAL DRAFT

CHAPTER 24

EDITING THE BRIEF

Now that you have a complete draft of the brief, turn your attention to editing. Put the document aside for a day or two, if you can, and try to read the document with fresh eyes. Seek feedback from a colleague if collaboration is permitted by your assignment. Before you go further in this chapter, return to Chapters 14 and 15. Use those chapters as checklists to edit your usage, style, citation form, and quotations. Once you have completed those tasks, edit the following aspects of your brief.

I. PERSUASIVE STYLE

A. Degree of Formality

Customarily, a brief reflects professional formality. This means, for instance, that the document normally doesn't contain contractions, slang, or humor.[1] It normally shouldn't contain references to you, the judge, or opposing counsel unless the references are necessary for the legal discussion of the issues. For examples of traditional professional formality, review the level of formality used in the sample briefs in Appendices D, E, and F.

---

1. Unless, of course, the document is quoting another speaker or writer and the substance of the quotation is legally relevant.

B. Competence and Clarity

Communicating clearly and convincing the judge of your competence are two of an advocate's most important persuasive techniques. In addition to the items contained in Chapters 14 and 15, here are four editing strategies to increase clarity and send the message of competence:

1. Tabulate. When your document deals with several items (such as elements of a rule, factors, guidelines, categories of facts), consider tabulating the items:

> A lawyer has a responsibility to undertake legal service in the public interest. Among the possible avenues of service are (1) free or reduced-fee representation of the poor; (2) free or reduced-fee representation of public service organizations; (3) participating in activities designed to improve the legal system; or (4) financially supporting legal services programs.

Tabulating helps the judge navigate through the substance of your text. It also demonstrates that you are controlling the substance rather than the other way around. The judge will be more willing to follow you along your line of reasoning if she finds you an effective leader.

2. Where helpful, create shortened forms of reference. This is another technique for sending the message that you are in control of the material. Introduce the shortened reference at the earliest feasible occasion, and maintain consistency of reference from then on. If you will use several shortened references, consider a paragraph or footnote early in the text introducing all of them.

> This brief will refer to Defendants Carter, Colham, Tellerhoff, and Winston, in combination, as "the employers," and to Defendants Allen, Rakestraw, and Vernon, in combination, as "the employees." The brief also refers to 42 U.S.C. § 2000e-17 by its popular name "Title VII," and to 42 U.S.C. § 1983 by its popular reference "Section 1983."

Where possible, select a shortened reference that will facilitate your theory of the case. Avoid references that will work at odds with your theory of the case.

3. Add explanatory parentheticals to citations. Go back through your citations to find any authorities that could use an explanatory parenthetical.[2] A citation might profit from a parenthetical if you aren't discussing its facts and reasoning in the text. Here are examples of such times:

- when you're citing simply as additional authority for a point primarily supported in some other way
- when you're citing as support for a minor and uncontested proposition

You can use the parenthetical to quote a nugget of language or to highlight examples of relevant facts from the cited case. Here are two examples:

---

2. ALWD Citation Manual, R. 12.11; Bluebook, R. 10.6.

a. Following a discussion of several cases dealing with the evidentiary significance of racial statements by supervisors:

> *See also* Slack v. Havens, 7 F.E.P. 885, 885 (S.D. Cal. 1973) *aff'd as modified*, 522 F.2d 1091 (9th Cir. 1975) ("Colored folks are hired to clean because they clean better.").

b. Where the ineffectuality of serving process by trickery is a minor and uncontested point:

> Courts have held that a defendant who resides out of state cannot be lured into the state by fraud or trickery and then served with process. *McClellan v. Rowell*, 99 So. 2d 653 (Miss. 1958) (petitioner told his ex-wife that his mother was dying and wanted to see the couple's child one last time); *Zenker v. Zenker*, 72 N.W.2d 809 (Neb. 1955) (plaintiff told defendant that his presence was needed to convey certain real estate).

4. Purge your document of vague references like these:

this matter	with regard to
it involves	it deals with
it pertains to	it concerns

Writing peppered with these phrases forces the reader to struggle to understand the reference and to wonder whether the writer is in control of the material. It's as if the writer is saying "There is some kind of relationship between these two things, but I'm not sure what it is, so I'll just point off into the fog." Instead, try to specify the relationship you're referring to. Here's a simple example:

Edit this: "The statute involves adverse employment actions based on gender."

Into this: "The statute prohibits adverse employment actions based on gender."

C. Tact and Good Judgment

Here are four "attitude" problems to watch for and edit out.

1. Don't tell a court what it "must" do or what it "cannot" do.   Use less confrontational language when referring to limits on the court's authority or power. For instance, avoid:

The Court must reverse the trial court's order.
The Court cannot grant the defendant's motion.
The Court is not permitted to consider subsequent negotiations.

Here are some better options:

   a. Shift the focus to a tactful statement of another court's error.

The lower court erred in ordering that . . .

   b. Use a passive-voiced verb to avoid identifying the court as the actor. Substitute "should" for "cannot." Switch to a permissive statement (what the court *should* do) rather than a prohibitory statement (what the court *shouldn't* do).

The defendant's motion should be denied . . .

   c. Focus on the rule that governs the issue rather than on the entity that must follow the rule.

The rule permits consideration of subsequent negotiations only where . . .

2. **Edit out signs of negative emotion.**   Cool reason is much more persuasive than sarcasm or anger. Cool reason says to the judge, "The law and the facts are on my side, so I don't have to be disturbed by the opposing side's position."

3. **Focus on the judge, not the opposing party or the opposing lawyer.**   A brief-writer's focus can be distracted by seeing the case as a battle with opposing parties or their lawyers. Don't let your day-to-day contact with the parties and their lawyers cause you to forget that the judge is the primary focus of your brief.

4. **Make a final check on your perspective, and moderate any exaggeration of the law or the facts.**   A necessary part of the advocacy process is the shift from an objective perspective to a partisan perspective. But you still must evaluate the final draft of the brief with an objective eye, being careful not to overstate the law or the facts. Remember that a judge who suspects that something has been exaggerated will doubt all the other points as well.

II. WRITING WITH CONFIDENCE

As you are first learning to write briefs, you're learning the basic requirements and expectations, and these things are complicated enough for your initial focus. But as you master those entry-level tasks, you can turn your attention to writing not only for technical compliance but also for interest and for confident tone. Writing with respectful confidence makes the judge more confident in your work.

   Writing with confidence is difficult to describe, but almost always, confident writing is interesting writing. Here are some characteristics shared by many of the best legal writers, but be careful not to overuse these techniques.

Also, take special care to ensure that your writing is otherwise without reproach.

- Interesting verbs (disrupts; highlights; eviscerates; frustrates; obscures; threatens; seized upon; abdicated; pioneered)
- Cultural references and commonsense metaphors (muddy waters; scapegoat; train wreck; marathon; a recipe for confusion)
- Slightly less formal language here and there (swamped; without blinking an eye; hoodwinked; the doctrine is dead and the time for its burial has come)
- Short, simple, slightly conversational language (pocket the profits; ride shotgun, recite the creed)
- Occasional very short sentences (This argument fails. Neither party so claims. The manager gave his word.)

As you develop more confidence and refine your rhetorical judgment, you may even be able to use a rhetorical question here and there, begin a few sentences with a conjunction, or even leave out a few words in a parallel structure. But for now, opt for the more conservative style. You'll soon know whether and when you can choose a more poetic style.

FINAL CHECKLIST

1. Look one last time at the court rules governing briefs. Does your brief comply with all of them?
2. Check the listings and page numbers in the Table of Contents. Are they still complete and accurate after the final edit?
3. Check the listings and page numbers in the Table of Authorities. Are they still complete, accurate, and in proper alphabetical order after the final edit?
4. Check the citations to the record in the Statement of Facts and in the rule application sections of the Argument. Confirm that any necessary additions to the record (such as affidavits to be filed simultaneously with the brief) are prepared and ready.
5. Confirm that any appendices are complete and attached to the brief.
6. Confirm that a proper Certificate of Service is appended.
7. Do a final check for spelling and typographical errors.
8. Sign the signature line, remembering that your signature constitutes your representation that the brief is not being submitted for any improper purpose, that the contentions are not frivolous, and that the facts alleged are consistent with the evidence.[3]

---

3. Fed. R. Civ. P. 11.

CHAPTER 25

ORAL ARGUMENT

This chapter and your first law school oral argument provide only a glimpse of actual appellate practice. Appellate lawyers must know much more than any introduction can provide, so consider taking a course in appellate practice and procedure. The first time you handle a case on appeal, you'll be glad to have had that important training.

The sections of this chapter are designed for an appellate oral argument in your legal writing class. In law practice, some details of presentation and formality might differ from those expected in a law school setting, but the fundamental concepts presented here will apply equally. So what are those fundamental concepts?

I. THE PURPOSE OF ORAL ARGUMENT

Before you plunge into preparing your oral argument, consider its purpose. An oral argument is not just an opportunity to say orally what you have already said in writing. If that were the purpose, judges would not waste your time or theirs. They'd just read the briefs and decide the case.

Rather, an oral argument is *an opportunity for the judges to ask you questions*. They want to clarify their understanding of your arguments. They want to give you a chance to alleviate their concerns about adopting the position you advocate. They want to have a conversation. As your only chance to speak directly with those who will decide your case, oral argument is an important opportunity.

Oral argument also gives you a chance to return the judges' attention to the big picture. You'll have the chance to emphasize the narrative themes and policy rationales that underlie your legal argument. These themes show not just how the law *does* support your position, but also why it *should*. Direct, eye-to-eye contact can be the best way to bring home the importance of those fundamental themes.

II. FORMALITIES AND ORGANIZATION OF ORAL ARGUMENT

First, become familiar with the formalities you'll encounter and the overall organization your argument should follow. Here is an overview of the oral argument:

1. Preliminary formalities.   Usually you'll be seated at counsel table, waiting for the judges to enter and call your case. A bailiff will announce the entry of the judges, perhaps with ritual language like this:

> Oyez, oyez, oyez. All rise. The First Circuit Court of . . . is now in session. All those with business before this Honorable Court may now draw near.

As soon as the bailiff begins this speech, stand up and remain standing until the judges are seated and the chief judge tells you to be seated. The chief judge will then call your case and ask if the lawyers are ready, saying something like this:

> The Court calls the case of *Giray v. Cole*. Is counsel for the appellant ready? . . . Is counsel for the appellee ready?

When the judge asks you if you are ready, stand up and say "Ready, Your Honor." The chief judge will then instruct counsel for the appellant to proceed.

2. The appellant's argument.   Counsel for the appellant goes first. You might be the only lawyer for the appellant, or you might have co-counsel arguing one of the issues. Use the following structure, leaving out the mention of co-counsel if you are arguing alone:

> May it please the Court. May name is Russell Stege, and along with my co-counsel, Susan Marks, I represent the Appellant, Paul Giray. I would ask the Court for permission to reserve two minutes for rebuttal. [Pause to allow the Chief Justice to respond.]
>
> Thank you, your Honor. Mr. Giray respectfully asks this Court to . . . [state in one or two phrases the ruling you seek, for example, "reverse the trial court's entry of summary judgment and remand the case for trial"].
>
> The issue(s) before the Court is/are whether . . . [state each issue in one sentence, phrased favorably to your side[1]]. I will argue the adverse possession issue, and Ms. Marks will argue the damages issue.

---

1. Use the same techniques you used to phrase favorably the Questions Presented in your brief. See Chapter 21.

Then give the court a short overview of the arguments you will make.

> Your Honors, Mr. Giray will show that the undisputed facts in this case simply are not adequate to establish the elements of adverse possession. [In two or three sentences, state a summary of your argument so the judges will have a sense of the arguments you will make and the order in which you will present them. This is also a good spot to introduce your narrative theme, as described in Section III below.]
>
> Your Honors, the facts are these: . . . [Inform the court of the relevant facts, and then begin the main section of your argument, as described in Section III.]

3. **Argument of co-counsel for the appellant.** If you are co-counsel arguing a second issue for the appellant, you'll argue next. Go to the podium as soon as your co-counsel leaves it. Don't wait for an invitation from the judges. If the judges are still writing or conversing when you arrive at the podium, wait until they are ready or until one of them tells you that you may begin. Then introduce yourself and identify your client, as the first lawyer did. You don't need to introduce your co-counsel from whom the court has already heard. Nor do you need to repeat the request to reserve time for rebuttal. Proceed to a short overview of the arguments you'll make:

> May it please the Court, my name is Susan Marks, and I also represent Paul Giray. I will argue the issue of the adequacy of money damages in this case. Your Honors, even if the undisputed facts were sufficient to establish a claim for adverse possession, an award of money damages would be more than sufficient in this case. [In two or three sentences, state a summary of your argument.]

Your co-counsel has already stated the facts, so you don't need to repeat them. Simply begin your legal argument, including your narrative theme. The rest of your argument should proceed just as described above.

4. **The appellee's argument.** Go to the podium as soon as counsel for the appellant steps away. If the judges are still writing or conversing, wait a moment until they are ready or until one of them tells you that you may begin. Then introduce yourself, your co-counsel, if any, and your client, just as the first lawyer did. As counsel for the appellee, you don't have a rebuttal, so you don't need to reserve any time. Then give the court a short overview of the arguments you'll make:

> May it please the Court, my name is Elizabeth Tunnesen, and along with Jason Kennedy, I represent Carol Cole. Ms. Cole requests the Court to affirm the trial court's order granting summary judgment. Mr. Kennedy will argue the damages issue, and I will argue the adverse possession issue. I will show that the undisputed facts are more than sufficient to establish each element of adverse possession.

Give the court a short overview of the arguments you'll make and introduce your narrative theme. Counsel for the appellant has already provided the facts of the case, so don't repeat those facts. Add or clarify any *important* fact omitted from the appellant's fact statement.

> Ms. Cole agrees with the facts as stated by the Appellant. However, the Court should also be aware that . . . .

If you don't need to clarify or add an important fact, simply proceed to the rest of your argument, following the format described above.

5. Argument of co-counsel for the appellee. Your argument should follow the format described for the second lawyer for the appellant.

6. Concluding the argument. No matter whether you argue for the appellant or the appellee, you'll have to reach a graceful and persuasive ending while negotiating the constraints of the time cards (or some other mechanism for informing you of how much time remains). Have a prepared conclusion consisting of a short summary (three to five sentences) of your best points, phrased compellingly, and a request for the relief you seek:

> [A summary of your strongest arguments]. . . . Therefore, the appellant requests that the Court reverse the trial court's entry of summary judgment and remand the case for trial on the adverse possession claim. Thank you, Your Honors.

Try to be ready to begin your conclusion when the one-minute card goes up. When the "zero" card is raised, you may finish your sentence, but then you must stop. Simply say, "Thank you, Your Honors," and sit down. If you are in the middle of answering a judge's question when the zero card goes up, stop and say to the chief judge:

> Your Honor, I see that my time is up. May I finish answering Judge Nottingham's question and have a moment to conclude?

The chief judge will probably say "Yes." If so, finish your answer and take *no more than forty-five seconds* to deliver your conclusion. If the chief judge declines your request, simply say "Thank you, Your Honors," and sit down.

7. Rebuttal. After counsel for the appellee has finished arguing, one of the lawyers for the appellant will give a rebuttal. If you'll be delivering the rebuttal, listen carefully during the appellee's argument to identify a weak point or a point on which opposing counsel has damaged your case but which you can remedy with a strong, extremely brief rebuttal. When counsel for the appellee concludes, go to the podium and deliver your rebuttal in one to two minutes (however long you reserved), say "Thank you, Your Honors," and sit down. The goal is to make your point in a compelling way and to sit down without prompting further questioning from the bench. Have one rebuttal prepared in advance, and use this prepared rebuttal in case you panic and can't

put together a compelling rebuttal based on what you just heard in the appellant's argument.

III. THE CONTENT OF THE ARGUMENT

The following procedural facets of your case will be crucial. You must know how these concepts apply to your case and be able to phrase your arguments accurately, given that application.

1. The standard of review.   The standard of review governs how much deference the appellate court must give to the decision below. Review the material on the standard of review in Chapter 21. If the standard of review is favorable to your side, be especially sure to phrase your argument in its terms. If it's not favorable to your side, you might choose to omit it from your prepared remarks, but you'll need to be ready to deal with it, nonetheless, because your opponent will probably emphasize it. No matter how much you choose to emphasize the standard, be ready to respond clearly and succinctly to a judge's question regarding the appropriate standard.

2. The burden of proof.   Be sure you know the relevant burden of proof on the issue you're arguing. The burden of proof identifies the party who has the responsibility of proving the necessary facts in the trial court and persuading the court on the issues. Usually the plaintiff bears the burden of proving the elements of the cause of action, and the defendant bears the burden of proving an affirmative defense. On a procedural issue, the moving party often bears the burden. For example, on a motion to compel discovery, the moving party would bear the burden of proof. Check the authorities on your legal issue to be sure you know which party bears the burden of proving each aspect of the case.

3. The trial-level procedural posture.   Finally, your argument might be affected by the procedural posture of the trial-level decision being appealed. The trial-level procedural posture applied to the legal question when it was before the trial court, so the appellate court will be evaluating the trial court's decision given that procedural posture.

For example, if the appeal is from a ruling granting summary judgment, the question before the trial judge was whether the undisputed facts (the facts established before trial) were enough to decide the case before trial. The appellate court's job, then, is to decide whether the trial judge ruled correctly *on that legal question in that procedural posture.* An appellate judge doesn't decide what she would have done if she had been in the trial judge's shoes. She decides whether a reasonable judge could have made the ruling, even if the appellate judge would have made a different decision. In other words, she decides whether the trial judge's decision was supported by enough evidence.

Here's another example. If the appeal is from a judge's decision after a bench (nonjury) trial, the question is whether the facts in the trial record are sufficient to justify the ruling—in other words, whether a reasonable judge, after presiding over that trial, could have decided the case in the way this judge did. Once again, the appellate judge doesn't decide how she would have ruled. She decides whether a reasonable judge could have ruled as this judge did.

Check the authorities to be sure of the implications of your case's trial-level procedural posture, and frame your arguments and your answers with that posture in mind.

4. Themes.   Your case needs a theme, the overriding point of your argument. Ask yourself what's at stake from you client's perspective? What is this case about? Your theme should be the most persuasive big-picture point you have. Choose a narrative theme if the most powerful part of your argument is based on your client's compelling facts:

> Your Honors, this is a case about a record title-holder who sat by and watched his neighbor build a garage, knowing that the neighbor believed the garage to be properly located on his own land. Then, just as the garage was completed, the record title-holder told his neighbor that the garage was 6 inches over the property line and demanded that the neighbor tear it down.

If the most compelling point of your argument is a policy implication, select a theme based on that policy:

> Even if a minor is less than completely candid about his age, the law should still require a merchant to take the remarkably simple precaution of asking to see the minor's driver's license. Such a requirement does not burden the merchant at all, and it protects against the very real danger that a merchant might find it profitable to be too easily convinced of an eager young customer's age.

If the most compelling part of your argument is the strength of the law on your side, select a theme that capitalizes on this strength:

> Despite the plaintiff's admittedly sympathetic facts, the law in this jurisdiction could not be more clear. A wrongful death action simply cannot be sustained for the death of a nonviable fetus. The legislature of this state has expressly declared this to be the law, and no fewer than five rulings of the Supreme Court have agreed.

If the most compelling part of your argument is the procedural posture of the trial court decision on which the appeal is based, select a theme that keeps bringing the discussion back to that procedural posture:

> The defendant strenuously disagrees with the inferences the plaintiff asks the Court to draw from the affidavits. However, even if the affidavits did support the plaintiff's inferences, the fact remains that this case comes before the Court on appeal from a summary judgment ruling. The question is not whether the plaintiff's inferences are possible, or even whether they are the most likely, but rather whether they are the *only* possible inferences. Clearly they are not.

IV. PREPARATION

1. The Record.   Thoroughly know the facts in the record. Know them well enough that you can even cite to the page on which the most important facts appear. State the facts accurately. Don't overstate the facts, and don't state inferences as facts. If you misstate facts, you'll lose all credibility with the court, and if you misstate facts intentionally, you will have acted unethically.[2]

2. Outline your argument.   Usually the outline of your argument should mirror the large-scale organization of your brief. The first level of headings should articulate your position on each relevant element of the governing rule. Under each heading, note each argument you'll make on that point.

3. Prepare an argument folder.   Prepare a folder with your notes for oral argument. You can use a file folder and small index cards. Open the folder and use both sides for your opening and closing language (in case you panic) and for the outline of your argument. Also note any important facts you might need (like dates and numbers you might not remember).

Consider including two outlines, one for a cold bench (a bench that asks few questions) and one for a hot bench (a bench that leaves you little time for your scripted material). The outline for the cold bench is your expanded out-line—the one you'll use if the judges are quiet and you have time to present most of your prepared material. The outline for the hot bench is compressed into just the main points you want to make if you have only a few minutes. You can start with the expanded outline but shift to the compressed outline as necessary during the argument.

Reserve one area of the folder for the index cards. For each important case, statute, or regulation, summarize on a card the important information from that source and quote any key language. Tape the cards on top of each other with the bottom of each card protruding a quarter of an inch from beneath the card on top of it. Write the statute or case name on that bottom edge, so you can easily find the card you need. Tape the cards to the folder along the card's top edge, so the cards can be flipped up like an address file. Practice finding the information on the cards and in the other parts of the folder quickly and easily.

4. Script the entire opening, the conclusion, and your prepared rebuttal. You can't and shouldn't try to script the body of the argument, because you're hoping for a conversation with the judges. But you can script an opening and closing. Memorize it, but deliver it with full eye contact, as if you were not delivering a prepared script. This preparation will guarantee that you say what you want to say and that you say it smoothly and effectively. Although your

---

2. See Chapter 17.

extemporaneous responses might not always be smooth, your beginnings and endings can and should be both poised and persuasive.

5. Practice.   Practice delivering your argument to friends. Have the friends question you just as they would if they were the appellate judges. Practice at least five or six times, more if possible. Go through the whole argument each time, and then ask for feedback. Use these practice benches to improve both your knowledge of the case and the smoothness of your delivery.

6. Visit the courtroom.   Familiarize yourself with the room where you'll argue. Imagine yourself delivering your argument there, and remind yourself that you belong there, advocating for your client. Psychologically claim the space.

V. HANDLING QUESTIONS FROM THE BENCH

The most important purpose of oral argument is to answer the judges' questions, so get ready to provide those answers. Here are some points to guide your preparation.

1. Anticipate questions.   Ask yourself what you would want to know if you were a judge hearing the case. What parts of the argument would be hard to accept and why? What will your opponent argue? What key cases or statutes will the court be most concerned about? Pay close attention to the questions you receive in your practice rounds. Prepare your best answers for all these questions.

2. Attitude.   The judges will ask you questions and they'll often interrupt you to do it. This is part of the role of a judge. It's efficient and it saves you precious time. When a judge interrupts you, stop talking *immediately* and listen to what the judge is saying. Then answer the judge's question as best you can. Treat the question for what it is—a valuable opportunity to clarify a point about which the judge is concerned. Never appear to be rushing through the answer so you can get back into your prepared argument. The judge's question is much more important than your prepared argument.

The right to interrupt belongs only to the judge, however. Never interrupt a judge. No matter how badly you want to speak, wait patiently until the judge has finished speaking before you utter a sound.

3. Recognize types of questions.   You'll experience three basic kinds of questions:

- friendly questions,
- questions genuinely seeking clarification of information, and
- adversarial questions.

A *friendly question* is designed to help you. It's a sign that the judge is giving you a chance to present an argument or make an additional point. Be happy. A judge might want you to make a certain point primarily for the benefit of another judge, or a judge might simply be pleased to have thought of another point and might want to share it. Be sure to recognize a friendly question and to make use of the opportunity it gives you to agree with a judge and to articulate and validate the judge's point.

A question genuinely seeking information is an chance to help a judge who needs a point clarified. Again, be happy. Answer whatever the judge is asking. If you have an additional point to make about that subject, you can use this chance to make it, but only after you've answered the judge's question.

An adversarial question comes from a judge who is skeptical of your position. Most of the questions you receive might be adversarial, designed to test your arguments. Again, be happy. Despite their threatening nature, these are the questions you should welcome most. These are the questions that give you the chance to resolve the concerns that could stand in the way of winning. Often these questions will be phrased politely, but sometimes a judge will use an intimidating or even rude manner. Your job is to answer politely but firmly, ignoring the packaging of the question and responding only to its content. Never respond in anger, even if you are feeling angry. Remain outwardly calm and answer the question as best you can:

> Your Honor, I must respectfully disagree. In the *Jones* case, the Supreme Court did not hold that . . . . Rather, ... And this is precisely why . . . .

4. **Listen carefully to the question.**   You might find that your nervousness interferes with your ability to listen carefully to the question. This is a common and completely understandable problem for many of us as we first learn to be oral advocates. After you hear the first part of the question, you might assume you know what the judge will be asking, and you might stop listening as you begin scrambling to think of an answer. Yet you can't answer a question that you've misunderstood. When a judge begins to speak, remember to listen carefully to the whole question before you answer.

5. **Clarify the question.**   Sometimes you won't understand a question even when you've listened carefully. This could happen because you are nervous or because the judge hasn't articulated the question clearly. Admit that you did not understand the question, apologize, and ask the judge to repeat it. If you think that you might have understood it but you aren't sure, you can clarify your understanding: "Is Your Honor asking whether . . . ?"

6. **Begin with a clear, direct answer.**   The judge should know within roughly your first ten words what your answer to the question will be, so always begin with a very short, direct answer to the question in the form in which the judge posed it:

> "Yes, Your Honor."
> "No, Your Honor, I must respectfully disagree."
> "Your Honor, that has sometimes been the case, but not always."

Once you've given your short, direct response, explain the answer. The judge will give you much more latitude to explain if you've given the judge the courtesy of a direct answer first.

7. Returning to your prepared presentation. When you've finished answering a question, return immediately to your prepared presentation. Don't wait for the judge to respond or to give you permission to return to your prepared material. Try to find a way to connect the ending of your answer to an entry point into your argument so the answer seamlessly weaves you right back into your prepared material. But if you cannot think of a connection on the spot, it's fine to just return to your argument.

8. Handling questions on your co-counsel's issue. Sometimes a judge will ask you a question about the issue your co-counsel has already argued or will shortly argue. Try to answer it if you can, but qualify your answer by admitting that your co-counsel might be able to provide a better answer. This should minimize the chance that the judge will pursue the matter further.

> Your Honor, since *Home Finders* dealt with the issue of sufficiency of money damages, my co-counsel may be the best person to assist the Court on this question. However, I believe that the court there held that. . . .

9. Handling a question for which you don't have an answer. Your hard work should prepare you for most questions, but you might be asked a question that takes you by surprise. It has happened to everyone. A judge might ask you about an unexpected case or statute; about how your issue compares to a comparable issue in some other area of law; or about how some procedural practice would affect your position. Even experienced appellate attorneys aren't familiar with all aspects of the law. If you don't know the answer, admit it. Don't try to bluff your way through. Apologize and offer to find the answer and provide it to the court promptly after the argument concludes:

> Your Honor, I regret that I am not familiar with *Hatcher v. Norman*. However, if the Court allows, I will provide the Court with an answer to this question within 24 hours after today's argument concludes.

10. Agreeing when you can. Remember that you'll probably receive a friendly question here and there, so don't automatically disagree each time the judge engages you. You can even agree partially with the concerns underlying some adversary questions as well, but go on to show why that valid concern doesn't defeat your position.

> Yes, your Honor, I agree that this is a legitimate concern. However, . . .

11. Referring to earlier questions or comments from the bench. Remember the questions that were already directed to you or to your opponent. You can refer to them when appropriate in your argument. If a judge has asked you

a friendly question or made a friendly comment, you can refer to it later in the argument. You can also refer to the adversarial questions or comments directed to opposing counsel.

As Justice Bailey pointed out, ...

Use this technique sparingly though. Some judges might be irritated to hear their own words used in this manner more than once or, at most, twice during an argument.

VI. PRESENTATION

1. Dress.   Wear a conservative suit.

2. Body, hands, and eyes.   Stand straight, with your weight equally placed on both feet, and remain behind the podium. Maintain eye contact with the judges, and include the whole bench in that eye contact. Don't read your argument. Speak to the judges conversationally, looking down at your notes now and then. Lay your hands on the podium, and use them only moderately for occasional small gestures. Don't grip the podium. Don't put your hands in your pockets or clasp them behind your back.

3. Voice.   Speak at a moderate pace. Don't allow your nervousness to cause you to speak too quickly, but do speak with a degree of energy appropriate for discussion of an important matter about which you and your client care deeply. Speak firmly and loudly enough to be heard.

4. References.   Refer to the bench as "Your Honors" or "the Court." Refer to individual judges as "Your Honor" or "Justice [last name]." Refer to clients by their last name preceded by "Mr." or "Ms." or by other appropriate titles, such as "Dr." Refer to other lawyers as "counsel for Appellant/Appellee" or as "opposing counsel."

5. Nervousness.   Oral argument will probably make you a little nervous, but remember that judges are human beings. Like you, they are trying to do a hard job well, and they will sometimes fall short. Although they have more experience than you do at this point in your legal career, they probably remember when they did not. All they ask of you, and all you need ask of yourself, is to do your best.

APPENDICES

SAMPLE OFFICE MEMORANDUM

This office memo applies a three-element conjunctive rule to a set of facts. Notice that the predictions on the three elements reach different degrees of certainty. In addition to rule-based reasoning, it uses analogies, disanalogies, policy-based reasoning, and factual inferences. See if you can identify instances of each.

To:	Requesting Attorney
From:	Summer Clerk
Date:	November 9, 2005

Re: Beth Buckley; file # 756385; stolen car; whether Buckley can disaffirm purchase of car based on her minority

QUESTION PRESENTED

Can Buckley, a minor, disaffirm the purchase of a car when she misunderstood the sales agent's question and therefore accidentally misrepresented her age as eighteen?

BRIEF ANSWER

Probably yes. A minor can disaffirm a contract unless the minor's fraudulent misrepresentation induced the other party to rely justifiably on the representation. On Buckley's facts, a court would probably rule

-1-

that an innocent misrepresentation such as Buckley's is not fraudulent and therefore would not prevent a minor from disaffirming a contract. A court might also rule that the seller did not justifiably rely on Buckley's representation.

FACTS

Our client, Beth Buckley, is seventeen and a high school senior. She will turn eighteen on December 15. Two months ago she bought a used car for $3,000 from Willis Chevrolet. She paid cash, using the money she had saved from her summer job. Buckley purchased collision insurance for the car, but she did not insure against theft. Last week the car was stolen, and Buckley has asked what she can do about her loss.

When Buckley first looked at cars on the lot, the sales agent asked if she was old enough to buy a car. Buckley did not realize that she had to be eighteen to enter into a contract, even when paying cash. She thought the sales agent was asking whether she was old enough to drive, so she said "yes." The agent did not ask to see any identification and did not raise the subject of age again.

The next day Buckley returned to the lot, selected the car she wanted to purchase, and completed the transaction. She recalls "signing a bunch of papers," but she did not read them and does not know what they said. She says that the sales agent did not attempt to explain the documents. He simply showed her where to sign, and she signed on those lines. She does not know if she still has copies of the documents, but she will look among her papers and let us know.

DISCUSSION

I. Can Beth Buckley disaffirm the contract?

Generally, one who is a minor at the time of making a contract can disaffirm the contract within a reasonable time after reaching the age of majority. O.C.G.A. § 13-3-20 (1982); *Merritt v. Jowers*, 193 S.E. 238 (Ga. 1937). The rationale for the rule is the recognition that minors have not yet attained sufficient maturity to be responsible for the decisions they make, so the rule protects them from at least some of the consequences of bad decisions. *See generally White v. Sikes*, 59 S.E. 228 (Ga. 1907). However, a minor is estopped from disaffirming a contract if (a) the minor made a false and fraudulent representation of his or her age; (b) the contracting party justifiably relied on the minor's representation; and (c) the minor had reached the age of discretion. *Carney v. Southland Loan Co.*, 88 S.E.2d 805 (Ga. 1955). Thus, if Willis Chevrolet can establish these three elements, Buckley would be estopped from disaffirming the contract. Because the first element is the most problematic in Buckley's case, the memo will discuss it first.

A. Buckley's unintentional misrepresentation of her age probably is insufficient to constitute fraudulent misrepresentation. ↗First element

The first element necessary for estoppel is a false and fraudulent representation. A minor makes a false and fraudulent representation when the minor affirmatively and intentionally states a false age, intending that the seller rely on the information. *Id.* at 805. For instance, in *Carney*, the minor told the car sales agent that he was twenty-two, the agent recorded that information on the loan application, and the minor signed the application to purchase the car. The court affirmed the trial court's holding that the minor had fraudulently misrepresented his age and was estopped from disaffirming the contract. *Id.* at 807-808.

Similarly, in *Clemons v. Olshine*, 187 S.E. 711 (Ga. Ct. App. 1936), the minor told the clothing sales agent that he was twenty-one and signed a contract confirming the representation. The court held that his fraudulent misrepresentation estopped him from disaffirming. In *Watters v. Arrington*, 146 S.E. 773 (Ga. Ct. App. 1929), another car purchase case, several agents of the seller testified that the minor had twice affirmatively stated his age to be twenty-one. The court affirmed the jury's verdict for the seller, holding that the minor had fraudulently misrepresented his age and was therefore estopped from disaffirming the contract.

The courts distinguish this kind of intentional, knowing misrepresentation from unintentional, even negligent misrepresentations of age. For instance, in *Woodall v. Grant Co.*, 9 S.E.2d 95 (Ga. Ct. App. 1940), the minor had simply signed a form contract without reading its representation that he was of age. There the court held that the representation in the contract did not estop the minor because the minor had not read the contract. The court reasoned that minors are not required to read contracts. *Id.* at 95. The *Carney* decision distinguished *Woodall* by pointing out that in *Woodall*, "the minor's only sin, if any, was his failure to read a contract which . . . stated that he was of age, while in [*Carney*] the minor falsely gave the information put into the contract." *Carney*, 88 S.E.2d at 808.

The most recent relevant case, *Siegelstein v. Fenner Beane*, 17 S.E.2d 907 (Ga. Ct. App. 1941), reaffirmed the *Carney/Woodall* distinction. In *Siegelstein*, the jury returned a verdict for the defendant, and the appellate court reversed on other grounds. However, the appellate court affirmed the trial court's jury instruction, stating that a minor's false representation of age "will not affect his power to disaffirm a contract unless [the representation] was made *fraudulently*." *Id.* at 910 (emphasis supplied).

The rule holding minors responsible only for intentional affirmative misrepresentations is consistent with the policy behind allowing minors to disaffirm their contracts. Minors, by definition, are both more likely than adults to enter into unwise contracts and more likely to make errors and other innocent misrepresentations in the process. Given this symmetry of rationale, the courts are likely to continue allowing minors to disaffirm despite innocent, even negligent, misrepresentations.

Here, the sales agent simply asked Buckley whether she was old enough to buy a car. Buckley misunderstood the question, thinking that the agent was asking whether she was old enough to drive. Thus she innocently answered "yes." She did not affirmatively state an age at all. This kind of misunderstanding is exactly the sort of confusion a minor is likely to experience.

Buckley's representation that she was old enough to buy a car is significantly different from the representations in the cases holding that the minor cannot disaffirm. Unlike the minors in *Carney, Clemons,* and *Watters,* Buckley never stated her age at all. Also, unlike the facts in those cases, Buckley's assertion, taken to mean what she intended it to mean (that she was old enough to drive), was not even false. Further, Buckley made only this single, ambiguous statement, in comparison to the several oral and written assertions of a specific age found in *Carney, Clemons,* and *Watters.*

Buckley's statement is much closer to the situation in *Woodall,* in which the minor made the representation unknowingly. In *Woodall,* the minor did not know that he was making the representation because he did not read the form contract he was signing. Buckley did not know that she might be making a representation that she was eighteen because she misunderstood the agent's question. In both cases, the requisite intent to deceive is absent. Since Buckley did not intend to deceive Willis Chevrolet, a court would probably allow her to disaffirm the contract.

However, Buckley must realize that the sales agent's testimony describing their conversation may differ from hers. The agent may remember the conversation differently or may testify falsely. Others may claim to have overheard the conversation. One way or another, Buckley's testimony may be controverted. Further, the documents Buckley signed may have contained representations of age, and other witnesses may testify that Buckley read them. If we decide to proceed with Buckley's case, we will need to learn what testimony Willis Chevrolet will offer and

Application

-4-

what the documents contain. On the facts we now have, however, a court would probably conclude that Buckley did not fraudulently misrepresent her age.

first element concl.

B. Willis Chevrolet's reliance on Buckley's representation was probably reasonable.

second element

The next element requires the injured party to have justifiably relied on the representation. *Carney,* 88 S.E.2d at 808. The cases describing this element allude to the minor's physical appearance, the minor's life circumstances known to the injured party, the lack of any reason to cause the party to suspect the representation, and the lack of a ready means of confirming the representation. *Clemons,* 187 S.E. at 712-713; *Hood,* 125 S.E. at 788; *Carney,* 88 S.E.2d at 808; *Watters,* 146 S.E. at 773-774.

For instance, in *Carney,* the court pointed out that the minor was married, was a father, and appeared to be of the age of majority. 88 S.E.2d at 808. In *Hood,* the court pointed to the minor's physical appearance and to the seller's knowledge that the minor had been married and living independently with his wife for about four years. 125 S.E. at 788. While the decisions sometimes articulate the standard as whether the defendant "failed to use all ready means" to ascertain the truth, *see, e.g., Carney,* 88 S.E.2d at 808, none of the reported decisions have found circumstances requiring the defendant to go further than the minor's representation. In fact, *Clemons* specifically held that a contracting party need not undertake an affirmative investigation beyond the representation of age when the contracting party has no reason to doubt the representation. 187 S.E. at 713-714.

Buckley's facts do not indicate whether the sales agent knew anything about Buckley's life circumstances that would lead the agent to suspect that Buckley might not be eighteen. The facts also do not include a physical description of Buckley, although we can infer that she looks young, since the agent questioned her about her age. Although this issue would be a question of fact at trial, the facts seem similar to the facts in the reported cases. Contrary to the facts in *Hood,* Buckley is close enough to eighteen that an agent probably would not be expected to know that she was a minor simply from her appearance. Also unlike the *Hood* facts, we have no reason to believe that the agent knew anything about Buckley's life, nor that he had any reason other than her appearance to suspect that she was a minor. Therefore, the facts may not be sufficient to require the agent to go further than questioning Buckley.

APP.

However, one might argue that the agent had at least one "ready means" to verify Buckley's answer, namely asking to see her driver's license.

-5-

No prior case discusses requiring this simple verification, but at least for some of them, that may be because drivers licenses were not required at the time those cases were decided. Not only would this solution have been simple, but requiring it would facilitate an important policy rationale for the rule. The rule is designed to discourage sellers from being too ready to make sales by contracting with minors. Requiring sellers to verify the ages of buyers who appear young would counteract the possible tendency of sellers to be too easily convinced of a buyer's majority.

concl.

The court's ruling on the second element would depend primarily on the facts elicited at trial. On the facts as we now know them, a court would probably rule that Willis Chevrolet's reliance on Buckley's representation was reasonable.

third elem.

C. Buckley had almost certainly reached the age of discretion when she made the representation of her age.

A minor cannot be held responsible for a misrepresentation unless the minor had reached the age of discretion when he or she made the misrepresentation. *Carney,* 88 S.E.2d at 808; *Clemons,* 187 S.E. at 713. A minor reaches the age of discretion when the minor has developed the capacity to conceive a fraudulent intent. *Clemons* pointed out that most minors have reached the age of discretion for criminal prosecution for fraud at least by the age of fourteen, though probably not by the age of ten. *Clemons* concluded that the eighteen-year-old minor in that case was well within the age of discretion. *Id.* at 713.

app.

Buckley was seventeen when she bought the car, just a few months away from the age of majority. She is three years older than the presumptive age of discretion for criminal prosecution, and criminal prosecution probably requires more assurance of sufficient age than does simple estoppel in a contract action. A court almost certainly would conclude that Buckley had reached the age of discretion.

CONCLUSION

Buckley can disaffirm unless (1) she fraudulently misrepresented her age, (2) Willis Chevrolet justifiably relied upon the misrepresentation, and (3) Buckley had reached the age of discretion. On the facts as we presently understand them, a court would probably rule that Buckley did not misrepresent her age. A court might also rule that Willis Chevrolet was not justified in relying on Buckley's representation. Given the probable absence of one element required to prevent disaffirmance and the possible absence of another, Buckley can probably disaffirm the contract.

SAMPLE OFFICE MEMORANDUM

This office memo analyzes a rule with factors. Can you tell how the discussion's organization differs from the organization of the memo in Appendix A (analyzing a rule with elements)? In addition to rule-based reasoning, this analysis uses primarily analogies and disanalogies. Can you locate all of these case comparisons? What is their function?

This memo covers the first factor in four paragraphs, the second factor in two paragraphs, and the third factor in one paragraph. If the writer had more to say about these factors, the writer might have chosen to organize by explaining and applying each factor before going on to the next factor. In that case, subheadings would have helped a busy reader navigate through the analysis. Here, for this shorter analysis, notice how the signposts at the beginning of most paragraphs function much like subheadings. A law-trained reader looks for these signposts. Do they work here?

When a memo addresses only one issue, some lawyers omit a formal point heading. Notice that this writer has made that choice.

This writer has chosen to forego a formal section labeled "Conclusion," probably because that section essentially would repeat the last paragraph of the Discussion section. Another option would have been simply to label the last paragraph "Conclusion." A conclusion serves an important summarizing function. Would this memo be easier to read if the writer had added a Conclusion section?

MEMORANDUM

To: Rebecca Cuellar
From: Phil Brown
Date: May 5, 2005
Re: Sgt. Joseph Jackson; tort claim against Air Force; whether
           Jackson's FTCA claim is barred under the *Feres* doctrine
           because he was acting incident to service.

QUESTION PRESENTED

Whether Jackson was acting "incident to service" and, therefore, will be barred by the *Feres* doctrine from bringing an action under the Federal Tort Claims Act (FTCA) when, at the time of his injury, (1) he was off-duty for the weekend but not on a leave, pass, furlough, or any other kind of leave status requiring special permission; (2) he was on the base; and (3) he was returning to his on-base residence after bowling in a civilian league.

BRIEF ANSWER

Probably yes. The FTCA waives the government's sovereign immunity for some kinds of tort liability. Under the *Feres* doctrine, however, immunity is not waived where the plaintiff is a member of the military acting "incident to service." To decide whether a plaintiff was acting incident to service, the court will examine three factors: (a) the plaintiff's duty status at the time of the accident; (b) the location of the accident; and (c) the activity in which the plaintiff was engaged. At the time of the accident, Jackson was "on liberty," meaning that he was not scheduled to work but had been granted no formal absence status. Further, the accident occurred on the base. Finally, although Jackson was returning from bowling at a civilian-owned lane, his team was composed entirely of members of his squadron, and they bowled at the civilian-owned alley primarily as practice for a military bowling tournament they hoped to win. Given the combination of these factors, a court likely would conclude that at the time of the accident, Jackson was acting incident to service.

FACTS

On Friday, February 14, 2005, Staff Sergeant Joseph Jackson was on active duty as a member of the Air Force, stationed at Robins Air Force Base. He had completed his normal work shift for the week and was not scheduled to work until the following Monday morning. He was on the base and driving to his on-base residence when his vehicle was struck by an Air Force truck. It is undisputed that the accident was caused by the driver of the truck.

At the time of the accident, Jackson was returning from bowling in a league that included both military and civilian teams. His team was composed entirely of members of his squadron, who paid their own expenses and bowled during their free time. They planned to compete for the base championship that year, and for practice, they bowled both on base and at the civilian-owned lanes. Every year, the Air Force sends the base championship team to represent the base in a national military tournament. Jackson's team hoped to win that honor.

To recover for his injuries, Jackson would like to file suit against the Air Force under the FTCA. His action will be barred, however, if he was acting incident to his military service.

DISCUSSION

The Federal Tort Claims Act (FTCA) waives sovereign immunity for certain kinds of negligence actions brought against the United States. 28 U.S.C. § 1346(b)(1) (2001). The United States Supreme Court created an exception to the FTCA, however, when it held that a claim is barred if it is deemed "incident to military service." *Feres v. U.S.*, 340 U.S. 135, 146 (1950). The *Feres* exception recognizes that service members have an alternate remedy (veterans' benefits) for injuries related to their military service. The exception also recognizes that fear of possible civil liability might impair discipline and, therefore, limit military effectiveness. *Stencel Aero Eng'g Corp. v. U.S.*, 431 U.S. 666, 671-72 (1977).

To determine whether a particular claim is barred under *Feres*, the Eleventh Circuit considers three factors: (1) the plaintiff's duty status at the time of the accident; (2) the location of the accident; and (3) the activity in which the plaintiff was engaged. *Whitley v. U.S.*, 170 F.3d 1061, 1070 (11th Cir. 1999). No one factor will be determinative; the court will examine the totality of the circumstances in each case. *Pierce v. U.S.*, 813 F.2d 349, 354 (11th Cir. 1987).

Under the first factor, the court examines the plaintiff's duty status at the time of the accident. *Whitley*, 170 F.3d at 1070. The length of the time off-duty is not the operative question. *Compare Watkins v. U.S.*, 462 F. Supp. 980, 988 (S.D. Ga. 1977) (off for weekend; claim barred) *with Hand v. U.S.*, 260 F. Supp. 38, 41 (off for 24 hours; claim permitted) *and Pierce*, 813 F.2d 349, 350 (off for several hours; claim permitted). Rather, the critical question is whether the time off-duty was part of the service member's normal work schedule, as opposed to a specially requested time away from work. *See Parker v. U.S.*, 611 F.2d 1007, 1011 (5th Cir. 1980).

For instance, in *Parker*, the service member had sought and been granted four days off to move his family to a new residence. 611 F.2d at 1008. While he was on his way home for this four-day period, his car was struck by a military vehicle. *Id*. The court held that the service member's status was closer to being on a pass or a furlough than to merely being off-duty for the day. Therefore, the court held that the first factor weighed against finding the accident incident to service. *Id*. at 1013-14.

Similarly, in *Pierce*, 813 F.2d at 350, the service member had requested and received permission to leave his normal work duties that day to run personal errands. He was expected to return in several hours to complete the rest of the work day. Although he was technically not on either furlough or leave, he had been granted "the right to be absent from regular duty," and the court equated that status with being on furlough. *Id*. at 353. The court, therefore, held that the duty status factor weighed against finding the accident incident to service. *Id*.

In contrast, a service member who is merely off-duty for the day, in the normal course of the work schedule, usually is found to be acting incident to service. *Parker*, 611 F.2d at 1013; *see also Flowers v. U.S.*, 764 F.2d at 760 (11th Cir. 1985). For instance, in *Flowers*, the service member was injured while he was off-duty for the day and driving home from the grocery store. 764 F.2d at 760. In *Watkins*, the service member had completed his normal week's work schedule and was off-duty for the weekend. 462 F. Supp. 980, 986. In both cases, the courts held that the duty status factor indicated that the activity was incident to service. *Flowers*, 764 F.2d at 761; *Watkins*, 462 F. Supp. at 988.

The second factor a court considers is the location of the accident. If an accident occurs on the base, the location factor weighs in favor of finding the activity incident to service. *Parker*, 611 F.2d at 1014. In *Flowers*, for example, the location factor weighed toward finding the accident incident to service where the service member was on-base, driving from the grocery store to his on-base home. 764 F.2d at 761. In *Watkins*, the on-base location weighed toward finding the accident incident to service where the service member was leaving recreational softball practice at an army field. 462 F. Supp. at 986.

Occurrence on-base does not automatically make an activity incident to service, however. *Parker*, 611 F.2d at 1014; *see also Hand*, 260 F. Supp. at 42. In both *Parker* and *Hand*, claims for on-base accidents were permitted. In *Parker*, the plaintiff had been dismissed from work and was driving to his off-base residence. He had not yet left the base when the accident occurred. 611 F.2d at 1008. In *Hand*, the plaintiff was driving from his off-base residence to the location where he planned to hunt. The most direct path between the two points took him through the base, and the accident occurred there. 260 F. Supp. at 39. In both cases, despite the on-base location, the court looked to the other two factors and found the accident not incident to service. *Hand*, 260 F. Supp. at 42; *Parker*, 611 F.2d at 1015. If the accident occurred on-base, however, and the service member was on a normal duty status, the combination of these two factors will almost surely bar the claim. *Watkins*, 462 F. Supp. at 987 ("Where the claimant is injured on base while on 'active duty,' *Feres* applies virtually as a matter of law.").

Finally, a court examines the link between the activity and the service member's military service. The court will consider the degree to which the service member was directly subject to military control or was performing a military task. *Parker*, 611 F.2d at 1014-15. In evaluating the service member's activity, however, a court will consider that a service member is subject to military control at all times and especially when on the base. *See Watkins*, 462 F. Supp. at 988. Assessing the activity factor, then, will necessarily require gauging the relative *degree* of the relationship to the plaintiff's military service.

Here, Jackson's claim would probably be barred. First, Jackson was "on liberty," that is, on a *routinely* authorized absence. He had completed his work shift for the week and was not scheduled to report for work until the following Monday. This time off occurred as part of his normal work schedule, however, and not as a result of a request for a special leave. Thus, his duty status facts are identical to those in *Watkins*, where the accident occurred on a Friday evening, after the service member had completed his normal work week and while he was on his regularly scheduled weekend break. 462 F. Supp. at 986. There, the court concluded that the duty status factor pointed toward a finding that the plaintiff was acting incident to service. *Id*. at 988. A court likely would conclude the same about Jackson's duty status.

Second, Jackson's injuries occurred on the base, as he was returning to his on-base housing. These facts are most similar to those in *Flowers*, where the accident also occurred on-base while the plaintiff was returning to on-base housing. *Flowers*, 764 F.2d at 761 (claim barred); *see also Watkins*, 462 F. Supp. 980 (claim for on-base accident barred). A court would, therefore, hold that the second factor points toward a finding that Jackson was injured while acting incident to service.

Third, Jackson's activity was partly personal and partly military-related. Jackson certainly can argue that he was returning from a voluntary recreational activity, undertaken on his time off, held at a civilian-owned facility, and done in conjunction with civilians. However, the activity was not utterly unrelated to his military life. Jackson's team was composed entirely of service members from his squadron, and together they were practicing to compete in the on-base tournament sponsored by the Air Force. The purpose of the on-base tournament was to select the championship team that, at Air Force expense, would represent Robins Air Force Base in competition against teams from other bases. Under these circumstances, a court would probably conclude that participation in the civilian league was at least partly related to Jackson's military service.

Thus, weighing all three factors together, a court is likely to conclude that Jackson's claim is barred under the *Feres* doctrine. The accident occurred on Robins Air Force Base at a time when Jackson was "on liberty" but not on any kind of a special leave, pass, or furlough. Because both the duty status factor and the location factor weigh against Jackson's claim, it is almost certain that a court would find his injuries incident to service. *See Watkins,* 462 F. Supp. at 986. The analysis of the third factor—the activity factor—probably does not yield a result compelling enough to overcome the first two factors here. The activity itself, while not sponsored by the military, was undertaken together with other squadron members as practice for an on-base Air Force event. Even if a court could be persuaded to give some significance to the civilian aspects of the activity, the first two factors weigh so clearly against Jackson that his claim most likely will be barred.

SAMPLE LETTERS

RETAINER LETTER

[date]

Ms. Elizabeth S. Bradenton
Pinnellas Landscaping, Inc.
8537 South Washington St.
Newton, TX 65432

Dear Ms. Bradenton:

It was a pleasure meeting with you in our office this week. We appreciate your selection of Harris, Felton, and Cox to represent Pinnellas Landscaping, Inc. in a breach of contract action against Charles and Dorothy Cott. This letter confirms my understanding of the legal matter and the terms on which we agreed.

I understand that the Cotts contracted with Pinnellas Landscaping to landscape their commercial properties. After the work was completed, the Cotts refused to pay for the work, claiming that both the plants and the labor were inferior. You have attempted to resolve the matter informally, but the Cotts continue to refuse any payment. You would like our firm to represent Pinnellas Landscaping and, if necessary, to file a complaint against the Cotts to collect the contract price as well as any other damages to which Pinnellas may be entitled.

Our fee will be based on the amount of time we devote to the case. An hourly fee arrangement insures that Pinnellas Landscaping will not be required to pay for any more services than are actually required for its case. My hourly rate is $200, and the hourly rate for my paralegal is $80.00. It is impossible to determine in advance how much time will be needed, but we will do our best to minimize the time required while still providing Pinnellas Landscaping with diligent and competent representation. In addition, Pinnellas Landscaping will be responsible for costs our firm incurs on its behalf. These costs may include such charges as filing fees, service-of-process fees, telephone and travel costs, and costs for depositions. By this agreement, you are appointing us as agents for Pinnellas Landscaping and authorizing us to make expenditures on its behalf. I will obtain in advance your specific authorization for any expenditures in excess of $1,000.

As I explained, it is our custom to charge a retainer in commercial litigation. For this case, a retainer of $3,000 will be sufficient to commence the representation. We will apply the retainer to fees and costs as they accrue, and we will ask Pinnellas Landscaping to renew the retainer when its balance falls below $500. Each month, I will send a statement itemizing the fees and costs incurred that month so you can monitor both the expenses of the litigation and the substantive developments on the case. Any credit balance remaining at the conclusion of the matter will be refunded promptly.

I am enclosing a copy of this retainer letter and a pre-addressed envelope. If these arrangements are satisfactory, please sign the copy in the space provided and return the signed copy along with the retainer. Upon receipt of the signed retainer letter and the retainer fee, the representation will commence. We will first attempt to settle the claim without the need for litigation, and we will relay any settlement offers to you for your consideration. Sometimes parties who have been unwilling to settle a dispute previously will change their minds once an attorney is retained. However, if the Cotts remain unwilling to settle the matter fairly, we will file suit on Pinnellas Landscaping's behalf and seek all remedies allowed by law.

I look forward to working with you to resolve this matter as quickly and favorably as possible. Should you at any time have questions about these arrangements, please feel free to call me.

Very truly yours,

Keith Salter
Attorney at Law

INFORMAL ADVICE LETTER

[date]

Mr. Joseph S. Crimshaw
Crimshaw Plumbing Supply
1245 Glenwood Dr.
Gooding, New State 55832

RE: Crimshaw Plumbing Supply; personnel matter

Dear Joe:

Last week, I said that I would research the question of whether you can require an existing sales employee to sign a covenant not to compete to retain his employment. My research indicates that you can require the employee to sign a noncompetition covenant as long as the employee is an "at will" employee and as long as the terms of the covenant are reasonable. I will explain that conclusion more fully below, but first let me summarize my understanding of the facts that have raised this question for you.

Facts: I understand that about a year ago, you hired Steven Lewis to call on potential customers and take orders for plumbing supply products. Lewis told you that he had been selling plumbing supply products for ten years for another company but was recently laid off when that company reduced its workforce. He told you orally that he wished to go to work for another established company and stay there until he retires in ten years. I understand that you did not offer him any particular term of employment and that he did not make any promises to you about how long he would stay or whether he would leave and compete against Crimshaw Plumbing Supply. You have now heard a rumor indicating that Lewis is planning to open his own plumbing supply business in about a year and that he will be directly competing against Crimshaw Plumbing. You would like to require Crimshaw to sign a covenant not to compete with Crimshaw for three years after he leaves Crimshaw's employment.

Issues: These facts raise two issues: (1) whether a current employee can be required to sign a covenant not to compete; and (2) what covenant terms are enforceable.

Research and Legal Conclusions: On the first issue, no statute or reported case in our state has addressed the question of whether continuation of employment can be conditioned on the signing of a covenant not to compete. However, all employment contracts are treated as "at will" employment unless the contract specifies otherwise. Assuming that you did not offer Lewis employment for any particular period of time, he is an "at will" employee. You can terminate an "at will" employee at any time as long as the termination is not for a particular prohibited reason, such as the employee's race, religion, or sex.

While no reported cases in our jurisdiction have dealt with requiring an employee to sign a noncompetition covenant, several cases did deal with requiring a current "at will" employee to abide by other kinds of newly instituted rules of employment such as new attendance or dress requirements or new rules requiring particular training or certifications. These cases have uniformly upheld an employer's right to institute new employment rules or requirements and to condition continued employment on compliance with those rules.

Further, I was able to find several cases in other jurisdictions that dealt specifically with requiring a current employee to sign a covenant not to compete, and those cases all permitted the requirement. In those cases, the courts stated that there was no significant difference between requiring the signing of a noncompetition covenant and requiring the employee to abide by other newly instituted rules. While a court in our state would not be required to follow the ruling of a case from another state, these cases do provide additional support for our position.

On the second issue, the cases in our state uniformly hold that a signed covenant not to compete is enforceable if its terms are reasonable. Customary terms set out the geographic area of the restriction, the duration of the restriction, and a description of the restricted activities. The opinions all recite that the restrictions should not be broader than necessary to protect the employer's business. Commonly, durational terms do not exceed one year, and geographic restrictions do not exceed the area of the employer's primary market. The restricted activities are limited to the activities the employee performed for the former employer plus any additional activities for which the employee could profitably use confidential information obtained from the former employer (such as a customer list). Consequently, if you are going to require Lewis to sign a covenant, we should carefully discuss its terms, and I would recommend that you allow our firm to draft the agreement for you so we can help you create terms a court would enforce.

Advice: First, if competition from former sales employees is a concern, as I suspect it is, I suggest that you ask all new sales employees to sign a noncompetition agreement with carefully drafted terms. This will prevent future occasions in which the current delicate situation arises.

Second, it appears that legally you can condition Lewis's continued employment on the signing of a covenant not to compete. However, you might want to think carefully about whether to bring the issue to a head in this way. If Lewis has not yet decided whether to start his own business, presenting him with a covenant at this point could push him to decide to leave and begin to compete immediately. Further, presenting him with a legal document and requiring him to either sign it or be fired could cause him to react emotionally. He might feel both strong-armed and suspected of wrong-doing, in which case he may react by doing exactly what you are trying to prevent. Therefore, you will need to assess carefully the risks of acting as compared to the risks of waiting.

If you decide to ask for the noncompetition agreement, I suggest that you consider two possible strategies. If Lewis is a valuable employee you would like to keep, consider whether you can devise a promotion or some other increase in status or benefits and present the covenant as part of that new position. If a promotion or increase in benefits is not feasible, you might present the covenant as a new policy applying to a whole category of employees so Lewis does not feel singled out and personally offended.

I hope this information is helpful. I would be happy to discuss this matter with you further. Let me know if you would like us to assist in any other way.

Very truly yours,

Keith Salter
Attorney at Law

STATUS LETTER

[date]

Ms. Elizabeth S. Bradenton
Pinnellas Landscaping, Inc.
8537 South Washington St.
Newton, TX 65432

RE: Pinnellas Landscaping, Inc. v. Charles and Dorothy Cott

Dear Beth:

As you know, we have filed a set of interrogatories and scheduled the defendants' depositions for June 12. Yesterday we received word that the Cotts' attorney plans to set your deposition for June 12 immediately following the defendants' depositions. Since you had already planned to attend the Cotts' depositions on that day, I presume you are available for your own deposition that day as well. Let me know right away if that is not the case.

We should meet prior to the 12th to discuss all three depositions. Your help will be important in preparing me to depose the Cotts, and I will help you prepare for your own deposition as well. In case you have not ever been deposed, let me tell you that you need not worry about the experience. I will be with you throughout the process, and I will handle any objections to the questions you are asked. In our meeting, I'll explain what to expect and help you anticipate the questions and think through your answers. Please call my secretary in the next several days to schedule a time for us to prepare for the depositions, and don't hesitate to call me if you have questions or concerns we should address before that meeting.

Very truly yours,

Keith Salter
Attorney at Law

DEMAND LETTER

March 20, 2003

CERTIFIED MAIL
RETURN RECEIPT REQUESTED

Harold M. Lawler
Susan S. Lawler
9754 West 14th St.
Newton, TX 65432

RE: State Bank Loan Account 12345

Dear Mr. and Mrs. Lawler:

Your loan with State Bank, account number 12345, is delinquent in the amount of $1,489.78. Since this delinquency represents four months of missed payments, State Bank is exercising its right under the contract to declare the entire balance of the loan due. Our firm has been retained to collect the balance of your loan plus all late fees and accrued interest. As of today, that amount is $17,225.51.

State Bank has authorized us to file suit against you and to seek all lawful remedies for your breach as well as your payment of our attorneys' fees for collecting the loan balance. If you wish to avoid a lawsuit and liability for our fees, you must pay the sum of $17,225.51 to this office on or before April 2, 2003. You must pay this amount by certified check or money order made out to State Bank. If you do not pay this amount on or before April 2, we will have no recourse other than to file suit against you. You are hereby instructed to direct all further communication about this matter to our firm and not to State Bank or any of its employees.

Very truly yours,

Keith Salter
Attorney at Law

cc: Charles A. Miller
    State Bank Credit Dept.

SAMPLE TRIAL-LEVEL BRIEF

TRIAL-LEVEL BRIEF

The umbrella rule for this brief is a procedural rule that incorporates the substantive rule within it. Because no trial has yet occurred, the argument relies on facts asserted in an affidavit. The first subpart of the umbrella rule applies a set of factors to the client's situation, using a series of precedential cases to explain each of the factors. Observe these characteristics and notice the role each plays in the analysis.

IN THE UNITED STATES DISTRICT COURT
FOR THE DISTRICT OF COLORADO

RANDALL BROWNLEY,
    Plaintiff

    v.

SCOTT DUNN, d/b/a DUNN CREDIT
BUREAU,
    Defendant.

Civ. No. 95-14867

BRIEF IN SUPPORT OF DEFENDANT'S MOTION
TO SET ASIDE DEFAULT JUDGMENT

INTRODUCTION

This is an action alleging a violation of Section 607(b) of the Fair Credit Reporting Act (FCRA), 15 U.S.C. § 1681e(b) (1995). The Complaint was filed and served upon Scott Dunn on October 27, 1995. Default judgment was entered six days ago, on November 17, 1995, just one day after the expiration of Mr. Dunn's time to answer the Complaint. Mr. Dunn now files a motion to set aside this default judgment, along with a supporting affidavit and a proposed Answer to the Complaint. This brief is filed in support of Mr. Dunn's Motion.

STATEMENT OF FACTS

In September 1995, a potential lender contacted Dunn Credit Bureau requesting a credit report on the Plaintiff. Aff. Scott Dunn ¶ 10 (Nov. 26, 1995). The Credit Bureau prepared the report, and it contained a reference to an unpaid department store account. Aff. Scott Dunn ¶ 11. Upon the discovery of this item on his credit report, the Plaintiff contacted Mr. Dunn to demand that the item be removed, arguing that the charged merchandise had been defective and that the defect was the reason for his nonpayment. Aff. Scott Dunn ¶ 12. Mr. Dunn asked the Plaintiff to provide this explanation in writing and promised to include it along with the store's version of the account. Aff. Scott Dunn ¶ 13.

The Plaintiff refused to provide the written explanation, again demanding that the item be removed entirely. Aff. Scott Dunn ¶ 14. Mr. Dunn replied by letter, declining to delete the item entirely but repeating the offer to include the Plaintiff's defense. Aff. Scott Dunn ¶ 14. The Plaintiff did not respond to Mr. Dunn's letter, and Mr. Dunn did not hear from the Plaintiff again. Aff. Scott Dunn ¶ 15.

On October 27, 1995, copies of the Summons and Complaint in this action were served at Mr. Dunn's home by leaving them with Mr. Dunn's sixteen-year-old son, Gregory. (Ret. of Serv. Oct. 30, 1995.) On that day, Mr. Dunn and his wife had traveled to Denver, planning to return the next day. Aff. Scott Dunn ¶ 3.

However, on the evening of October 27, Mrs. Dunn suffered a serious heart attack and was hospitalized. Aff. Scott Dunn ¶ 4. Gregory left immediately for Denver. In the midst of the crisis surrounding his mother's heart attack, Gregory did not think to tell his father about the delivery of an envelope to the family home. Aff. Scott Dunn ¶ 6.

Mr. Dunn remained in Denver with his wife for two weeks until Mrs. Dunn was released from the hospital to return home. Aff. Scott Dunn ¶ 5. Upon his return, Mr. Dunn began going in to his office part-time, while continuing to care for his wife. Aff. Scott Dunn ¶ 7. Mr. Dunn did not find the envelope until November 20, 1995. On that day, Mr. Dunn moved a stack of papers on the table in the family room and found the envelope there. Aff. Scott Dunn ¶ 8.

Mr. Dunn immediately called his attorney and began the preparations to file an Answer to the Complaint. Aff. Scott Dunn ¶ 9. Shortly after the initial telephone conversation with his attorney, Mr. Dunn learned that a default judgment had been entered three days earlier. Aff. Scott Dunn ¶ 9. Mr. Dunn now seeks an order, pursuant to Fed. R. Civ. P. 60(b), setting aside this default judgment.

ARGUMENT

I. THE DEFAULT JUDGMENT SHOULD BE SET ASIDE BECAUSE IT WAS ENTERED AS A RESULT OF INADVERTENCE OR EXCUSABLE NEGLECT AND BECAUSE THE DEFENDANT HAS A MERITORIOUS DEFENSE TO THE PLAINTIFF'S ALLEGATIONS.

Rule 60(b) of the Federal Rules of Civil Procedure invests the Court with the discretion to relieve a party from a final judgment entered as a result of inadvertence or excusable neglect. When the judgment was entered upon the moving party's default, the moving party must also demonstrate the existence of a potentially meritorious defense. *In re Stone,* 588 F.2d 1316, 1319 (10th Cir. 1978). Rule 60(b) is to be liberally construed. *Pierce v. Cook Co.,* 518 F.2d 720, 722 (10th Cir. 1975). Doubts are to be resolved in favor of adjudication on the merits. *In re Roxford Foods, Inc.,* 12 F.3d 875, 879 (9th Cir. 1993); *Tolson v. Hodge,* 411 F.2d 123, 130 (4th Cir. 1969).

A. The Defendant's Default Resulted from Excusable Neglect Because Service Was Effected upon the Defendant's Minor Son and the Crisis of His Mother's Heart Attack Caused the Son to Forget to Inform His Father of the Service.

Mr. Dunn meets the first requirement for Rule 60(b) relief because the default resulted from excusable neglect. The United States Supreme Court has defined the term "excusable neglect," in the context of bankruptcy filings, to include giving "little attention or respect" or "leav[ing] undone or unattended . . . esp[ecially] through carelessness." *Pioneer Inv. Servs. Co. v. Brunswick Assocs. Ltd. Partnership,* 507 U.S. 380 (1993). Last year the Tenth Circuit adopted this definition of excusable neglect in the context of a Rule 60(b) motion. *City of Chanute, Kansas v. Williams Nat. Gas Co.,* 31 F.3d 1041 (10th Cir. 1994). The Tenth Circuit specifically held that Rule 60(b) relief is not limited to circumstances beyond the moving party's control. *Id.* at 1046.

-2-

The Tenth Circuit's analysis of excusable neglect considers four factors: (1) the potential prejudice to the nonmoving party; (2) the length of delay; (3) the reason for the delay; and (4) the degree of good faith of the moving party. *Id.* at 1046-47.

The first factor, the prejudice to the nonmoving party, must amount to more than simply delaying enforcement of the judgment. *Feliciano v. Reliant Tooling Co.*, 691 F.2d 653, 656-57 (3d Cir. 1982). Usually cognizable prejudice involves some change of position in reliance on the judgment. The second factor, the length of delay, measures both the time since the entry of judgment and the time since the party became aware of the judgment. *See Lasky v. International Union*, 27 Fed. R. Serv. 2d 473, 477 (E.D. Mich. 1978), *aff'd*, 638 7.2d 954 (6th Cir. 1981). For instance, a delay of thirty-one days might be well within acceptable limits. *City of Chanute*, 31 F.3d at 1047.

The third factor examines the validity of the reason for the delay and whether the delay was willful. The Tenth Circuit has consistently affirmed orders setting aside default judgments entered as a result of understandable error or inadvertence as opposed to willful action by the defendant. For example, the court affirmed a decision to set aside a default judgment entered while the plaintiff believed that his new attorney was negotiating a settlement that would resolve the litigation. *Thompson v. Kerr-McGee Ref. Corp.*, 660 F.2d 1380 (10th Cir. 1981). The Tenth Circuit also affirmed an order granting Rule 60(b) relief from a judgment caused by confusion about filing a notice of appeal. *Romero v. Peterson*, 930 F.2d 1502 (10th Cir. 1991).

The excusable reasons for delay in these cases contrast with cases in which the default resulted from a willful decision by the defendant. For example, in *Cessna Fin. Corp. v. Bielenberg Masonry Contracting, Inc.*, 715 F.2d 1442 (10th Cir. 1983), the court affirmed the trial court's decision denying relief to a corporate defendant whose representatives had decided not to answer the complaint because they believed that the corporate defendant would escape liability in bankruptcy. In *United States v. Theodorovich*, 102 F.R.D. 587 (D.D.C. 1984), the court denied relief because the default judgment had resulted from defendant's willful decision not to attend his own properly scheduled deposition.

The final factor asks whether the defendant has acted in good faith. This factor invites the court to consider the broad equitable question of whether the moving party has dealt in good faith with the court and with the other parties to the litigation.

A court can consider equitable matters as well. For instance, it may overlook the defendant's neglect if an order requiring the defendant to pay the plaintiff's costs would sufficiently alleviate any prejudice to the plaintiff. *Littlefield v. Walt Flanagan and Co.*, 498 F.2d 1133 (10th Cir. 1974).

Applying these four factors to the present case demonstrates that Rule 60(b) relief is certainly appropriate here. First, granting the Defendant's Motion would not cause the Plaintiff to suffer any cognizable prejudice. The default judgment was entered less than one week ago. The only cognizable prejudice that would result from setting aside the judgment stems from the costs the Plaintiff incurred in seeking the entry of the judgment. The Defendant has offered to pay those reasonable costs, Aff. Scott Dunn ¶ 16, and an order to that effect would sufficiently relieve the Plaintiff of even this small prejudice. *Id.*

The "length of delay" factor also weighs in favor of granting the motion. Only three days elapsed between the entry of the default judgment and the Defendant's discovery of the litigation. Only three additional days elapsed between the Defendant's discovery and the filing of this motion and supporting documents. By comparison, the Tenth Circuit found a delay of thirty-one days "short." *City of Chanute*, 31 F.3d at 1047. A six-day delay is well within permissible bounds.

The third factor, the validity of the reason for delay, is often the most important factor. In the present case, this critical factor is the most compelling of all. Here, the delay was caused by the sudden and serious heart attack of Mr. Dunn's wife and Gregory's mother. Aff. Scott Dunn ¶¶ 4-9. That a teenager should forget under such circumstances to tell his father about the delivery of an unopened envelope is certainly understandable. This situation is precisely the sort of omission that Rule 60(b) is designed to forgive.

Mr. Dunn's good faith also argues for relieving the Defendant from judgment. Mr. Dunn has dealt with both the Court and the Plaintiff entirely in good faith. The delay was not caused by any stratagem or artifice. Mr. Dunn was entirely unaware of the litigation. Immediately upon learning of the Complaint, Mr. Dunn hurriedly contacted his attorney and began the process of responding. Aff. Scott Dunn ¶ 9. Mr. Dunn's offer to bear the Plaintiff's costs is further evidence of his good faith.

Thus all four factors of the Rule 60(b) analysis place the Defendant's situation squarely within the parameters for Rule 60(b) relief and establish that Mr. Dunn meets the first requirement for setting aside the default judgment.

B. <u>The Defendant Has a Meritorious Defense to the Complaint Because the Credit Report Accurately Reflects the Plaintiff's Admitted Failure to Pay the Account.</u>

Mr. Dunn also meets the second requirement for Rule 60(b) relief, the existence of a meritorious defense. A plaintiff alleging a violation of 15 U.S.C. § 1681e(b) must establish two elements: (1) that the credit report is inaccurate; and (2) that the inaccuracy flows from the reporting agency's failure to follow reasonable procedures. *Cahlin v. General Motors Corp.*, 936 F.2d 1151, 1156 (11th Cir. 1991). Establishing inaccuracy is a threshold requirement for a Section 1681e(b) claim. *Id.* at 1156.

The accuracy requirement of the FCRA does not require the credit reporting agency to delete all reference to an unpaid account merely because it is disputed. This is true even if the consumer ultimately pays the account. *Id.* In *Cahlin*, the plaintiff's credit report included reference to a disputed account. Initially the account was unpaid, but after it appeared on the credit report, the consumer settled the account for partial payment. The consumer then demanded that the credit agency delete all reference to the account. *Id.* at 1155. The Eleventh Circuit held that Section 607(b) does not require a credit reporting agency to report only favorable information. The court specifically held that the agency need not delete the reference to the disputed account even though the dispute was settled, explaining that such an interpretation would gut the very purpose of a credit report. *Id.* at 1158.

Here the Plaintiff's credit report accurately reflects his failure to pay the balance owed on a department store charge account. Aff. Scott Dunn ¶ 11. Further, unlike the account in *Cahlin*, the Plaintiff's account remains unpaid. The Credit Bureau offered to include the consumer's written statement describing the dispute, as required by 15 U.S.C. § 1681*i*(b) (1995). The Plaintiff refused to provide a statement of defense. This refusal is the only impediment to a more complete description of the Plaintiff's dispute with the account holder. The Plaintiff's demand that the item be removed entirely would have decreased rather than increased the report's accuracy because it would have omitted all reference to an admittedly unpaid debt. The Act simply does not require this sort of concealment of a consumer's true credit history.

Thus, the Plaintiff's credit report is accurate, and the Credit Bureau did not violate FCRA. Mr. Dunn has a meritorious defense to the Plaintiff's Complaint.

CONCLUSION

Mr. Dunn meets both requirements for Rule 60(b) relief. All four factors for evaluating inadvertence or excusable neglect strongly argue in favor of granting Mr. Dunn relief under Rule 60(b). Further, the Plaintiff's credit report met the accuracy requirement under FCRA, and thus Mr. Dunn has a meritorious defense to the complaint. Mr. Dunn respectfully requests the Court to enter an order setting aside the judgment and allowing him to file his Answer and to otherwise defend this action.

DATED: _____   _____

Attorney for the Defendant

CERTIFICATE OF SERVICE

I, _____, attorney for the Defendant, do hereby certify that I have served upon the Plaintiff a complete and accurate copy of this Brief in Support of the Defendant's Motion to Set Aside Default Judgment, by placing the copy in the United States Mail, sufficient postage affixed and addressed as follows:

[name and address of Plaintiff's attorney]

DATED: _____   _____

Attorney for the Defendant

SAMPLE APPELLATE BRIEF

This appellate brief addresses a pure question of law. It sets out two alternative arguments for the relief sought. The second of these is phrased so as to avoid undercutting the first (see Summary of Argument). Both arguments rely on techniques of statutory construction and policy rationales.

IN THE UNITED STATES COURT OF APPEALS
FOR THE FIFTEENTH[1] CIRCUIT

DR. JUNE TEMPLE AND
NORTHPARK FAMILY CLINIC,
INC.,
    Appellants
  v.
  RICHARD SINGER,
    Appellee.

Docket No. 92-1939

BRIEF FOR APPELLANTS[2]

---

1. This is a hypothetical circuit.
2. This brief is adapted from a student brief written by Phillip C. Griffeth, Donna G. Hedgepeth, and Angela D. Medders.

TABLE OF CONTENTS

TABLE OF AUTHORITIES

QUESTIONS PRESENTED

1. Can a plaintiff enforce an offer of judgment made pursuant to Fed. R. Civ. P. 68 when the plaintiff responded to the offer with a counter-offer rather than an acceptance and when the plaintiff did not specify an intention to take the offer under advisement?

2. Can a plaintiff enforce a Rule 68 offer of judgment when the plaintiff did not accept the offer until after the court adjudicated the plaintiff's claims by granting summary judgment?

STATUTE INVOLVED

Rule 68 of the Federal Rules of Civil Procedure provides as follows:

> At any time more than 10 days before the trial begins, a party defending against a claim may serve upon the adverse party an offer to allow judgment to be taken against the defending party for the money or property or to the effect specified in the offer, with costs then accrued. If within 10 days after the service of the offer the adverse party serves written notice that the offer is accepted, either party may then file the offer and notice of acceptance together with proof of service thereof and thereupon the clerk shall enter judgment. An offer not accepted shall be deemed withdrawn and evidence thereof is not admissible except in a proceeding to determine costs. If the judgment finally obtained by the offeree is not more favorable than the offer, the offeree must pay the costs incurred after the making of the offer. The fact that an offer is made but not accepted does not preclude a subsequent offer. When the liability of one party to another has been determined by verdict or order or judgment, but the amount or extent of the liability remains to be determined by further proceedings, the party adjudged liable may make an offer of judgment, which shall have the same effect as an offer made before trial if it is served within a reasonable time not less than 10 days prior to the commencement of hearings to determine the amount or extent of liability.

JURISDICTION

The jurisdiction of this Court is invoked pursuant to 28 U.S.C. §1291 (1988).

STATEMENT OF THE CASE

On August 3, 1991, the Plaintiff filed this diversity action alleging medical malpractice against Dr. June Temple and the Northpark Family Clinic. (R. 1.) On January 17, 1992, after extensive discovery, the

Defendants moved for summary judgment. (R. 11.) The District Court took the motion under advisement.

On June 1, 1992, while the motion was pending, the Defendants made an Offer of Judgment in the amount of $100,000, pursuant to Fed. R. Civ. P. 68. (R. 24.) The Plaintiff did not accept the offer. Rather, on June 4, he served a document entitled "Plaintiff's Offer of Judgment." (R. 27.) The document purported to be a Rule 68 offer to accept the entry of judgment in the amount of $225,000. The Plaintiff never specified that he was still considering the Defendants' initial Offer. (R. 27.)

On June 7, the District Court granted the Defendants' Motion for Summary Judgment. (R. 18-23.) After learning of the Order granting summary judgment against him, the Plaintiff attempted to accept the Defendants' initial Offer of Judgment by serving an Acceptance of Offer of Judgment on June 8, 1992. (R. 25.) The Defendants moved for an order striking the Plaintiff's Acceptance. (R. 26.) After hearing argument, the District Court denied the motion to strike and entered judgment in favor of the Plaintiff for $100,000 plus costs. (R. 34.) The Defendants have filed this appeal seeking reversal of the District Court's order enforcing the Offer of Judgment.

SUMMARY OF ARGUMENT

The Plaintiff's counteroffer constituted a rejection of the Defendants' Offer of Judgment and thus extinguished it. This interpretation is consistent with the policies and purposes behind Rule 68 and with existing case law and commentary upon the Rule. Further, this interpretation is consistent with long-standing contract principles, which establish that a counteroffer terminates the offeree's power to accept the original offer. In addition, interpreting Rule 68 to permit an absolute ten-day period within which a plaintiff can consider acceptance would exceed the Court's judicial authority under the Rules Enabling Act.

Even if the counteroffer had not extinguished the initial Offer, the District Court's order granting summary judgment would have extinguished it. The order constituted an adjudication on the merits and terminated any rights the Plaintiff may have had to enforce the original Offer. Interpreting the Rule to allow acceptance after an order granting summary judgment would do nothing to further the Rule's purpose of encouraging settlement of pending litigation. Further, such an interpretation would create unfair tactical advantages for plaintiffs at the expense of defendants.

ARGUMENT

The Defendants' Offer of Judgment was extinguished either by the Plaintiff's counteroffer or by the District Court's Summary Judgment Order. The facts surrounding these two events are undisputed, and the determination of the issues raised by this appeal will not require the application of law to fact. Therefore, both issues are pure questions of law, to which a de novo standard of review applies, *Traywick v. Juhola*, 922 F.2d 786, 787 (11th Cir. 1991).

I. THE ORDER ENFORCING THE DEFENDANTS' OFFER OF JUDG-MENT SHOULD BE REVERSED BECAUSE THE PLAINTIFF'S COUNTEROFFER HAD ALREADY EXTINGUISHED THE DEFEN-DANTS' OFFER.

Rule 68 provides that a defendant may serve upon the plaintiff an offer to allow judgment to be taken against the defendant upon the terms specified in the offer. If the plaintiff accepts the offer within ten days, the agreement becomes binding, and the court enters judgment. Fed. R. Civ. P. 68 (1995). An offer not accepted within ten days is deemed withdrawn. *Id.* If the judgment ultimately entered is not more favorable than the offer, the plaintiff must pay any litigation costs incurred by the defendant after the offer was made. *Id.* The Rule's purpose is to encourage parties to settle litigation. *Marek v. Chesney*, 473 U.S. 1, 5 (1985); *Delta Air Lines, Inc. v. August*, 450 U.S. 346, 352 (1981).

Any response to a Rule 68 offer other than an unqualified accep-tance operates as a rejection. *Rateree v. Rockett*, 668 F. Supp. 1155 (N.D. Ill. 1987); Roy D. Simon, Jr., *Rule 68 at the Crossroads: The Relationship Between Offers of Judgment and Statutory Attorney's Fees*, 53 U. Cin. L. Rev. 889, 921 (1984). In *Rateree*, the court noted that, consistent with the Supreme Court's guidelines in *Marek*, "a plaintiff cannot do anything except simply say 'I accept' if he or she expects to enforce the offer under Rule 68." *Id.* at 1158.

Once a plaintiff responds with anything other than an acceptance, the original offer is deemed withdrawn. The Rule allows a plaintiff a ten-day *maximum* period during which the plaintiff can consider the offer. However, the Rule does not *require* a plaintiff to use the entire ten days allotted by the Rule.

The Rules Advisory Committee also understood the present language of Rule 68 to mean that an attempted counteroffer operates as a rejection of the initial offer. In 1984, the Committee proposed amendments to Rule 68. In a note explaining the proposed changes, the Committee explained

-5-

that under the proposed Rule "a written counteroffer would not constitute a rejection unless it expressly so stated." Committee on Rules of Practice and Procedure of the Judicial Conference of the United States, Preliminary Draft of Proposed Amendments to the Federal Rules of Civil Procedure (Sept. 1984), *reprinted in* 102 F.R.D. 407, 435 (1985). The Committee's explanation of the proposed amendment (never adopted) demonstrates that under the present version of Rule 68, a counteroffer *does* constitute a rejection. Further, the fact that the proposed amendment was not adopted demonstrates that such a construction of Rule 68 has been specifically considered and rejected.

If the express language of the Rule does not resolve a question of interpretation, the court should look to related state law for guidance. To whatever extent the language of the Rule does not specifically address the effect of a counteroffer, the court's interpretation creates a common law construction that is essentially federal in character. *See generally Kamen v. Kemper Fin. Servs., Inc.*, 111 S. Ct. 1711, 1717 (1991). In *Kamen*, the Supreme Court observed that such constructions of federal law should not be "wholly the product of a federal court's devising." Rather, the Supreme Court cautioned that the federal court should "fill the interstices of a federal . . . scheme" by incorporating state law. *Id.* at 1717. This presumption is especially strong when the parties have reason to believe that state law rather than federal law will apply to their rights and obligations. *Id.* at 1717.

In the case of Rule 68, the relevant body of state law is contract law. Rule 68 is a process by which the parties can achieve a private contractual agreement. *Greenwood v. Stevenson*, 88 F.R.D. 225, 229 (D.R.I. 1980). Therefore, courts have consistently held that general contract principles determine whether an offer or acceptance complies with the Rule's requirements. *Radecki v. Amoco Oil Co.*, 858 F.2d 397, 400 (8th Cir. 1988). *See also Johnson v. University College of the Univ. of Ala.*, 706 F.2d 1205, 1209 (11th Cir.), *cert.denied*, 464 U.S. 994 (1983); *Adams v. Wolff*, 110 F.R.D. 291, 293 (D. Nev. 1986); *Bentley v. Bolger*, 110 F.R.D. 108, 113-14 (C.D. Ill. 1986); *Boorstein v. City of New York*, 107 F.R.D. 31, 33-34 (S.D.N.Y. 1985). Parties utilizing Rule 68 have long had reason to believe that general contract principles will apply to their Rule 68 filings. Since the presumption to incorporate state law is especially strong in such cases, a federal court should fill the interstices of Rule 68 by incorporating the substantive law of contracts.

It is a rudimentary contract principle that a counteroffer terminates the power to accept the previously made offer. Restatement (Second) of Contracts, §§ 36(1) & 39(2) (1981); 1 Arthur L. Corbin, *Corbin on*

Contracts § 90 (1963). *See also* 1 Walter H.E. Jaeger, *Williston on Contracts* § 51 (3d ed. 1959). Only a counteroffer that specifies an intention to take the original offer under advisement would not have the effect of extinguishing the original offer. Restatement (Second) of Contracts § 39(2) (1981). *See also* 1 Corbin, *Contracts* § 92.

For instance, in *Collins v. Thompson*, 679 F.2d 168 (9th Cir. 1982), a suit by prison inmates, the parties reached a settlement and the State filed the terms in a proposed consent decree. Subsequently, the State submitted a revised proposal with a later compliance date. The prisoners moved to enforce the first proposed decree or, in the alternative, for amended notice to class members of the later date. *Id.* at 169. The court observed that, by their alternative motion, the prisoners had indicated their continued interest in accepting the later date should the earlier date not be enforceable. *Id.* at 172.

Further, if Rule 68 created an absolute ten-day period, the Rule would exceed the Court's authority under the Rules Enabling Act, 28 U.S.C. § 2072 (1995). The Act gives the Supreme Court the power to prescribe general rules of procedure for the federal courts. However, the Act specifically cautions that "[s]uch rules shall not abridge, enlarge or modify any substantive right." 28 U.S.C. § 2072(a)-(b).

The Supreme Court has defined "substantive rights" as used in the Act to mean those "rights conferred by law to be protected and enforced in accordance with the adjective law of judicial procedure." *Sibbach v. Wilson Co., Inc.*, 312 U.S. 1, 13 (1941). According to the Supreme Court, the test is whether the rule regulates "the judicial process for enforcing rights and duties" or whether the rule regulates the substantive law that grants those rights and duties. *Id.* at 14.

A construction of Rule 68 that caused an offer to survive a counteroffer would "abridge, enlarge, or modify" substantive rights. Under the Rule, the district court plays a minor role in the actual settlement negotiations. A defending party does not file the Offer with the court, but rather serves it upon the adverse party. Fed. R. Civ. P. 68. The court does not even become aware of the Offer unless the parties reach an agreement. *Id.* The district court only "formaliz[es] the agreement hammered out by the parties." *Greenwood*, 88 F.R.D. at 229. Thus, a defendant's right to contract for settlement is a substantive right, and a construction of Rule 68 that caused a settlement offer to survive a counteroffer would abridge those substantive rights.

Here, the Plaintiff's counteroffer operated as a rejection of the Defendants' Offer and thus extinguished it. Defendants' Offer of Judgment under Rule 68 created a power of acceptance in the Plaintiff.

If the Plaintiff had any interest in keeping the Offer alive, he had several options: He could have chosen to accept the Offer on its terms; he could have filed no formal response to the Offer but negotiated with the Defendants outside the constraints of Rule 68; or he could have filed a counteroffer specifically indicating his intention to continue considering the original Offer.

Instead, three days after receiving the Offer, he served a counteroffer. (R. 27.) His counteroffer made no mention of the original Offer and did not specify any intention of taking that Offer under advisement. Further, the counteroffer specified an amount more than twice the amount of the initial Offer. (R. 27.) His action can only be construed as a rejection of the original Offer, thus terminating his power of acceptance.

The Plaintiff did not have to respond to the Offer at all; however, he chose to do so. He cannot later change his mind, after learning that the District Court had granted summary judgment against him, and attempt to accept the Offer he had already rejected.

II. THE ORDER ENFORCING THE DEFENDANTS' OFFER OF JUDGMENT SHOULD BE REVERSED BECAUSE THE COURT'S SUMMARY JUDGMENT ORDER EXTINGUISHED ANY OFFER OF JUDGMENT STILL OUTSTANDING.

The District Court's order granting summary judgment was an adjudication on the merits of the case and a final decision of the rights and liabilities of the parties. Therefore, it terminated any remaining right the Plaintiff may have had to enforce the original Offer.

Rule 68 encourages settlement of pending controversies by allowing litigants to balance the risks and costs of litigation with their chances for success. *Marek v. Chesney*, 473 U.S. 1, 5 (1985). The Rule is not intended to permit acceptance of an offer of judgment after the court has resolved the case. At that point, settlement of the dispute is no longer an option for the loser, because a legal dispute no longer exists.

Further, allowing a plaintiff to accept an offer after the court has decided the case would unfairly advantage the plaintiff over the defendant. The Supreme Court has held that the Rule's "policy of encouraging settlements is neutral, favoring neither plaintiffs nor defendants." *Marek*, 473 U.S. at 10. Permitting acceptance of the original offer of judgment after the granting of summary judgment would frustrate this policy by giving significant tactical advantages to the plaintiff.

These tactical advantages are demonstrated by the policy rationale behind another provision of Rule 68—the provision that prohibits offers made within ten days of trial. This prohibition dovetails with the allowance of ten days in which to respond to an offer. *Greenwood*, 88 F.R.D. at 228 (citing 12 Charles A. Wright & Arthur R. Miller, *Federal Practice and Procedure* § 3003 (1973)). The purpose of the ten-day prohibition is to insure that the Rule 68 process is completed while the parties have an equal opportunity to assess the risks of continuing the litigation. One judge aptly illustrated the result the ten-day prohibition is intended to avoid:

> [Otherwise an offeree could] watch how the case is unfolding and weigh the probabilities. If the trial is going well, the offer can simply be ignored; if things begin to look grim, the offeree can decide to go with the sure thing. . . . [L]ocking one side into a settlement offer while the other side assesses the ongoing trial is, purely and simply, stacking the deck.

Greenwood, 88 F.R.D. 225, 228-229 (D.R.I. 1980).

The "deck stacking" that would result from allowing a plaintiff to accept an offer after a final adjudication would be far worse than the "deck stacking" described in *Greenwood*. The ten-day prohibition is intended to prevent the plaintiff from having a better opportunity to assess the probabilities of losing; however, at least under the *Greenwood* scenario, both parties would still be assessing *probabilities*.

Here, the Plaintiff asks the Court to allow a procedural favoritism far worse than that prevented by the ten-day prohibition. He asks the Court to allow him to wait until the litigation probabilities have become *certainties*. As the Supreme Court has cautioned, it is "inappropriate for the Judiciary, without legislative guidance, to reallocate the burdens of litigation." *Alyeska Pipeline Serv. Co. v. Wilderness Soc'y*, 421 U.S. 240, 247 (1975). Allowing a plaintiff to wait until *after* the case is resolved before accepting an offer the defendant made *before* the case was resolved would do just that.

This Court should not condone manipulations of Rule 68 that would so distort the Rule's fundamental policy of neutrality. The Rule was never intended to allow the result the Plaintiff urges. Rather, the Rule was intended to allow the parties to traverse Rule 68 terrain on equal footing. Once the rights and liabilities of the parties have been adjudicated by the court, any pending Rule 68 offer is extinguished. Therefore, the Court should hold that the entry of the trial court's order granting summary judgment extinguished the Defendant's offer of judgment.

CONCLUSION

For the foregoing reasons, Appellants request that the Judgment of the District Court be reversed and that the case be remanded with instructions to the District Court to enter judgment in favor of the Defendants.

Respectfully submitted,

DATED: _____

_____
Attorney for the Appellants

CERTIFICATE OF SERVICE

I, _____, do hereby certify that I have this date served a true and correct copy of the Appellants' Brief upon the Appellee's counsel by placing a true copy of the Appellants' Brief in the United States mail, with sufficient postage affixed, and addressed as follows:

William J. Beck
P.O. Box 1670
Hutchfield, [state]

DATED: _____

_____
Attorney for the Appellants

SAMPLE APPELLATE BRIEF

The issue addressed in this brief is essentially a pure question of law, requiring interpretation of a rule of evidence. Therefore, the rule explanation sections focus primarily on the language of the rule, the intent of the rule's drafters, and the policies served by adhering to the rule's plain language. The writer relies on case authorities as well, but since the cases are not mandatory authority for this court, the writer presents the cases as further support for the primary arguments of plain meaning, intent of the drafters, and policy.

In both the "plain language" section and the "intent of the drafters" section, notice how closely the writer focuses on the actual words of Rule 615. If the case authority had defined the Rule's terms more fully, the writer would have relied primarily on case authority for the definitions of the words used in the Rule. Even without strong case authority defining the terms, however, a writer can use legal and other dictionaries to parse each word of a rule or statute, as the writer has done here.

In the "intent of the drafters" section, the writer casts the Rule as primarily defining what restrictions a party can force on other parties as a matter of course, without justifying the need for the restrictions. This section expressly articulates the primary theme of the brief, contrasting the trial court's powers with the powers given to parties. The section relies on a canon of statutory construction to point out not only what is included in the Rule's plain language, but also what is omitted. The writer also discusses the Rule's silence on important questions that would arise routinely if the Rule had been intended to have the scope urged by the appellant. This section ends by pointing out that the trial court, which presumably knew what it meant by its own order, did not intend that the order apply in the manner the appellant has proposed, thus harkening back to the theme of reliance on the court's trial management powers.

Then, after the rule explanation sections, the writer applies the Rule to the facts of the case before the court. The way the Rule will apply to these facts is clear, but the writer uses the rule application section as an opportunity to reinforce the points made in the rule explanation sections and to reassure the court that justice will not be infringed by a ruling in the appellee's favor.

IN THE UNITED STATES COURT OF APPEALS
FOR THE FIFTEENTH[1] CIRCUIT

DENNIS IRVING,
    Appellant

v.

Docket No. 04-1234

THE UNITED STATES
  OF AMERICA,
    Appellee.

BRIEF OF THE APPELLEE[2]

---

1. This is a hypothetical circuit.

2. This brief is based on briefs written by students in the Spring 2005 Advanced Writing Groups at Mercer University School of Law. Professor Beth Cook of the Pennsylvania State University Dickinson School of Law graciously allowed the use of the problem that was adapted for that class.

TABLE OF CONTENTS

TABLE OF AUTHORITIES

QUESTION PRESENTED

Whether Rule 615 of the Federal Rules of Evidence should be expanded to apply to communications outside the courtroom where (1) the trial court did not intend that its routine Rule 615 order should limit outside conversation; (2) the defendant never requested a broad sequestration order; (3) the court did not instruct witnesses to refrain from discussing their testimony; (4) a police officer spoke about his testimony to his co-worker; and (5) during the co-worker's subsequent testimony, the defendant was able to cross-examine the co-worker about the conversation.

RULE OF EVIDENCE INVOLVED

Federal Rule of Evidence 615 provides:

> At the request of a party the court shall order witnesses excluded so that they cannot hear the testimony of other witnesses, and it may make the order of its own motion. This rule does not authorize exclusion of (1) a party who is a natural person, or (2) an officer or employee of a party which is not a natural person designated as its representative by its attorney, or (3) a person whose presence is shown by a party to be essential to the presentation of the party's cause, or (4) a person authorized by statute to be present.

STANDARD OF REVIEW

Because rulings on motions to exclude testimony raise predominately legal questions regarding the interpretation of the Federal Rules of Evidence, the appellate court reviews those evidentiary rulings de novo. *U.S. v. Angwin*, 271 F.3d 786, 798 (9th Cir. 2001).

STATEMENT OF THE CASE

On May 8, 2004, the Defendant, Dennis Irving, sold to Nathan Roberts more than 50 grams of methamphetamine, a Schedule II controlled substance. (R. 1.) Officers Miller and Nelson witnessed the transaction and immediately arrested both men. (R. 1.) Subsequently, a grand jury indicted the Defendant for offenses involving the possession and distribution of methamphetamine. (R. 2.)

In pretrial proceedings, the district court granted the Defendant's Motion to Exclude Witnesses Pursuant to Rule 615 of the Federal Rules of Evidence and specifically ordered all prospective witnesses to leave the courtroom. (R. 4.) The court, however, did not instruct the witnesses or counsel that witnesses were prohibited from discussing their testimony with each other. (R. 4.)

On September 22, 2004, the trial began. That day, during the government's case-in-chief, Officer Nelson testified that he had seen the Defendant hand to Roberts the envelope containing the drugs. (R. 5.) Later that evening, Officer Nelson had dinner with Officer Miller, who was scheduled to testify the following day. (R. 6.) A research assistant for the Defendant's attorney was seated nearby. (R. 7.) According to the research assistant, as the officers ate dinner, Officer Nelson described the testimony he had given at trial that morning. (R. 7.) In pre-trial statements, Officer Miller had described first seeing the two men at the point where the envelope was already in Roberts' hand. (R. 7.) Allegedly, after hearing a description of Officer Nelson's testimony, Officer Miller stated that he now remembered seeing the Defendant hand the envelope to Roberts. (R. 7.)

The next day, the Defendant moved to exclude Officer Miller's testimony, arguing that the dinner conversation between Officers Nelson and Miller the previous evening violated the court's Rule 615 order to exclude witnesses from the courtroom. (R. 5.) The district court heard argument and denied Defendant's motion. (R. 6.) The court reasoned that a witness's refreshed recollection of events (1) was common when talking to another person involved in the same incident; (2) was not evidence that the witness planned to perjure himself; and (3) did not violate the court's Rule 615 order, which barred witnesses only from being physically present in the courtroom. (R. 6.)

Later that day, Officer Miller testified at trial. (R. 7.) The Defendant's attorney cross-examined Officer Miller, confronting him with his previous statements and questioning him about his conversation with Officer Nelson the previous evening. (R. 6.) After hearing this cross-examination and all of the other evidence in the case, the jury convicted the Defendant on all counts. (R. 7.) The District Judge sentenced the Defendant to serve 56 months in a federal prison (R. 7.), and the Defendant has now filed this appeal.

SUMMARY OF THE ARGUMENT

Federal Rule of Evidence 615 provides that upon the request of a party, the trial court "shall order witnesses excluded so that they cannot hear the testimony of other witnesses." Fed. R. Evid. 615. The Appellant asks this Court to hold that a routine Rule 615 order also prohibits witnesses from discussing their testimony with each other. Neither the plain meaning of the Rule, nor the intent of its drafters, nor sound public policy support the Appellant's argument.

First, the plain meaning of Rule 615 is limited to physical presence in the courtroom. The Rule provides that witnesses shall be "excluded," meaning "expelled" or "barred" —a reference to physical presence, not to communication. The Rule sets out the reason for the exclusion, "so that" they do not "hear testimony." The word "testimony" means sworn statements of a competent witness in a trial, affidavit, or deposition. Therefore, by definition, witnesses cannot "hear testimony" unless they are present when the testimony is being given. Several courts, including the First and Eighth Circuits, have so held.

Further, the plain language of the Rule indicates the drafter's intention to limit only presence in the courtroom. Since a trial court already has the power to restrict witness communication as part of its inherent authority to manage proceedings before it, the Rule's primary purpose is to define the restrictions a *party* can impose unilaterally upon other parties. By expressly delineating the power to exclude witnesses from the courtroom, the Rule impliedly withholds from parties other, broader powers. Also, the drafters did not address several key questions that would arise regularly if Rule 615 had been intended to apply beyond the courtroom, such as exactly what witnesses are prohibited from saying and whether the prohibition precludes attorneys from preparing witnesses for their testimony.

Finally, application of Rule 615 beyond its express terms would disrupt the Rule's carefully crafted balance of the rights of parties and the efficient administration of trials. Broad witness sequestration is available outside Rule 615 in those cases where restrictions on witness communication are appropriate. Blanket restrictions, however, would be burdensome to witnesses and unworkable for the trial court. Enforcement proceedings would interrupt trials and squander judicial resources. Without guidance about what sorts of communications are prohibited, outcomes of these hearings would be unpredictable. Witnesses unwilling to risk charges of contempt of court would be inclined not to testify at all.

According to its express terms, the drafter's intent, and sound policy rationales, a routine Rule 615 order is limited to excluding witnesses from physical presence in the courtroom and does not apply to conversations between witnesses. Therefore, the Rule 615 order below did not prohibit the conversation between Officers Nelson and Miller. The Government respectfully requests this Court to affirm the trial court's denial of the Defendant's motion to exclude testimony.

<u>ARGUMENT</u>

I. THE COURT SHOULD AFFIRM THE TRIAL COURT'S DECISION BECAUSE RULE 615 PROHIBITS ONLY PHYSICAL PRESENCE IN THE COURTROOM AND THEREFORE DOES NOT APPLY TO OUTSIDE COMMUNICATIONS SUCH AS THE DINNER CONVERSATION BETWEEN OFFICERS NELSON AND MILLER.

Rule 615 provides that, upon a party's request, the trial court "shall order witnesses *excluded* so that they cannot hear the *testimony* of other witnesses." Fed. R. Evid. 615 (emphasis added). According to the Rule's plain language, a Rule 615 order bans prospective witnesses from the courtroom, but does not restrict communication outside the courtroom. The Defendant seeks to extend the scope of Rule 615 beyond its plain language, in contravention of the intent of the Rule's drafters and in derogation of the trial court's inherent discretionary authority to manage its courtroom. The district court rejected such an interpretation of the rule, and this Court should affirm the district court's ruling.

A. <u>The Plain Language of Rule 615 Applies Only to a Witness's Physical Presence in the Courtroom.</u>

The first step in interpreting a rule is to examine the language itself. If the language is plain and unambiguous, a court should not look past this plain meaning. *Shotz v. City of Plantation*, 344 F.3d 1161, 1167 (11th Cir. 2003); *Thompson v. Goeztmann*, 337 F.3d 489 (5th Cir. 2003). Dictionaries often are used to confirm the plain meaning of statutory text.

The issue before the Court concerns only one sentence of Rule 615: "At the request of a party the court shall order witnesses excluded so that they cannot hear the testimony of other witnesses, and it may make the order of its own motion." Fed. R. Evid. 615. The phrase at issue is *"exclude[]* so that they cannot *hear . . . testimony."* *Id.* (emphasis added). "Exclude" means to "expel or ban." *Merriam-Webster's Collegiate Dictionary* (11th ed. 2003). "Testimony" means "evidence that a competent witness under oath or affirmation gives at trial or in an affidavit or deposition." *Black's Law Dictionary* 1485 (Bryan A. Garner ed., 7th ed., West 2000). The plain, ordinary, straightforward language of the rule, therefore, provides only that witnesses are banned from the courtroom so they do not hear other witnesses *as they testify.*

The Rule goes on to identify the reason for exclusion from the courtroom: "so that they cannot hear the testimony of other witnesses." This phrase does not define a broad category of situations to which the Rule will apply. Rather, the phrase expressly uses the language of purpose ("so that") to set out the reason for the exclusion from the courtroom. The plain language of Rule 615, therefore, says nothing at all about what a witness may say or do outside the courtroom. *See U.S. v. Scharstein*, 531 F. Supp. 460, 462-63 (E.D. Ky. 1982).

Even if the word "exclude" could be redefined to refer to something other than banning an individual from the courtroom, Rule 615, by its own terms, would apply only to hearing *testimony*. A participant in a restaurant conversation over dinner is not "hearing testimony." In that setting, no one is under oath, no one is being questioned by an attorney, and no rules of evidence apply. The express language of Rule 615 does not apply to communications of that sort. *See* 29 Charles Alan Wright & Victor James Gold, *Federal Practice and Procedure* § 6243, at 57 ("Testimony is given only in a formal legal context such as a deposition, hearing, or trial. Thus witness communication outside that context does not enable witnesses to 'hear testimony.' ").

Several courts have held that the language of Rule 615 limits only physical presence of witnesses in the courtroom. For instance, in *Sepulveda v. U.S.*, 15 F.3d 1161, 1176 (1st Cir. 1993), the First Circuit held the Rule inapplicable to extra-courtroom communication. In that case, the defendants had been charged with offenses relating to the distribution of cocaine, and the trial court had issued a Rule 615 order before trial began. *Id.* at 1176. Later in the trial, the defendants alleged that extra-courtroom witness contact had violated the Rule 615 order. The court held that a Rule 615 order does not prohibit witness communication, stating that the Rule 615 order had "plowed a straight furrow in line with Rule 615 itself [and therefore] did not extend beyond the courtroom." *Id.* at 1176.

The Eighth Circuit also has held Rule 615 inapplicable to extra-courtroom communications. *U.S. v. Smith*, 578 F.2d 1227, 1235 (8th Cir. 1978). In *Smith*, defendants were on trial for offenses associated with the distribution of heroin. *Id.* at 1229. Early in the trial, the court had issued a Rule 615 order excluding witnesses from the courtroom. As trial progressed, a police officer took notes and relayed information to government witnesses waiting to testify. *Id.* at 1234. The trial court held that this conduct did not violate the Rule 615 order because Rule 615 only excludes witnesses from the courtroom. *Id.* The Eighth Circuit affirmed the trial court's holding, noting that the defendants had not requested additional restrictions beyond Rule 615. *Id.* at 1235. The appellate court stated that the question of whether to instruct witnesses not to communicate with other witnesses is within a trial court's discretion. *Id.* at 1235.

Such a discretionary instruction is not, therefore, mandated by the plain language of Rule 615.

Similarly, the court in *Scharstein* held that the plain language of Rule 615 limits only physical presence in the courtroom. 531 F. Supp. at 463-64. In *Scharstein*, defendants had been charged with illegally manufacturing, storing, and transporting explosives. *Id.* at 461. The court declined to expand the application of Rule 615 to prohibit witnesses from conferring with each other outside the courtroom. The court stated, "[T]his court believes that there is no reason to go beyond the plain language of the Rule," observing that the question of whether to instruct witnesses not to discuss their testimony is within the court's discretion and not required by Rule 615. *Id.* at 463; *see also Lapenna v. Upjohn Co.*, 665 F. Supp. 412, 413 (E.D. Pa. 1987) (declining to apply Rule 615 "beyond the literal meaning of the rule").

B. The Drafters Did Not Intend Rule 615 to Apply Broadly to Communication Outside the Courtroom

Not only does the plain language of Rule 615 call for affirmance here, but indications of the drafters' intent support that result as well. Since a trial court already has inherent power to limit witness communication outside the courtroom, *Sepulveda*, 15 F.3d at 1176, the primary purpose of Rule 615 is to identify the restrictions *a party* can impose unilaterally on other trial participants. Therefore, the key inquiry is what unilateral and unrestrained powers the Rule's drafters intended to give to parties.

The drafters of the Rule rightly limited the unrestrained power the Rule would give to parties. At common law, when a court ordered sequestration, the order could include (1) preventing witnesses from hearing other witnesses testify; and (2) preventing prospective witnesses from consulting other witnesses. *Sepulveda*, 15 F.3d at 1176 (citing 6 John Wigmore, *Evidence* § 1840). When the drafters expressly included in Rule 615 the power to "exclude" witnesses, they impliedly excluded the right to impose other more intrusive limitations. According to the canon of statutory construction *expressio unius est exclusio alterius*, the expression of one thing implies the exclusion of another. *Thompson*, 337 F.3d at 499. Rule 615, therefore, does not give parties the unilateral power to prohibit communication outside the courtroom. That power remains within the discretion of the trial court.

In fact, Rule 615 does not use the term "sequester" at all. *Black's Law Dictionary* defines "sequester" to mean "to segregate or isolate [a witness] during trial." *Black's Law Dictionary* 1370 (Bryan A. Garner, ed., 7th ed., West 2000). Tellingly, the drafters did not use the term "sequester" in Rule 615. Rather, they selected only the first aspect of common law sequestration (the aspect that does not "segregate or isolate a witness") and refrained from using the term "sequester" to describe the scope of Rule 615. These drafting decisions provide further indication of an intent to withhold broad sequestration powers from the scope of Rule 615. *Scharstein*, 531 F. Supp. at 464.

Further, the drafters did not define categories of communication allegedly prohibited by the Rule—as they surely would have done had they intended to restrict communication. Violation of a trial court's order constitutes contempt of court, rendering the offending person at risk of fine or imprisonment. *U.S. v. Johnston*, 578 F.2d 1352 (10th Cir. 1978). A reading of Rule 615 to prohibit certain kinds of communication outside the courtroom would mean that witnesses who spoke outside the courtroom would be subject to contempt proceedings. If the drafters had intended to impose such serious individual liability for trial witnesses, they surely would have set out the prohibition clearly and defined its parameters unambiguously. The Appellant's proposed construction would render trial witnesses vulnerable to contempt proceedings without fair notice of what they must not do or what the penalties might be. The drafters cannot have intended such a result.

If the drafters had intended the construction urged by the Appellant, they also would have had to address the question of whether trial attorneys could continue preparing witnesses for their testimony. To prepare a witness to testify, any competent attorney confers with the witness about the status of the trial proceedings and about the testimony to come. *See generally U.S. v. De Jongh*, 937 F.2d 1, 3 (1st Cir. 1991) (A lawyer "would be foolhardy to call an important witness without attempting, first, to debrief the witness."). Because parties adjust their strategies as the trial progresses, these witness conferences are an essential part of trying a case. *Scharstein*, 531 F. Supp. at 463. In fact, the right to prepare a witness for his or her testimony is so fundamental that deprivation of this right may raise Due Process concerns. *Scharstein*, 531 F. Supp. at 463-64 (citing *Potashnic v. Port City Construction Company*, 609 F.2d 1001 (5th Cir. 1980)).

Had the drafters intended Rule 615 to limit extra-courtroom communication, they could have chosen either to prohibit trial attorneys from preparing witnesses or to exempt trial attorneys. Exempting trial attorneys would have rendered the proposed construction of Rule 615 pointless, however. Witnesses who have already testified would be precluded from speaking to prospective witnesses, but trial counsel could still describe prior testimony freely. In fact, since attorneys know precisely what will be most relevant in future testimony, allowing attorneys to describe prior testimony would be far more problematic than allowing other witnesses to describe their own testimony. To hold that Rule 615 prohibits witnesses from talking to each other but allows attorneys to prepare prospective witnesses for their testimony "would be an exercise in futility." *Scharstein*, 531 F. Supp. at 464.

Prohibiting trial attorneys from preparing witnesses, on the other hand, would have resulted in a sea change in standard trial preparation. Again, like the question of individual witness liability, such a drastic result would have called for express language in the Rule itself, language clearly applying the Rule to attorney conduct and identifying what attorneys could and could not say during witness preparation. Since the drafters did not address the question of whether and how Rule 615 would apply to communication with attorneys, it is most likely that the drafters did not intend to apply Rule 615 to extra-courtroom communication.

Finally, the intent of the Rule's drafters is not the only intent relevant to the question before this Court. The trial court issued its order under the authority of Rule 615, but an order limiting outside communication could have been issued as part of the court's inherent powers of trial management. *Sepulveda*, 15 F.3d at 1176. Therefore, the more important inquiry may be what the *trial court intended* by its order. A court's interpretation of its own order is given great weight. *Sepulveda*, 15 F.3d at 1177; *U.S. v. Smith*, 578 F.2d at 1235 ("holding that it is within the discretion of the trial court to determine whether or not a sequestration order has been violated"). If, as here, the *trial court* did not intend its order to constrain conversation outside the courtroom, that order should not be redefined on appeal.

Both the intent of the drafters and the intent of the trial court issuing the order demonstrate that the conversation at issue did not violate the court's order. Neither the provisions of Rule 615 nor the court's own language reflect an intent to reach beyond the courtroom doors.

C. <u>Expanding Rule 615 Beyond Its Express Terms Would Disrupt the Rule's Balance Between Providing Truth-Testing Strategies and Minimizing Unnecessary Litigation Costs.</u>

The purposes of the Federal Rules of Evidence are to secure fairness in administration, eliminate unjustifiable expense and delay, ascertain the truth, and determine proceedings fairly. Fed. R. Evid. 102. The Rules aim to balance the need for legitimate truth-testing strategies with the need to minimize unnecessary expense. Expanding the scope of Rule 615 would unnecessarily disrupt the delicate balance Rule 615 has achieved.

Applying Rule 615 to out-of-court conduct is not necessary to obtain truthful testimony. Barring witnesses from the courtroom prevents them from hearing testimony directly, so their only knowledge of prior testimony will be by the general recollection of others. In most cases, this limitation will be sufficient. *Sepulveda*, 15 F.3d at 1176. Further, a party suspecting that witness contact may have influenced testimony is free to cross-examine a witness about that contact and its content, as occurred in the case before the Court. For cases in which greater protection is appropriate, the trial court can, *sua sponte* or on proper motion, impose greater limitations, including ordering witnesses not to disclose their testimony. In fact, this reliance on the discretion of the trial court is fundamental to the federal trial process. *Scharstein*, 531 F. Supp. at 464 ("The general approach of the Federal Rules of Evidence is to place heavy reliance on the discretion of the trial court in conducting a fair trial."). Thus, the very protection the Appellant seeks is already available without stretching Rule 615 beyond its intended application.

Not only is expansion of the Rule's scope unnecessary, but application to out-of-court communications would result in significant and often unnecessary administrative costs. First, enforcement would be extremely difficult. A court can easily enforce an order banning witnesses from the courtroom, but violations outside the judge's presence are difficult to discover. 29 Charles Alan Wright & Victor James Gold, *Federal Practice and Procedure*, § 6243, at 63 (West 1997). Further, enforcing routine orders prohibiting witness contact would require the court to undertake "an undue amount of supervision" over witnesses, distracting the court from its primary function. *Scharstein*, 531 F. Supp. at 464 n.7.

Second, extension of the Rule would result in long delays during trials. Each time two witnesses talked, there could be grounds for a motion alleging a violation of Rule 615 and a resulting evidentiary hearing to learn the content of the conversation. Witnesses would be called upon to disclose publically everything they had said to each other. These hearings would occur frequently, especially in long trials with many witnesses. *Id.* at 464. Constant interruptions would impede trial management, increase litigation costs, and absorb significant judicial resources. Courts would be "bogged down in numerous inquiries . . . when there is no genuine need to do so." *Id.*

Third, the outcome of these hearings would be uncertain at best. The Rule does not define what kinds of communication would be prohibited. Neither parties nor witnesses nor the district court itself would know whether a violation had occurred if a witness stated that she had testified; that her testimony was over; that the cross-examination had been brief; that she had been nervous; that she had testified about a particular topic; or that a particular question had been asked. With no clear standard of what could and could not be said, hearings would be numerous and issues would be difficult to resolve. *Id.*; 29 Wright, *Federal Practice* at § 6243.

Fourth, extension of the Rule would place unrealistic hardships on witnesses. An order limiting out-of-court communication between witnesses places far greater burdens on witnesses than does mere exclusion from the courtroom. Wright, *Federal Practice* at § 6243. Witnesses testifying in the same case often are spouses or co-workers. Communication between spouses or other close associates should be restricted only when absolutely necessary, not any time a party decides to invoke Rule 615.

Fifth, extending the Rule to out-of-court statements would render witnesses vulnerable to contempt proceedings. The combination of this vulnerability and the lack of clarity about what kinds of communication are prohibited would discourage witnesses from testifying. Discouraging testimony would impede the goal of obtaining truthful testimony to a far greater degree than would a decision to keep Rule 615 within its intended bounds.

Sixth, to apply Rule 615 to out-of-court conversations would be to give any party, as a matter of right, the ability to impose significant limitations on all witnesses in the case, including spouses and co-workers who must continue to have close daily contact with each other as the trial progresses. A party could use Rule 615 as another way to make the trial experience as unpleasant as possible for opposing parties and witnesses. This approach to trial management does not assist in achieving just and fair results at trial.

Only one circumstance—the reading of transcripts of actual testimony—justifies the application of Rule 615 beyond its express terms. In *Miller v. U.S.*, 650 F.2d 1365, 1367 (5th Cir. 1981), the trial court had entered an order excluding witnesses under Rule 615. *Id.* at 1372. During the trial, however, the defendant's expert witness was provided with daily transcripts of the trial testimony. The district court held that providing transcripts of testimony violated the Rule 615 order, and the appellate court affirmed, explaining that the harm of *reading* testimony is potentially greater than the harm of *hearing* testimony. *Id.* Accordingly, the court held that a Rule 615 order prohibits witnesses from reading trial transcripts prior to testifying. *Id.* at 1373.

The *Miller* exception does not apply to conversation outside the courtroom, however. The court in *Miller* compared hearing actual testimony with reading a transcript and found the key difference to be that a listener would have to rely on his or her memory of the testimony while a reader would not. *Id.* at 1372. This key distinction does not apply to conversation outside the courtroom. Unlike the reader of a transcript, who can thoroughly study the actual testimony, a participant in a conversation must rely on his or her memory of the conversation. Perhaps more significantly, the *speaker* must rely on memories of the testimony as well. By the very rationale explained in *Miller*, therefore, the danger of casual conversation outside the courtroom is considerably smaller than the danger Rule 615 is designed to prevent. Thus, the *Miller* exception does not apply to extra-courtroom conversation. In fact, *Miller's* very rationale demonstrates a key reason for limiting Rule 615 to "testimony" rather than to mere recollections of testimony.

Further, the narrow *Miller* exception is consistent with the rationales on which Rule 615 is based. The *Miller* exception does not impose the administrative costs and personal impositions on witnesses that the Appellant's construction would impose. Prohibiting the reading of transcripts creates a bright-line test, easily applied in enforcement proceedings. Witnesses need not wonder what they may and may not say. Parties need not wonder what conduct may violate the Rule 615 order. Also, a witness has access to trial transcripts only through trial attorneys, who are officers of the court and therefore more easily and effectively governed by trial court orders. Further, the prohibition on reading transcripts does not interfere with normal daily interactions between witnesses who live or work together or who encounter each other in casual interactions in the hallway.

In all other circumstances, trial judges have broad discretion to limit contact between witnesses when appropriate. *Sepulveda*, 15 F.3d at 1176. In those few cases in which a small nuance in testimony may determine the outcome, a Rule 615 exclusion of witnesses may be insufficient. *Scharstein*, 531 F. Supp. at 464. In such cases, the trial court can use its broad case management powers to determine whether "extra-courtroom prophylaxis" is necessary and what means best accomplishes the goal in that case. *Sepulveda*, 15 F.3d at 1176 (citing *U.S. v. Arias-Santana*, 964 F.2d 1262, 1266 (1st Cir. 1992)). Since trial courts already have the power to restrict communication when appropriate, the only effect of broadening Rule 615 to include such restrictions would be to shift the power from the trial court's discretion and place it instead in the unrestrained hands of a party. Nothing in the language or history of Rule 615 indicates that the drafters intended such a result.

D. The Casual Dinner Conversation of Officers Nelson, and Miller Did Not Violate the Rule 615 order.

On September 22, 2004, Officers Nelson and Miller had dinner together. (R. 6.) During their meal, the conversation ranged over topics of common interest. Officer Nelson had testified in the Irving trial that day. (R. 7.) He related to his dinner companion his recollection of his testimony, including his testimony of having seen Irving hand the drug-filled envelope to Roberts. Officer Nelson's description prompted Officer Miller to recall that he had seen the transfer as well. (R. 7.)

This dinner conversation between the officers did not violate the Rule 615 order. The trial court's order made reference only to whether and when witnesses could be in the courtroom, exactly as the plain language of Rule 615 provides. At no time during the trial did the court instruct witnesses not to speak to each other. This was no mere inadvertent omission by the court. As demonstrated by the court's denial of defendant's motion to exclude, the trial court did not *intend* that its order should apply to communication outside the courtroom.

Nor does this case fall within the narrow *Miller* exception. In *Miller*, the reading of daily transcripts was held to violate Rule 615. 650 F.2d at 1374. The court concluded that reading transcripts eliminated the need to rely on memory and was thus more dangerous than actual witness presence in the courtroom. Here, however, Officer Nelson had to rely on his recollection of his testimony. Then, Officer Miller had to rely on *his* recollection of what Officer Nelson had recalled. These key differences render the officers' conversation far less problematic than either physical presence in the courtroom or the reading of trial transcripts.

In fact, this double reliance on memory is even less problematic than the situation the Eighth Circuit permitted in *U.S. v. Smith*, 578 F.2d 1227, where an officer in the courtroom was taking notes and relaying information to prospective witnesses. Here, no one was planted in the courtroom taking notes. There was no plot to circumvent the prohibition on access to actual testimony. Two co-workers simply had dinner together and spoke of their day's events, as friends and co-workers often do.

Additionally, prohibiting these officers from speaking to each other likely would have made no difference here. Officers Nelson and Miller had worked together on this case for months. Together, they had arrested the Defendant and worked with the prosecutor to prepare the case for trial. During that process, they would have seen each other daily. Undoubtedly, they had discussed the case on countless occasions. They may well have discussed the case immediately before trial began. Whether or not the officers communicated on September 22, no doubt the prosecutor would have carefully prepared Officer Miller for his testimony the next day. The prosecutor would have highlighted the factual question of the drug transfer and would have told Officer Miller about the status of the testimony on that point. Officer Miller's recollection would have been just as refreshed by that description as it was by the description of his co-worker the night before. In such a circumstance, there is little point in prohibiting a discussion on September 22nd that normally could have happened both on September 21st and on September 23rd.

Further, whether the conversation occurred before or after trial began, the Defendant would have been able to confront Officer Miller with his prior statements and question him about conversations with others—just as the Defendant did. Thus, in either case, the jury would have been fully informed of the circumstances surrounding Officer Miller's testimony. In neither case would there be reason to second-guess the jury's ability to gauge the officer's credibility and the accuracy of his recollection.

Finally, reading Rule 615 beyond its express terms is not necessary to preserve the availability of broad sequestration in appropriate cases. As part of its inherent authority, the court below had the power to impose, *sua sponte*, extra-courtroom restrictions on witnesses. The court did not find those restrictions necessary here. If the Defendant disagreed, the Defendant had the opportunity to request those restrictions, but the Defendant did not make the request. Had counsel sought such an order, and had the trial court issued it, Officers Nelson and Miller certainly would have complied. The Defendant did not seek the order, however, and cannot now bootstrap a routine Rule 615 order into the order Defendant wishes he had sought.

CONCLUSION

Both the plain language of Rule 615 and all available indicators of the drafters' intent show that the Rule governs only physical presence in the courtroom and not conversations such as that between Officers Nelson and Miller. Further, application of Rule 615 according to its express terms preserves the Rule's carefully crafted balance of the rights of parties and the efficient administration of trials. Therefore, the Government respect-fully requests this Court to affirm the trial court's denial of the Defendant's motion to exclude testimony.

_____

Counsel for the United States

CASES USED IN THE TEXT'S EXAMPLES AND EXERCISES[1]

COFFEE SYSTEM OF ATLANTA V. FOX
226 Ga. 593, 176 S.E.2d 71 (1970)

Supreme Court of Georgia

HAWES, Justice.

The appeal here is from the final judgment and order dismissing the complaint for failure to state a claim upon which relief can be granted. Coffee System of Atlanta sued Fox and Intercontinental Coffee Service Plan seeking damages and a temporary and permanent injunction against the continued violation of a restrictive covenant entered into between Fox and the plaintiff as a part of an employment contract. Under the contract, Fox was employed by Coffee System, Inc., as a senior sales representative "to offer, on its behalf, its 'Coffee System' service, and to sell its replacement kits, within" the territory of Fulton, DeKalb, Cobb and ten other named counties in the State of Georgia. The trial court issued a temporary ex parte restraining order on the 7th day of January, 1970. On January 26, 1970, the matter came on for a hearing on the question of whether the temporary injunction should be granted, and at that time the defendant Fox filed a written motion to dismiss the complaint for failure to state a claim. The judge, before whom the matter was heard, passed an order, which, insofar as is pertinent, reads: "After hearing argument of counsel for defendant and plaintiff, . . . it appearing that the restrictions in the contract under consideration . . . are uncertain, indefinite, unreasonable, and impose upon the employee greater limitations than are necessary for the

---

1. [Citations and footnotes within the cases reprinted here have been deleted without indication. Where footnotes are included, the original footnote numbers have been retained.]

protection of the employer, they are therefore illegal, unenforceable, null and void . . . .Therefore, it is hereby ordered, adjudged and decreed that the complaint be, and it is hereby, dismissed for failure to state a claim upon which relief can be granted."

The material and relevant parts of the contract sued on provide that Fox "agrees to use his best efforts to the exclusion of all other employment, in order to promote and solicit sales of the company's coffee system service in the aforesaid territory, and to perform any and all other services reasonably required by company in connection with the merchandising of such service . . . [He] agrees that, for the term of this agreement and for one (1) year following the termination hereof, he will not, directly or indirectly in any capacity, solicit or accept orders of business located within the area assigned to [him] during any part of the two (2) year period immediately preceding the termination of his employment for any program, service, equipment or product similar to or competitive with the business of the company from any organization or individual which or who has been a customer of the company during any part of the two (2) year period immediately preceding termination of his employment, or who or which was actively solicited as a customer by company during the period of this agreement . . . .That he will not, during the term of his employment, and for a period of one year thereafter divulge to anyone other than an authorized employee of employer, and after the term of his employment will not use any information or knowledge relating to sales prospects, business methods and/or techniques which were acquired by him during the term of his employment."

1. Among those contracts which are against public policy and which cannot be enforced are contracts in general restraint of trade. Code § 20-504. However, "a contract only in partial restraint may be upheld, 'provided the restraint be reasonable,' and the contract be valid in other essentials. A contract concerning a lawful and useful business in partial restraint of trade and reasonably limited as to time and territory, and otherwise reasonable, is not void."

2. An examination of the decided cases on restrictive covenants reveals that this court has customarily considered three separate elements of such contracts in determining whether they are reasonable or not. These three elements may be categorized as (1) the restraint in the activity of the employee, or former employee, imposed by the contract; (2) the territorial or geographic restraint; and (3) the length of time during which the covenant seeks to impose the restraint. It has been said that no better test can be applied to the question of whether a restrictive covenant is reasonable or not than by considering whether the restraint "is such only as to afford a fair protection to the interest of the party in favor of whom it is given, and not so large as to interfere with the interest of the public. Whatever restraint is larger than the necessary protection of the party can be of no benefit to either; it can only be oppressive, and if oppressive, it is in the eye of the law unreasonable . . . .There can be no doubt that an agreement that during the term of the service, and for a

reasonable period thereafter, the employee shall not become interested in or engage in a rival business, is reasonable and valid, the contract being otherwise legal and not in general restraint of trade. This is the rule followed by a majority of the American Courts and is supported by reason . . . .This court seems to be committed to the rule that the contract must be limited both as to time and territory, and not otherwise unreasonable. If limited as to both time and territory, the contract is illegal if it be unreasonable in other respects. And, with respect to restrictive agreements ancillary to a contract of employment, the mere fact that the contract is unlimited as to either time or territory is sufficient to condemn it as unreasonable." Shirk v. Loftis Bros. & Co., 148 Ga. 500, 504, 97 S.E. 66.

3. Two of the elements referred to in the preceding division lend themselves to more or less exact comparison with the yardstick laid down by previous cases. The proscription against competition by the defendant embodied in the restrictive covenant in this case extends to 13 named counties in the State of Georgia. Insofar as geographic area is concerned, this is undoubtedly a reasonable restriction to be upheld by the courts if the contract is otherwise reasonable and not oppressive. The limitation as to the time within which the defendant may not engage in a competitive employment or enterprise, being one year from the termination of his employment with the plaintiff, is reasonable and not such a restriction as would render the contract void.

4. We now turn to the question of the reasonableness of the restriction against the activities of the defendant as contained in the covenant. The defendant Fox was employed by the defendant as a sales representative to offer on behalf of the plaintiff its "'Coffee System' service, and to sell its replacement kits." He agreed that he would not, directly or indirectly, in any capacity, solicit or accept orders of business located within the area assigned to him (that is, the 13 named counties) during his employment with the plaintiff and for one year thereafter "for any program, service, equipment or product similar to or competitive with the business of" the plaintiff, and that he would refrain from doing this with respect to any organization which, or individual who, had been a customer or had been solicited as a customer of plaintiff during that term. It must be noted that the contract does not restrict the plaintiff from accepting *employment* with a competitor, so long as such employment does not involve the direct or indirect solicitation and acceptance of orders from customers or those solicited as customers of the plaintiff. Even if the enforcement of the broad language forbidding the use by the defendant of business methods and techniques acquired during his employment with the plaintiff should, if enforced, effectively prevent the defendant from accepting employment with any other competitor of the plaintiff within the limited area and time of the operation of the contract, it would not render the contract void as a matter of law. See Shirk v. Loftis Bros. & Co., supra, where a contract in which the employee covenanted that he would "not directly or indirectly, under any circumstances or conditions whatsoever, for himself [or] for any other person,

firm, or corporation, engage in or be or become interested or be employed, directly or indirectly . . . as an individual, partner, stockholder, director, officer, clerk, salesman, buyer, principal, agent, employee, trustee, or in any relation or capacity whatsoever, in the line of business carried on by" the plaintiff. That contract was upheld by this court as not imposing too broad a restriction on the defendant since the proscription of the contract only related to Fulton County and was limited as to time to four years. As a general rule, this court seems to have established the principle in cases of this kind that, where the restraint as to time and territory is reasonably limited, a general prohibition against soliciting customers and accounts of the employer will be upheld. We need hold no more than that in this case.

With respect to the definition or description of the business engaged in by the plaintiff and which the defendant was employed by the plaintiff to conduct, the contract only refers to it as a "Coffee System Service," but we think this is enough. This court has upheld restrictive covenants where the description of the business was no more specific. The restraint imposed by the contract in this case is no more than is reasonably necessary to afford fair protection to the interests of the employer and is not unduly oppressive of the employee. It is not void for any reason urged by the appellee.

5. It follows that the trial court erred in sustaining the motion to dismiss and in dismissing the complaint. It should be kept in mind that this case was brought under the Civil Practice Act, and that the former rules of strict pleading no longer apply. We have looked only to the contract, as it is apparent the trial court did, in reaching the conclusion we have reached. The complaint, itself, sufficiently sets forth the existence of the contract and a breach thereof and it was not subject to being dismissed for failure to state a claim. From the language of the order appealed from, it is clear that the trial judge did not reach the question of whether to grant or deny a temporary injunction. Therefore, no question in that regard is presented for our decision on this appeal.

Judgment reversed.

All the Justices concur.

GOLDMAN v. KANE

3 Mass. App. Ct. 336, 329 N.E.2d 770 (1975)

Massachusetts Appeals Court

HALE, Chief Justice.

[Barry Kane represented Lawrence Hill, a law school graduate but not a lawyer. Kane had represented Hill for several years on various matters. In April 1971, Hill signed an agreement to purchase a boat for $31,500 and paid a deposit of $3,150. Hill agreed to pay the balance on May 17. Kane advised Hill about miscellaneous legal matters pertaining to the purchase and registration of the boat. Hill also asked Kane to arrange for the financing of the balance of the purchase price. When Kane could not arrange a loan through a bank, Hill told Kane to sell a piece of real property Hill owned. Kane put the property on the market, but the property did not sell. With one day to go before losing the deposit, Hill told Kane that he was in dire need of the money to complete the sale. Kane told Hill that the timing and Hill's financial circumstances made it "virtually impossible" to get a loan. After several telephone conversations, Kane offered to arrange for Kane's corporation to lend Hill $30,000. However, Hill would have to transfer to Kane's corporation absolute title to the unsold real property, to all of the personal property located on the real property, and to a smaller boat Hill owned. In addition, Hill would have to secure the loan with a mortgage on the new boat. Kane urged Hill not to accept these terms, but Hill insisted. In July 1971, Kane's corporation sold the real property and the personal property located on it for $86,000. Subsequently, Hill defaulted on the loan. Kane seized the boat and sold it. Hill's estate thereafter sued Kane and his corporation, alleging that Kane had breached his fiduciary duty as Hill's attorney. Judgment for the plaintiff; defendants appealed.]

The defendants argue that even if an attorney-client relationship existed the record does not support the conclusion that there was a breach of that relationship. We disagree. The relationship of attorney and client is highly fiduciary in nature. "Unflinching fidelity to their genuine interests is the duty of every attorney to his clients. Public policy hardly can touch matters of more general concern than the maintenance of an untarnished standard of conduct by the attorney at law toward his client."

The law looks with great disfavor upon an attorney who has business dealings with his client which result in gains to the attorney at the expense of the client. "The attorney is not permitted by the law to take any advantage of his client. The principles holding the attorney to a conspicuous degree of faithfulness and forbidding him to take personal advantage of his client are thoroughly established." When an attorney bargains with his client in a business transaction in a manner which is advantageous to himself, and if that transaction is later called into question, the court will subject it to close scrutiny. In such a case, the attorney has the burden of showing that the transaction "was in all respects fairly and equitably conducted; that he fully and faithfully discharged all his duties to his client, not only by refraining from any misrepresentation or concealment of any material fact, but by active diligence to see that his client was fully informed of the nature and effect of the transaction proposed and of his own rights and interests in the subject matter involved, and by seeing to it that his client either has independent advice in the matter or else receives from the attorney such advice as the latter would have been expected to give had the transaction been one between his client and a stranger."

Applying these principles to the case at bar, it is clear that the judge was correct in concluding that Kane, by entering into the transaction, breached his fiduciary duty to Hill. While the defendants contend that Kane's conduct did not constitute a breach of his fiduciary duty because Hill fully understood the

fundamentally unfair

nature and effect of the transaction and because Kane advised Hill against it, in the circumstances of this case, Kane's full disclosure and his advice were not sufficient to immunize him from liability. The fundamental unfairness of the transaction and the egregious overreaching by Kane in his dealings with Hill are self-evident. In light of the nature of the transaction, Kane, at a bare minimum, was under a duty not to proceed with the loan until he was satisfied that Hill had obtained independent advice on the matter. The purpose of such requirement is to be certain that in a situation where an attorney deals with a client in a business relationship to the attorney's advantage, the "presumed influence resulting from the relationship has been neutralized." . . .

Judgment affirmed.

CLEIN V. KAPILOFF
213 Ga. 369, 98 S.E.2d 897 (1957)

Supreme Court of Georgia

ALMAND, Justice.

The bill of exceptions assigns error on orders overruling general demurrers to an equitable petition, and granting an interlocutory injunction.

The petition of Harry Kapiloff and Sam Turetsky sought to restrain the defendant Sidney A. Clein from engaging in the retail clothing business in violation of a restrictive covenant entered into by the defendant Clein and other named defendants with the plaintiffs. In substance, the petition alleged: that the plaintiffs, prior to August 28, 1950, owned and controlled Macey's, Inc., a corporation engaged in the retail jewelry business at 110 Whitehall Street in the City of Atlanta; that the plaintiffs sold said business to Sterling Jewelry Company, a corporation owned and controlled by the named defendants; that the written contract of sale, signed by both corporations through the plaintiff Kapiloff as president of Macey's, Inc., and the defendant Clein as vice-president of Sterling Jewelry Company, Inc., contained the following covenant: "4. *Restrictive covenants.* Seller covenants and agrees that it will not, throughout the term of the lease assigned hereunder [July 31, 1959], engage in the retail jewelry business, or in the sale of any items normally sold by a retail jewelry company, other than television sets, within a radius of one mile from the premises herein described, and *buyer covenants that it will not engage in the operation of a retail clothing business on the premises, nor will it engage in the sale of items normally sold in a retail clothing store on the premises or within a radius of one-half mile of the premises, throughout the term of the lease* [July 31, 1959] *herein assigned.*" (Italics and brackets supplied.) Following the corporate signatures in the contract of sale, all of the named plaintiffs and defendants agreed in writing that the "restrictive covenants mentioned in paragraph 4 of the within agreement are hereby adopted and agreed to by us individually, and any one acting for us, or any firm, corporation, or partnership in which any of us may have an interest." The seller conveyed to the buyer all of his accounts receivable, the plaintiff Kapiloff agreed to assign the lease in 110 Whitehall Street to the buyer, and the defendant Clein agreed to endorse the purchase money notes. At the time of the sale, the plaintiffs were engaged in the retail clothing business at 114 Whitehall Street under the name of Hollywood Credit Clothiers. It was alleged that, at the time of the sale, the defendants "knew that the accounts of customers of said jewelry business were in a great part the same as the accounts of the petitioners' retail credit clothing business and petitions as a consideration of said sale and agreement insisted that defendants covenant not to engage in the clothing business because a great number of the accounts of the two said stores were of the same customers. Petitioners show that defendants knew that if they were allowed to sell clothing to petitioners' jewelry accounts after said jewelry business was sold to them, that they would be dealing with many of the customers of petitioners' said credit clothing business, as aforesaid, and they knew that petitioners insisted upon said covenant to protect themselves from that situation." It was further alleged that the defendant Clein is now engaged in the business of selling clothing at retail at 132 Whitehall Street, which is within one-half mile of the premises at 110 Whitehall Street, in violation of this covenant, and that the defendant Clein, by engaging in the retail clothing business in competition with the plaintiffs, will cause them irreparable damage and injury.

1. As a general rule, a contract in general restraint of trade is void, but a contract only in partial restraint may be upheld provided the restraint is reasonable and the contract is valid in the other essentials. In determining the reasonableness of a restrictive covenant, a greater latitude is allowed when the covenant relates to the sale of a business than in cases where the covenant is ancillary to a contract of employment. The agreement must be considered with reference to the situation, business and objects of the parties in light of all of the surrounding circumstances. The restrictive covenant in the instant case is reasonable as to time and territory, its area of operation being within a radius of one-half mile, and its time being limited to July 31, 1959. The true test of the validity of the contract is whether it is supported by a sufficient consideration and whether the restraint is reasonable. In determining whether the covenant is "otherwise reasonable," the covenant must be reasonably necessary to protect the interests of the party in whose favor it is imposed, and must not unduly prejudice the interests of the public, and must not impose greater restrictions than are necessary for the protection of the promisee.

In this case, the plaintiffs bound themselves not to compete with the defendants in the retail jewelry business within one mile of 110 Whitehall Street during a period ending July 31, 1959, and the defendants, knowing that the plaintiffs were then engaged in the retail clothing business at 114 Whitehall Street, agreed that, within a like period of time, they would not engage in the retail clothing business within one-half mile of 110 Whitehall Street. The covenant is reasonable in all respects, and there are no allegations in the petition which indicate that the public would suffer in having one less retail clothing store in this limited area for the time specified. We have here simply a case where the sellers and the buyers of a business have entered into a valid contract containing mutual obligations, and one party has chosen to ignore his obligation. In such a case, equity will exercise its restraining arm and require him to abide by his promise.

The petition sets forth a cause of action for the relief prayed, and the court did not err in overruling the general demurrers of Clein.

2. On the interlocutory hearing, the case was submitted upon an agreed stipulation of facts. Under the evidence submitted, the court did not err in granting an interlocutory injunction.

Judgment affirmed.

All the Justices concur.

JACOBSON V. KAMERINSKY[2]

Karen Jacobson had gallbladder surgery on June 30, 1984. Her doctor negligently left a surgical sponge in the surgery site when he closed the incision. The sponge caused Jacobson considerable physical difficulty and subsequently resulted in a second surgery to remove it. After the second surgery Jacobson decided to seek legal representation for a medical malpractice claim against her first surgeon. She saw Kamerinsky's office sign, sought his advice, and agreed to retain him to bring her claim. Kamerinsky had been admitted to practice law only ten weeks when he accepted Jacobson's case.

Kamerinsky correctly realized that the surgeon was clearly liable for Jacobson's damages. He tried to negotiate a settlement of the claim with the surgeon and the surgeon's insurance carrier so that litigation would not be necessary. As the weeks and months went by, Jacobson contacted Kamerinsky periodically to learn whether there was any progress on her claim. He would tell her that negotiations were proceeding well and that he should have a settlement for her soon. Several times he told her that he had obtained an expert opinion that leaving a surgical sponge inside the body was clearly medical malpractice. He explained that he had not yet filed suit because, since liability was so clear, he hoped to negotiate a settlement without the necessity of filing suit.

Shortly before the statute of limitations expired, when negotiations had not been successful, Kamerinsky filed suit in the appropriate state trial court. However, he had failed to research the requirements for bringing a medical malpractice action. State law requires that prior to filing suit a medical malpractice plaintiff must first file a charge before the medical Malpractice Screening Panel, complete the Panel's discovery and hearing process, and

---

2. [This is a hypothetical case based on several real cases.]

obtain a decision from the Panel. [citation omitted] Failure to go through these steps results in the dismissal of the plaintiff's court action. [citation omitted] The lawyer for the doctor successfully moved for the dismissal of the plaintiff's claim, and the plaintiff was precluded from completing the Screening Panel process and refiling the suit because by then the statute of limitations had expired and the medical malpractice claim was barred.

Ms. Jacobson brought this legal malpractice claim against Kamerinsky, arguing that Kamerinsky's failure to file a charge before the Screening Panel constituted legal malpractice and resulted in $500,000 damage to Jacobson. A jury found in favor of Jacobson and awarded her $425,000 in damages. Kamerinsky appeals, arguing that his error did not constitute malpractice.

A lawyer is held to a standard of competency that meets or exceeds the professional skill and diligence commonly exercised by reasonable and prudent lawyers in this state [citation to state's highest court]. Lawyers are not guarantors of a successful result; nor are they required to surpass human limitations. Lawyers are often called upon to exercise professional judgment in representing and advising clients. A good faith error in judgment is not legal malpractice as long as the lawyer's judgment was reasonable under the circumstances.

Kamerinsky's failure was more than an error in judgment, however. The failure to comply with the filing requirements was readily preventable by proper legal research. The Medical Malpractice Act creates the Screening Panel and the requirement of completing the Panel's hearing process before suit is filed. The debate and ultimate passage of the Act had been covered by the press extensively, the Screening Panel requirement being the most controversial provision of the Act. Even if Kamerinsky was not aware of the Act from the public press coverage, he certainly should have been aware of the Act and its requirements as a result of the prominent coverage of the new requirements by the State Bar Journal and the several Continuing Legal Education programs that explained the Act's provisions.

However, no lawyer should rely on press or state bar journalists to keep apace with statutory changes. Kamerinsky had a duty to conduct thorough legal research concerning statutory requirements for filing a lawsuit. Filing lawsuits is something general practitioners are familiar with doing, and it is well within the area of competence required of all lawyers.

Kamerinsky argues that medical malpractice litigation is a complex and difficult area of the law and that he, as a novice lawyer, should not be held to the standard of an experienced litigator. As we established above, researching and complying with statutory requirements for filing a lawsuit are tasks well within the standard of practice expected of all lawyers. However, even if they were not, Kamerinsky cannot undertake representation on a case without being held to the standard expected of all lawyers practicing in this state. A lawyer must either decline the representation or meet the appropriate standard of competence required for the representation. If bringing a medical malpractice claim requires knowledge or experience that Kamerinsky did not already have or could not obtain, he had no business accepting the case. All clients are entitled to at least the minimum standard of knowledge, skill, and diligence. Further, allowing lawyers to meet a lower standard if they can demonstrate a lower level of skill or knowledge would not encourage lawyers to develop their levels of skill, knowledge, and experience.

Judgment affirmed.

LUCY V. ZEHMER
196 Va. 493, 84 S.E.2d 516 (1954)

Supreme Court of Appeals of Virginia

BUCHANAN, Justice.

This suit was instituted by W.O. Lucy and J.C. Lucy, complainants, against A.H. Zehmer and Ida S. Zehmer, his wife, defendants, to have specific performance of a contract by which it was alleged the Zehmers had sold to W.O. Lucy a tract of land owned by A.H. Zehmer in Dinwiddie county containing 471.6 acres, more or less, known as the Ferguson farm, for $50,000. J.C. Lucy, the other complainant, is a brother of W.O. Lucy, to whom W.O. Lucy transferred a half interest in his alleged purchase.

The instrument sought to be enforced was written by A.H. Zehmer on [Saturday,] December 20, 1952, in these words: "We hereby agree to sell to W.O. Lucy the Ferguson Farm complete for $50,000.00, title satisfactory to buyer," and signed by the defendants, A.H. Zehmer and Ida S. Zehmer.

The answer of A.H. Zehmer admitted that at the time mentioned W.O. Lucy offered him $50,000 cash for the farm, but that he, Zehmer, considered that the offer was made in jest; that so thinking, and both he and Lucy having had several drinks, he wrote out "the memorandum" quoted above and induced his wife to sign it; that he did not deliver the memorandum to Lucy, but that Lucy picked it up, read it, put it in his pocket, attempted to offer Zehmer $5 to bind the bargain, which Zehmer refused to accept, and realizing for the first time that Lucy was serious, Zehmer assured him that he had no intention of selling the farm and that the whole matter was a joke. Lucy left the premises insisting that he had purchased the farm.

Depositions were taken and the decree appealed from was entered holding that the complainants had failed to establish their right to specific performance, and dismissing their bill. The assignment of error is to this action of the court . . . .

The defendants insist that the evidence was ample to support their contention that the writing sought to be enforced was prepared as a bluff or dare to force Lucy to admit that he did not have $50,000; that the whole matter was a joke; that the writing was not delivered to Lucy and no binding contract was ever made between the parties.

It is an unusual, if not bizarre, defense. When made to the writing admittedly prepared by one of the defendants and signed by both, clear evidence is required to sustain it.

In his testimony Zehmer claimed that he "was high as a Georgia pine," and that the transaction "was just a bunch of two doggoned drunks bluffing to see who could talk the biggest and say the most." That claim is inconsistent with his attempt to testify in great detail as to what was said and what was done. It is contradicted by other evidence as to the condition of both parties, and rendered of no weight by the testimony of his wife that when Lucy left the restaurant she suggested that Zehmer drive him home. The record is convincing that Zehmer was not intoxicated to the extent of being unable to comprehend the nature and consequences of the instrument he executed, and hence that instrument is not to be invalidated on that ground. It was in fact conceded by defendants' counsel in oral argument that under the evidence Zehmer was not too drunk to make a valid contact.

The evidence is convincing also that Zehmer wrote two agreements, the first one beginning "I hereby agree to sell." Zehmer first said he could not remember about that, then that "I don't think I wrote but one out." Mrs. Zehmer said that what he wrote was "I hereby agree," but that "I" was changed to "We" after that night. The agreement that was written and signed is in the record and indicates no such change. Neither are the mistakes in spelling that Zehmer sought to point out readily apparent.

The appearance of the contract, the fact that it was under discussion for forty minutes or more before it was signed; Lucy's objection to the first draft because it was written in the singular, and he wanted Mrs. Zehmer to sign it also; the rewriting to meet that objection and the signing by Mrs. Zehmer; the discussion of what was to be included in the sale, the provision for the examination of the title, the completeness of the instrument that was executed, the taking possession of it by Lucy with no request or suggestion by either of the defendants that he give it back, are facts which furnish persuasive evidence that the execution of the contract was a serious business transaction rather than a casual, jesting matter as defendants now contend . . . .

If it be assumed, contrary to what we think the evidence shows, that Zehmer was jesting about selling his farm to Lucy and that the transaction was intended by him to be a joke, nevertheless the evidence shows that Lucy did not so understand it but considered it to be a serious business transaction and the contract to be binding on the Zehmers as well as on himself. The very next day he arranged with his brother to put up half the money and take a half interest in the land. The day after that he employed an attorney to examine the title. The next night, Tuesday, he was back at Zehmer's place and there Zehmer told him for the first time, Lucy said, that he wasn't going to sell and he told Zehmer, "You know you sold that place fair and square." After receiving the report from his attorney that the title was good he wrote to Zehmer that he was ready to close the deal.

Not only did Lucy actually believe, but the evidence shows he was warranted in believing that the contract represented a serious business transaction and a good faith sale and purchase of the farm.

In the field of contracts, as generally elsewhere, "We must look to the outward expression of a person as manifesting his intention rather than to his secret and unexpressed intention. 'The law imputes to a person an intention corresponding to the reasonable meaning of his words and acts.'"

At no time prior to the execution of the contract had Zehmer indicated to Lucy by word or act that he was not in earnest about selling the farm. They had argued about it and discussed its terms, as Zehmer admitted, for a long time. Lucy testified that if there was any jesting it was about paying $50,000 that night. The contract and the evidence show that he was not expected to pay the money that night. Zehmer said that after the writing was signed he laid it down on the counter in front of Lucy. Lucy said Zehmer handed it to him. In any event there had been what appeared to be a good faith offer and a good faith acceptance, followed by the execution and apparent delivery of a written contract. Both said that Lucy put the writing in his pocket and then offered Zehmer $5 to seal the bargain. Not until then, even under the defendants' evidence, was anything said or done to indicate that the matter was a joke. Both of the Zehmers testified that when Zehmer asked his wife to sign he whispered that it was a joke so Lucy wouldn't hear and that it was not intended that he should hear.

The mental assent of the parties is not requisite for the formation of a contract. If the words or other acts of one of the parties have but one reasonable meaning, his undisclosed intention is immaterial except when an unreasonable meaning which he attaches to his manifestations is known to the other party. " . . . The law, therefore, judges of an agreement between two persons exclusively from those expressions of their intentions which are communicated between them . . . ."

An agreement or mutual assent is of course essential to a valid contract, but the law imputes to a person an intention corresponding to the reasonable meaning of his words and acts. If his words and acts, judged by a reasonable standard, manifest an intention to agree, it is immaterial what may be the real but unexpressed state of his mind.

So a person cannot set up that he was merely jesting when his conduct and words would warrant a reasonable person in believing that he intended a real agreement.

Whether the writing signed by the defendants and now sought to be enforced by the complainants was the result of a serious offer by Lucy and a serious acceptance by the defendants, or was a serious offer by Lucy and an acceptance in secret jest by the defendants, in either event it constituted a binding contract of sale between the parties . . .

The complainants are entitled to have specific performance of the contract sued on. The decree appealed from is therefore reversed and the cause is remanded for the entry of a proper decree requiring the defendants to perform the contract in accordance with the prayer of the bill.

Reversed and remanded.

INDEX